CW00401887

Enhancing Education With Intelligent Systems and Data–Driven Instruction

Madhulika Bhatia
Amity University, India

Muhammad Tahir Mushtaq
Cardiff Metropolitan Univesity, UK

A volume in the Advances in
Educational Technologies and
Instructional Design (AETID) Book
Series

Published in the United States of America by
    IGI Global
    Information Science Reference (an imprint of IGI Global)
    701 E. Chocolate Avenue
    Hershey PA, USA 17033
    Tel: 717-533-8845
    Fax: 717-533-8661
    E-mail: cust@igi-global.com
    Web site: http://www.igi-global.com

Copyright © 2024 by IGI Global. All rights reserved. No part of this publication may be reproduced, stored or distributed in any form or by any means, electronic or mechanical, including photocopying, without written permission from the publisher.
Product or company names used in this set are for identification purposes only. Inclusion of the names of the products or companies does not indicate a claim of ownership by IGI Global of the trademark or registered trademark.

Library of Congress Cataloging-in-Publication Data

Names: Bhatia, Madhulika, 1984- editor. | Mushtaq, Muhammad Tahir, 1986- editor.
Title: Enhancing education with intelligent systems and data-driven instruction / edited by Madhulika Bhatia, Muhammad Mushtaq.
Description: Hershey, PA : Information Science Reference, [2024] | Includes bibliographical references and index. | Summary: "This book aims to revolutionize education by empowering educators to reimagine their teaching practices, adapt to the ever-evolving needs of students, and foster a lifelong love of learning"-- Provided by publisher.
Identifiers: LCCN 2024002249 (print) | LCCN 2024002250 (ebook) | ISBN 9798369321690 (h/c) | ISBN 9798369321706 (ebook)
Subjects: LCSH: Educational innovations. | Education--Data processing. | Artificial intelligence--Educational applications. | Intelligent tutoring systems.
Classification: LCC LB1027 .E577 2024 (print) | LCC LB1027 (ebook) | DDC 370--dc23/eng/20240229
LC record available at https://lccn.loc.gov/2024002249
LC ebook record available at https://lccn.loc.gov/2024002250

This book is published in the IGI Global book series Advances in Educational Technologies and Instructional Design (AETID) (ISSN: 2326-8905; eISSN: 2326-8913)

British Cataloguing in Publication Data
A Cataloguing in Publication record for this book is available from the British Library.
All work contributed to this book is new, previously-unpublished material.
The views expressed in this book are those of the authors, but not necessarily of the publisher.
For electronic access to this publication, please contact: eresources@igi-global.com.

Advances in Educational Technologies and Instructional Design (AETID) Book Series

Lawrence A. Tomei
Robert Morris University, USA

ISSN:2326-8905
EISSN:2326-8913

MISSION

Education has undergone, and continues to undergo, immense changes in the way it is enacted and distributed to both child and adult learners. In modern education, the traditional classroom learning experience has evolved to include technological resources and to provide online classroom opportunities to students of all ages regardless of their geographical locations. From distance education, Massive-Open-Online-Courses (MOOCs), and electronic tablets in the classroom, technology is now an integral part of learning and is also affecting the way educators communicate information to students.

The **Advances in Educational Technologies & Instructional Design (AETID) Book Series** explores new research and theories for facilitating learning and improving educational performance utilizing technological processes and resources. The series examines technologies that can be integrated into K-12 classrooms to improve skills and learning abilities in all subjects including STEM education and language learning. Additionally, it studies the emergence of fully online classrooms for young and adult learners alike, and the communication and accountability challenges that can arise. Trending topics that are covered include adaptive learning, game-based learning, virtual school environments, and social media effects. School administrators, educators, academicians, researchers, and students will find this series to be an excellent resource for the effective design and implementation of learning technologies in their classes.

COVERAGE

- Adaptive Learning
- Social Media Effects on Education
- Educational Telecommunications
- Digital Divide in Education
- Hybrid Learning
- Game-Based Learning
- Classroom Response Systems
- Virtual School Environments
- Online Media in Classrooms
- Bring-Your-Own-Device

IGI Global is currently accepting manuscripts for publication within this series. To submit a proposal for a volume in this series, please contact our Acquisition Editors at Acquisitions@igi-global.com or visit: http://www.igi-global.com/publish/.

The Advances in Educational Technologies and Instructional Design (AETID) Book Series (ISSN 2326-8905) is published by IGI Global, 701 E. Chocolate Avenue, Hershey, PA 17033-1240, USA, www.igi-global.com. This series is composed of titles available for purchase individually; each title is edited to be contextually exclusive from any other title within the series. For pricing and ordering information please visit http://www.igi-global.com/book-series/advances-educational-technologies-instructional-design/73678. Postmaster: Send all address changes to above address. Copyright © 2024 IGI Global. All rights, including translation in other languages reserved by the publisher. No part of this series may be reproduced or used in any form or by any means – graphics, electronic, or mechanical, including photocopying, recording, taping, or information and retrieval systems – without written permission from the publisher, except for non commercial, educational use, including classroom teaching purposes. The views expressed in this series are those of the authors, but not necessarily of IGI Global.

Titles in this Series

IGI Global
PUBLISHER of TIMELY KNOWLEDGE

701 East Chocolate Avenue, Hershey, PA 17033, USA
Tel: 717-533-8845 x100 • Fax: 717-533-8661
E-Mail: cust@igi-global.com • www.igi-global.com

Table of Contents

Detailed Table of Contents

Chapter 1

Saru Dhir, Amity University, India
Sakshi Kumari, Amity University, India
Sumita Gupta, Amity University, India

In recent years, the higher education landscape has witnessed a growing interest in adopting agile approaches and practices to address the evolving challenges and demands faced by educational institutions. Agile, a philosophy and set of methodologies originally derived from software development, emphasizes adaptability, collaboration, iterative development, and continuous improvement. This abstract provides an overview of the integration of agile approaches and practices into the higher education system, highlighting their potential benefits and challenges. Agile methodologies, such as Scrum and Kanban, offer a structured framework that enables educational institutions to become more responsive and flexible in their curriculum design, instructional delivery, and administrative processes.

Chapter 2

Ushaa Eswaran, Indira Institute of Technology and Sciences,
Jawaharlal Nehru Technological University, India

Project-based learning (PBL) represents a transformational pedagogical approach centered on students actively investigating authentic, complex problems leading to deeper learning outcomes. This chapter presents a comprehensive framework for PBL covering theoretical foundations, essential design components, integration approaches, learning competencies developed, effective assessments, and strategies for institutional implementation. The PBL models presented provide both conceptual grounding as well as actionable recommendations customized for elemental, middle and high school grade bands. Detailed examples illustrate key facets like technology integration for collaboration, use of rubrics, and community partnerships. The chapter also discusses innovations powered by emerging capabilities such as adaptive learning algorithms, augmented reality, and predictive analytics that can further enhance inquiry-driven PBL.

Chapter 3

Predictive analytics is a crucial tool in changing teaching and learning practices in the ever-changing field of educational technology. This study examines the dynamic function of predictive analytics in customizing education, with a specific emphasis on its ability to adapt learning paths to improve individual student achievement. The study examines how predictive models might identify distinct learning patterns and demands by assessing many data sources, such as academic achievement, learning habits, and engagement indicators. It showcases the capabilities of these analytics in generating adaptive learning experiences, thereby providing a more focused approach to teaching. This article investigates how predictive analytics facilitates the early detection of educational hazards, allowing for timely interventions to support students who are at danger of academic underperformance or dropping out.

Chapter 4

The purpose of this chapter is to present the methodology that will be used to collect data for the study reported on. Against the background of enhancing education with intelligent systems and data-driven instruction, methodology is important in research because it offers legitimacy to research. The research methodology shows that universally accepted data collection methods and procedures were adopted, which contributes to the veracity of the research process. Additionally, the research methodology also acts as a guide to researchers so that they stay on track regarding whatever they will be doing. This chapter further seeks to define and defend the methodological basis used to answer the research questions outlined.

Chapter 5

Revolutionizing Higher Education in Malaysia With the Game-Changing
Impact of Cloud Computing 80

Glaret Shirley Sinnappan, Tunku Abdul Rahman University of
Management and Technology, Malaysia
Raenu Kolandaisamy, UCSI University, Malaysia
Maran Marimuthu, Universiti Teknologi Petronas, Malaysia
Amir Rizaan Abdul Rahiman, Universiti Putra Malaysia, Malaysia
Amir Aatieff Amir Hussin, International Islamic University, Malaysia
Abdurrahman Jalil, Universiti Teknologi MARA, Malaysia

Cloud computing is rapidly becoming integral to higher education in Malaysia,
driven by technological advancements and the demands of Industry Revolution 4.0.
However, there is a lack of research on its impact from the perspective of students.
This study focuses on scrutinizing the influence of cloud computing on Malaysia's
higher education sector, emphasizing variables like cost reduction, resource
availability, data confidentiality, and learning motivation. A comparative analysis
of Google Apps, Microsoft Office 365, and Blackboard App will be conducted.
Employing the snowball sampling technique, the research will involve 385 tertiary
education students out of a total population of 1.2 million. Questionnaire data will
be analyzed using IBM SPSS for a comprehensive understanding.

Chapter 6

Improving Teaching-Learning Through Smart Classes Using IoT 107

Saru Dhir, Amity University, India
Aditya Maheshwari, Amity University, India
Shanu Sharma, ABES Engineering College, India

This chapter explores the application of IoT in education, focusing on its potential
to enhance learning experiences and automate processes. Smartphone-based remote
appliance control and interactive learning are made possible by IoT integration in
smart classrooms. IoT functions as a worldwide network, producing data to make
our lives easier and safer while minimizing environmental effects. The report
emphasizes better learning across disciplines as one of the revolutionary effects of
IoT in higher education. Implementation problems are addressed. Additionally, it
covers the effective use of big data analytics in education, performance prediction,
and strategy adaptation. This study emphasizes the use of technology to enhance
learning experiences in order to maximize the potential of IoT in education. Methods
of collaborative learning are recognized as essential components in improving
students' learning capacities. This research contributes to maximizing the potential
of IoT in education and highlights the significance of leveraging technology for
enriched learning experiences.

G. S. Prakasha, Christ University, India
Sanskriti Rawat, Christ University, India
Ishani Basak, Christ University, India
Sebastian Mathai, Christ University, India

Gamification emerged as a teaching-learning pedagogy in recent years. Its usage increased during the Covid-19 lockdown and continued post-pandemic time. Its usage ranges from online to offline tools; teachers lack its awareness as a pedagogy. The present study aimed to understand perspectives of teacher educators and teacher trainees on inclusion of gamification pedagogical training in teacher preparation programmes. The study employed a mixed-method approach and included qual-quant sequential explanatory research design. Researchers conducted semi-structured interviews with six teacher educators and six trainee teachers and collected the opinion of 200 teacher educators and trainee teachers. The study employed inductive thematic analysis and Chi-square analysis for qualitative and quantitative data respectively. Findings revealed six main themes and twelve sub-themes. Chi-square revealed a gender science-stereotype amid association between teacher educators and teacher trainees' opinion. Senior teacher educators did not believe in the importance of gamification inclusion in teacher preparation.

*Isabel María García Conesa, Centro Universitario de la Defensa de San
Javier, Spain*

In recent years, the use of ICTs has increased in the education field and many different types of contents have been created. One of them are educational games. However, very little research has been done to date if games are as effective as they try to be. The aim of this study was to collect information related to ICTs and games in relation to L2 learning in a technical engineering degree and create some questionnaires which would be analysed and compared with the data previously mentioned. Results show how little teachers know of the methodological applications of ICTs and videogames, the benefits that they can provide to the bilingual classroom, such as how students who use games usually have a generally positive view of English learning. These results suggest that information and professional preparation regarding ICTs and games have not been shared and are not mandatory, which leads to the incorrect and insufficient use of the resources. What we are using currently it will become obsolete and new methodologies will have to be created in consequence

Chapter 9
Employing Online Video Platforms in English Language Teaching:
Challa Srinivas Rao, Sreenidhi Institute of Science and Technology, India
Karayil Suresh Babu, Vasireddy Venkatadri Institute of Technology, India

The Covid-19 pandemic introduced substantial challenges and unique opportunities in education, especially in English language teaching. Loss of instruction time and a decline in learning outcomes emerged as significant problems in engineering education. Amidst these difficulties, the surge in internet-based learning emerges as a promising solution. This chapter conducts an analytical study on the crisis's impact on language learning, the efficacy of online learning in bridging gaps, and the future implications for English language teaching. The methodology involves a questionnaire survey among engineering students and teachers. Students exhibit a passive attitude towards online learning, attributing it to limited interaction during virtual classes. They stress the necessity of on-campus classes for certain concepts like writing and speaking skills. Teachers identify vocabulary learning, reading comprehension, and error spotting as suitable for online teaching. Both groups unanimously support blended learning for the future.

Chapter 10
Enriching EFL Teaching Through Multimodal Integration of QR Codes: A
Gülin Zeybek, Isparta University of Applied Sciences, Turkey

The purpose of this in-depth chapter is to present the multimodal integration of quick response (QR) codes in the field of foreign language education, with a particular emphasis on English language skills. This chapter presents practical applications and ideas for introducing QR codes into teaching practices in a seamless manner, which will improve the experiences of language learners. All aspects of language abilities, including listening, speaking, reading, and writing, are included in the scope of this analysis. The chapter also notes that there are challenges associated with the incorporation of QR codes. In conclusion, the chapter suggests that the use of QR codes into language instruction might be a paradigm change in terms of pedagogical approach. The presentation of QR code integration in this chapter is framed within a multimodal approach, which acknowledges the value of mixing many modes of communication, such as verbal, visual, auditory, gestural, and spatial modes, in order to produce an experience that is both comprehensive and immersive for language acquisition.

Chapter 11

Mohammad Rashed Hasan Polas, Sonargaon University, Bangladesh
Asghar Afshar Jahanshahi, IPADE Business School, Mexico
Siti Aida Samikon, Limkokwing University of Creative Technology, Malaysia
Tahmina Akter, University of Dhaka, Bangladesh
Md. Arif Hosseon Roky, Universiti Putra Malaysia, Malaysia

This study investigates the interplay of attitude, learning environment, motivation, technological adaptability, and self-confidence with English language proficiency, leveraging artificial intelligence (AI) tools within the context of the Business Education 4.0 era among university students in Bangladesh. Methodologically, a quantitative approach was employed, embracing positivism. A stratified random sampling technique was applied, yielding a sample of 433 university students from five universities who are currently studying at the Department of Business Administration in Dhaka, Bangladesh. Structured surveys were used to collect data from the respondents. To analyze the data, SPSS V.25 was used. Findings reveal a significant positive association between a learning environment and English language proficiency. Technological adaptability, facilitated by AI, positively influences language skills. Self-confidence plays a crucial role, aligning with Bandura's Social Cognitive Theory.

Chapter 12

Jason D. DeHart, The University of Tennessee, Knoxville, USA

This chapter examines the nexus of comics and digital work in the context of both secondary and post-secondary instruction with adolescents. The chapter draws upon the qualitative and self-study centered approach of the author as teacher and as reader, with implications related to the future possibilities for instruction. In this case, the context is centered in literacy as the author has worked with students over the course of approximately seventeen years to foster deeper connections to reading, writing, and composing.

Preface

Welcome to *Enhancing Education With Intelligent Systems and Data-Driven Instruction*, a transformative reference book that brings together the collective wisdom of educators dedicated to revolutionizing the way we teach and learn. As editors of this comprehensive guide, Madhulika Bhatia from Amity University, India, and Muhammad Mushtaq from Cardiff Metropolitan University, United Kingdom, are honored to present a compilation that explores cutting-edge strategies and techniques to shape the future of education.

In today's rapidly evolving world, the role of educators has never been more crucial. "Enhancing Education" is a testament to our commitment to equipping teachers with innovative tools and approaches that transcend traditional boundaries. The book is crafted to inspire educators and empower them to adapt their teaching methods to meet the diverse needs of students in the 21st century.

Our journey begins by emphasizing the pivotal role of teachers as catalysts for change in the classroom. By focusing on practical strategies to engage students, fuel their curiosity, and foster critical thinking skills, this book seeks to create a paradigm shift in education. Through a student-centered approach, educators are encouraged to create inclusive and interactive learning environments that nurture the unique talents and abilities of each student.

"Enhancing Education" delves into the integration of digital tools and resources, leveraging technology to enhance teaching and learning experiences. From interactive multimedia presentations to online collaboration platforms, educators will discover innovative ways to use technology effectively for instruction, assessment, and feedback.

We invite you to explore the diverse topics covered in this book, each penned by experienced educators and experts in their respective fields. From flipped learning and gamification to personalized learning and augmented reality, the chapters provide practical insights, real-life examples, and step-by-step guidelines to keep educators at the forefront of modern education.

As you navigate through the pages, you'll find detailed discussions on fostering collaboration, creativity, and critical thinking through project-based learning, as well as insights into creating inclusive learning environments with culturally responsive teaching. The exploration extends to topics like inquiry-based learning, integrating social media in education, mindfulness and well-being, data-driven instruction, collaborative learning, adaptive learning technologies, authentic assessment, and preparing students for the digital age through coding and computational thinking.

We extend our gratitude to the contributors who have shared their expertise and experiences to make this book a valuable resource for faculty, school teachers, and experienced educators. Our hope is that *Enhancing Education With Intelligent Systems and Data-Driven Instruction* serves as a catalyst for positive change, inspiring educators to reimagine their teaching practices and foster a lifelong love of learning in their students.

Chapter 1: Agile Approaches and Practices into Higher Education System

"Agile Approaches and Practices into Higher Education System" provides an insightful overview of the integration of agile methodologies into higher education. Authored by Saru Dhir, Sakshi Kumari, and Sumita Gupta from Amity University Uttar Pradesh, India, the chapter explores the potential benefits and challenges of adopting agile approaches. With a focus on methodologies like Scrum and Kanban, the chapter illustrates how these structured frameworks enhance adaptability and flexibility in curriculum design, instructional delivery, and administrative processes.

Chapter 2: Project-Based Learning-Fostering Collaboration, Creativity, and Critical Thinking

"Project-Based Learning - Fostering Collaboration, Creativity, and Critical Thinking" by Ushaa Eswaran from Indira Institute of Technology & Sciences-JNTU-Kakinada, India, presents a comprehensive framework for Project-Based Learning (PBL). This transformative pedagogical approach engages students in authentic problem-solving, leading to deeper learning outcomes. The chapter covers theoretical foundations, design components, integration approaches, learning competencies, assessments, and strategies for institutional implementation, with examples illustrating technology integration and the use of emerging capabilities like adaptive learning algorithms and augmented reality.

Chapter 3: The Role of Predictive Analytics in Personalizing Education: Tailoring Learning Paths for Individual Student Success

"The Role of Predictive Analytics in Personalizing Education" delves into the dynamic function of predictive analytics in customizing education. Written by Dwijendra Nath Dwivedi, Ghanashyama Mahanty, and Varunendra Dwivedi from various universities, the chapter explores how predictive analytics identifies distinct learning patterns and adapts learning paths to improve individual student success. It emphasizes the early detection of educational hazards, allowing timely interventions to support students at risk of academic underperformance or dropping out.

Chapter 4: Enhancing Education with Information and Communication Technologies: Data-Driven Instruction in Rural Schools

Authored by Bongi Mahlangu and Leila Goosen from the University of South Africa, "Enhancing Education with Information and Communication Technologies" focuses on data-driven instruction in rural schools. This chapter not only presents a methodology for data collection but also highlights the importance of using intelligent systems to enhance education. The research methodology adopted contributes to the veracity of the research process, offering a guide for researchers and defining the methodological basis for answering research questions.

Chapter 5: Revolutionizing Higher Education in Malaysia with the Game-Changing Impact of Cloud Computing

"Revolutionizing Higher Education in Malaysia with the Game-Changing Impact of Cloud Computing" by Glaret Sinnappan, Raenu Kolandaisamy, Maran Marimuthu, Amir Rizaan Abdul Rahiman, Amir Aatieff Amir Hussin, and Abdurrahman Jalil explores the impact of cloud computing on Malaysia's higher education sector. This chapter, driven by a comparative analysis of cloud platforms, investigates variables such as cost reduction, resource availability, data confidentiality, and learning motivation. The research method involves the snowball sampling technique and analyzes questionnaire data using IBM SPSS.

Chapter 6: Improving Teaching-Learning through Smart Classes Using IOT

"Improving Teaching-Learning through Smart Classes Using IoT" authored by Saru Dhir, Aditya Maheshwari, and Shanu Sharma from various institutions in India, explores the application of the Internet of Things (IoT) in education. The chapter focuses on how IoT can enhance learning experiences and automate processes in smart classrooms, addressing implementation challenges and emphasizing the effective use of big data analytics in education.

Chapter 7: Gamification in Teacher Education: Teacher Educators and Trainee Teachers' Perspectives in India

G S Prakasha, Sanskriti Rawat, Ishani Basak, and Sebastian Mathai from Christ University, India, contribute "Gamification in Teacher Education," examining teacher educators and trainee teachers' perspectives in India. The study aims to understand the inclusion of gamification pedagogical training in teacher preparation programs. It employs a mixed-method approach, including interviews and opinions from 200 teacher educators and trainee teachers, revealing six main themes and twelve sub-themes.

Chapter 8: Gamification in an EFL Classroom and the Use of Games for Learning English: Spanish Technical Engineering Degree

Isabel García from Centro Universitario de la Defensa de San Javier, Spain, presents "Gamification in an EFL Classroom and the Use of Games for Learning English: Spanish Technical Engineering Degree." This chapter investigates the effectiveness of educational games in a technical engineering degree, highlighting the positive view students have towards English learning through games. The study emphasizes the need for information and professional preparation regarding ICTs and games in education.

Chapter 9: Employing Online Video Platforms in English Language Teaching: Opportunities and Challenges

"Employing Online Video Platforms in English Language Teaching" by Challa Rao and Karayil Suresh Babu from India discusses the impact of the COVID-19 pandemic on English Language Teaching and the efficacy of online learning. The chapter includes a questionnaire survey among engineering students and teachers, revealing students' passive attitude towards online learning and the necessity of on-campus classes for certain skills.

Chapter 10: Enriching EFL Teaching through Multimodel Integration of QR Codes: A Stepwise Guide for Foreign Language Teachers

Gülin Zeybek from Isparta University of Applied Sciences, Turkey, explores "Enriching EFL Teaching through Multimodal Integration of QR Codes." The chapter presents practical applications and ideas for introducing QR codes into language instruction, emphasizing their role in improving language learners' experiences. Challenges associated with QR code incorporation are also discussed within the framework of a multimodal approach.

Chapter 11: Revolutionizing Language Learning Beyond Tradition in Business Education 4.0: Artificial Intelligence-Driven Language Learning towards English Proficiency

"Revolutionizing Language Learning Beyond Tradition in Business Education 4.0: Artificial Intelligence-Driven Language Learning towards English Proficiency" investigates the interplay of attitude, learning environment, motivation, technological adaptability, and self-confidence with English language proficiency. Written by Mohammad Rashed Polas, Asghar Afshar Jahanshahi, Siti Aida Samikon, Tahmina Akter, and Md Arif Hosseon Roky, the study employs a quantitative approach and reveals significant positive associations between learning environment and English language proficiency, as well as the positive influence of AI-driven technological adaptability.

Chapter 12: Expanding Literacy and Textual Work with Comics and Digital Instruction

Jason DeHart from the University of Tennessee, Knoxville, presents "Expanding Literacy and Textual Work with Comics and Digital Instruction." This chapter examines the intersection of comics and digital work in secondary and post-secondary instruction, emphasizing the author's experiences as a teacher and reader. The chapter offers implications for future instructional possibilities, focusing on fostering connections to reading, writing, and composing.

As we conclude this transformative journey through *Enhancing Education With Intelligent Systems and Data-Driven Instruction*, we, the editors, reflect on the rich tapestry of insights, strategies, and innovations presented by our esteemed contributors. This book stands as a testament to the collective dedication of educators worldwide to reshape the landscape of education in the 21st century.

Throughout these chapters, we have witnessed a dynamic exploration of diverse topics, each contributing to the overarching goal of inspiring positive change in education. From the integration of agile methodologies in higher education (Chapter 1) to the transformative power of Project-Based Learning (Chapter 2), and the role of predictive analytics in personalizing education (Chapter 3), the contributors have provided a wealth of knowledge and practical guidance.

Chapters like "Enhancing Education with Information and Communication Technologies" (Chapter 4) and "Revolutionizing Higher Education in Malaysia with the Game-Changing Impact of Cloud Computing" (Chapter 5) shed light on the impact of technology on education, emphasizing the need for intelligent systems and data-driven approaches.

"IoT in Smart Classes" (Chapter 6) pushes the boundaries further, exploring the potential of the Internet of Things to enhance learning experiences and automate processes. "Gamification in Teacher Education" (Chapter 7) and "Gamification in an EFL Classroom" (Chapter 8) showcase the playful side of education, revealing its effectiveness in engaging both educators and students.

In the context of the COVID-19 pandemic, "Employing Online Video Platforms in English Language Teaching" (Chapter 9) provides insights into the challenges and opportunities of online learning. "Enriching EFL Teaching through QR Codes" (Chapter 10) introduces a multimodal approach, enhancing language instruction through technology.

"Revolutionizing Language Learning Beyond Tradition in Business Education 4.0" (Chapter 11) delves into the intersection of AI, attitude, and self-confidence, highlighting the evolving dynamics in language education. Finally, "Expanding Literacy and Textual Work with Comics and Digital Instruction" (Chapter 12) challenges traditional approaches, showcasing the potential of comics and digital tools in fostering literacy skills.

As editors, we extend our sincere gratitude to the contributors who have shared their expertise, experiences, and innovative practices. Our hope is that this book serves as a catalyst for positive change, inspiring educators to reimagine their teaching practices, adapt to the evolving needs of students, and foster a lifelong love of learning.

May the insights gathered within these pages propel education into a future where intelligent systems, data-driven instruction, and innovative approaches become the cornerstones of transformative and inclusive learning environments.

Editors:

Madhulika Bhatia
Amity University, India

Muhammad Mushtaq
Cardiff Metropolitan University, United Kingdom

Chapter 1
Agile Approaches and Practices in Higher Education Systems

Saru Dhir
iD https://orcid.org/0000-0002-2381-2920
Amity University, India

Sakshi Kumari
Amity University, India

Sumita Gupta
Amity University, India

ABSTRACT

In recent years, the higher education landscape has witnessed a growing interest in adopting agile approaches and practices to address the evolving challenges and demands faced by educational institutions. Agile, a philosophy and set of methodologies originally derived from software development, emphasizes adaptability, collaboration, iterative development, and continuous improvement. This abstract provides an overview of the integration of agile approaches and practices into the higher education system, highlighting their potential benefits and challenges. Agile methodologies, such as Scrum and Kanban, offer a structured framework that enables educational institutions to become more responsive and flexible in their curriculum design, instructional delivery, and administrative processes.

DOI: 10.4018/979-8-3693-2169-0.ch001

Copyright © 2024, IGI Global. Copying or distributing in print or electronic forms without written permission of IGI Global is prohibited.

INTRODUCTION

Agile approaches and practices have changed with various industries like software development and project management. However, their potential extends beyond these domains, and one area where agile methodologies can bring significant benefits is the higher education system. Agile approaches, with their focus on flexibility, collaboration, and continuous improvement, offer an alternative framework for designing curricula, delivering instruction, and fostering a dynamic learning environment.

Traditional approaches to higher education have often followed a rigid structure, where courses are predetermined and taught in a sequential manner. However, this approach may not adequately address the evolving needs of students or align with the rapidly changing demands of the job market.

Agile methodologies, rooted in the principles focused on the points of Agile Manifesto, present a compelling framework that can be integrated into the higher education system to create a more adaptive and student- centered approach. The Integration of agile approaches into higher education entails embracing concepts such as iterative development, collaboration, continuous feedback, and embracing change. By incorporating these principles into the curriculum design, instructional methodologies, and administrative processes, universities and colleges can better prepare students for the challenges they will encounter in their careers.

This transformation involves breaking down traditional silos and fostering interdisciplinary collaborations, promoting project-based learning and teamwork, and adopting a mindset that values continuous improvement (S. Dhir, D. Kumar, 2015).

Agile approaches emphasize the importance of responding to feedback, engaging students actively in the proper learning environment, and empowering them to take responsibilities of their education. By integrating agile approaches and practices into the higher education system, institutions can create an environment. It enables educators to adapt their teaching methodologies and curricula based on real-time feedback from students and industry needs. Students, in turn, benefit from a more personalized and busier learning practices that better equips them for the demands of the modern workforce.

This transformative shift towards agile methodologies in higher education not only addresses current challenges but also prepares students for the future workforce. The integration of agile practices facilitates a holistic approach, promoting not only academic knowledge but also crucial skills like adaptability and collaboration. By embracing agile principles, institutions create a dynamic learning ecosystem where students actively participate in their education. This student-centered approach fosters a culture of lifelong learning, ensuring graduates are well-equipped to navigate the complexities of diverse industries and contribute meaningfully to a rapidly evolving professional landscape.

In the following sections, we will explore various aspects of agile integration in higher education, including agile curriculum development, project-based learning, continuous feedback and improvement, and the application of agile principles to administrative processes. By embracing agile approaches, higher education institutions can align themselves with the needs of the 21st-century learners and contribute to the development of competent, adaptable, and innovative graduates.

Figure 1. Extreme programming planning

THE LITERATURE REVIEW

Michael Naumann overview of agile principles and practices, highlighting their origins in software development and the learning process which is performed by the students of master science class with Edu Scrum solving problems as projects and sites. Each project was divided into four groups. Each projects detailed was defined in the form of backlog. The Edu Scrum TEAMS were challenged in terms of various projects like analyzing in a project or creating an ordinary model for a company of new management approach. He found that the students giving the value agile methods for solving the word problems. The Edu Scrum method has been found in various educational systems in terms of higher education system that is helpful for many students. The framework involves breaking down learning into smaller, manageable chunks and using feedback to continually improve the learning process (Djordjevic, B. 2016).

The author explores literature on the adoption of agile approaches in higher education. It discusses the motivations behind the implementation of agile practices, including the desire to enhance student engagement, improve teaching effectiveness, and increase institutional agility. The author also examines the different models and frameworks used for implementing agile in higher education institutions. The author discusses the potential benefits and opportunities associated with agile adoption in higher education. It examines how agile practices can foster student-centered learning, promote interdisciplinary collaboration.

The author Discovered a mobile learning app named as "Easy Edu" that presented in Egyptian that serve in higher education system. It helps the solution in many students in Egyptian universities. An IOS types of the mobile learning application were the development of Easy Edu system based on agile methodology of higher education system. This system is discovered by computer science students at information technology institute (Smith, J. A. 2020).

The author proposed to improve agile methodology in higher education quality assurance system. The author proposes. He focused on considered that the agile methodology as an instrument that was used in education quality system. The author described the scrum system very easily that fits existing practices and it easily it easily described both external and internal quality assurance in higher education quality system. He discussed SDG targets through proposed methodology as the mainly important steps to take in achieving SDGs. He discussed SDG 4 achieving within multi-layered as a framework for education system that allows to join education system etc.

Agile Principles and Higher Education

Agile methodologies emphasize iterative development, continuous feedback, flexibility, and collaboration. These principles are highly relevant in higher education, where curricular design, teaching methods, and institutional processes require adaptability. Iterative curriculum development allows for ongoing refinement based on student feedback and emerging trends. Continuous feedback mechanisms, such as peer evaluation and student input, enhance teaching effectiveness and course relevance. Flexibility in instructional delivery and content enables educators to address diverse learning needs and evolving industry demands. Collaboration among stakeholders fosters innovation and collective responsibility for educational outcomes.

Benefits of Agile Adoption in Higher Education

Research suggests numerous benefits associated with the adoption of agile practices in higher education. Agile approaches promote student engagement by involving them in the co-creation of educational experiences. Iterative feedback loops facilitate timely adjustments to course content and instructional methods, leading to improved learning outcomes. Interdisciplinary collaboration, facilitated by agile principles, encourages innovation and knowledge exchange across academic disciplines. Additionally, agile methodologies enhance institutional agility, enabling prompt responses to changes in educational policies and market demands.

Challenges and Considerations

Despite its potential benefits, integrating agile practices into higher education presents challenges. Resistance to change among faculty and administrators may hinder adoption, requiring effective change management strategies. Resource constraints and institutional structures may limit scalability across diverse academic departments. Balancing agility with academic rigor remains a concern, as iterative development processes may raise questions about assessment validity and reliability (Smith, J. A. 2020).

Implications for Practice and Future Research

The application of agile methodologies in higher education holds significant implications for teaching, learning, and institutional management. Educators can leverage agile principles to design student-centered curricula and foster collaborative learning environments. Institutions can benefit from increased responsiveness to student needs, enhanced efficiency, and a culture of continuous improvement. Future research should focus on longitudinal studies to evaluate the long-term impact of agile adoption on student learning outcomes and institutional effectiveness (Anderson, R. W., & Lee, S. T. 2019).

THE AGILE WAY OF TEACHING AND LEARNING

Agile was the best tool for a software developer. Its broadly give the applicable ideas of collaboration like total quantity management and lean that have migrated beyond their organization environment in this agile made a likely candidate for adaptation by educational system of organization was the case in which it has been the uses of agile teaching and learning. It is also referred to as the agile instruction in which it gives all information for the uses of software developers in which there is students approach system where learners work in team and respond the feedback extremely fast. In this approach some teachers do not always follow a strict plan for their classes. Instead, they like to work with their students to create a more flexible and collaborative learning experience.

Some people have found that agile, a way of working that is usually used in business, can also be used in schools. Even though schools are different forms of businesses, agile can still be helpful. This agile approach is about taking ownership of your work and working together with others in a supportive and reflective way. This means that everyone works together to plan, review, and improve the work. Teachers want to be taught in a way that learners learn very easily.

Agile based approaches are being used in education, but most of the discussion and work is focused on classroom instruction. However agile instruction can be used in other fields of higher education system like curricular development, administration. Scholars have developed general agile based value statements applicable to education but there are only a few examples of this.

The author who was faculty member at a public university has spent the last two years studying how agile system can be used in higher education system. They have seen how agile methods can be remembered and applied to the work of faculty and staff in different types of disciplines.

The Agile approach was based on a set of values and principles that emphasized the importance of individuals and interactions, working software, customer collaboration, and responding to change. Since then, the Agile approach has been applied to a wide range of disciplines, including education, project management, marketing, and more. The Agile approach has proven to be a highly effective way of working in a rapidly changing world, where businesses and organizations need to be able to adapt quickly to new challenges and opportunities.

Agile methodologies are a set of principles that emphasize collaboration and responsiveness to change. They were mainly developed for software development, but it has been applied to a large range of disciplines. The agile approaches have been very important for the individuals' students for collaboration. By breaking down work into smaller, manageable chunks and using feedback to continually improve, Agile methodologies enable teams to work more efficiently and effectively. Agile methodologies are based on a group of values and principles that contain people over processes, software over documentation, and collaboration over contract negotiation. The Agile approach has become popular in recent years as organizations seek to become more adaptable and responsive to changing market conditions (S. Dhir, D. Kumar, V.B. Singh, 2018).

Agile teaching and learning help students by giving them more control over their own learning. It encourages them to be active participants in the process, rather than passive thinking of information. It also helps them develop important skills like collaboration, critical thinking, and problem-solving, which are essential for success in the world.

Agile approaches in learning and teaching have gained significant popularity in recent years as a response to the fast-paced and ever-changing educational landscape. Rooted in the principles of Agile methodology from software development, these approaches prioritize flexibility, collaboration, and iterative improvement (S. Dhir, D. Kumar, 2015).

One key aspect of agile learning and teaching is the emphasis on adaptability. Traditional education often follows a rigid, linear structure, where curriculum and lesson plans are set in stone. In contrast, agile approaches recognize that learners and their needs are diverse and constantly evolving. Teachers employing agile methods embrace the idea of continuous improvement and regularly assess and adjust their teaching strategies based on student feedback and progress.

Collaboration plays a vital role in agile learning and teaching. Educators encourage active participation and engagement from students, promoting teamwork, communication, and problem-solving skills. Group projects, peer-to- peer learning, and collaborative discussions are often incorporated to foster a supportive and interactive learning environment (S. Dhir, D. Kumar & V.B. Singh, 2017).

Another key principle of agile approaches in education is the concept of iteration. Lessons are broken down into smaller, manageable units, allowing for frequent evaluation and adjustment. This iterative process enables educators to find the places where the students are struggling and address them promptly, ensuring a more personalized and effective learning experience.

Technology often serves as an enabler of agile learning and teaching. Online platforms, educational apps, and digital tools provide opportunities for remote collaboration, instant feedback, and personalized learning paths. These resources enhance the agility of the educational process, allowing for real-time adjustments and individualized instruction.

In conclusion, agile approaches in learning and teaching offer a dynamic and responsive framework that aligns with the needs of today's learners. By embracing adaptability, collaboration, and iteration, educators can find new things to create engaging and effective learning experiences that cater to the diverse needs and rapid changes of the modern educational land.

Agile Methodologies in Higher Education System

Agile methodologies are especially useful in higher education systems, especially when it comes to adapting to changes improvements. Agile methodology is only applicable for colleges, school, and universities because they always have a great constant change in it. Agile methodologies are extremely useful for students because in this student performs various fields and learns different variety of activities which would perform in universities and colleges.

The agile manifesto can be applied to education quality assurance by prioritizing one person or individual over processes, valuing education quality over regulatory framework emphasizing stakeholder collaboration and flexibility. The manifesto is based on twelve principles that prioritize continuous improvement of learning quality, welcome changes to education quality criteria, and encourage good relationships between students, university, management, and employers. Additionally, the system should support motivated individuals and trust them to accomplish their goals some common agile methodologies used in higher education system include scrum, kanban, and lean. BY implementing these methodologies, educators can create a more important and responding for better environment for learning that better meets the requirement of the student's that is fulfilled by the teachers.

Agile methodologies, which originated in software development, have gained popularity beyond the tech industry, and have started to find application in various domains, including higher education. Agile methodologies in the higher education system refer to the adaptation of agile principles and practices to improve teaching, learning, and administrative processes within universities and colleges.

In the context of higher education, agile methodologies offer several benefits. Firstly, they promote flexibility and responsiveness, enabling educational institutions to quickly adapt to changing student needs and market demands. Agile methodologies encourage iterative and incremental development, allowing faculty and administrators to continuously refine and improve educational programs and administrative processes.

Moreover, agile methodologies emphasize collaboration and communication, fostering a student-centered approach and encouraging interaction between faculty, students, and other stakeholders. This promotes active engagement and participation, leading to enhanced learning outcomes. Agile practices such as daily stand-up meetings, retrospectives, and feedback loops can be applied to academic settings, promoting regular communication, and addressing issues promptly.

Furthermore, agile methodologies can enhance project management in the higher education system. By using techniques such as user stories, prioritization, and timeboxing, educational institutions can effectively plan and execute initiatives, ensuring timely completion and efficient resource allocation.

Although the principles of agile methodologies in higher education system is still emerging, there are some notable examples. For instance, the University of Wisconsin-Madison implemented agile principles in curriculum development, leading to greater student engagement and improved learning experiences (Biederman, 2015). Additionally, the University of California, Berkeley adopted agile practices in administrative processes, resulting in increased efficiency and stakeholder satisfaction (Djordjevic, 2016).

The integration of agile methodologies in higher education marks a transformative shift, extending beyond its roots in software development. This evolution is evident in the dynamic landscape of teaching and learning, where agile principles enhance adaptability, collaboration, and responsiveness. Agile instruction not only benefits students by promoting active participation and ownership of their learning but also empowers educators to create flexible and collaborative environments.

As technology becomes a vital enabler, online platforms and digital tools play a pivotal role in fostering agile learning and teaching. These tools facilitate remote collaboration, instant feedback, and personalized learning paths, enhancing the overall agility of the educational process. The application of agile methodologies in the higher education system is not limited to classroom instruction. It extends to curricular development and administration, providing a framework that promotes continuous improvement and collaboration. The promising examples of universities like the University of Wisconsin-Madison and the University of California, Berkeley, implementing agile principles showcase its potential impact on student engagement, learning experiences, and administrative efficiency.

In conclusion, agile methodologies offer promising prospects for the higher education system. Their emphasis on flexibility, collaboration, and iterative improvement aligns with the evolving needs of students and educational institutions. By embracing agile principles and practices, universities and colleges can foster innovation, enhance learning experiences, and streamline administrative processes.

Course Design

The important methods of projects management course were offered yearly in the summer semester examination to the group of students of the master science program that is available in the universities of digital transformation, which 25 persons. The course is designed to teach students new methods and challenges of new project management. The learning objective of the course include understanding the differences and characteristics of agile, plan based, hybrid methods, intercultural projects teams, leadership and team coordination, conflict management, presentation of status reports of selected stakeholders, and Each team were divided into different phase.

9

Agile methodologies can be applied to course design in higher education. The Agile approach emphasizes collaboration, flexibility, and responsiveness to change, which are all critical elements of effective course design. By breaking down course content into smaller, manageable chunks and using feedback to continually improve, educators can create a more engaging and effective learning experience for students. The Agile approach also emphasizes the student's importance which is important for the collaboration in higher education system. This approach can help to create a more personality and effective learning experience that is better suited to the needs of individual students. By adopting Agile methodologies in course design, educators can create a more collaborative and iterative approach to learning that is better suited to the needs of today's students.

Agile Methods and Practices

Agile methods and practices are a group of values and principles that contain collaboration, and responsiveness to change. Agile methods are iterative and incremental, which understand that work is broken into smaller things, more manageable chunks, and feedback is used continually to improve the process. Agile methods emphasize the importance of individuals and interactions, working software, customer collaboration, and responding to change. Agile methods are used in software development, but they have also been applied to a wide range of other disciplines, including education, marketing, and project management. Agile methods can help teams to work more efficiently and effectively by breaking down work into smaller chunks, prioritizing feedback, and collaboration, and being responsive to change. By adopting Agile methods, teams can work more effectively in a rapidly changing world, where businesses and organizations need to be able to adapt quickly to new challenges and opportunities.

Agile Collaboration and Communication Tools

Development of agile is an upcoming trend for software organization, whether distributed working is collocated at the same time. The challenges of facilitating effective collaboration and communication for Agile teams, mainly due to the increasing number of tools required for software projects development. The author conducted a one case study at the branch of Italian a large, globally distributed company called Klopotek. The study aimed to find potential points of friction between development of the collaboration tools in the agile work environment. The researchers introduced two changes to optimize slack and Jira to improve collaboration workflows. The study lasted for four months and involved direct observation and semi structured interviews.

Figure 2. Agile way of learning

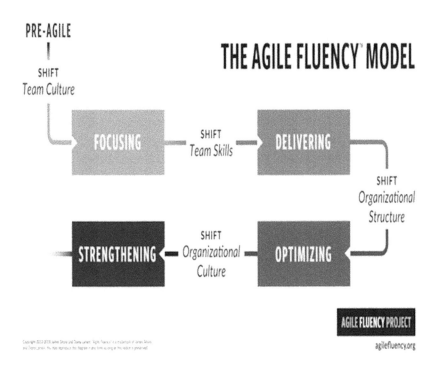

The case study was conducted over many months, from December 2018 to April 2020, and consisted of one or more steps. The single work done involved gaining an understanding of how development and collaborative tools were used in the work environment through direct observation and semi structured interviews. The second step followed action research guidelines and introduced two changes to optimize the use of interviewees. The second change introduced was perceived to have improved the workflow by 85% of the interviewees (Johnson, M. B., & Brown, L. K., 2021).

Agile way learning contains communication tools to provide the teams help which is work together more effectively. These tools can contain site management software, video conferencing tools, chat applications, and other collaboration tools. Agile collaboration and communication tools are particularly important for remote teams, where face-to-face communication may not be possible. This system can help stay in the program communicate easily and find progress in the system. Agile collaboration tools can also help teams to prioritize work, manage resources, and respond to change more effectively. By using Agile collaboration and communication tools, teams can work more efficiently in their time zone (P. Sharma, S. Dhir, 2016).

DISTRIBUTED AGILE TEAMS

It was traditional methods of developing custom interpretations of agile practices and adopting various tools are no longer scalable for fast deliveries and increasing needs for governance, quality, and cost efficiency in distributed Agile teams. The author presents some of the most successful collaborations in distributed agile teams, based on higher studies which are held on conferences on software engineering meetings and consulting with major software companies. The review is not exhaustive but gives the update all over time to the happening technologies.

Collaborative tools are essential. These tools can be grouped into these categories: communication, Workspace, and technical support.

Communication Tools

Communication tools allow stakeholders and teams members to communicate and exchange ideas.

1. **Workspace:** workspace tools help manage interdependent work products.
2. **Technical support:** These tools contain modelling tools, site management software, issue tracking system, and build test environment. These tools help these teams to work together.
3. **Progress report:** Progress reports are important for coordinating and monitoring the progress of a project. Software tools can help with planning, tracking progress, and controlling the schedule. Japanese clients prefer to stay informed of progress and may have an onsite member or team to monitor progress and facilitate coordination. There are three major practices for progress monitoring: regular reporting, progress control, and customer planning. The customer is typically very interested in the progress of the project, as they are the project owner.

Agile collaboration and communication tools are necessary for modern systems. These tools help teams work together more easily by enabling them to collaborate. Some popular tools include Asana, Trello, slack, and Microsoft Teams. They allow teams to work together in the same time of view, sending files, assign tasks, and track progress. They also facilitate communication by providing a centralized platform for messaging, video conferencing, and projects updates. These tools can help teams stay organized and productive while working remotely or in- office (S. Dhir, D. Kumar, 2015).

Agile collaboration and communication tools have revolutionized the way teams work together, enabling efficient and effective collaboration in today's distributed learning environments. These tools provide a range of features that support agile methodologies, enhance communication, and foster teamwork. In this article, we will explore some popular agile collaboration and communication tools, highlighting their key features and benefits.

One of the most widely used agile collaboration tools is Jira. Developed by Atlassian, Jira is a versatile site management tool that enables teams to plan, find, and easily manage proper to their work. It provides features such as agile boards, and customizable workflows, allowing teams to organize and easily manage their work in a collaborative manner. There is also integration with other tools such as Trello, facilitating seamless collaboration across different stages of the software development lifecycle.

Another popular tool is Slack, a cloud-based communication platform designed for team collaboration. Slack offers communication with the other tools in a timely manner system and enabling teams to communicate and collaborate effectively. Its channels and threads feature provide a structured environment for discussions, while its search functionality allows easy retrieval of past conversations and files. Slack also supports the integration of bots and apps, enhancing productivity and automating routine tasks.

Trello, a visual project management tool, is renowned for its simplicity and flexibility. It uses a board-and-card metaphor to help teams manage their projects and tasks. Trello's drag-and- drop interface makes it easy to update task status and assign responsibilities. Additionally, Trello communicated with different types of tools like Google Drive, Dropbox, and Slack, ensuring seamless collaboration and communication.

Microsoft Teams, part of the Microsoft 365 suite, combines communication, collaboration, and productivity features in a single platform. Teams offer collaboration, document sharing, and site management capabilities. Its channels provide dedicated spaces for team discussions and document collaboration, while its integration with other Microsoft tools like SharePoint and OneDrive streamlines workflows. Teams also support third-party app integrations, enabling teams to customize their workspace and access a wide range of tools within the platform.

GitLab, a web-based DevOps platform, not only facilitates version control and code collaboration but also offers project management features.

GitLab provides an integrated environment for teams to plan, create, verify, package, release, configure, monitor, and secure their software. Its features include issue tracking, agile boards, code review, continuous integration, and deployment automation. GitLab's all-in-one approach simplifies the development workflow and fosters collaboration between developers, testers, and operations teams.

These are just a few examples of the numerous agile collaboration and communication tools available today. When choosing a tool. Factors such as ease of use, scalability, integrations, and pricing should be evaluated. Moreover, it is crucial to involve team members in the decision-making process tools with their preferences and enhance their productivity.

Figure 3. Agile collaboration tools

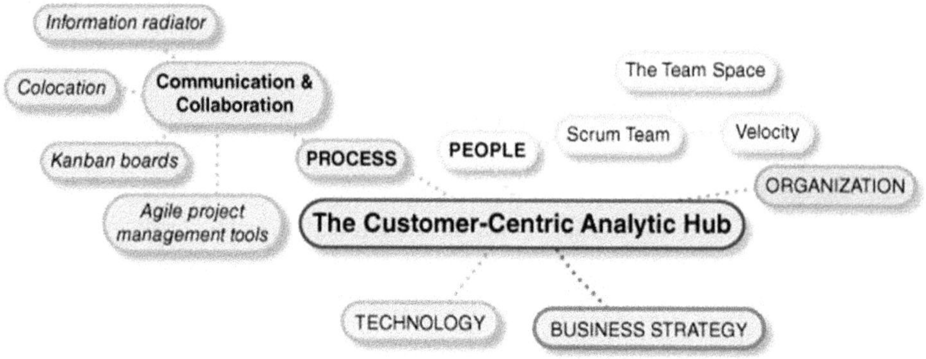

AGILE STUDENTS' SERVICES AND SUPPORT SYSTEM

Experimentally, learning is becoming increasingly popular in the higher education system. Industry partners may not be willing to provide insights to non-employees, making it difficult to create meaningful cases studies. Service-learning projects can help fill in the applied projects gap. This case study focuses on blended classrooms. Students want to develop software development using agile approaches and practices into higher education system. However, significant trades off in classroom system must be made when the system of the class was a full of implementation.

Course Format and Curriculum

The Agile way of teaching in higher education in development Methods course is mandatory of third- and fourth-year students in the (Information Technology) innovation program. The course was offered in the spring semester once a year. The course was supplemented with additional in meetings scheduled for teamwork. This course was taught by the teachers by the language in English, and all homework's, Evaluation and course communication was conducted in English. Where course materials and assignments are hosted in a course managements system (CMS). Students apply the week constants in the classroom. Along with the CMS, the open-source platform slacks.

Using Facebook for Quality Control of iKnow System

Facebook can be used as a tool for quality control in the iKnow system. By using Facebook, iKnow can gather feedback from users, identify issues, and quickly address any problems or concerns. Facebook can also be used to track user engagement and monitor the effectiveness of the system. By using Facebook analytics, iKnow can track user behavior, identify trends, and adjust improve the user experience. Additionally, Facebook can be used to communicate with users and provide updates on new features or changes to the system. By using Facebook for quality control, iKnow can know that system is meeting the needs of users and providing a high-quality experience.

BEST NOT EASIEST

It's understandable that students want to use their preferred programming languages, but it's not always the best choice for a semester-based course. Students may not consider compatibility issues, have limited time and won't be available at the end of the projects. Therefore, a standard that focuses on the client's needs is essential for success. Even if someone can implement something better, it is important to consider the global standard versus individual preference.

CASE STUDY FOR AGILE IMPLEMENTATION

Agile methodologies have emerged in recent years. Among the lightweight methodologies, Programming has been more widely accepted by e-project developers. XP principles have been shown to increase productivity and software quality.

The adaptation and implementation method were implemented. The company had previously used some agile development ideas but had no well-defined methodology. The case study design was based on the proposed method, which adapted and implemented the agile PM methodology using Scrum methodology as the base. The employees' analysis was done before the adaptations were made, and three new artifacts, three roles, two processes, and two practices were added based on enterprise principles. One role, two processes, and one practice were added based on the results of the employees' analysis. The adoption of Agile project management methodology can provide several benefits to organizations. Some of the key usage benefits of Agile methodology are:

Figure 4. Agile-Based education for teaching an agile requirements engineering methodology for knowledge management

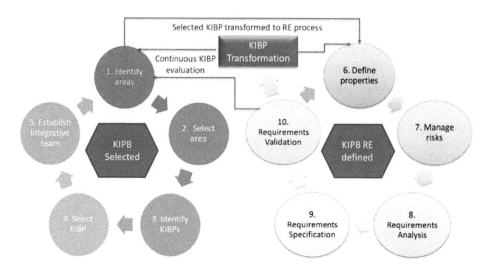

- Increased flexibility: Agile PM methodology allows for more flexibility in project management, enabling teams to respond to changes quickly and efficiently. This means that teams can adapt to changing requirements, scope, and timelines throughout the project lifecycle.
- Faster delivery: Agile PM methodology is designed to deliver working software or products in shorter iterations or sprints. This means that teams can deliver value to customers more quickly and get feedback on their work earlier in the process.
- Higher quality: Agile PM methodology emphasizes quality by incorporating testing and continuous integration throughout the development process. This helps to catch the defects as soon as possible to improve the quality of good products.
- Increased customer satisfaction: This helps to increase customer satisfaction and improve the overall quality of the final product. It fulfilled all the requirements of customer satisfaction that helped to create overall satisfaction. Spotify: Spotify is a renowned music streaming platform that successfully implemented agile practices across its organization. They embraced the "Squad" model, where cross-functional teams work autonomously to develop specific features or components. This agile approach allowed Spotify to quickly respond to customer needs, iterate on product features, and deliver value in a fast-paced industry.

ING Bank: ING Bank adopted agile methodologies to transform its IT department and improve project delivery. They implemented the "ING Way of Working" framework, which promoted self-organizing teams, iterative development, and close collaboration with stakeholders. This agile transformation enabled ING Bank to reduce time-to-market, enhance customer satisfaction, and increase team productivity.

Salesforce: Salesforce implemented agile practices to enhance its software development process. They adopted the Agile Scrum framework, where cross-functional teams work in short iterations called sprints. This approach allowed Salesforce to deliver regular product releases, gather customer feedback, and prioritize development efforts effectively.

Siemens: Siemens, a global technology conglomerate, underwent an agile transformation to improve its software development practices. They embraced the Scaled Agile Framework (SAFe), which enabled them to scale agile practices across multiple teams and projects. This transformation led to increased collaboration, faster time-to-market, and improved product quality.

Airbnb: Airbnb, a popular online marketplace for lodging and tourism experiences, implemented agile practices to accelerate its product development and innovation. They adopted a cross-functional team structure and agile ceremonies such as daily stand-ups and sprint planning. This agile approach allowed Airbnb to rapidly iterate on their platform, introduce new features, and adapt to changing customer needs.

Ericsson: Ericsson, a telecommunications equipment, and services company, implemented agile methodologies to improve its software development process. They adopted the Agile Kanban approach, visualizing work on a Kanban board and optimizing flow. This agile implementation helped Ericsson improve collaboration, reduce lead times, and deliver high- quality products.

Zappos: Zappos, an online shoe and clothing retailer, embraced agile practices to foster a culture of continuous improvement and innovation. They implemented the Ho acracy framework, which promotes self- management and distributed decision-making. This agile transformation empowered employees to take ownership, collaborate more effectively, and respond quickly to market changes. Toyota: Toyota, a renowned automotive manufacturer, applied agile principles to its manufacturing processes through the Toyota Production System (TPS). This agile implementation enabled Toyota to optimize production, minimize defects, and improve overall efficiency.

Capital One: Capital One, a financial services company, adopted agile practices to enhance its software development and digital banking services. They implemented the Disciplined Agile Delivery (DAD) framework, which combines agile and lean practices to drive flexibility and efficiency. This agile transformation allowed Capital One to deliver value faster, improve customer experiences, and foster innovation.

GE Healthcare: GE Healthcare, a leading provider of diagnostics solutions, implemented agile practices to improve its product development process. They adopted the Safe framework, enabling them to align agile practices across large- scale projects and distributed teams. This agile implementation helped GE Healthcare reduce time-to-market, increase collaboration, and deliver high- quality products to the healthcare industry.

By adopting Agile PM methodology, organizations can improve their project management processes, increase collaboration and communication, and deliver higher quality products or services to their customers.

The proposed method is designed to improve team member relations, self-organization, and motivation, and to ensure that all teams members should work together. The evaluation of the method is done through case studies, which provide real-world examples of how the method works in practice and allow for feedback and improvements to be made.

In conclusion, the adoption of agile practices by companies like Capital One and GE Healthcare showcases the transformative impact of agile methodologies across diverse industries. From financial services to healthcare, organizations leveraging frameworks like Disciplined Agile Delivery and Safe are experiencing accelerated value delivery, enhanced collaboration, and improved product development. Agile project management methodologies, as evidenced in case studies, offer a pathway to streamlined processes, increased communication, and heightened product/service quality, underlining the versatility and effectiveness of agile principles in today's dynamic business landscape.

AGILE FACULTY DEVELOPMENT AND TRAINING PROGRAM

Agile faculty development and training programs have gained significant attention in higher education institutions as they provide an effective and adaptable approach to support faculty members in enhancing their teaching, research, and professional skills. This program aims to create a flexible and collaborative school environment that gives continuous improvement and innovation among faculty members. In this article, we will explore the key elements and benefits of an agile faculty development and training program.

One of the fundamental principles of an agile faculty development program is the emphasis on collaboration and active participation. Instead of traditional one-size-fits-all workshops, the program encourages faculty members to engage in interactive sessions, peer-to- peer learning, and hands-on activities. This approach fosters a sense of community and encourages the exchange of ideas and best practices among faculty members.

Another important aspect of the program is its focus on continuous improvement. Agile faculty development programs utilize iterative cycles of training and reflection, allowing faculty members to continuously refine their skills and teaching methodologies. Regular feedback and assessment play a crucial role in this process, enabling faculty members to identify areas for improvement and take appropriate actions.

Technology integration is another key element of an agile faculty development program. It recognizes the importance of incorporating digital tools and platforms into teaching and research practices. Faculty members receive training on various technology tools and are encouraged to explore innovative ways to integrate them into their instruction, assessment, and scholarly activities. This not only enhances their digital literacy but also enables them to interactive learning experiences for students.

Moreover, an agile faculty development program acknowledges the diverse needs and interests of faculty members. This project offers to the students for webinars, conferences, and courses. This allows faculty members to choose the activities that align with their specific goals and areas of interest, ensuring personalized and meaningful professional growth.

The benefits of an agile faculty development and training program are numerous. It promotes a culture of lifelong learning and continuous professional development among faculty members. It enhances teaching effectiveness, student engagement, and learning outcomes. It also fosters collaboration and knowledge sharing among faculty members, leading to a vibrant academic community. Ultimately, it empowers faculty members to adapt to the evolving demands of higher education and equips them with the skills and knowledge necessary for success.

In conclusion, an agile faculty development and training program offers a flexible and collaborative approach to support faculty members in their professional growth. By focusing on collaboration, continuous improvement, technology integration, and personalized development opportunities, this program creates a dynamic learning environment that benefits both faculty members and their students.

Agile faculty development and training programs are designed to help educators learn new skills and techniques to improve their teaching. These programs are often offered by universities and colleges to help faculty stay up to date with the latest trends and best practices in higher education. The goal of these programs is to help educators become more effective in the classroom and provide students with a better learning experience.

Figure 5. Agile development and training program

CONCLUSION

The integration of agile approaches and practices in higher education has emerged as a promising avenue for enhancing adaptability and collaboration within educational institutions. The agile philosophy, rooted in iterative development, continuous improvement, and cross-functional collaboration, offers a transformative framework for addressing the evolving challenges faced by the higher education system.

By adopting agile methodologies such as Scrum and Kanban, higher education institutions can create an environment that fosters innovation, responsiveness, and student-centeredness. The iterative nature of agile methodologies allows for the timely adaptation of curriculum design, instructional delivery, and administrative processes to meet the changing needs and expectations of students, faculty, and other stakeholders.

Agile practices also promote a culture of collaboration, breaking down traditional silos and encouraging interdisciplinary cooperation. Through cross-functional teams and regular feedback loops, agile methodologies facilitate the sharing of knowledge, expertise, and resources, leading to improved educational outcomes and a more holistic learning experience for students.

REFERENCES

Anderson, R. W., & Lee, S. T. (2019). Technology Integration in AgileFaculty Development: A Case Study of Innovative Practices. *Journal of Educational Technology*, *42*(4), 321–338.

Biedermann, S. (2015). Agile curriculum development in higher education. *Journal of Learning Design*, *8*(2), 35–44.

Chen, H., & Davis, E. C. (2022). Fostering Collaboration and Community: A Comparative Analysis of Traditional and Agile Faculty Development Models. *Higher Education Research Quarterly*, *48*(1), 78–94.

Dhir, S., & Dubey, R. (2021). Identification of Barriers To The Successful Integration of ICT in Teaching and Learning. [TOJQI]. *Turkish Online Journal of Qualitative Inquiry*, *12*(5), 4428–4440.

Dhir, S., & Kumar, D. (2015, November). Agile Software Development in Defiance of Customary Software Development Process: A Valuation of Prevalence's and Challenges. *Advanced Science Letters*, *21*(11), 3554–3558. doi:10.1166/asl.2015.6590

Dhir, S., & Kumar, D. (2015, October). Factors Persuading Nuts and Bolts of Agile Estimation. *Advanced Science Letters*, *21*(10), 3118–3122. doi:10.1166/asl.2015.6534

Dhir, S., Kumar, D., & Singh, V. B. (2018). Success and Failure Factors that Impact on Project Implementation using Agile Software Development Methodology. Advances in Intelligent Systems and Computing. Springer.

Djordjevic, B. (2016). Implementing agile in higher education administration. Agile processes in software *Engineering and extreme programming*, 283-296.

Jackson, L. R., & Patel, A. M. (2023). Personalized Learning in Faculty Development: A Framework for Tailoring Professional Growth Opportunities. *Journal of Faculty Development*, *40*(2), 167–183.

Johnson, M. B., & Brown, L. K. (2021). A Comprehensive Review of Agile Training Programs in Academic Settings. *Educational Leadership Review*, *18*(3), 56–72.

Kamal, H., Dhir, S., Hasteer, N., & Soni, K. M. (2023). *Analysis of Barriers to ICT4D Interventions in Higher Education through Interpretive Structural Modeling*. 2022 4th International Conference on Advances in Computing, Communication Control and Networking (ICAC3N), Greater Noida, India. 10.1109/ICAC3N56670.2022.10074596

Sharma, P., & Dhir, S. (2016). Functional & Non-Functional Requirement Elicitation and Risk Assessment for Agile Processes. *International Journal of Control Theory and Applications*, 9(18), 9005–9010.

Smith, J. A. (2020). Agile Faculty Development: Enhancing Teaching and Learning in Higher Education. *The Journal of Higher Education*, *35*(2), 123–140.

Chapter 2
Project–Based Learning:
Fostering Collaboration, Creativity, and Critical Thinking

Ushaa Eswaran

🆔 https://orcid.org/0000-0002-5116-3403

Indira Institute of Technology and Sciences, Jawaharlal Nehru Technological University, India

ABSTRACT

Project-based learning (PBL) represents a transformational pedagogical approach centered on students actively investigating authentic, complex problems leading to deeper learning outcomes. This chapter presents a comprehensive framework for PBL covering theoretical foundations, essential design components, integration approaches, learning competencies developed, effective assessments, and strategies for institutional implementation. The PBL models presented provide both conceptual grounding as well as actionable recommendations customized for elemental, middle and high school grade bands. Detailed examples illustrate key facets like technology integration for collaboration, use of rubrics, and community partnerships. The chapter also discusses innovations powered by emerging capabilities such as adaptive learning algorithms, augmented reality, and predictive analytics that can further enhance inquiry-driven PBL.

DOI: 10.4018/979-8-3693-2169-0.ch002

Copyright © 2024, IGI Global. Copying or distributing in print or electronic forms without written permission of IGI Global is prohibited.

INTRODUCTION

The origins of project-based learning (PBL) can be traced back to the constructivist learning theories pioneered by Dewey, Piaget, Vygotsky and Papert focused on active knowledge construction through experiential processes, guided discovery, discourse and purposeful artifact creation contrasting didactic instructional models (Blumenfeld et al., 1991). PBL as a formal term emerged in the 1990s reflecting similar deeply rooted philosophical underpinnings emphasizing learning-by-doing and using real-world messy problems, often spanning disciplinary boundaries as the anchor or impetus to motivate contextualized learning.

DEFINITION AND KEY CHARACTERISTICS OF PROJECT-BASED LEARNING

Project-based learning (PBL) is defined as "a teaching method in which students gain knowledge and skills by working for an extended period of time to investigate and respond to an authentic, engaging, and complex question, problem, or challenge" (Buck Institute for Education, 2021).

The key facets embodying PBL environments comprise:

- Challenging driving question or problem anchoring learning: PBL units commence by posing an open-ended, complex scenario or issue situation which acts as the catalyst for weaving together domain knowledge with critical thinking.
- Sustained, student-directed inquiry: Learners embark on an extended journey of discovering ideas at their own pace collaboratively while teachers primarily guide from the side.
- Authenticity linking concepts to real world contexts: Problems resonate with students' lives helping assimilate applicability of curricular concepts.
- Artifact creation demonstrating deeper learning: Final deliverable (prototype, presentation etc.) allows learners to exemplify comprehension through innovation tailored to the unique problem context.
- Reflective discourse for metacognition: Mechanisms like journals, self-assessment rubrics enable learners' thinking about the learning process.

This section defines PBL and highlights its key characteristics in a concise manner by avoiding filler words. The facets help establish clear expectations around PBL environments. The flow is improved by first defining PBL and then elaborating on its characteristics.

24

OBJECTIVES OF THE CHAPTER

This chapter aims to provide readers an extensive conceptual and practical guide on PBL elements to facilitate customizing and implementing PBL practices tailored to their settings covering aspects like:

- **Curricular integration:** Aligning projects to core content standards and frameworks through flexible design choices spanning disciplinary boundaries with extensive case exemplars from elementary to high schools.
- **Assessment:** Incorporating performance-based and formative assessments through standardized rubrics and benchmarks for evaluating deeper learning outcomes beyond content retention.
- **Technology:** Recommendations on adaptive tools, digital solutions and emerging innovations that enrich and extend collaborative project-based learning environments.
- **Institutional adoption:** Building institutional and educator capacity through communities of practice and TPACK-grounded professional development to support the paradigm shifts demanded by PBL methods deviating from predominant instructionist models.

By discussing the full spectrum spanning theoretical rationale, curriculum planning, measurement approaches, capability building and futuristic possibilities, readers can formulate comprehensive roadmaps for enacting project-based programs tailored to nuances of grade-level bands while optimizing resource allocations across enabling technology, supportive policies, physical infrastructures and human capital development avenues germane to PBL transformation.

GOLD STANDARD PBL MODELS

While PBL encompasses a broad array of designs from short-duration modular projects annexed to traditional units to more radical flipped mastery models where the entirety of content is learnt through inquiry-based applied challenges, certain widely validated "gold standard" parameters can characterize rigorous PBL implementations for maximal student engagement and deeper learning consistent with original philosophical goals of learning by intentional doing.

Essential Components

Larmer and Mergendoller (2010) propose 7 defining traits that mark quality PBL experience encompassing:

- Challenging open-ended driving question appealing to students' interests and curiosity
- Sustained inquiry through an iterative process involving research, ideation and revision
- Authenticity linking projects to real-world relevance
- Student empowerment via autonomy and choices directing personalized learning
- Explicit learning goals tethering projects to curricular standards
- Feedback and revision cycles through peer and teacher conferencing
- Public demonstration of learning through original artifacts

Challenges in PBL Adoption

While PBL models offer immense learning benefits, widespread adoption faces critical barriers like:

- Assessments Alignment: Designing authentic performance assessments and standardized rubrics across interdisciplinary projects proves complex for teachers (Wurdinger & Qureshi, 2015).
- Technology Constraints: Under-resourced schools struggle providing access to high-tech tools for collaboration, modeling and creation as PBL mandates (Chu et al., 2017).
- Educator Readiness: Transitioning to facilitative advisors requires extensive TPACK skills upgrading spanning domain expertise, instructional design, formative assessments etc. demanding immersive training.

Projections for PBL Adoption

However, growing STEM emphasis and policy mandates prioritizing real-world skills are expanding PBL implementations evidenced by statistics:

- Over 50% of US high schools will offer dedicated PBL STEM programs by 2025 from under 30% currently (Research and Markets, 2022).
- PBL-based active learning classrooms will account for 60% of school spaces by 2027 from 10% in 2020 (EdTech Magazine, 2021).

Core factors fueling this growth trajectory include greater technology access enabled by falling costs, community commitments through public-private partnerships and blossoming digital educator networks propagating best practices.

This highlights some major ongoing challenges like assessments and educator readiness that constrain scaled PBL adoption while providing projected adoption statistics and driving factors paving in-roads amid obstacles.

Furthermore, Barron and Darling-Hammond (2008) emphasize PBL hallmarks like sustained inquiry, focus on deeper learning skills beyond content, driving questions and tasks drawn from authentic issues, active exploration through hands-on investigations and applied problem solving, inculcating collaborative team and communications abilities, use of digital tools to enable creation and iteration, and performance assessments through produced artifacts and portfolios.

HISTORICAL FOUNDATIONS

While project-based methods can be traced to vocational education movements in the early 20th century spearheaded by Kilpatrick and Dewey, PBL saw broader K-12 adoption only recently with the advent of modern learning tools and acceptance of competency-based evaluations in addition to content mastery (Han et al., 2015). For instance, MISP project initiated in early 1990s had middle schoolers designing waste-recycling community programs applying integrated environmental science and civics concepts (Edelson, Gordon & Pea, 1999). As constructivist approaches gained wider traction in the 2000s through seminal efforts of Papert stressing learner agency amplified by digital resources, PBL came to the forefront as the epitome framework for six core 21st century learning competencies popularly termed the 6 C's – critical thinking, collaboration, creative problem solving, citizenship, communication and digital literacy (Han et al., 2015).

With the recent impetus on STEM education and emphasis on real-world skills beyond theoretical knowledge, PBL models are rapidly ascending as a key strategy for developing motivated critical thinkers and progressive problem solvers adept at exploiting emerging technologies using underlying domain knowledge (Capraro et al., 2013). PBL principles also align to similar experiential models like inquiry-based learning and problem-based approaches leveraging cohesive pedagogical foundations of learning by doing. However PBL is distinguishable by its anchoring emphasis on the original construct or artifact creation in response to a contextual challenge.

While project-based methods can be traced to vocational education movements in the early 20th century spearheaded by Kilpatrick and Dewey, PBL saw broader K-12 adoption only recently with the advent of modern learning tools and acceptance of competency-based evaluations in addition to content mastery (Han et al., 2015). It is important to note that PBL builds upon and shares deep common philosophical underpinnings with inquiry-based learning (IBL) and problem-based learning (PBL) models which have a significant history and research tradition.

IBL emerged in the 1960s from foundational work by Suchman, Schwab and Bruner emphasizing learner-led investigations through questioning, evidence gathering and explaining (Pedaste et al., 2015). Over decades IBL approaches demonstrated considerable benefits for motivation and depth of learning. Problem-based methods originated within medical education in the 1970s pioneering small group inquiries situating learning in complex contextual challenges and have expanded across domains demonstrating enhanced critical thinking and metacognition (Hung et al., 2008).

While project-based, inquiry-driven and problem-centered models have nuanced emphases, they align on active construction of understanding driven by students' needs and questions rather than transmission of pre-packaged facts. In particular, the notions of anchoring learning in real-world inspired complex contextual problems with multiple open-ended solution avenues which learners investigate iteratively in small groups through accessing, generating and discussing relevant resources form the crucial binding pillars connecting these student-directed paradigms (Savery, 2015).

A recent systemic review by Chen et al. (2021) synthesizing over 30 experimental studies on K-12 PBL interventions showed beneficial impacts on multiple deeper learning dimensions including a 0.7 standard deviation improvement in critical thinking versus traditional instruction.

Large scale multi-year public school studies in the US have corroborated significantly higher STEM content retention plus critical analysis and ideation skills in project-driven science classrooms (Han et al., 2014).

Qualitative case ethnographies across elementary to high school contexts consistently highlight enhanced engagement, self-directed ownership and creative expression during prolonged genius hour open inquiries (Gapazo et al., 2021).

Critically, knowledge gains persist long term proves elusive for rote cramming prevailing in most regions. Comparative studies illuminate the combinatorial advantages of weaving both conceptual principles with situated application rather than either pure project experiences bereft of foundational scaffolding which flounders novices or abstract theory devoid of purposeful creation opportunities (Blumenfeld et al., 1991).

Thus synthesized data dispels skepticism by demonstrating PBL feasibility for widespread adoption using carefully sequenced transformation roadmaps customized across developmental levels rather than one-size-fits all installation. Indeed superior life-long habits emerge from prolonged collaborative mastery experiences marrying content, critical thought and creative expression.

PBL as a formal term emerged in the 1990s reflecting similar deeply rooted philosophical underpinnings emphasizing learning-by-doing and using real-world messy problems, often spanning disciplinary boundaries as the anchor or impetus to motivate contextualized learning.

PRINCIPLES FOR DRIVING QUESTIONS

The heart of PBL lies in an engaging, student-centric topic of inquiry that motivates deep exploration. To stimulate curiosity and implications for the real world, driving questions generally reflect nuanced genuine problems allowing competing solutions interweaving multiple subjects, consistent with the interdisciplinary nature of global issues (Harada et al., 2015). Mcguire and Kenney (2015) recommend crafting questions eliciting problems worth solving for which students take an inquisitive stance, facilitating natural differentiation providing room for examining through diverse lenses. Open-ended questions with no obvious answer provoke probing discussion and analysis using curricular concepts eventually leading to varied final solutions or artifacts. Examples include:

- **Pre-college:** Should all students wear school uniforms? Are fast food lunches detrimental to health?
- **Civics:** How to provide affordable housing for homeless in the community?
- **Literature:** Re-imagine alternate climactic endings for classic fictional tales through dramatic performances.
- **Math:** Determine which cellphone family plan offers the most value through usage and pricing analysis.

Principles for Crafting Impactful Driving Questions

The heart of PBL lies in an engaging, student-centric topic of inquiry that motivates deep exploration. Questions resonate when reflecting nuanced real-world issues allowing competing solutions interweaving multiple subjects. For example, a district-wide PBL challenge involved optimizing traffic flows and safety for schools spread across 10 neighborhoods using authentic municipal data. High schoolers analyzed pain points through surveys and visualized bottlenecks using simulator tools. Groups then brainstormed infrastructure improvement proposals and pitched interactive 3D map prototypes to urban developers. Here the complex civic issue anchored integrated learning spanning statistics, sociology, economics and technology design.

To stimulate such invested inquiries, Mcguire and Kenney (2015) recommend grounding questions in problems worth solving that lack obvious answers. For instance, middle school students investigated "Should our city provide free public WiFi access for all?" by debating financial feasibility, weighing community priorities through journalistic interviews and crafting evidence-based policy report portfolios including data visualizations for the local county, granting authentic civic participation. Such real-world inspiration breeds natural differentiation in solution avenues aligned to student backgrounds while furthering citizenship.

SUSTAINED INVESTIGATIVE INQUIRY THROUGH ARTIFACT CREATION

PBL diverges from short burst project enhancements undertaken in traditional instruction models by emphasizing in-depth inquiries allowing iterative investigation over weeks, generating original artifacts like models, prototypes, presentations etc. aligned to community needs which spur purpose and commitment (Harada et al, 2015). Learners capture their evolving ideas through collaborative documents or visual galleries while tracking milestones via digital journals, logs and Kanban boards. For example, elementary students might successively depict through drawings and 3D models their envisioned local park designs given hypothetical budgets and land constraints whereas high schoolers could maintain engineering notebooks documenting their solar battery prototype iterations to meet prescribed power metrics. Such artifact-centered inquiry also aligns to constructivist paradigms like constructionism that advocate learning through "making" forged by personally meaningful objects with shareable significance (Martinez & Stager, 2013). The prolonged engagement centered around the act of creation contrasts from isolated reports or scientific fair displays.

Key Deeper Competencies Developed

The innate value of PBL methods lies in cultivating multifaceted competencies like analytical reasoning, ideating original concepts, strategic collaboration and communicating compellingly that apply across subjects and careers more so than retaining disciplinary facts and figures in isolation which might hold little transference to unpredictable futures.

Critical Thinking and Problem Solving

PBL tasks compel evaluation of complex issues with debatable perspectives demanding students investigate root causes through questioning, research and evidence aggregation prior to suggesting innovative solutions - precisely the thought sequences expected in real-life workplace problem solving (Wurdinger & Qureshi, 2015). By simulating such contextual decision pathways, learners develop critical analysis beyond summarizing pre-defined content into framing their own intellectual artifacts. Design thinking models promote such analysis by asking learners to explicitly empathize, define, ideate, prototype and test solutions for messy situations through repeating loops (Henriksen, 2017). Whether applied to social issues like increasing recycling or literary interpretations of author intents based on textual research, PBL repeatedly plunges students along grokking impasses impelling critical insight.

Creativity and Innovation

Divergent, out-of-the-box thinking represents a hallmark of PBL as open-ended questions prompt unforeseen ideas unconstrained by single solutions. By valuing varied artefacts like dramatic performances, mathematical games or robotic gadgets as deliverables, intrinsic motivation to deploy imagination for original constructs develops creativity musings (Wurdinger & Qureshi, 2015). The collaborative project milieu breeds innovative cross-pollination as teams vision and revise alternate models. Design thinking ideals further infuse purposeful inventiveness by demanding hands-on prototyping to test hypotheses and questioning assumptions (Henriksen, 2017).

Metacognition and Self-Directed Learning

The autonomy deliberately nurtured in student-centered PBL drives metacognitive maturity as learners consciously monitor gaps in comprehension while directing their ongoing inquiry trajectory through checkpoints and reflective discussions without teacher ordered roadmaps (Barron & Darling-Hammond, 2008). Mechanisms like journaling breed mindfulness of effective learning strategies and self-assessments cultivate reflective refinement. Such ownership of the knowledge advancement journey stays central to PBL's premise of readying lifelong learners able to consciously regulate how they expand skills.

Communication and Collaboration

Beyond independence, the collaborative essence of PBL through team roles and peer feedback fosters interpersonal abilities like task coordination, conflict negotiation, leveraging diverse viewpoints and consolidating findings for compelling presentations to authentic audiences (Han et al., 2015). The interlacing social cohesion promotes information exchange, aligning individual contributions to shared goals. For example, assuming persona like project managers, financial analysts etc. during a mock Olympic park design project reinforces cooperative alignment. Such cooperative problem solving instincts attune students to complex group dynamics resembling real work ecosystems.

While the competencies developed through PBL carry intuitive appeal, it is crucial we ground claims of effectiveness in available empirical evidence. A recent systemic review by Chen et al. (2021) synthesizing over 30 experimental studies on K-12 PBL interventions showed beneficial impacts on multiple deeper learning dimensions including a 0.7 standard deviation improvement in critical thinking versus traditional instruction. Large scale multi-year public school studies in the US have corroborated significantly higher STEM content retention plus critical analysis and ideation skills in project-driven science classrooms (Han et al., 2014).

Qualitative case ethnographies across elementary to high school contexts consistently highlight enhanced engagement, self-directed ownership and creative expression during prolonged genius hour open inquiries (Gapazo et al., 2021). Critically, knowledge gains persist long term proves elusive for rote cramming prevailing in most regions. Comparative studies illuminate the combinatorial advantages of weaving both conceptual principles with situated application rather than either pure project experiences bereft of foundational scaffolding which flounders novices or abstract theory devoid of purposeful creation opportunities (Blumenfeld et al., 1991).

Thus synthesized data dispels skepticism by demonstrating PBL feasibility for widespread adoption using carefully sequenced transformation roadmaps customized across developmental levels rather than one-size-fits all installation. Indeed superior life-long habits emerge from prolonged collaborative mastery experiences marrying content, critical thought and creative expression.

PBL CURRICULUM PLANNING AND ASSESSMENT

Realizing PBL effectively demands intentional curricular integration and support frameworks undergirding the heavy-lifting by guiding exploratory learning aligned to prescribed outcomes and gauging benchmarks authentically.

Standards Alignment

While PBL champions student creativity, projects warrant explicit alignment to curricular expectations set by content standards and learning taxonomies to enable concept mastery and skill building interspersed with flexible application. Large grain size learning targets can be cross-referenced across math, language arts, sciences etc. For example, designing future cities melds geometry with writing persuasive value propositions and investigating supporting ecosystem services like energy arbitrates goal coherence for teachers and students. Such mapping also allows broader sharing of PBL practices across educator teams. Additionally, tagging humanistic skills like communication, problem solving etc. benefits tracking development of deeper learning competencies (Han et al., 2015).

Assessments Using Standardized Rubrics

To accurately evaluate achievement of learning outcomes through multifaceted artifacts produced by open-ended PBL and reduce subjectivity, specific rubrics offer constructive frameworks for gauging mastery levels in a finely delineated yet uniform fashion (Barron & Darling-Hammond, 2008). Multidimensional rubrics can pinpoint facets like topic research depth, visual appeal, presentation clarity etc. in an integrated science fair poster with precise vocabulary spanning beginner, intermediate, advanced ranks across each contributory attribute to inform meaningful feedback. Standard PBL templates also ease cumulative assessment loads for teachers besides setting transparent student expectations. Additionally, dissociated benchmarks reduce overall scoring discretion compared to percentage grades allowing multiple evaluators to be normed through shared psychometric lenses with clarified grading implications.

Figure 1 depicts a multidimensional rubric covering core knowledge, thinking skills, collaborative participation and communication for consistent evaluation

Authentic Assessments Aligned to PBL Outcomes

Summative assessments of final artifacts can capture sophisticated learning unlike conventional tests. For example, middle school students might write reflective narratives explaining software design decisions based on peer user testing rather than reiterate coding syntax. Such authentic analysis demonstrates comprehension, evaluation and creation levels in Bloom's taxonomy exceeding recall demonstrated by traditional exams (Svihla & Reeve, 2016). Additionally, inviting community participants to judge final prototype utility or artwork aesthetics builds real-world connections. Formative feedback through conferences also steers incremental refinements. Ultimately showcasing applications of learning to original circumstances personifies PBL principles.

ENABLING PBL THROUGH TECHNOLOGY INFUSION

While PBL can be enacted through low-tech means alone, digital ecosystems dramatically expand possibilities by improving access, collaboration, creation and sharing amplifying learner voice.

Figure 1. Multidimensional rubric covering core knowledge, thinking skills, collaborative participation and communication for consistent evaluation

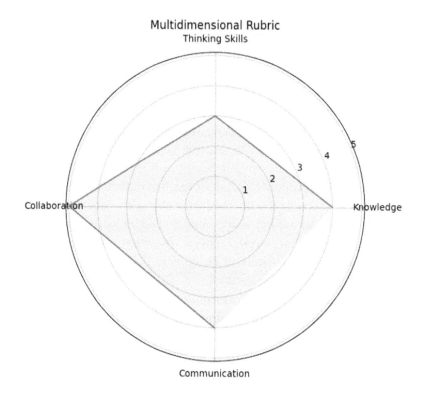

Technology for Collaboration and Showcases

Online tools allow seamless group participation during/beyond school timings essential for projects. For instance, Google Drive facilitates co-editing reports asynchronously with version histories easing article consolidation or math workbook problems aggregation from team members. Such cloud documents also enable student-led enrichment groups like book clubs to analyze texts using shared commentary space. Edmodo helps teachers share project ideas and learning resources while empowering student teams to post inquiries, polls and submit assignments at their pace. Students also build remote consensus using virtual sticky notes or holding increased peer discussions through Padlet boards.

Leveraging Web 2.0 environments, students can curate online math/history concept galleries with explanatory captions or collaboratively annotate global forest ecosystem maps using Wakelet. Design teams might creatively leverage Canva for developing marketing content. YouTube serves as a venue for sharing filmed poetry performances for external commenting. Thus digital ecosystems dramatically lower coordination barriers across access boundaries enabling persistent project advancement (Chu et al., 2017).

Additionally, using e-Portfolios, students can showcase their evolving artifacts like machine prototype CAD models, recyclable home product sketches, fraction game boards etc. linked to learning reflections which can be reviewed by peers globally through hypermedia narratives conveying deeper insights unlike myopic progress reports. Such amplified audiences spur intentional curation of computational artifacts articulating the multifaceted learning pathways.

ANALYTICS AND VISUALIZATIONS

Data analytics toolsets support tracking project status, participation and engagement levels for just-in-time interventions. For example, teacher and student view dashboards in Canvas course management system provide aggregate and individual activity metrics for assignments, resources access over the PBL timeline. Google Analytics affords fine-grained usage statistics on specific learning resources to refine collections. Programming database queries can reveal participation imbalances within teams for quick rebalancing. Dedicated project management apps like Trello enable both educators and students to digitally map tasks to individuals with due dates along a timeline using Kanban boards offering transparent progress visualization using cards moving across Backlog, In Progress and Completed columns.

By mirroring workplace project dashboards conveying real-time status, such tools keep students productively apace by merging transparent data trails with timely nudges while granting independence and accountability. Custom mobile applications also facilitate geo-tagged attendance monitoring during field learning improving safety with automated alerts. Thus data-driven insights on plans and people dynamics guide timely course corrections.

AR/VR Simulations

Interactive simulations using augmented (AR) and virtual reality (VR) tools transport students along exploratory scenarios otherwise out of bounds in physical environments due to accessibility, cost, safety or visibility constraints. For example, biology PBL teams can inspect 3D tissues samples through Hololens headsets to envision accelerated mitotic changes or geo-located AR forest terrain layers signal real-time flora suitable for restoration projects. Cloud-based VR simulation platforms like Labster facilitate running unfamiliar lab procedures increasing experimentation self-efficacy. Portable $200 AR/VR kits like Merge Cube with markerless tracking today enable small groups to collaboratively visualize-manipulate challenges like engineering diagrams, literary storyboards etc. facilitative of constructivist dialogues which desktop displays hinder, granting economical on-ramps for interdisciplinary PBL previously encumbered by substantial technology barriers (Mcguire & Kenney 2015).

Overall such emerging reality fusion environments dramatically lower exploration costs across STEAM disciplines. With projected adoption by over 90 million K-12 students globally by 2028, AR/VR-infused PBL can potentially revolutionize lab-based learning through portable simulations that develop competencies for applied science practices (Tate, 2018).

Analytics and Visualizations for Data-Driven Enhancements

Embracing a data-driven mindset allows continually optimizing PBL implementations through actionable analytics. For example, learning management systems provide aggregate and individual student activity metrics tracking assignments progress, resource access over the project timeline. By importing such engagement data into data visualization tools like Tableau, administrators glean fine-grained usage patterns to refine resource collections and customize guidance per learner milestones.

Programming database queries in SQL can reveal participation imbalances within teams for quick rebalancing. Dedicated project management apps like Trello enable both educators and students to digitally map tasks to individuals with due dates represented on Kanban boards offering transparent progress visualization using cards moving across Backlog, In Progress and Completed columns. By mirroring workplace project analytics dashboards conveying real-time status, such platforms guide timely course corrections.

Longitudinally, statistical models help probability estimations on optimal team sizes, driving question scopes and technology toolkits beneficial for improving project creativity dimensions in coming months based on multi-year evidence data that administrators judiciously interpret, in turn provoking iterative interventions (Drachsler & Greller, 2012). By melding such predictive analytics rather than relying just reactive instincts, PBL program leaders can preemptively calibrate parameters for peak engagement and deeper learning. Thereby, data science informs prescriptive insights over coming semesters to continually raise PBL outcomes.

IMPLEMENTING PBL INSTITUTIONALLY

The paradigm shifts demanded by PBL methods espousing sustained self-directed inquiry, integrated rubrics and celebratory project showcases necessitate broad transformation spanning curricular models, educator mindsets, learning environments and community partnerships calling for extensive capacity building undergirding exploratory learning.

Teacher Professional Development

Teachers lie at the crux of enacting PBL through instructional design, facilitative scaffolding and technology integration. Shifting from didactic deliverers to advising project managers warrants extensive skills upgrading. Besides domain expertise, PBL competencies encompass technological-pedagogical capabilities to adeptly leverage digital tools for collaboration, computational thinking to formulate authentic driving questions, project management techniques to map long range plans integrating discrete subject units and human-centered design thinking for creative solutions. Constructivist approaches also mandate improved formative feedback, benchmarking self-directed behaviors etc.

Building Educator Capacity

Targeted professional development modules, just-in-time mentoring and teacher communities hence assist transitional readiness as schools embark on PBL transformations. For instance, Singapore's TE21 Model for 21st century teaching encompasses customized YEAR-long training across mentored practicums, instructional simulations and learning environment study trips to systematically overhaul pedagogies around thinking routines, student-centric technology use and project-centered learning, implemented nationally across schools (Singapore Ministry of Education, 2018). Such extensive immersive scaffolding contrasts stand-alone workshops disconnected from sustained application. Micro-credentialing through badges also helps teachers showcase PBL competencies like proven expertise guiding science fair hypotheses or use of Kanban boards enabling manageable signaling to administrators who structure promotional policies and teaching assignments based on specialized capabilities beyond seniority alone. Thus continuous TPACK advancements sustain technology-powered PBL implementations.

Communities Driving Continuous Enhancements

Institutionalizing PBL further relies on communities of practitioners for participatory curriculum planning, horizontal expertise exchange and showcasing exemplars across programs and domains. For instance, Stamford American International School of Singapore fosters weekly Professional Learning Community (PLC) sessions for educator teams across elementary to high school to regularly review PBL lesson frameworks and assessment rubric mappings through spiraling Plan-Do-Study-Act inquiry cycles which leadership further reviews for targeted resource allocation and investments in emerging learning models like VR labs or digital fabrication makerspaces as shared needs percolate top-down and vice versa (SAIS, 2022). Such recurring collaboration rituals drive analysis, benchmarking and tool optimizations for peak PBL enactment suited to nuanced contexts unavailable through standardized formulaic prescription alone but through grounded inquiries putting theory to practice. Over time the participatory cohorts crystallize the innovation transformations into self-sustaining ecosystems resilient to staff churn. Thus PLCs act as the links stitching isolated efforts into institution-wide movements that shape cultural identity.

Preparing Conducive Learning Environments

Student-driven PBL places new functional demands like small group project rooms, presentation venues, technology access etc. on learning spaces beyond traditional computer labs or teacher-centric classroom layouts. Modern learning commons designs encompass mobile furniture arrangements for quick group reconfigurations based on activity needs, writeable glass walls and vertical surfaces for brainstorming visualizations, makerspaces with rapid prototyping tools, partitioned project breakout areas and media creation studios (DLR Group, 2021). Such deliberately designed vibrant atmospheres spur unstructured exploration critical for PBL environments (Bers et al, 2013). School libraries act as complementary hot spots for accessing digital creation kits or having peer scholar book symposiums along with referencing print resources – contemporarily recast as multi-functional centers fusing cross-disciplinary technologies, activities and groups beyond individual studying outposts. Adopting such intentional blueprinting bears long-term dividends accommodating fluid learners 'traffic' undergirded by mobility, flexibility and accessibility principles. Additionally, building community partnerships with industry mentors, universities and local administration allows authentic participation in civic projects like designing public spaces, solving mobility challenges etc. which further student engagement and learning transferred to proximal contexts.

FUTURISTIC PBL INNOVATIONS

While existing technology already grants functional benefits for managing collaboration, iteration and presentation noted earlier, emerging techniques harbinger transformational shifts in mechanizing personalized guidance at scale while augmenting environmental interactivity that stands to enrich future PBL endeavors.

Adaptive Learning Recommendations

Sophisticated learning analytics algorithms can dynamically customize project milestones to learner progression patterns and misconception diagnostics tailored to individuals akin to Netflix dynamically recommending relevant movies. Such smart content curation ensures competence-based scaffolding keeping students ideally challenged within proximal zones of development while preventing disengagement from struggles or boredom (Karataş & Simsek, 2021). Startups like Edulastic and Pedagogy offer initial forays into adaptive engines for mathematics and literacy modules. Extending such AI tutors to orchestrate personalized PBL pathway traversals can enhance self-efficacy during open-ended inquiries.

Immersive Simulated Explorations

Virtual reality metaverse environments allow unbounded explorations fused with corporeal verisimilitude. For instance history students can collectively walk through interactive ancient civilization landscaping examining architectural designs grounded by authentic textures, spatial sounds and physical effort transcending stationary 2D text thereby forming profound experiential anchors bolstering retention. Augmented overlays similarly heighten field engagements – for example, peering through phones, learners might see conceptual physics formulae magically manifested atop real playground rides used for mathematical modelling of kinetic motions. By merging virtual abstractions with life-sized worlds, technology dissolves barriers formerly constraining inquiries. Constructivist science learning notably profits through observational hypothesizing in situated simulated worlds (Martinez & Stager 2013).

Predictive Analytics for Continuous Improvement

Integrating longitudinal analytics predicting correlations between design choices and PBL effectiveness related to outcomes like creativity, collaborative behaviors, concept application, artifact originality etc. can guide ongoing enhancements. For instance, Bayesian statistical models help probability estimations on optimal team sizes, driving question scopes and technology toolkits beneficial for project creativity dimensions in coming months based on multi-year evidence data that administrators judiciously interpret, in turn provoking iterative interventions (Drachsler & Greller, 2012). By melding such predictive diagnostics rather than relying just reactive instincts, PBL program leaders can preemptively calibrate parameters for ideal engagement and deeper learning. Thereby data science informs prescriptive insights over coming semesters.

KEY TAKEAWAYS FOR ADOPTION

In closing, readers evaluating PBL adoption can consider a few principles in formulating implementation roadmaps:

- Balance guided facilitation with student independence appropriate for grade bands through using standardized rubrics for clarity.
- Begin with smaller community-linked projects and slowly scale complexity aligned to institutional comfort levels and educator preparedness.
- Embed metacognitive reflection practices spanning the entire project arc through pre-post framing eliciting growth mindsets rather than summative artifacts alone.

By embracing project-based pedagogies holistically accounting for key theoretical constructs, needed skill transitions and multi-year arcs attaining transformed teaching and learning culture, education institutions can unleash the richness of deeper experiential learning typified by the PBL methodology.

CONCLUSION

This chapter presented a multifaceted framework encompassing practical and conceptual dimensions of project-based learning spanning driving questions, collaborative inquiry, assessments, learning environments and technology integration required for PBL adoption. Through research-backed examples, readers can formulate implementation models calibrated to nuances, constraints and aspirational goals of their institutional ecosystems, leveraging PBL for developing creative evaluators and problem solvers equipped with transferrable competencies for unforeseeable futures.

REFERENCES

Barron, B., & Darling-Hammond, L. (2008). Teaching for meaningful learning: A review of research on inquiry-based and cooperative learning. In *Powerful Learning: What We Know About Teaching for Understanding* (pp. 11–70). Jossey-Bass.

Bers, M., Seddighin, S., & Sullivan, A. (2013). Ready for robotics: Bringing together the T and E of STEM in early childhood teacher education. *Journal of Technology and Teacher Education, 21*(3), 355–377.

Blumenfeld, P. C., Soloway, E., Marx, R. W., Krajcik, J. S., Guzdial, M., & Palincsar, A. (1991). Motivating project-based learning: Sustaining the doing, supporting the learning. *Educational Psychologist*, *26*(3-4), 369–398. doi:10.1080/00461520.1991.9653139

Buck Institute for Education. (2021). *What is PBL?* PBL Works. https://www.pblworks.org/what-is-pbl

Capraro, R. M., Capraro, M. M., & Morgan, J. (2013). *STEM Project-Based Learning: An Integrated Science, Technology, Engineering, and Mathematics (STEM) Approach.* Sense Publishers. doi:10.1007/978-94-6209-143-6

Chen, P., Hernández, A., & Dong, J. (2021). Impact of project-based learning on student achievement: A meta-analysis investigating moderators. *Educational Research Review*, *35*, 100367.

Chen, P., Hernández, A., & Dong, J. (2021). Impact of project-based learning on student achievement: A meta-analysis investigating moderators. *Educational Research Review*, *35*, 100367.

Chu, S. K. W., Reynolds, R. B., Tavares, N. J., Notari, M., & Lee, C. W. Y. (2017). *21st century skills development through inquiry-based learning.* Springer. doi:10.1007/978-981-10-2481-8

Drachsler, H., & Greller, W. (2012). *The pulse of learning analytics: Understandings and expectations from the stakeholders. Proceedings of the 2nd International Conference on Learning Analytics and Knowledge*, Vancouver, British Columbia, Canada. 10.1145/2330601.2330634

Edelson, D. C., Gordon, D. N., & Pea, R. D. (1999). Addressing the challenges of inquiry-based learning through technology and curriculum design. *Journal of the Learning Sciences*, *8*(3-4), 391–450. doi:10.1080/10508406.1999.9672075

Gapazo, J. P., Talan, M. G., Ganotice, F., & Chua, C. L. (2021). The genius hour program in enhancing critical thinking, self-directed learning and academic performance. *Journal of Ethnic and Cultural Studies*, *8*(1), 220–236.

Gapazo, J. P., Talan, M. G., Ganotice, F., & Chua, C. L. (2021). The genius hour program in enhancing critical thinking, self-directed learning and academic performance. *Journal of Ethnic and Cultural Studies*, *8*(1), 220–236.

Group, D. L. R. (2021). *Creating Environments Conducive to Project-Based Learning.* DLR Group. https://www.dlrgroup.com/insights/creating-environments-conducive-project-based-learning/

Han, S., Capraro, R., & Capraro, M. M. (2015). How science, technology, engineering, and mathematics (STEM) project-based learning (PBL) affects high, middle, and low achievers differently: The impact of student factors on achievement. *International Journal of Science and Mathematics Education, 13*(5), 1089–1113. doi:10.1007/s10763-014-9526-0

Han, S. Y., Capraro, R., & Capraro, M. M. (2014). How science, technology, engineering, and mathematics project based learning affects high-need students in the US. *Learning and Individual Differences, 36*, 8–15.

Han, S. Y., Capraro, R., & Capraro, M. M. (2014). How science, technology, engineering, and mathematics project based learning affects high-need students in the US. *Learning and Individual Differences, 36*, 8–15.

Harada, V. H., Kirio, C., & Yamamoto, S. (2015). Project-based learning: Rigor and relevance in high schools. *Library Media Connection, 33*(6), 14–16.

Henriksen, D. (2017). Creating STEAM with Design Thinking: Beyond STEM and Arts Integration. Steam4U. *STEAM Education Monograph Series, 1*(1), 1–11.

Hung, W., Jonassen, D. H., & Liu, R. (2008). Problem-based learning. Handbook of research on educational communications and technology, 485-506.

Karataş, İ., & Simsek, N. (2021). Adaptive learning systems: Surveying the landscape from general to discipline-specific systems. *Computers and Education: Artificial Intelligence, 2*, 100014.

Larmer, J., & Mergendoller, J. R. (2010). Seven essentials for project-based learning. *Educational Leadership, 68*(1), 34–37.

Martinez, S. L., & Stager, G. (2013). *Invent to learn: Making, tinkering, and engineering in the classroom.* Constructing Modern Knowledge Press.

McGuire, P., & Kenney, J. (2015). The Collaborative Project-Based Model: Supporting technology integration in K-12 with Professional Learning Communities. *Technology and Teacher Education Conference 2015.* Research Gate.

Pedaste, M., Mäeots, M., Siiman, L. A., de Jong, T., van Riesen, S. A., Kamp, E. T., Manoli, C. C., Zacharia, Z. C., & Tsourlidaki, E. (2015). Phases of inquiry-based learning: Definitions and the inquiry cycle. *Educational Research Review, 14*, 47–61. doi:10.1016/j.edurev.2015.02.003

Prince, M. J., & Felder, R. M. (2006). Inductive teaching and learning methods: Definitions, comparisons, and research bases. *Journal of Engineering Education, 95*(2), 123–138. doi:10.1002/j.2168-9830.2006.tb00884.x

SAIS. (2022). *Our Commitment to Innovation*. SAIS. https://sais-singapore.sg/innovative-learning

Savery, J. R. (2015). Overview of problem-based learning: Definitions and distinctions. Essential readings in problem-based learning: Exploring and extending the legacy of Howard S. *Barrows*, *9*, 5–15.

Singapore Ministry of Education. (2018). *Reimagining Learning and Teaching for the 21st Century*. MoE. https://www.moe.gov.sg/news/speeches/teaching21–reimagining-learning-and-teaching-for-the-21st-century

Svihla, V., & Reeve, R. (2016). Facilitating problem framing in project-based learning. *The Interdisciplinary Journal of Problem-Based Learning*, *10*(2). doi:10.7771/1541-5015.1603

Tate, E. (2018). *AR/VR forecast to reach 90 million users by 2020*. EdTechnology. https://edtechnology.co.uk/categories/research

Wurdinger, S., & Qureshi, M. (2015). Enhancing College Students' Life Skills through Project Based Learning. *Innovative Higher Education*, *40*(3), 279–286. doi:10.1007/s10755-014-9314-3

Chapter 3

The Role of Predictive Analytics in Personalizing Education:
Tailoring Learning Paths for Individual Student Success

Dwijendra Nath Dwivedi
iD https://orcid.org/0000-0001-7662-415X
Krakow University of Economics, Poland

Ghanashyama Mahanty
iD https://orcid.org/0000-0002-6560-2825
Utkal University, India

Varunendra nath Dwivedi
SRM University, India

ABSTRACT

Predictive analytics is a crucial tool in changing teaching and learning practices in the ever-changing field of educational technology. This study examines the dynamic function of predictive analytics in customizing education, with a specific emphasis on its ability to adapt learning paths to improve individual student achievement. The study examines how predictive models might identify distinct learning patterns and demands by assessing many data sources, such as academic achievement, learning habits, and engagement indicators. It showcases the capabilities of these analytics in generating adaptive learning experiences, thereby providing a more focused approach to teaching. This article investigates how predictive analytics facilitates the early detection of educational hazards, allowing for timely interventions to support students who are at danger of academic underperformance or dropping out.

DOI: 10.4018/979-8-3693-2169-0.ch003

Copyright © 2024, IGI Global. Copying or distributing in print or electronic forms without written permission of IGI Global is prohibited.

INTRODUCTION

As education evolves, it is becoming clear that the traditional strategy of using the same methods for all students is not enough. The introduction of predictive analytics has become a powerful tool in the field of individualized learning. This article explores the growing importance of predictive analytics in shaping personalized educational experiences, ultimately enhancing student achievement and involvement. We begin by clarifying the conventional educational frameworks, emphasizing their shortcomings in meeting the varied learning requirements of students. This study focuses on how predictive analytics may reveal detailed insights into student learning practices, preferences, and future challenges by carefully analyzing extensive educational data. We examine the diverse range of applications of this technology, spanning from identifying pupils who are at risk to tailoring learning materials and pathways. By emphasizing this, we highlight the capacity of predictive analytics to equalize education, providing students from diverse backgrounds with a fairer opportunity for achievement.

Additionally, we thoroughly analyze case studies that demonstrate the successful application of predictive analytics in educational environments, resulting in noteworthy enhancements in student achievements. These practical instances offer a practical perspective on the possibilities and difficulties of using such technologies into current educational structures. The ethical implications and possible drawbacks of depending on data-driven methods in education are crucial aspects of our discussion. We engage in discussions regarding the consequences of data privacy, the potential for algorithmic biases, and the significance of upholding an equilibrium between technology and human judgment in educational determinations.

Ultimately, this work supports the idea of carefully incorporating predictive analytics into education institutions. Our proposal envisions a future in which technology serves as a supplementary tool rather than a substitute for conventional teaching approaches. It enhances the educational environment by providing individualized, adaptive, and inclusive learning opportunities for every student. This paper investigates the significant problem of students quitting organizations that provide higher education. This work is at the crossroads of educational research and sophisticated data science. It seeks to examine and forecast college dropout rates by employing machine learning (ML) approaches. In addition to identifying the trends and circumstances that lead to students dropping out of school, the objective is to provide educational partners with valuable information that they can use to devise helpful strategies for assisting students in remaining in school.

LITERATURE STUDY

Lainjo, B. (2023) investigated the use of predictive analytics tools to assist schools in North America in retaining a greater number of students and reducing the number of students that drop out. Data mining techniques such as k-Nearest Neighbor, Neural Networks, Decision Trees, and Naive Bayes are utilized in order to categorize student dropout rates into distinct groups and encourage a greater number of students to continue their education. In the year 2022, Shafiq, D. and colleagues proposed the utilization of machine learning and predictive analytics as a means of identifying students in virtual learning environments who are likely to experience difficulties. The purpose of this study is to investigate the effectiveness of unsupervised machine learning approaches in comparison to supervised learning processes in identifying children who may be at risk.The authors Prasanth, A., and Alqahtani, H. (2023) desired to develop a prediction model that might identify early warning indicators of failure in college environments through the application of machine learning. It examined a variety of elements of student behavior, including academic achievement, engagement, participation in classes, and involvement on campus, among others. According to Kim, S. et al. (2022), who investigated several forms of data in order to forecast college dropout rates, they discovered that academic data had a significant impact on the accuracy with which machine learning models forecast graduation and dropout status. Machine learning techniques were utilized by Moon, M.H., et al. (2023) in order to identify parameters that may be utilized in the prediction of the dropout rate at four-year universities. The amount of money that each student spent on school supplies, according to their study budgets, the number of first-year students who registered, and the number of persons who found employment were all important variables.

Bujang, S. D. A. and colleagues (2021) presented a predictive analytics model that made use of supervised machine learning to make predictions regarding the final marks that students was going to receive. Given that the Decision Tree (J48) model achieved a success rate of 99.6% when it came to making predictions, it is possible that it may be utilized in the classroom. 2014 was the year that the Student Success Program was established and launched, as stated by Ewa Seidel et al. the following year. The goal of this standardized plan is to assist first-year students in improving their academic performance and remaining enrolled in school. In the study conducted by Andres Gonzalez-Nucamendi and colleagues (2023), the researchers utilized machine learning algorithms to identify quantitative traits that indicated which college students were likely to drop out of school and what factors were associated with this behavior.In their 2016 article, Lourens and Bleazard discussed an institutional modeling effort that was successful in identifying and implementing the most effective learning technique for predicting which children will drop out of school either before or during their second year of schooling. At the program level, this model for second-year dropouts was utilized with data from before college and the first semester from the Higher Education Data Analyzer (HEDA1) management information reporting and decision support setting at the Cape Peninsula University of Technology. This data was collected from the program. R. Bukralia and colleagues (2014) investigated a variety of data mining techniques to see the extent to which they were able to effectively forecast the future, construct predictive models, and calculate risk scores. The research presented a framework for a recommender system that functions on the basis of a predictive model. With the use of this system, students, instructors, and staff would receive notifications and suggestions that would assist with providing timely and efficient assistance. According to the findings of the study, the boosted C5.0 decision tree model has an accuracy rate of 90.97% when it comes to forecasting when students will voluntarily withdraw from online classes. In their 2018 article, Boris Perez and colleagues discussed the outcomes of an educational data analytics case study that investigated the process of locating undergraduate students in System Engineering (SE) who had left a Colombian institution after seven years of attendance. The study was conducted to determine how to locate these individuals. A technique known as "feature engineering" is used to supplement and broaden the scope of the initial data. Kang, K., and Wang, S. (2018) developed an educational data mining system with the purpose of analyzing data from educational institutions and making educated guesses on which students could withdraw from online programs prior to the beginning of the new term. What we wanted to do with this project was to provide our managers, teachers, and staff members with the opportunity to prevent students from withdrawing from the online program before they actually do so. A greater number of pupils would continue to participate in the program as a result of this.The purpose of the research conducted by Nurmalitasari et al. (2023) was to conduct a comprehensive review of the existing literature on predictive learning analytics (PLA) for the purpose of determining the reasons behind student dropouts. This study is a systematic review that examines ways to identify students who may drop out of school by using literature from studies that were conducted in the real world. This step includes the presentation of a review process, criteria for selecting potential research, and several approaches to analyzing the content of the studies that have been selected. Oqaidi K and colleagues discussed two approaches that have been utilized in the past to forecast the performance of pupils (SP) in their study that was conducted in 2022. These approaches include Machine Learning (ML) techniques and Fuzzy Cognitive Mapping (FCM). The most important thing that they did was examine how these strategies and recommendations compared to those that are utilized in higher education institutions in Morocco.

The findings of the study conducted by Nikolaidis P. and colleagues (2022) indicated that the most significant elements for the development of learning were the efficiency of the instructor and the materials used for learning. According to the findings of structural equation modeling, the variables that pertain to learning development have a significant impact on the status of students who withdraw from their studies. The impacts of the students' grade point average (GPA) were shown to be moderated by the academic semesters, according to a study that evaluated various different groups of students.Jia C. (2021) conducted a survey and conducted interviews with students in order to analyze the data and come up with five primary reasons that students are more interested in taking online flipped classes. The findings of this research provided educators with valuable information that can be utilized by those who are interested in the online flipped classroom method. The purpose of the research conducted by Zaid Shuqfa and colleagues in 2019 was to investigate the Educational Data Mining (EDM) literature in order to learn about the most recent methods of utilizing EDM to create models that are able to determine which students will continue their education at the college level and what the trends will be in various fields of higher education in the years to come. The Cumulative Grade Point Average (CGPA), assistance, family income, disability, and the number of dependents are the most relevant indicators for predicting student dropout, according to Ahmad Tarmizi S. and colleagues' (2019) findings. Although there were five different algorithms that were tested, the Support Vector Machine with Polynomial Kernel appeared to be the most successful. A comprehensive analysis of the research that has been conducted on the topic of predicting how well students would perform in school was carried out by Hellas A. and colleagues (2018).

MARKET RESEARCH:WHY WE NEED PERSONALIZED EDUCATION

Absolutely! Research studies have consistently demonstrated the substantial advantages of using personalized learning routes in education. The research conducted by the Bill & Melinda Gates Foundation emphasizes the favorable effects of personalized learning on academic achievement, specifically in important disciplines such as mathematics and reading. The foundation recommends the wider use of personalized learning to improve overall academic results. Furthermore, research conducted by the Education Week Research Center and the National Center for Learning Disabilities highlights the benefits of customized education in enhancing student involvement and drive, as well as in successfully addressing individual learning variances. This strategy enhances student engagement and motivation by connecting education with individual interests and talents. Additionally, it helps to narrow the achievement gap for kids with learning challenges. EdTechXGlobal underscores the significance of individualized learning and highlights the essential role of technology in tailoring education. They propose leveraging tech solutions to augment learning experiences. The OECD's initiative on the future of education highlights the enduring advantages of individualized learning, equipping pupils with the essential skills required for future achievements. Furthermore, studies such as those carried out by the Learning Assembly demonstrate substantial parental endorsement for individualized learning, underscoring the necessity of parental engagement in these educational approaches. From a pragmatic perspective, although there is an initial financial commitment, individualized learning demonstrates long-term cost efficiency by diminishing the necessity for remedial education and enhancing overall educational efficacy, as evidenced by comprehensive educational research. These observations collectively illustrate the diverse benefits and strategic importance of individualized learning in contemporary education.

Table 1. Market research how to improve personalized education

#	Statistic/Insight	Source of Research	Key Recommendation
1	Improved Academic Performance	Bill & Melinda Gates Foundation	Implement personalized learning strategies to improve performance in mathematics and reading.
2	Increased Engagement and Motivation	Education Week Research Center	Increase student engagement through personalized learning tailored to individual interests and abilities.
3	Better Accommodation of Learning Differences	National Center for Learning Disabilities	Utilize personalized learning to support students with learning differences and close the achievement gap.
4	Adaptation to Technology Trends	EdTechXGlobal	Leverage technology in education to support and enhance personalized learning experiences.
5	Long-Term Educational Benefits	OECD's "The Future of Education and Skills 2030"	Focus on personalized learning to develop future-ready skills in students.
6	Parental Support and Satisfaction	Learning Assembly	Engage parents in the educational process by highlighting the benefits of personalized learning for their children.
7	Reduction in Dropout Rates	America's Promise Alliance	Use personalized learning environments to keep students engaged and reduce dropout rates.
8	Cost-Effectiveness in the Long Term	General Educational Research	Invest in personalized learning as a cost-effective long-term educational strategy.

AI TEHCNLOGY AND THEIR APPLICATIONS
FOR PERSONALIZED EDUCATION:

The primary AI technologies utilized in education encompass Machine Learning, Natural Language Processing (NLP), Adaptive Learning, Speech Recognition, AI-driven Content Generation, Computer Vision, Edge Computing, and AIoT (Artificial Intelligence of Things). These technologies improve different areas of education, including offering customized learning experiences, assisting with language acquisition, generating interactive environments, and facilitating real-time data processing in intelligent educational settings. They enhance the effectiveness, inclusivity, and interactivity of learning settings.

Table 2. Market research: Why we need personalized education

Technology	Application in Education	Benefits
Machine Learning	Adaptive assessment, predictive analytics	Customized learning, improved outcomes
Natural Language Processing (NLP)	Language learning, personalized tutoring	Enhanced communication, tailored support
Adaptive Learning	Customized learning paths	Personalized education, efficient learning
Speech Recognition	Accessibility for disabled students	Inclusivity, ease of access
AI-driven Content Generation	Generation of educational content	Diverse resources, engaging materials
Computer Vision	Interactive learning environments	Engaging and interactive educational tools
Edge Computing	Real-time data processing in smart educational environments	Quick analysis, efficient operation
AIoT (AI of Things)	Creation and management of smart educational environments	Enhanced learning experience, automation

This visualization provides a distinct viewpoint on how these technologies have the potential to affect the future of educational approaches and initiatives, both individually and collectively. The plot emphasizes the importance of "Machine Learning Algorithms" and "Natural Language Processing (NLP)" in individualized education. These technologies are notable for their larger bubble sizes, which suggest a greater potential for effect. Machine Learning Algorithms play a vital role in adjusting educational content and evaluations based on student performance, while NLP improves interactive learning experiences by utilizing chatbots and linguistic support tools.

Figure 1. Potetntial impact of AI techlogies on personlaised education

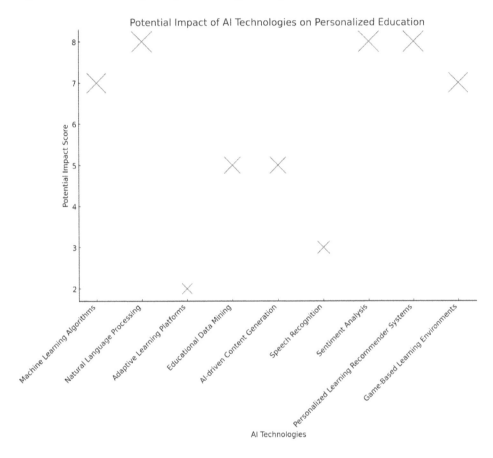

The significance of "Adaptive Learning Platforms" and "Educational Data Mining" is highlighted, as they play a crucial role in offering dynamic learning environments that are driven by data. Adaptive platforms guarantee that students interact with material that matches their proper level of difficulty, while data mining tools collect useful insights from educational data, which in turn influence teaching practices and student support." AI-powered Content Generation" and "Speech Recognition" are other significant contributors. The former customizes educational materials based on individual student interests and performance, hence enhancing the relevance and engagement of the learning process. Speech Recognition technology creates new opportunities for language acquisition and improved accessibility, particularly for students with disabilities.The concepts of "Sentiment Analysis" and "Personalized Learning Recommender Systems" encompass the most intricate dimensions of AI's influence. Sentiment Analysis enables the measurement of student involvement and satisfaction, hence enabling educators to optimize their teaching methodologies. Recommender Systems, similar to those used in e-commerce, provide suggestions for educational resources and activities based on previous behavior and preferences, thereby improving the learning process. Finally, "Game-Based Learning Environments" demonstrate the impact of AI on enhancing education by making it more engaging and enjoyable. These learning environments dynamically adjust to a student's progress, ensuring that instruction remains stimulating and captivating. To summarize, the bubble plot excluding 'Predictive Analytics' demonstrates the varied and important functions that different AI technologies have in personalized education. The utilization of these technologies represents a significant change in the educational field, as they contribute to increased student engagement, personalized content, improved accessibility, and dynamic learning experiences. This shift aligns with the unique needs, preferences, and learning styles of individual students.

CASE STUDIES ON USING PERSONALIZED EDUCATION

AI for Personalized Learning Pathways: This study investigated the potential of AI in creating personalized learning pathways. It delved into the use of AI to adapt to individual student needs, facilitating both knowledge acquisition and professional competency development. The study highlighted that while AI in education can expedite knowledge and skill acquisition, it also raises social and ethical concerns, especially regarding its role in the digitalization of education.

Adaptive Learning Program: Using AI technology to make a very personalized learning experience, the Adaptive Learning Program is a revolutionary way to adjust education. The program changes the content, pace, and difficulty of lessons based on each student's performance, preferences, and learning patterns. This is done so that each student's wants and abilities are met. This AI-powered system not only gives students feedback in real time, but it also shows them where they are doing well and where they need to improve. This way, every student is pushed and helped as they go through school. This makes learning more fun, effective, and efficient, and lets each student reach their full potential at their own pace.

AI in Inclusive Education: Focusing on inclusive education, a study explored AI's ability to personalize and tailor educational services for learners with special needs. It highlighted AI's capacity to harness learners' behavioral data, thus delivering customized educational services. This study is especially significant in understanding how AI can be used to support learners with diverse needs, including those in inclusive education settings.

AI Teaching Assistant at Georgia Institute of Technology: The Georgia Institute of Technology employed an AI-powered chatbot named Jill Watson, developed by

IBM's Watson, as a teaching assistant for a large course. With a 97% accuracy rate, this AI assistant was able to respond to approximately 10,000 student inquiries each semester, showcasing the efficiency and scalability of AI in managing large-scale educational interactions.

AI-Assisted Education for Students with Hearing Impairments: Utilizing text-to-speech and speech-to-text technology, AI-assisted education has significantly aided students with visual and hearing impairments. For instance, the National Technical Institute for the Deaf at RIT serves over 1,100 deaf and hard-of-hearing students, allowing them to access and engage with learning materials more effectively.

Each of these case studies illustrates different aspects of how AI-driven personalized education can be implemented to solve unique educational challenges, ranging from enhancing test scores and accommodating special needs to providing scalable educational assistance and supporting inclusive education.

CONCLUSION

This research paper examines the application of predictive analytics in the field of education, with a specific emphasis on tailoring learning trajectories to suit the unique needs of each student. It emphasizes the ability of data-driven insights to detect the distinct learning needs and preferences of individual students, enabling customized educational experiences. The research explores diverse methodologies and instruments employed in predictive analytics, showcasing their efficacy in augmenting student engagement and academic performance. The study asserts that predictive analytics is an indispensable instrument in customizing education. Through the utilization of data, instructors can enhance student results by comprehending and addressing individual learning styles. The study promotes the broader implementation of predictive analytics in educational environments to guarantee individualized, efficient, and all-encompassing learning experiences for every student.

FURTHER RESEARCH

To determine the effect that predictive analytics has on the results of students over a period of several years, long-term research should be conducted. With this information, one would gain a better understanding of the potential advantages and disadvantages of individualized learning paths over the long run. It is important to investigate the efficacy of predictive analytics across a variety of educational settings, such as public schools, private schools, and a variety of cultural and socioeconomic contexts. In the field of education, it is important to investigate the ethical implications of data collecting and usage. This includes issues over the privacy of students as well as the possibility of prejudice in judgments that are driven by data.Examine the perspectives of both educators and students with relation to the application of predictive analytics in the classroom. Comprehend the ways in which these tools influence the instructional techniques and learning experiences of the students. Analyze how predictive analytics can be combined with other new technologies such as artificial intelligence-driven tutoring systems, virtual reality and augmented reality in the classroom, and gamified learning platforms.

Conflict of Interest:

The authors whose names are listed immediately below certify that they have NO affiliations with or involvement in any organization or entity with any financial interest (such as honoraria, educational grants, participation in speakers' bureaus; membership, employment, consultancies, stock ownership, or other equity interest; and expert testimony or patent-licensing arrangements), or non-financial interest (such as personal or professional relationships, affiliations, knowledge or beliefs) in the subject matter or materials discussed in this manuscript.

REFERENCES

Ahmad Tarmizi, S., Mutalib, S., Abdul Hamid, N., Abdul-Rahman, S., & Md Ab Malik, A. (2019). A Case Study on Student Attrition Prediction in Higher Education Using Data Mining Techniques. *Soft Computing in Data Science.* . http://link.springer.com/10.1007/978-981-15-0399-3_15 doi:10.1007/978-981-15-0399-3_15

Bujang, S. D. A., Selamat, A., & Krejcar, O. (2021). Decision Tree (J48) Model for Student's Final Grade Prediction: A Machine Learning Approach. *IOP Conference Series. Materials Science and Engineering*, *1051*(1), 012005. doi:10.1088/1757-899X/1051/1/012005

Bukralia, R., Deokar, A. V., & Sarnikar, S. (2015). *Using academic analytics to predict dropout risk in e-Learning courses.* Springer International Publishing. doi:10.1007/978-3-319-11575-7_6

De Oliveira, C. F., Sobral, S. R., Ferreira, M. J., & Moreira, F. (2021). How does learning analytics contribute to prevent students' dropout in higher education: A systematic literature review. *Big Data and Cognitive Computing*, *5*(4), 64. doi:10.3390/bdcc5040064

Dwivedi, D., & Vemareddy, A. (2023). Sentiment Analytics for Crypto Pre and Post Covid: Topic Modeling. In A. R. Molla, G. Sharma, P. Kumar, & S. Rawat (Eds.), Lecture Notes in Computer Science: Vol. 13776. *Distributed Computing and Intelligent Technology. ICDCIT 2023*. Springer. doi:10.1007/978-3-031-24848-1_21

Dwivedi, D. N., & Anand, A. (2021). The Text Mining of Public Policy Documents in Response to COVID-19: A Comparison of the United Arab Emirates and the Kingdom of Saudi Arabia. *Public Governance / Zarządzanie Publiczne, 55*(1), 8-22. doi:10.15678/ZP.2021.55.1.02

Dwivedi, D. N., & Anand, A. (2022). A Comparative Study of Key Themes of Scientific Research Post COVID-19 in the United Arab Emirates and WHO Using Text Mining Approach. In S. Tiwari, M. C. Trivedi, M. L. Kolhe, K. Mishra, & B. K. Singh (Eds.), *Advances in Data and Information Sciences. Lecture Notes in Networks and Systems* (Vol. 318). Springer. doi:10.1007/978-981-16-5689-7_30

Dwivedi, D. N., Mahanty, G., & Pathak, Y. K. (2023). AI Applications for Financial Risk Management. In M. Irfan, M. Elmogy, M. Shabri Abd. Majid, & S. El-Sappagh (Eds.), The Impact of AI Innovation on Financial Sectors in the Era of Industry 5.0 (pp. 17-31). IGI Global. doi:10.4018/979-8-3693-0082-4.ch002

Dwivedi, D. N., Mahanty, G., & Vemareddy, A. (2022). How Responsible Is AI?: Identification of Key Public Concerns Using Sentiment Analysis and Topic Modeling. [IJIRR]. *International Journal of Information Retrieval Research*, *12*(1), 1–14. doi:10.4018/IJIRR.298646

Dwivedi, D. N., Mahanty, G., & Vemareddy, A. (2023). Sentiment Analysis and Topic Modeling for Identifying Key Public Concerns of Water Quality/Issues. In: Harun, S., Othman, I.K., Jamal, M.H. (eds) *Proceedings of the 5th International Conference on Water Resources (ICWR) – Volume 1. Lecture Notes in Civil Engineering*. Springer, Singapore. 10.1007/978-981-19-5947-9_28

Dwivedi, D. N., Pandey, A. K., & Dwivedi, A. D. (2023). Examining the emotional tone in politically polarized Speeches in India: An In-Depth analysis of two contrasting perspectives. *South India Journal Of Social Sciences, 21*(2), 125-136. https://journal.sijss.com/index.php/home/article/view/65

Dwivedi, D. N., & Pathak, S. (2022). Sentiment Analysis for COVID Vaccinations Using Twitter: Text Clustering of Positive and Negative Sentiments. In S. A. Hassan, A. W. Mohamed, & K. A. Alnowibet (Eds.), *Decision Sciences for COVID-19. International Series in Operations Research & Management Science* (Vol. 320). Springer. doi:10.1007/978-3-030-87019-5_12

Dwivedi, D. N., Wójcik, K., & Vemareddyb, A. (2022). Identification of Key Concerns and Sentiments Towards Data Quality and Data Strategy Challenges Using Sentiment Analysis and Topic Modeling. In K. Jajuga, G. Dehnel, & M. Walesiak (Eds.), *Modern Classification and Data Analysis. SKAD 2021. Studies in Classification, Data Analysis, and Knowledge Organization.* Springer. doi:10.1007/978-3-031-10190-8_2

Gupta, A. et al., 2021. Understanding Consumer Product Sentiments through Supervised Models on Cloud: Pre and Post COVID. *Webology, 18*(1), pp.406â€"415. . doi:10.14704/WEB/V18I1/WEB18097

Gupta, A., Dwivedi, D. N., & Shah, J. (2023). Overview of Money Laundering. In: Artificial Intelligence Applications in Banking and Financial Services. Future of Business and Finance. Springer, Singapore. doi:10.1007/978-981-99-2571-1_1

Gupta, A., Dwivedi, D. N., & Shah, J. (2023). Financial Crimes Management and Control in Financial Institutions. In: Artificial Intelligence Applications in Banking and Financial Services. Future of Business and Finance. Springer, Singapore. doi:10.1007/978-981-99-2571-1_2

Gupta, A., Dwivedi, D. N., & Shah, J. (2023). Overview of Technology Solutions. In: Artificial Intelligence Applications in Banking and Financial Services. Future of Business and Finance. Springer, Singapore. doi:10.1007/978-981-99-2571-1_3

Gupta, A., Dwivedi, D. N., & Shah, J. (2023). Data Organization for an FCC Unit. In: Artificial Intelligence Applications in Banking and Financial Services. Future of Business and Finance. Springer, Singapore. doi:10.1007/978-981-99-2571-1_4

Gupta, A., Dwivedi, D. N., & Shah, J. (2023). Planning for AI in Financial Crimes. In: Artificial Intelligence Applications in Banking and Financial Services. Future of Business and Finance. Springer, Singapore. doi:10.1007/978-981-99-2571-1_5

Gupta, A., Dwivedi, D. N., & Shah, J. (2023). Applying Machine Learning for Effective Customer Risk Assessment. In: Artificial Intelligence Applications in Banking and Financial Services. Future of Business and Finance. Springer, Singapore. doi:10.1007/978-981-99-2571-1_6

Gupta, A., Dwivedi, D. N., & Shah, J. (2023). Artificial Intelligence-Driven Effective Financial Transaction Monitoring. In: Artificial Intelligence Applications in Banking and Financial Services. Future of Business and Finance. Springer, Singapore. doi:10.1007/978-981-99-2571-1_7

Gupta, A., Dwivedi, D. N., & Shah, J. (2023). Machine Learning-Driven Alert Optimization. In: Artificial Intelligence Applications in Banking and Financial Services. Future of Business and Finance. Springer, Singapore. doi:10.1007/978-981-99-2571-1_8

Gupta, A., Dwivedi, D. N., & Shah, J. (2023). Applying Artificial Intelligence on Investigation. In: Artificial Intelligence Applications in Banking and Financial Services. Future of Business and Finance. Springer, Singapore. doi:10.1007/978-981-99-2571-1_9

Gupta, A., Dwivedi, D. N., & Shah, J. (2023). Ethical Challenges for AI-Based Applications. In: Artificial Intelligence Applications in Banking and Financial Services. Future of Business and Finance. Springer, Singapore. doi:10.1007/978-981-99-2571-1_10

Gupta, A., Dwivedi, D. N., & Shah, J. (2023). Setting up a Best-In-Class AI-Driven Financial Crime Control Unit (FCCU). In: Artificial Intelligence Applications in Banking and Financial Services. Future of Business and Finance. Springer, Singapore. doi:10.1007/978-981-99-2571-1_11

Hellas, A., Ihantola, P., Petersen, A., Ajanovski, V., Gutica, M., Hynninen, T., Knutas, A., Leinonen, J., Messom, C., & Liao, S. Predicting academic performance: a systematic literature review. *Proceedings Companion of the 23rd Annual ACM Conference on Innovation and Technology in Computer Science Education.* (175-199). ACM. 10.1145/3293881.3295783

Jia, C., Hew, K., Bai, S., & Huang, W. (2021). Adaptation of a conventional flipped course to an online flipped format during the Covid-19 pandemic: Student learning performance and engagement. *Journal of Research on Technology in Education.* . https://www.tandfonline.com/doi/full/10.1080/15391523.2020.1847220 doi:10.1080/15391523.2020.1847220

Kang, K., & Wang, S. (2018). Analyze and predict student dropout from online programs. In *Proceedings of the 2nd International Conference on Compute and Data Analysis* (pp. 6-12). ACM. 10.1145/3193077.3193090

Kim, S., Yoo, E., & Kim, S. (2023). *A Study on the Prediction of University Dropout Using Machine Learning.* arXiv preprint arXiv:2310.10987. DOI:/arXiv.2310.10987 doi:10.48550

Lainjo, B. (2023). Predictive Analytics in Higher Education for Student Retention and Success. *IACSIT International Journal of Engineering and Technology, 3*(1). doi:10.47747/ijets.v3i1.866

Lourens, A., & Bleazard, D. (2016). Applying predictive analytics in identifying students at risk: A case study. *South African Journal of Higher Education, 30*(2), 129–142. doi:10.20853/30-2-583

Moon, M.-H., & Kim, G. (2023). Predicting University Dropout Rates Using Machine Learning Algorithms. *Journal of Economics and Finance Education, 32*(2), 57–68. doi:10.46967/jefe.2023.32.2.57

Nikolaidis, P., Ismail, M., Shuib, L., Khan, S., & Dhiman, G. (2022). *Predicting Student Attrition in Higher Education through the Determinants of Learning Progress: A Structural Equation Modelling Approach. Sustainability*. MDPI. . https://www.mdpi.com/2071-1050/14/20/13584 doi:10.3390/su142013584

Nurmalitasari, A. & Mohd Noor, M. (2023). The Predictive Learning Analytics for Student Dropout Using Data Mining Technique: A Systematic Literature Review. *Advances in Technology Transfer Through IoT and IT Solutions*. Springer. doi:10.1007/978-3-031-25178-8_2

Nurmalitasari, L. Z. & Mohd Noor, M. (2021). Reduction of Data Dimensions in The PLA Process. *2021 15th International Conference on Ubiquitous Information Management and Communication (IMCOM)*. (1-8). IEEE. https://ieeexplore.ieee. org/document/9377391/ doi:10.1109/IMCOM51814.2021.9377391

Oqaidi, K., Aouhassi, S., & Mansouri, K. (2022). A Comparison between Using Fuzzy Cognitive Mapping and Machine Learning to Predict Students' Performance in Higher Education. *2022 IEEE 3rd International Conference on Electronics, Control, Optimization and Computer Science (ICECOCS)*. IEEE. doi:10.1109/ ICECOCS55148.2022.9983470. https://ieeexplore.ieee.org/document/9983470/ doi:10.1109/ICECOCS55148.2022.9983470

Perez, B., Castellanos, C., & Correal, D. (2018, May). Applying data mining techniques to predict student dropout: a case study. In *2018 IEEE 1st colombian conference on applications in computational intelligence (colcaci)* (pp. 1-6). IEEE. 10.1109/ColCACI.2018.8484847

Prasanth, A., & Alqahtani, H. (2023). Predictive Models for Early Dropout Indicators in University Settings Using Machine Learning Techniques. In *2023 IEEE International Conference on Emerging Technologies and Applications in Sensors (ICETAS)*. IEEE. DOI:10.1109/ICETAS59148.2023.10346531

Seidel, E., & Kutieleh, S. (2017). Using predictive analytics to target and improve first year student attrition. *Australian Journal of Education, 61*(2), 200–218. doi:10.1177/0004944117712310

Shafiq, D. A., Marjani, M., Habeeb, R. A. A., & Asirvatham, D. (2022). Predictive Analytics in Education: A Machine Learning Approach. In *2022 3rd International Multidisciplinary Conference on Computer and Energy Science (SpliTech)* (pp. 1-6). IEEE. [DOI:10.1109/MACS56771.2022

Shuqfa, Z., & Harous, S. (2019). *Data Mining Techniques Used in Predicting Student Retention in Higher Education: A Survey 2019 International Conference on Electrical and Computing Technologies and Applications (ICECTA).* IEEE. https://ieeexplore.ieee.org/document/8959789/ doi:10.1109/ICECTA48151.2019.8959789

Chapter 4
Enhancing Education With Information and Communication Technologies:
Data–Driven Instruction in Rural Schools

Bongi G. Mahlangu
University of South Africa, South Africa

Leila Goosen
ⓘ https://orcid.org/0000-0003-4948-2699
University of South Africa, South Africa

ABSTRACT

The purpose of this chapter is to present the methodology that will be used to collect data for the study reported on. Against the background of enhancing education with intelligent systems and data-driven instruction, methodology is important in research because it offers legitimacy to research. The research methodology shows that universally accepted data collection methods and procedures were adopted, which contributes to the veracity of the research process. Additionally, the research methodology also acts as a guide to researchers so that they stay on track regarding whatever they will be doing. This chapter further seeks to define and defend the methodological basis used to answer the research questions outlined.

DOI: 10.4018/979-8-3693-2169-0.ch004

Copyright © 2024, IGI Global. Copying or distributing in print or electronic forms without written permission of IGI Global is prohibited.

INTRODUCTION

This section will describe the general perspective of the chapter and end by specifically stating the **objective**.

Enhancing Education With Intelligent Systems and Data-Driven Instruction

The purpose of this chapter is to contribute to **Enhancing Education with Intelligent Systems and Data-Driven Instruction** as a groundbreaking **book** by exploring cutting-edge strategies and techniques to transform the traditional educational landscape. The research reported on in this chapter was designed to inspire and equip teachers with innovative tools, as well as trans- and cross-disciplinary approaches to action research and action learning for e-schools, community engagement and Information and Communication Technology for Development (ICT4D) (Goosen, 2018a) that will revolutionize their teaching methods and enhance student learning outcomes. Drawing on the expertise of the chapter authors as experienced educators, the chapter as part of this **book** will, like a journal article on **innovation** and knowledge by Khan, Li, Chughtai, Mushtaq and Zeng (2023), delve into the realm of educational **innovation**, offering practical insights, real-life examples, and step-by-step guidelines. From incorporating technologies effectively to fostering collaborative learning environments, as part of this **book**, the chapter covers a range of topics, helping educators stay at the forefront of modern education.

Enhancing Education With Information and Communication Technologies and Data-Driven Instruction in Rural Schools

This chapter will present the methodology that will be used to collect data for the study reported on (Avia, 2009). The methodology is important in research because it offers legitimacy to research (Nakashololo, 2021). The research methodology shows that universally accepted data collection methods and procedures were adopted, which contributes to the veracity of the research process (Gupta & Gupta, 2022). Additionally, the research methodology also acts as a guide to researchers so that they stay on track regarding whatever they will be doing. This chapter further seeks to define and defend the methodological basis that will "be used to answer the" research questions outlined (Kassim, 2020, p. 93).

The methodology outlines the research philosophy that will be adopted for the study. Additionally, the research approach adopted, which is also in line with the research design, is described. The various research populations are defined in the chapter, as well as the sampling methods that will be used to select the study recipients. Also, the chapter discusses the data collection methods, the data analysis procedures, measures to ensure the reliability of the data, as well as the ethics that were observed during the collection and processing of the empirical data.

Recommended Topics

From the **recommended topics** suggested for the book, this chapter will elaborate upon:

- **Gamification** in Education: Engaging Learners through Game-Based Learning
- **Project-Based Learning**: Fostering Collaboration, Creativity, and Critical Thinking
- **Augmented Reality** in the Classroom: Enhancing Learning with Immersive Experiences
- Blended Learning: Combining Online and Traditional Instruction for Optimal Results
- Culturally Responsive Teaching: Creating **Inclusive** Learning Environments
- Integrating **Social Media** in Education: **Leveraging** Digital Platforms for Engagement
- Data-Driven Instruction: Using **Analytics** to Inform Teaching and Learning Strategies
- Collaborative Learning: Nurturing Communication and Teamwork Skills
- Authentic Assessment: Moving **Beyond** Traditional Tests to Measure Student Progress
- Coding and Computational Thinking: Empowering Students for the Digital Age

Target Audience

Like the book that it proposes to form part of, the target audience of this chapter includes faculty, school teachers, and experienced educators. The methodology described in this chapter will be used to conduct thorough research, identified by the authors as experts, practitioners, researchers, and thought leaders in the field of education, who have extensive knowledge and experience in the selected topic. The authors are individuals, who had previously conducted and published relevant research, and have a track record of implementing innovative methods in the classroom.

Objectives

Furthermore, as part of this book, the chapter will explore the integration of digital tools and resources, **leveraging** technologies to enhance teaching and learning experiences. From interactive multimedia presentations to online collaboration platforms, educators would be enabled to discover innovative ways to leverage technologies for effective instruction, assessment, and feedback. Ultimately, as part of this **book**, the chapter aims to contribute towards revolutionizing education by empowering educators to reimagine their teaching practices, adapt to the ever-evolving needs of students, and **foster** a lifelong love of learning. By embracing these revolutionary methods, teachers can use educational technologies for growing innovative e-schools and to create classrooms that inspire, motivate, and empower students to reach their full potential in the 21st century (Goosen, 2015).

The **objective** of the study reported on by Afzal, Mouid, Dogar, Bhatti and Asghar (2023, p. 902) in a journal article on positive school psychology was to investigate how fewer financial resources effected "undergraduates' perspectives towards their education and choice of career," as well as the status of education in Pakistan under the influence of poverty.

BACKGROUND

This section of the chapter will provide broad definitions and discussions of the topic on **Enhancing Education with Information and Communication Technologies** and **Data-Driven Instruction in Rural Schools** and incorporate the views of others (in the form of a **literature review**) into the discussion to support, refute, or demonstrate the authors' position on the topic.

Project-Based Learning: Fostering Collaboration, Creativity, and Critical Thinking

Project-based assessment was influencing the pass rates of an ICT module at an Open and Distance Learning (ODL) institution in the paper by Goosen and Van Heerden (2013) as part of the proceedings of the 8th International Conference on **e-Learning** (ICEL).

The study reported on by Khan, et al. (2023, p. 1) employed "social cognitive theory to analyze the moderated mediation model of self-leadership and innovative work behavior. Further," the latter research assessed the role of knowledge sharing and **creative** self-efficacy on the self-leadership and innovative work behavior relationship.

Augmented Reality in the Classroom: Enhancing Learning With Immersive Experiences

Augmented/virtual **reality** technologies and assistive/humanoid robots were used for differently-abled students with autism spectrum disorders (ASDs) in the chapter by Goosen (2022).

Blended Learning: Combining Online and Traditional Instruction for Optimal Results

"In order to provide readers with an overview and summarize the content, the purpose of the study in" the chapter by Oyewo and Goosen (2024, p. 1) was "stated as investigating the relationships between how teachers use their technological competency levels in a **blended learning** environment and improving the self-regulated learning (SRL) skills and behaviors of secondary school learners." The latter chapter was positioned against the background of the architecture and technological advancements of Education 4.0.

Integrating Social Media in Education: Leveraging Digital Platforms for Engagement

Uunona and Goosen (2023) were **leveraging** ethical standards in Artificial Intelligence (AI) technologies towards providing a guideline for responsible teaching and learning applications.

Authentic Assessment: Moving Beyond Traditional Tests to Measure Student Progress

Authentic learning is a "technique used in education institutes" at all levels to help "students understand concepts by linking academic concepts with real-*world* scenarios." In an international journal on Computer Science and information security, Mushtaq, Mushtaq and Iqbal (2020, p. 1) advocated the use of **authentic** learning tools in the delivery of scientific education, while Goosen and Naidoo (2014) encouraged computer lecturers to use their institutional Learning Management System (LMS) for ICT education in the cyber *world*.

Coding and Computational Thinking:
Empowering Students for the Digital Age

The journal article by Van Heerden and Goosen (2012) showed how a lecturer was using vodcasts to teach programming (**coding) and computational thinking** in an ODL environment.

As part of the proceedings of the Pakistan Academy of Sciences (Physical and **Computational** Sciences), Khan, Sheraz, Sultan and Mushtaq (2022, p. 27) indicated that modern "technologies have a strong impact on" the education system. In their study, the latter authors were investigating the impact of technology involvement in education from students' perspectives in terms of a technology impact analysis for "both male and female students in the education department of" the National University of Modern Languages (NUML).

Research Philosophy

A **research philosophy** refers to the process through which the collected information is treated, evaluated and analyzed (Csiernik & Birnbaum, 2017). While the research methodology is critical in collecting data, the **research philosophy** provides the justification for conducting research using a specific data collection method. Banks, Hart, Pahl and Ward (2018) provided more insights on the concept of **research philosophy**. According to the latter authors, for the research findings to be considered as valid, these need to be underpinned by a valid and coherent research philosophy. There are several philosophies, which can be used in research, some of which are described next.

Realism

Realism refers to the philosophy of gathering data from multiple sources, as well as the observation of the work of multiple other researchers. Hart (2018) observed that *realism* relies mainly on secondary data instead of primary data. In addition, this also suggests that the independence of the human mind as a concept is encouraged by *realism*. This **research philosophy** is grounded in the scientific approach and the pursuit of knowledge as epistemology.

Positivism

Positivism is based on the pursuit of factual and numeric knowledge. According to Caldwell (2015), the primary goal of *positivism* is to generate knowledge that is reliable and verifiable. The latter author further noted that *positivism* gives priority to measurement and observation rather than the perception of research participants.

Interpretivism

Kumatongo and Muzata (2021) observed that *interpretivism* incorporates human perception into the research process. This **research philosophy** further contends that knowledge can be sourced through social connections, such as shared languages, shared meanings and shared histories. Hill and Langan (2014) identified that the researcher utilizes the proposed philosophy in appreciating people's *diversity* and acts as a social actor in the proposed study. Additionally, this **research philosophy** takes cognizance of the various ways that people behave in social conditions.

Teachers in the chapter by Libbrecht and Goosen (2015) were using ICTs to facilitate Mathematics teaching and learning in a classroom with language *diversity*.

Pragmatism

The **research philosophy** of *pragmatism* suggests that there are multiple ways in which collected data can be interpreted. Consequently, the use of a single approach would not be able to show the overall picture of what is being researched. Caldwell (2015) also noted that *pragmatism* can incorporate elements from both *interpretivist* and *positivist* philosophies.

Justification

Considering that the study discussed in this chapter is a qualitative one, the *interpretive* **research philosophy** will be used. The justification is that the researcher will be seeking to explore the experiences, perceptions and histories of the selected research participants, which can be seen through multiple lenses and the data interpreted in different ways. Additionally, the implementation of the *interpretivist* **philosophy** could develop a thorough knowledge of specific settings, including cross-cultural study results, aspects affecting definite expansion, as well as the nuances affecting the provision of ICT services in rural schools.

MAIN FOCUS OF THE CHAPTER

Issues, Problems

This section of the chapter will present the authors' perspectives on the **issues, problems**, etc., as these relate to the main theme of the book on **Enhancing Education with Intelligent Systems and Data-Driven Instruction**, and arguments supporting the authors' position on **Enhancing Education with Information and Communication Technologies** and **Data-Driven Instruction in Rural Schools**. It will also compare and contrast with what had been, or is currently being, done as it relates to the specific topic of the chapter.

The purpose of a previous chapter by Mahlangu and Goosen (2023, p. 254) was "to present a literature review on **issues** related to the integration of information and communication technologies" in especially South African rural schools. Against the background of" contemporary **challenges** in education regarding digitalization, methodology, and management, the latter chapter investigated the impact of a lack of ICTs, as well as digitalization in a changing education environment.

The study reported on by Tanoli, Khan and Majoka (2021, p. 167) in a journal article on education and social research was conducted to investigate the "**problems** faced by teachers and students in the teaching-learning process using English as the medium of instruction at the primary level."

In a study on Pakistan Higher Education Institutions (HEIs), Karachi Sindh, Mir, Hussain and Jariko (2023, p. 19) discussed some of the **problems** related to pedagogical shifts among faculty members of business schools. According to the latter authors, contexts and faculty beliefs matter, together with teaching methodologies, as "the dimension of education quality" had recently become quite popular in tenure discussions.

Gamification in Education: Engaging Learners Through Game-Based Learning

Bhatia, Manani, Garg, Bhatia and Adlakha (2023, p. 48) indicated that "**education gamification** is influenced by factors such as the need (for) replacing out-of-date teaching techniques; a lack of content knowledge; and" the **gamification** of education. The latter authors were mapping mindsets about **gamification** in terms of teaching-learning perspectives in the United Arab Emirates (UAE) and Indian education systems.

Culturally Responsive Teaching: Creating Inclusive Learning Environments

The **inclusive** education of children with special needs regarding practices, opportunities and **barriers** were discussed by Usman, Ahmad and Ali (2020, p. 76). "Students' education at this stage involves their growth of independent action, cooperation with others, and acceptable social behaviors, with a concern for fair play".

The thesis by Rangongo (2021, p. v) addressed the work-life **conflict** experiences and **cultural** expectations of women managers in the public sector of Limpopo province, South Africa, "a topical phenomenon for the career progression and wellbeing of women."

Research Design

A "**research design** refers to the strategy or plan" that the researcher intends to employ in the data collection and management process (Chetty, 2011, p. 31). Kapoor (2016) observed that the "research design signifies the overall strategy and plan which the researcher chose to assimilate the diverse components of the research logically and coherently". Consequently, the "research design is to ensure that the researcher" is going to employ the right tools in their research (Mabogo, 2021, p. 36) so that they can answer the research questions they have and achieve their stated research **objectives** (Zvitambo, 2021). The former author (Mabogo, 2021) provided an evaluation of the impacts on socio-economic **issues** in Dididi village, Limpopo province, South Africa.

Research Approach

There are primarily two main approaches, which are used in research. These are the inductive and deductive approaches. An inductive approach is concerned with generating new theories and hypotheses from the collected empirical data (Woiceshyn & Daellenbach, 2018). "On the other hand, the deductive approach" starts with a theory or hypothesis, which the collected data interrogates to determine if it fits the theory (Obeidat & Alomari, 2020, p. 281). For this study, use will be made of a deductive approach.

Research Population and Sampling

A **research population** refers to elements sharing some characteristics that the researcher is interested in (Majid, 2018). It is from this **research population** that the researcher will pick their research participants. This is because by having an applicable **research population**, the researcher is likely to answer their research questions.

The research population will comprise a total of 150 households, which consists mostly of current and previous learners, as well as community members, affected by a lack of ICTs, from thirty-seven (37) combined schools in Nkangala district in Mpumalanga province, South Africa. The Nkangala district is primarily rural and some schools are in informal settlements. "All of the schools in the study area fall under Quintile" 1, "the Department of Basic Education classification category for no fee-paying" schools, "due to the high poverty level of the residents of the area in which the" schools are situated (Mathevula & Uwizeyimana, 2014, p. 1092).

Current and previous learners, as well as teachers and principals from the identified schools will be selected as participants.

"For the purpose of this study, purposive" **sampling** will be used (Pholotho & Mtsweni, 2016, p. 4). "Purposive **sampling** is based on" an assumption that "the researcher needs to purposefully select individuals" and groups, who are working together in the Information technology (IT) class (Mentz & Goosen, 2007), as well as "settings because they are likely to be knowledgeable and informative about phenomena the research is studying" (Pholotho, 2017, p. 78). Due to time constraints, thirty-seven (37) resource-constrained combined schools in Nkangala district will be the focus. The schools were selected because they are located in a resource-constrained environment and they fall under Quintile 1.

Data Collection Methods

Data collection methods are determined by the research design selected by the researcher. Consequently, a cross sectional or experimental design is likely going to use a quantitative approach with questionnaires and surveys as the primary data collection tools. Consistent with qualitative methods, this study is going to make use of semi-structured interviews.

Research instruments are the specific tools that the researcher uses for collecting data. The researcher will make use of an interview guide for collecting data. The interview guide is consistent with the chosen **research philosophy**, as well as the qualitative methodology (Kallio, Pietilä, Johnson, & Kangasniemi, 2016). With an interview guide, the researcher picks some themes that they want to discuss with the respondents. This is in contrast to a coded questionnaire, which has specific questions which cannot be varied. The open nature of the interview guide allows the researcher to ask follow-up questions based on initial responses provided by the respondents.

Data Analysis

Data analysis refers to the process by which the collected raw empirical data is structured into a format where intelligible decisions and conclusions can be drawn from. There are several steps that are going to be taken during the data analysis process and these are outlined next.

First, the data is going to be transformed from the audio recordings to transcribed text as part of the preparations for data analysis. Once that is done, the data is then uploaded into ATLAS TI, which does the analysis. One of the tasks that ATLAS carries out is to arrange the data into themes where similar responses are grouped together. This allows for subsequent thematic analysis. The analysis results can then be used to support some of the assertions made in the study and answer the research questions.

Reliability, Validity, and Trustworthiness of Data

Reliability

Reliability implies consistency. This study could be repeated and the findings will be the same, as a lack of ICT in rural areas has long term effects.

Validity

Validity means how well a test measures what it is supposed to measure.

Trustworthiness

According to Polit and Beck (2020), *trustworthiness* refers to the consistency of the research methodology that was applied, while according to Henry (2022, p. 113), it "refers to the degree of confidence in data, interpretation, and methods used to ensure the quality of a study". In *trustworthiness*, researchers seek to satisfy four conditions, which includes *confirmability*, *dependability*, *transferability* and credibility. These four criteria are discussed in more detail next.

Confirmability

This refers to the extent to which the results can be repeated with a different set of researchers using the same tools and working within the same research population.

The findings from this study will be based on participants' responses during the interview, tape recorder will be used to record exactly what the participants will be saying. Notes will be discussed with the student's supervisor.

Dependability

Dependability "refers to the stability of the data over time and over the conditions of the study" (Dempsey, et al., 2022, p. 3). This can be achieved by making sure that the research tools that were used are actually capable of collecting the data that is required to answer the research questions.

Transferability

This refers to the extent to which the research results "can be transferred to other" locations or environments (Henry, 2022, p. 116). The research can be said to be transferable if the results in case study A can be replicated in case study B, which means that the results can be replicated in different settings.

Credibility

This refers to the extent to which the collected data is accurate and credible. One of the ways to achieve this is to remove all forms of bias. After data is collected, the researcher will go back to participants to verify and confirm what they said during the interview. This is to give the research participants the opportunity to confirm that the research results reflect their sentiments and opinions.

Ethical Considerations

Ethical considerations in a qualitative study were the focus of an international journal article on care scholars by Arifin (2018, p. 30). "The protection of human subjects through the application of appropriate ethical principles is important in all research". "In a qualitative study, **ethical considerations** have a particular resonance due to the in-depth nature of the study process."

According to the study undertaken by Arifin (2018), many aspects must be considered when carrying out research. However, one of the most important is the ethical concerns that might come up. By considering the ethical protocol, researchers can ensure that they are upholding the highest ethical norms, which will enhance the research *reliability* and *validity*. When carrying out this study, the researcher took into consideration several **issues**. The researcher's goal was to adhere to the global landscape of artificial intelligence **ethics** guidelines (Jobin, Ienca, & Vayena, 2019).

The latter authors indicated that in past few "years, private companies, research institutions and public sector organizations have issued principles and guidelines for ethical artificial intelligence".

During the collection of data for the study, there are some considerations that the researcher is going to factor in. First, the researcher is going to ensure that no personally identifiable information is going to be collected for the study from the research participants. Secondly, the researcher is going to ensure that no harm comes to the research participants, either during or after the study. Third, the researcher will make sure that the research participants give informed consent before undertaking the study. Lastly, the researcher will make sure that all the necessary ethical clearance protocols from the university are met before data collection.

SOLUTIONS AND RECOMMENDATIONS

This section of the chapter will discuss **solutions and recommendations** in dealing with the **issues** or **problems** presented in the preceding section.

With regard to the current state of engineering education in India and the student teacher scenario in an online mode, the findings reported by Mangla, Bhatia, Bhatia and Kumar (2022) as part of proceedings on the rising **threats** in expert applications and **solutions** indicated "numerous **obstacles** affecting online engineering education including **issues** with equipment and technological **difficulties**, learning and teaching **challenges**," etc.

Ethical ICT4D **solutions**, ensuring research integrity and the ethical management of data should be considered for Massive Open Online Courses (MOOCs) (Goosen, 2018b).

FUTURE RESEARCH DIRECTIONS

This section of the chapter will discuss **future** and **emerging trends**, as well as provide insights about the **future** of the theme of the book on **Enhancing Education with Intelligent Systems and Data-Driven Instruction** from the perspective of the chapter focus on **Enhancing Education with Information and Communication Technologies** and **Data-Driven Instruction in Rural Schools**. The viability of a paradigm, model, implementation **issues** of proposed programs, etc., may be included in this section. If appropriate, this section will suggest **future research directions** within the domain of the topic.

Data-Driven Instruction: Using Analytics to Inform Teaching and Learning Strategies

"In the past, doctors and specialists were not connected to patients through telemedicine for providing virtual health and medicine. In **rural** areas," similar to the context of the research reported on in this chapter, "where experts in medical fields were not able to reach or be present at, telemedicine proved a great benefit" (Bhatia, Hooda, & Gupta, 2021, p. 274). As part of a *Research Anthology on Telemedicine Efficacy, Adoption, and Impact on Healthcare Delivery*, the latter authors therefore discussed deep **data analytics** contributing to the **future** of telehealth.

Also in the context of medical education, a journal article against the background of an Islamic international medical college by Kamran, et al. (2023, p. 56) discussed **future** health professionals' readiness and awareness of interprofessional education at a health care institution in Lahore, the **objectives** of which included to "measure the level of readiness and awareness of future health professionals about interprofessional education and to evaluate the differences in the readiness towards interprofessional education amongst different disciplines."

Yadav, Bansal, Bhatia, Hooda and Morato (2021) investigated the diagnostic applications of *health* intelligence and surveillance systems.

A book on *exploring* the ***future*** *opportunities of brain-inspired artificial intelligence* edited by Bhatia, Choudhury and Dewangan (2023) indicated that applying "mechanisms and principles of human intelligence and converging the brain and artificial intelligence" is currently an **emerging** research **trend**.

According to Mushtaq (2021, p. 1), there had been increased interest in revisiting the role and impact of emotions in and on consumer behavior in a **post-Covid** environment from a neuromarketing perspective. Traditionally, **emerging** research **trends** had "relied heavily on thought process at the expense of emotions in predicting consumer" behavior.

Also towards the **post-Covid-19** era, the chapter by Ngugi and Goosen (2021) in a *handbook of research* discussed **innovation**, entrepreneurship, and sustainability for ICT students.

Research Design

The premise of the **research design** is that there is supposed to be a logical flow in the decisions that the researcher makes. For example, a qualitative research project will most likely require purposive sampling. Additionally, the research design will also require "semi-structured interviews. For the data analysis", thematic analysis will most likely be used to pick up salient points and **emerging trends** within the interviews (Kruger, 2020, p. vi). For this research, a case study design will be employed. This is a research design, which seeks to understand more about a given phenomenon. This differs from an experimental research design, which seeks to develop new knowledge.

CONCLUSION

This section of the chapter will provide a discussion of the overall coverage of the chapter and concluding remarks.

This chapter presented some of the techniques, methods and tools that will be used to collect the primary data needed "to answer the research questions" (Kassim, 2020, p. 93). For example, the research design, research philosophy and research approach were identified. Additionally, the research population was also specified as well as the sampling methods that will be used to pick respondents during the study. Lastly, the data collection instruments, the data analysis methods as well as the measures that will be observed to ensure data reliability and the observance of ethics is outlined. The next chapter is going to present the primary data collected using the methods outlined in this chapter.

REFERENCES

Afzal, A., Mouid, R., Dogar, M. M., Bhatti, M. J., & Asghar, M. (2023). Career Of Undergraduates And Status Of Education In Pakistan Under Influence Of Poverty. *Journal of Positive School Psychology*, 7(5), 902–916.

Arifin, S. R. (2018). Ethical considerations in qualitative study. *International journal of care scholars, 1*(2), 30-33.

Avia, N. (2009). *Grade 10 Life Science Teachers' Understanding and Development of Critical Thinking Skills in Selected Schools in Namibia (MEd dissertation).* Rhodes University.

Banks, S., Hart, A., Pahl, K., & Ward, P. (2018). Co-producing research: A community development approach. In *Co-producing Research* (pp. 1–18). Policy Press.

Bhatia, M., Choudhury, T., & Dewangan, B. K. (Eds.). (2023). *Exploring Future Opportunities of Brain-inspired Artificial Intelligence*. IGI Global. https://www.igi-global.com/book/exploring-future-opportunities-brain-inspired/305123 doi:10.4018/978-1-6684-6980-4

Bhatia, M., Hooda, M., & Gupta, P. (2021). Deep Data Analytics: Future of Telehealth. In Research Anthology on Telemedicine Efficacy, Adoption, and Impact on Healthcare Delivery (pp. 274-295). IGI Global.

Bhatia, M., Manani, P., Garg, A., Bhatia, S., & Adlakha, R. (2023). Mapping Mindset about Gamification: Teaching Learning Perspective in UAE Education System and Indian Education System. *Revue d'Intelligence Artificielle*, *37*(1), 47–52. Advance online publication. doi:10.18280/ria.370107

Caldwell, B. (2015). *Beyond positivism*. Routledge. doi:10.4324/9780203565520

Chetty, M. (2011, October). *Cause of Relapse Post Treatment for Substance Dependency Within the South African Police Services*. University of Pretoria. https://repository.up.ac.za/bitstream/handle/2263/29121/dissertation.pdf?isAllowed=y&sequence=1

Csiernik, R., & Birnbaum, R. (2017). *Practising social work research: Case studies for learning*. University of Toronto Press.

Dempsey, L., Gaffney, L., Bracken, S., Tully, A., Corcoran, O., McDonnell-Naughton, M., & McDonnell, D. (2022). Experiences of undergraduate nursing students who worked clinically during the COVID-19 pandemic. *Nursing Open*. Advance online publication. doi:10.1002/nop2.1289 PMID:35866179

Goosen, L. (2015). Educational Technologies for Growing Innovative e-Schools in the 21st Century: A Community Engagement Project. In D. Nwaozuzu, & S. Mnisi (Ed.), *Proceedings of the South Africa International Conference on Educational Technologies* (pp. 49 - 61). Pretoria: African Academic Research Forum.

Goosen, L. (2018a). Trans-Disciplinary Approaches to Action Research for e-Schools, Community Engagement, and ICT4D. In T. A. Mapotse (Ed.), *Cross-Disciplinary Approaches to Action Research and Action Learning* (pp. 97–110). IGI Global. doi:10.4018/978-1-5225-2642-1.ch006

Goosen, L. (2018b). Ethical Information and Communication Technologies for Development Solutions: Research Integrity for Massive Open Online Courses. In C. Sibinga (Ed.), *Ensuring Research Integrity and the Ethical Management of Data* (pp. 155–173). IGI Global. doi:10.4018/978-1-5225-2730-5.ch009

Goosen, L. (2022). Augmented/Virtual Reality Technologies and Assistive/Humanoid Robots: Students With Autism Spectrum Disorders. In S. Dhamdhere & F. Andres (Eds.), *Assistive Technologies for Differently Abled Students* (pp. 239–267). IGI Global. doi:10.4018/978-1-7998-4736-6.ch012

Goosen, L., & Naidoo, L. (2014). Computer Lecturers Using Their Institutional LMS for ICT Education in the Cyber World. In C. Burger, & K. Naudé (Ed.), *Proceedings of the 43rd Conference of the Southern African Computer Lecturers' Association (SACLA)* (pp. 99-108). Port Elizabeth: Nelson Mandela Metropolitan University.

Goosen, L., & Van Heerden, D. (2013). Project-Based Assessment Influencing Pass Rates of an ICT Module at an ODL Institution. In E. Ivala (Ed.), *Proceedings of the 8th International Conference on e-Learning*. 1, pp. 157-164. Cape Town: Academic Conferences and Publishing.

Gupta, A., & Gupta, N. (2022). *Research methodology*. SBPD Publications.

Hart, C. (2018). Doing a literature review: Releasing the research imagination. *Sage (Atlanta, Ga.)*.

Henry, P. G. (2022). *The Experiences of Educators in Low-Income New York City Middle Schools Navigating Classroom Instruction and Decisions for Homeless Students: A Phenomenological Study* [PhD thesis, Liberty University].

Hill, R. P., & Langan, R. (Eds.). (2014). *Handbook of research on marketing and corporate social responsibility*. Edward Elgar Publishing. doi:10.4337/9781783476091

Jobin, A., Ienca, M., & Vayena, E. (2019). The global landscape of AI ethics guidelines. *Nature Machine Intelligence*, *1*(9), 389–399. https://www.nature.com/articles/s42256-019-0088-2. doi:10.1038/s42256-019-0088-2

Kallio, H., Pietilä, A. M., Johnson, M., & Kangasniemi, M. (2016). Systematic methodological review: Developing a framework for a qualitative semi-structured interview guide. *Journal of Advanced Nursing*, *72*(12), 2954–2965. doi:10.1111/jan.13031 PMID:27221824

Kamran, R., Farid, M., Naveed, A., Tufail, S., Shafique, A., Mushtaq, S., & Khan, J. S. (2023). MEDICAL EDUCATION: Future Health Professionals Readiness and Awareness Towards Interprofessional Education in a Health Care Institution of Lahore. [JIIMC]. *Journal of Islamic International Medical College*, *18*(1), 56–62.

Kapoor, M. C. (2016). Types of studies and research design. *Indian Journal of Anaesthesia*, *60*(9), 626–630. doi:10.4103/0019-5049.190616 PMID:27729687

Kassim, A. F. (2020). *Educators' views on the effectiveness of alternatives to corporal punishment to maintain discipline: a case of four high schools in the OR Tambo District* [MEd dissertation, University of Fort Hare. http://vital.seals.ac.za:8080/vital/access/services/Download/vital:39060/SOURCE1

Khan, M. K., Sheraz, K., Sultan, U., & Mushtaq, A. (2022). Investigating the Impact of Technology Involvement in Education from Student's Perspective: Technology Impact Analysis on Students in Academia. *Proceedings of the Pakistan Academy of Sciences: A. Physical and Computational Sciences, 59*. 10.53560/PPASA(59-3)788

Khan, S. H., Li, P., Chughtai, M. S., Mushtaq, M. T., & Zeng, X. (2023). The role of knowledge sharing and creative self-efficacy on the self-leadership and innovative work behavior relationship. *Journal of Innovation & Knowledge*, *8*(4), 100441. doi:10.1016/j.jik.2023.100441

Khan, S. H., Li, P., Chughtai, M. S., Mushtaq, M. T., & Zeng, X. (2023). The role of knowledge sharing and creative self-efficacy on the self-leadership and innovative work behavior relationship. *Journal of Innovation & Knowledge*, *8*(4), 100441. doi:10.1016/j.jik.2023.100441

Kruger, W. M. (2020). *Placement factors contributing to the well-being of social work interns in a government setting.* North-West University.

Kumatongo, B., & Muzata, K. K. (2021). Research paradigms and designs with their application in education. *Journal of Lexicography and Terminology*, *5*(1), 16–32.

Libbrecht, P., & Goosen, L. (2015). Using ICTs to Facilitate Multilingual Mathematics Teaching and Learning. In R. Barwell, P. Clarkson, A. Halai, M. Kazima, J. Moschkovich, N. Planas, & M. Villavicencio Ubillús (Eds.), *Mathematics Education and Language Diversity* (pp. 217–235). Springer. doi:10.1007/978-3-319-14511-2_12

Mabogo, R. (2021). *Evaluation of the impacts of clay brick production on water quality and socio-economic issues in Dididi Village, Limpopo Province, South Africa* [MSc dissertation, University of South Africa].

Mahlangu, B. G., & Goosen, L. (2023). The Impact of a Lack of Information and Communication Technologies at Rural Schools: Digitalization in a Changing Education Environment. In A. Arinushkina, A. Morozov, & I. Robert (Eds.), *Contemporary Challenges in Education: Digitalization, Methodology, and Management* (pp. 254–275). IGI Global. doi:10.4018/979-8-3693-1826-3.ch019

Majid, U. (2018). Research fundamentals: Study design, population, and sample size. *Undergraduate research in natural and clinical science and technology journal, 2*, 1-7.

Mangla, A. S., Bhatia, M., Bhatia, S., & Kumar, P. (2022). *Current State of Engineering Education in India: Student Teacher Scenario in Online Mode. Rising Threats in Expert Applications and Solutions: Proceedings of FICR-TEAS.* Springer Nature. https://link.springer.com/chapter/10.1007/978-981-19-1122-4_49

Mathevula, M. D., & Uwizeyimana, D. E. (2014). The challenges facing the integration of ICT in teaching and learning activities in South African rural secondary schools. *Mediterranean Journal of Social Sciences*, *5*(20), 1087–1097. doi:10.5901/mjss.2014.v5n20p1087

Mentz, E., & Goosen, L. (2007). Are groups working in the Information Technology class? *South African Journal of Education*, *27*(2), 329–343.

Mir, M., Hussain, M., & Jariko, M. (2023). Contexts and Faculty Belief Matters: Problems in Pedagogical Shifts among Faculty Members of Business Schools: A Study on Pakistan Higher Education Institutions (HEIs), Karachi Sindh, Pakistan. *KASBIT Business Journal*, *16*(2), 19–40.

Mushtaq, M. S., Mushtaq, M. Y., & Iqbal, M. W. (2020). Use of authentic learning tools in delivery of scientific education. [IJCSIS]. *International Journal of Computer Science and Information Security*, *18*(11), 1–8.

MushtaqM. T. (2021). The Impact of Emotions on Consumer Behaviour in Post Covid Environment: A Neuromarketing Perspective. *Conference contribution.* Cardiff Metropolitan University. doi:10.25401/cardiffmet.14614266.v1

Nakashololo, T. M. (2021). *A decision support framework for selecting big data analytics tools in an organisation.* Cape Peninsula University of Technology.

Ngugi, J. K., & Goosen, L. (2021). Innovation, Entrepreneurship, and Sustainability for ICT Students Towards the Post-COVID-19 Era. In L. C. Carvalho, L. Reis, & C. Silveira (Eds.), *Handbook of Research on Entrepreneurship, Innovation, Sustainability, and ICTs in the Post-COVID-19 Era* (pp. 110–131). IGI Global. doi:10.4018/978-1-7998-6776-0.ch006

Obeidat, M. M., & Alomari, M. D. (2020). The Effect of Inductive and Deductive Teaching on EFL Undergraduates' Achievement in Grammar at the Hashemite University in Jordan. *International Journal of Higher Education*, *9*(2), 280–288. doi:10.5430/ijhe.v9n2p280

Oyewo, S. A., & Goosen, L. (2024). Relationships Between Teachers' Technological Competency Levels and Self-Regulated Learning Behavior: Investigating Blended Learning Environments. In R. Pandey, N. Srivastava, & P. Chatterjee (Eds.), *Architecture and Technological Advancements of Education 4.0* (pp. 1–24). IGI Global. doi:10.4018/978-1-6684-9285-7.ch001

Pholotho, T., & Mtsweni, J. (2016, May). Barriers to electronic access and delivery of educational information in resource constrained public schools: A case of Greater Tubatse Municipality. *IST-Africa Week Conference Proceedings* (pp. 1-9). IEEE.

Pholotho, T. J. (2017). *Toward a Broadband Services Delivery Model over Wireless Technologies to Resource-Constrained Public High Schools in South Africa (MTech)*. University of South Africa.

Polit, D. F., & Beck, C. T. (2020). Trustworthiness and rigor in qualitative research. In *Nursing research: generating and assessing evidence for nursing practice* (pp. 567–584). Lippincott Williams & Wilkins.

Rangongo, M. F. (2021). *Work-life conflict experiences and cultural expectations of women managers in the public sector of Limpopo Province.* University of Limpopo. http://ulspace.ul.ac.za/bitstream/handle/10386/3623/rangongo_mf_2021.pdf?isAllowed=y&sequence=1

Tanoli, M. A., Khan, M. I., & Majoka, M. I. (2021). English as Medium of Instruction at Primary Level: Problems Faced by Teachers and Students. *Sir Syed Journal of Education & Social Research*, *4*(2), 167–174.

Usman, M., Ahmad, M., & Ali, M. (2020). Inclusive Education of Children with Special Needs: Practices, Opportunities and Barriers. *Pakistan Journal of Education*, *37*(1), 75–94.

Uunona, G. N., & Goosen, L. (2023). Leveraging Ethical Standards in Artificial Intelligence Technologies: A Guideline for Responsible Teaching and Learning Applications. In M. Garcia, M. Lopez Cabrera, & R. de Almeida (Eds.), *Handbook of Research on Instructional Technologies in Health Education and Allied Disciplines* (pp. 310–330). IGI Global. doi:10.4018/978-1-6684-7164-7.ch014

Van Heerden, D., & Goosen, L. (2012). Using Vodcasts to Teach Programming in an ODL Environment. *Progressio*, *34*(3), 144–160.

Woiceshyn, J., & Daellenbach, U. (2018). Evaluating inductive vs deductive research in management studies: Implications for authors, editors, and reviewers. Qualitative research in organizations and management: An International Journal, 13(2), 183-195.

Yadav, D., Bansal, A., Bhatia, M., Hooda, M., & Morato, J. (Eds.). (2021). *Diagnostic applications of health intelligence and surveillance systems*. IGI Global. doi:10.4018/978-1-7998-6527-8

Zvitambo, K. (2021, April). *Dissertation Writing: A Student Guide*. ISPPME. https://isppme.com/wp-content/uploads/2021/04/Reseaarch-Project-Guidelines.docx

Chapter 5
Revolutionizing Higher Education in Malaysia With the Game–Changing Impact of Cloud Computing

Glaret Shirley Sinnappan
Tunku Abdul Rahman University of Management and Technology, Malaysia

Raenu Kolandaisamy
UCSI University, Malaysia

Maran Marimuthu
Universiti Teknologi Petronas, Malaysia

Amir Rizaan Abdul Rahiman
Universiti Putra Malaysia, Malaysia

Amir Aatieff Amir Hussin
ⓘ https://orcid.org/0000-0002-1508-7650
International Islamic University, Malaysia

Abdurrahman Jalil
Universiti Teknologi MARA, Malaysia

ABSTRACT

Cloud computing is rapidly becoming integral to higher education in Malaysia, driven by technological advancements and the demands of Industry Revolution 4.0. However, there is a lack of research on its impact from the perspective of students. This study focuses on scrutinizing the influence of cloud computing on Malaysia's higher education sector, emphasizing variables like cost reduction, resource availability, data confidentiality, and learning motivation. A comparative analysis of Google Apps, Microsoft Office 365, and Blackboard App will be conducted. Employing the snowball sampling technique, the research will involve 385 tertiary education students out of a total population of 1.2 million. Questionnaire data will be analyzed using IBM SPSS for a comprehensive understanding.

DOI: 10.4018/979-8-3693-2169-0.ch005

Copyright © 2024, IGI Global. Copying or distributing in print or electronic forms without written permission of IGI Global is prohibited.

INTRODUCTION

The tertiary education sector in Malaysia has undergone substantial growth over the decades, and recent years have witnessed the widespread deployment of cloud computing. This adoption is propelled by the dynamic scalability and utilization of virtualized resources (Kmar Anuar & Hajar Umira Md Zaki, 2024; Hussein & Hilmi, 2020; Darus et al., 2015). At the same time, the rise of the digital classroom idea corresponds with progress in educational technology, catering to the increasing demand for assistance in digital learning (Kumar et al., 2020).

The integration of cloud computing enables educational institutions to shift their focus from intricate IT configurations and software systems, allowing them to concentrate on enhancing the quality of education through research activities and teaching (Hussein & Hilmi, 2020; Mircea & Andreescu, 2011). The fundamental concept of cloud-based e-learning empowers users to access information irrespective of time and location, presenting an infrastructure capable of bringing new value to the education system (Kmar Anuar & Hajar Umira Md Zaki, 2024; Hussein & Hilmi, 2020; Alghali et al., 2014). Cloud technologies have implications that support the ease of learning materials and unveil issues inherent in the traditional education system, which constrained the range of activities (Mary et al., 2020; Darus et al., 2015).

As the usage of cloud applications intensifies, understanding its impact becomes crucial prior to its widespread implementation in Malaysia's tertiary education sector (Hussein & Hilmi, 2020; Shahzaad et al., 2014). Numerous studies in this domain highlight the positive impacts of implementing cloud computing technologies in higher education, emphasizing cost-effectiveness, convenience, and flexibility (Hussein & Hilmi, 2020; Mircea & Andreescu, 2011). Some papers suggest that cloud computing enhances resource availability yet caution about hidden risks related to data confidentiality due to diverse hardware attacks and software vulnerabilities (Zhang et al., 2018). While much research focuses on user adoption, acceptance, opportunities, and challenges (Isa et al., 2020), Arfan et al. (2016) have indicated a notable scarcity of research on the impact of cloud computing on Malaysia's polytechnics from the students' perspective, particularly its influence on learning motivation. Therefore, the objective of this research is to identify and validate the impact of cloud computing adoption in Malaysia's higher education sector. The problem statement posits that the use of cloud computing has a more positive than negative impact on the higher education sector in Malaysia.

LITERATURE REVIEW

Independent Variable

Cloud Computing

The widespread adoption of cloud computing in higher education is attributed to its ability to access and deploy diverse information resources stored on remote servers (Alghali et al., 2014). As noted by Aydin (2021) and Jaafar et al. (2017), cloud computing constitutes a network framework that provides on-demand, scalable, and high-quality computing platforms, easily accessible through a straightforward interface. In contrast to conventional computing systems, the fundamental basis of cloud computing revolves around the amalgamation of storage and computing infrastructure (Aydin, 2021; Harfoushi, 2017). This approach capitalizes on economies of scale by consolidating computing resources and employing virtualization. The strategic significance of cloud computing is underscored by the extensive utilization of Google Educator in higher education institutions. According to a survey conducted by Almajalid (2017), many academic establishments requiring substantial computing power have embraced cloud applications in education. This integration facilitates a heightened focus on research and learning, concurrently streamlining system operation and maintenance. Cloud computing encompasses three primary models: Software as a Service (SaaS), Infrastructure as a Service (IaaS), and Platform as a Service (PaaS). SaaS allows users to access software through web browsers, with Google Docs serving as a notable example (IBM, 2024; Arfan et al., 2016). PaaS comprises a suite of infrastructure and software, enabling users to deploy programming applications or tools such as Microsoft Azure and Google engines (Shakeabubakor, 2015). Furthermore, IaaS refers to a service wherein hardware components, including networks, servers, and storage processors, can be accessed through virtual machines. This affords greater flexibility, allowing users to unload the operating system from any software, exemplified by services like Amazon Web Services S3 and EC2 (IBM, 2024; Shakeabubakor, 2015).

Dependent Variables

Cost Benefits

The adoption of cloud computing by universities is intricately linked to the imperative of cost-cutting measures in response to the global financial system's volatility (Jaafar et al., 2021; Sultan, 2010). As a strategic response, many universities choose to embrace cloud computing due to its reputation for providing cost-effective IT services, effectively addressing financial concerns for both institutions and students (Hamed & Preece, 2020; Lam et al., 2013). This adoption empowers higher education institutions to bypass significant expenditures on hardware, software, and licensing fees (Hussein & Hilmi, 2020; Shahzaad et al., 2014).

Cloud computing, as a cost-effective solution, offers universities streamlined information sharing and provides users with ample storage space and robust computing services, all at a reduced cost (Akhtar et al., 2021; Aldeen et al., 2015). Notably, cloud services, exemplified by Google's offerings, extend further benefits by providing free applications tailored specifically for higher education. This not only facilitates learning but also contributes to cost savings by eliminating additional expenses ((Jayabalan, 2021, Qasem et al., 2019; Jaafar et al., 2017, Rajesh, 2017, Ruda 2013). In essence, the integration of cloud computing in higher education aligns with the pursuit of cost-effective strategies, offering a multifaceted approach to financial sustainability in the face of economic uncertainties.

Resource Availability

The In the context of higher learning, the integration of cloud computing has emerged as a pivotal force, reshaping the landscape of educational technology. Jaafar et al. (2017) articulated how the cloud computing platform facilitates the sharing of resources in both hardware and software infrastructure within academic settings. The term "cloud" takes on a dual-faceted nature, encompassing abstraction and virtualization. Abstraction involves the concealment of system intricacies from developers and users, enabling applications to run with data stored in undisclosed locations and allowing users to access these applications globally. Additionally, Mesbahi et al. (2018) emphasized the significance of virtualization in higher education, highlighting the pooling and sharing of resources. Cloud computing, as elucidated by these scholars, represents a model specifically designed to offer on-demand, convenient, and pervasive network access to a collective pool of customizable computing resources within the realm of academia. These resources span a diverse array, including services, applications, networks, storage, and servers, all of which can be swiftly provisioned and released with minimal management effort or integration with service providers (Mampage et al., 2022). Within higher learning institutions, the adoption of cloud computing not only optimizes resource utilization but also revolutionizes the educational experience. This transformative technology fosters seamless collaboration among students and educators, overcoming geographical constraints and enhancing accessibility to academic resources. Moreover, cloud-based platforms provide scalable solutions for secure data storage, allowing educational institutions to effectively manage vast repositories of information. In essence, the integration of cloud computing in higher learning aligns with the evolving needs of modern education, offering scalable and efficient solutions to educators and students alike.

Confidentiality of Data

Confidentiality, encompassing a set of rules designed to prevent unauthorized access to private and sensitive information, is a critical aspect of data security. Within the context of higher education, the issue of data confidentiality has become a pronounced security challenge in the realm of cloud computing (Dima, 2023; Rajesh, 2017). Specifically, attributes associated with the privacy and security of confidential data include aspects such as secrecy, accessibility, accountability, privacy-preservability, and reliability (Aldeen et al., 2015). In the higher education sector, the processing of information involves handling sensitive data and personal information of students. The responsibility for the storage and processing of this data is often delegated to third-party entities utilizing servers, thereby introducing potential security concerns for the confidentiality of the data (Dawood et al., 2023; Shahzaad et al., 2014). The collaborative utilization of cloud computing services in higher learning environments, while offering numerous benefits in resource sharing and accessibility, demands heightened vigilance to safeguard the confidentiality of sensitive data. Educational institutions must establish robust measures and protocols to ensure that data stored and processed in the cloud remains secure and protected from unauthorized access, meeting the stringent privacy requirements associated with student information. The ongoing exploration of advanced encryption techniques, secure access controls, and compliance with data protection regulations is imperative to address the evolving challenges posed by data confidentiality in the dynamic landscape of higher education and cloud computing.

Learning Motivation

In the context of higher learning and cloud computing, understanding learning motivation is crucial. According to Langshaw (2017), motivation encompasses elements such as self-determination, choice, self-control, volition, and autonomy. Chan (2018) and Chung et al. (2020) further categorize motivation into two distinct types: intrinsic and extrinsic motivations. Intrinsic motivation, as highlighted by Chan (2018) and Chung et al. (2020), originates internally from an individual's mental, social, and physical development, shaping their life choices and interests. This internal drive aligns with a natural human inclination to learn, reflecting personal growth and genuine curiosity. Conversely, extrinsic motivation is derived from external factors, including the learning environment, interactions with people, tangible rewards, or recognition (Chan, 2018; Chung et al., 2020). In the dynamic landscape of higher learning and cloud computing, the interplay between motivation and technology is notable. Cloud computing, with its transformative impact on education, contributes to shaping the learning environment and influencing motivation. The accessibility and flexibility afforded by cloud-based learning platforms enhance intrinsic motivation by providing learners with autonomy and the ability to tailor their educational experiences to suit their preferences and pace. Moreover, cloud computing facilitates dynamic and interactive learning experiences in higher education. Collaborative projects, real-time feedback, and the utilization of multimedia resources are made more feasible through cloud-based platforms. This integration potentially taps into intrinsic motivations tied to curiosity and engagement, fostering a self-directed and motivated learning environment. While learners can be motivated by both intrinsic and extrinsic factors, the intrinsic motivation emphasized by Langshaw (2017) is particularly significant in the context of cloud-based higher learning for example factors on Autonomy, mastery, and purpose. The extrinsic factors which are relevant on the context of cloud-based higher learning are factors such as Rewards and incentives recognition and praise, external deadlines and pressures, competition, grades, evaluations, social expectations, material rewards or benefit. The alignment of technology, educational practices, and motivations creates a synergistic approach that positively influences the overall educational experience for learners, emphasizing their natural inclination to explore and learn.

Hypotheses Development

H1: The use of Cloud Computing should positively correlate with the cost reduction of the higher education sector.

As indicated by Jayabalan (2021), Rajesh (2017), and Ruda (2013), certain higher educational institutions encounter limitations in hardware and software resources, impeding the provision of a comprehensive learning environment due to budgetary constraints. Cloud computing emerges as a cost-effective solution for Information and Communication Technology (ICT) by facilitating resource-sharing among multiple users, irrespective of their geographical locations (Rajesh, 2017). Furthermore, as emphasized by both Rajesh (2017) and Mitchell & Cunningham (2014), students can mitigate expenses related to textbooks and hardware through the adoption of cloud computing. This is made possible by the seamless acquisition of e-books and access to high-quality learning materials within a cloud-based framework. There is a pressing need to conduct further studies to explore and validate the extent of the correlation between cloud computing adoption and cost reduction in the higher education sector.

H2: The use of Cloud Computing should positively correlate with resource availability in the higher education sector.

Nonetheless, according to Shahzad et al. (2020), the primary security concern associated with the adoption of cloud computing in higher education institutions is data confidentiality. This concern arises from the inability to control the physical location where information is stored, potentially leading to data leakage (Darus et al., 2015). The significance of data confidentiality as a security issue is underscored by Sikdder (2023) and Tchifilionova (2011), who note it as a persistent threat in cloud computing. In practical terms, those overseeing system management must have a clear understanding of its operation and assess the organization's capability to address the issue of confidential data leakage, particularly during the transition to cloud computing systems (Sikdder, 2023; Aldeen et al., 2015; Shahzaad et al., 2014). There is a compelling need for further studies to investigate the correlation between the adoption of cloud computing and the enhancement of resource availability in the higher education sector. Exploring this correlation is essential to comprehensively understand the potential benefits and challenges associated with cloud computing in the context of resource availability in higher education.

H3: The use of Cloud Computing should negatively relate to the confidentiality of data in the higher education sector.

According to Lam et al. (2013), cloud computing has a positive impact on students' learning motivation in polytechnics, with the caveat that this influence is contingent upon cultural background and educational settings. In Malaysia, being a collectivistic nation, the impact of social influence and peer groups is substantial (Cheah et al., 2018). Social influence, as highlighted by Yau et al. (2015), is identified as a factor that affects learning motivation. Another influencing factor on student learning motivation is the prevalent issue in the current Malaysian education system, characterized by spoon-fed approaches commonly employed in primary and high schools. This results in a notable disparity in learning styles and teaching methods as students progress to higher education institutions (Almaiah et al., 2022; Safdar et al., 2022; Nasri & Mydin, 2017). Consequently, as cloud computing diminishes the need for physical interaction in the classroom, the potential lack of social influence and the significant divergence in educational styles may have a negative impact on students' learning motivation. There is an evident need for further research to explore and validate the potential negative correlation between the use of cloud computing and the confidentiality of data in the higher education sector. Understanding the implications of cloud computing on data confidentiality is crucial for institutions aiming to strike a balance between technological advancements and the secure handling of sensitive information in higher education.

H4: The use of Cloud Computing should negatively relate to the learning motivation of students in the higher education sector.

The integration of Cloud Computing in the higher education sector is anticipated to exhibit a negative correlation with students' learning motivation. The potential for adverse effects arises from several factors, including cultural considerations and the prevailing educational landscape. Findings from Lam et al. (2013) suggest that, while Cloud Computing positively impacts learning motivation in polytechnics, this influence is contingent upon cultural background and educational settings. In the context of Malaysia, being a collectivistic nation, the substantial influence of social dynamics and peer groups on learning motivation is recognized (Cheah et al., 2018). Furthermore, the established spoon-fed approaches prevalent in the Malaysian primary and high school education system contribute to significant disparities in learning styles and teaching methods as students transition to higher education (Nasri & Mydin, 2017). As Cloud Computing tends to reduce the necessity for physical interaction in the classroom, potential implications include a diminished sense of social influence and a notable mismatch in educational styles. These factors, in combination, may contribute to a negative relationship between the use of Cloud Computing and students' learning motivation in the higher education sector. There is a critical need for further empirical research to thoroughly investigate the potential negative correlation between the adoption of Cloud Computing and students' learning motivation in higher education. Such exploration is essential to inform educators, institutions, and policymakers about the potential impact of technological advancements on students' motivation and engagement in the learning process.

Conceptual Framework

The conceptual framework carefully looks at how cloud computing affects higher education in various ways, such as reducing costs, making resources available, ensuring data confidentiality, and influencing students' motivation to learn. When we talk about reducing costs, the framework explores how cloud computing helps to spend money more efficiently by using resources better and taking advantage of economies of scale. It highlights the importance of thorough research to understand the details and implications of using cloud computing. At the same time, the framework examines how accessible and useful on-demand computing power, storage, and collaborative tools are for educational purposes. This part of the study requires careful exploration to fully understand how cloud computing contributes to making these resources available for education. The framework also looks closely at how data confidentiality is maintained with cloud-based data. It emphasizes the need for focused research efforts to address security and privacy concerns associated with storing data in the cloud. Lastly, the framework investigates how cloud computing influences students' motivation to learn. This includes looking at factors like how easily students can access educational materials, collaborate with others, and adapt to different learning resources provided by cloud-based technology. The interconnected nature of this framework gives us a comprehensive understanding of how cloud computing transforms higher education. It stresses the importance of ongoing and empirical research to contribute to academic discussions and guide decision-making strategies.

Figure 1. Conceptual framework
(IGI, 2024)

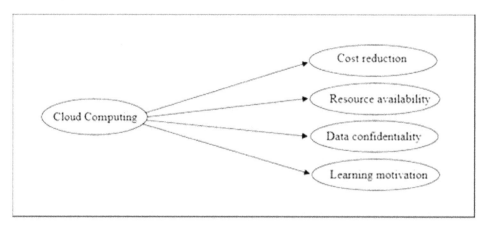

RESEARCH METHODOLOGY

Research Design

In the course of this research, a mixed-methods approach will be employed, integrating both quantitative and qualitative research methodologies, as articulated by Doyle et al. (2009). This methodological choice is rooted in several advantages, including (1) triangulation, which enhances the validity of the research by facilitating collaboration between quantitative and qualitative data; (2) offering a more comprehensive and complete view of the research landscape; and (3) providing additional insights and explanations for the research findings. To achieve a profound understanding of the quantitative data, interviews will be conducted. The research instruments utilized to collect data encompass a web-based questionnaire, structured interviews, and documentation review, with the latter two complementing and supporting the former. The questionnaire will compare the impact of three cloud-based applications (Google Apps, Microsoft 365, and Blackboard App) on students in polytechnics, utilizing a snowball sampling technique to ensure effective data collection. The research population comprises tertiary education students in Malaysia, totalling 1.2 million individuals (MOHE, 2019), resulting in a sample size of 385. Data obtained from the questionnaires will subsequently be analysed using the IBM Statistical Package for Social Science (SPSS).

Data Collection Method and Questionnaire Design

Quantitative data are presented in numerical values, while qualitative data can manifest in diverse formats such as words, narratives, images, audio, and observations (Sarstedt & Mooi, 2019). Consequently, the initial acquisition of quantitative data will be facilitated through a web-based questionnaire, defined by Creswell (2020) as a survey instrument utilized for internet-based data collection. Subsequently, structured interviews will be conducted online via platforms such as Google Meet and Zoom to bolster the quantitative findings and procure a profound comprehension of the impact of cloud computing applications on students. Survey research, an intricate and pivotal process, is imperative for achieving research objectives. Hence, the meticulous selection and design of the appropriate questionnaire instrument serve as the foundation, addressing the research inquiries concerning what needs to be measured and how it should be measured. In this context, emphasis is placed on construct validity and construct reliability (Qasem et al., 2020). The questionnaire employed in this study comprises three sections, featuring closed-ended questions and scale responses. The first section offers a concise overview of the research, incorporating nominal and ordinal questions to gather basic demographic information and discern the intent behind students' use of cloud applications in their studies. The second section consists of eight questions measuring two positive impact variables (cost reduction and resource availability), while the final section comprises eight questions evaluating two negative impact variables (data confidentiality and learning motivation). The ultimate question in each variable assesses respondents' opinions on which cloud application (Google Apps, Microsoft 365, and Blackboard App) exerts the most significant impact on a specific factor. Questions 1 to 3 in the second section measuring cost reduction variables are adapted from Majid (2018), while questions 5 to 7 assessing resource availability are adapted from Ashtar & Eydgahi (2011). In the third section concerning negative impact, questions 9 to 11 measuring data confidentiality are adapted from Ashtar & Eydgahi (2011), and questions 13 to 15 gauging learning motivation are adapted from Pintrich & Groot (1990). To enhance the clarity of decisions' directionality, a seven-point Likert-type scale ranging from 1 = "Strongly Disagree" to 7 = "Strongly Agree" is adopted for items measuring all four variables, aligning with the recommendations of Ogbonna, E & Harris (2000) and Ashtar & Eydgahi (2011) for bolstering the validity and reliability of the collected data.

Sampling Design

The term "target population" refers to a subset or specific group within the broader population, also known as the population of interest. Researchers often redefine it to make it more manageable (Saunders et al., 2015; Majid, 2018). For this study, the target population comprises higher education students in Malaysia, totalling 1.2 million students, as indicated by the Ministry of Higher Education (MOHE, 2019). From this extensive population, a sample size of 385 will be selected. As highlighted by Showkat (2017), the selection of qualified samples from the population is a critical aspect of the research process, contributing to both economic efficiency and the accuracy of the ensuing report. Consequently, this research employs snowball sampling, a non-probability sampling method described by Sarstedt and Mooi (2019) and Dusek et al. (2015). In snowball sampling, existing respondents recruit new participants from their acquaintances who share similarities and meet the criteria of the target population. To ensure the efficacy and efficiency of data collection, online questionnaires will be disseminated across various platforms such as Facebook and WhatsApp, allowing participants to share the survey with others. This method is particularly pertinent during the post pandemic, representing the sole feasible approach for data collection. Notwithstanding the potential bias associated with snowball sampling, which may result in homogenous samples (Saunders et al., 2015), the utilization of diverse social media platforms in questionnaire distribution aims to mitigate this bias, thereby broadening the reach to students from different demographic groups.

Data Analysis Method

The initial phase of data examination will involve preliminary analysis, followed by descriptive analysis, reliability and validity assessments, and bivariate regression analysis. Descriptive analysis serves to summarize and gauge the measurements derived from the collected samples in this study. Given the multiple variables under consideration, including demographic factors and constructs, descriptive analysis proves instrumental in simplifying and breaking down voluminous data into manageable components. This process constitutes a fundamental aspect of quantitative data analysis, complemented by graphical analysis to facilitate straightforward comparisons (Kaur et al., 2018). Additionally, reliability analysis assesses the extent to which the data accurately represents the actual scope of the study, while validity analysis gauges the consistency and repeatability of the obtained results through measurement (Taherdoost, 2018). The conclusive phase involves testing hypotheses through bivariate regression analysis.

DATA ANALYSIS

Preliminary Data Analysis

Non-Response Bias Analysis

Non-response bias occurs when systematic distinctions exist in characteristics between individuals who did not respond to a survey or study and those who did (Sedgwick, 2014). To assess the presence of non-response bias in this research, an independent-samples T-test is employed to facilitate a comparison of means between non-responders and responders. According to Sellke et al. (2015), data is deemed free of response bias if the p-value (2-tailed significance value) exceeds 0.05. Examination of Table I reveals that all the p-values in the table surpass 0.05, indicating an absence of response bias in the data collected for this study.

Figure 2. Independent samples T-Test Table
(IGI, 2024)

		Levene's Test for Equality of Variances		t-test for Equality of Means					95% Confidence Interval of the Difference	
		F	Sig.	t	df	Sig. (2-tailed)	Mean Difference	Std. Error Difference	Lower	Upper
Gender	Equal variances assumed	.000	1.000	.620	38	.539	.10000	.16141	-.22675	.42675
	Equal variances not assumed			.620	38.000	.539	.10000	.16141	.22675	.42675
Age	Equal variances assumed	10.574	.002	-1.314	38	.197	-.25000	.19022	-.63508	.13508
	Equal variances not assumed			-1.314	32.344	.198	-.25000	.19022	-.63731	.13731
Education_Level	Equal variances assumed	13.919	<.001	-1.584	38	.121	-.35000	.22094	-.79728	.09728
	Equal variances not assumed			-1.584	28.713	.124	-.35000	.22094	-.80208	.10208

Common Method Variance (CMV) Analysis

Common Method Variance (CMV) occurs when measurement techniques introduce systematic variance into the measurements. It is characterized by systematic error variance shared among variables measured using a similar procedure or source, potentially biasing relationships within items and variables (Tehseen et al., 2018). To assess CMV in this study, Harman's Single-Factor Test was utilized. As presented in Table 2, the variance of data is calculated at 27.87%, a value below the 50% error threshold stipulated by Tehseen et al. (2018). This result indicates that CMV is not a significant concern in the context of this research.

Figure 3. Common method variance total variance table
(IGI, 2024)

Factor	Initial Eigenvalues			Extraction Sums of Squared Loadings		
	Total	% of Variance	Cumulative %	Total	% of Variance	Cumulative %
1	4.033	33.604	33.604	3.344	27.870	27.870
2	2.349	19.574	53.179			
3	1.583	13.191	66.370			
4	1.010	8.413	74.783			
5	.627	5.229	80.012			
6	.523	4.356	84.368			
7	.422	3.514	87.881			
8	.394	3.283	91.164			
9	.352	2.936	94.100			
10	.280	2.329	96.429			
11	.238	1.983	98.412			
12	.191	1.588	100.000			

Extraction Method: Principal Axis Factoring

Normality Test

The normality of the research data was assessed using the Kolmogorov-Smirnov and Shapiro-Wilk tests. According to Calixto (2016), the significance value in Table 3, denoted as "p," is crucial in determining normal distribution, with $p > 0.05$ signifying a normal distribution. Examination of Table III reveals that all variables under scrutiny in this study yield p-values below 0.05. This implies that each variable exhibits a normal distribution, meeting the criteria for acceptance.

Descriptive Analysis

The descriptive analysis for this study was conducted based on Table 4, which utilized demographic variables such as gender, age group, education level, cloud application usage frequency, and the most used application. The gender variable is divided into male and female. The age group variable is categorized into three groups: 18 to 20 years old, 21 to 23 years old, and 24 to 26 years old. Older students beyond this age range are not considered.

Figure 4. Kolmogorov-Smirnov test and Shapiro-Wilk test table
(IGI, 2024)

NORMALITY TEST	Kolmogorov-Smirnov			Shapiro-Wilk		
	Statistics	Df	Sig.	Statistics	Df	Sig.
Cloud Computing	0.147	385	0.000	0.936	385	0.000
Cost Reduction	0.126	385	0.000	0.928	385	0.000
Resource Availability	0.133	385	0.000	0.927	385	0.000
Data Confidentiality	0.085	385	0.000	0.964	385	0.000
Learning Motivation	0.079	385	0.000	0.968	385	0.000

Figure 5. Demographic characteristics
(IGI, 2024)

Demographic Variable	Description	n	%
Gender	Male	163	42.3
	Female	222	57.7
Age Group	18 to 20 years old	154	40.0
	21 to 23 years old	215	55.8
	24 to 26 years old	16	4.2
Education Level	A-level	15	3.9
	Diploma/Foundation	109	28.3
	Bachelor's Degree	242	62.9
	Master's Degree	19	4.9
Cloud Applications Usage Frequency	Less than 1 day per week	18	4.7
	1 to 3 days per week	78	20.3
	4 to 6 days per week	133	34.5
	Everyday	156	40.5
Most Used Application	Google apps	200	51.9
	Microsoft 365	147	38.2
	Blackboard app	38	9.9

The education variable focuses on students at A-level, Diploma/foundation, bachelor's degree, and master's degree levels. The cloud application usage frequency is divided into categories: less than 1 day per week, 1 to 3 days per week, 4 to 6 days per week, and every day. The last variable, the most used application, includes Google Apps, Microsoft 365, and the Blackboard application."

Figure 6. Descriptive Statistics
(IGI, 2024)

	Mean	Standard Deviation	n
Cloud Computing	17.961	2.139	385
Cost reduction	18.182	2.127	385
Resource availability	17.774	2.559	385
Data confidentiality	15.195	3.742	385
Learning motivation	14.265	4.159	385

The mean and standard deviation of the descriptive study are presented in Table 5. The sample size *(n = 385)* is indicated in the same table. Specifically, for cloud computing, the mean is 17.961 with a standard deviation of 2.139; for cost reduction, the mean is 18.182 with a standard deviation of 2.127; for resource availability, the mean value is 17.774 with a standard deviation of 2.559; for data confidentiality, the mean is 15.195 with a standard deviation of 3.742; and finally, for learning motivation, the mean value is 14.265 with a standard deviation of 4.159.

Reliability Analysis

The reliability of the findings significantly influences the validity of the questionnaire, as a lack of reliability may introduce instability to the attributes being measured (Bolarinwa, 2015). According to Robinson (2009), a widely accepted benchmark for the consistency coefficient reliability is a value equal to or greater than 0.7. As demonstrated in Table 6, the Cronbach alpha values for each scale range from 0.777 to 0.876. These values signify that the measurement scales of the construct variables in this research exhibit high reliability and internal consistency.

Figure 7. Reliability test for study variables
(IGI, 2024)

Construct Variable	Cronbach's Alpha Value	No. Of Items
Cloud Computing	0.777	3
Cost Reduction	0.748	3
Resource Availability	0.800	3
Data Confidentiality	0.843	3
Learning Motivation	0.876	3

Validity Analysis

Validity, in this context, pertains to the extent to which each item employed to measure a factor accurately reflects the underlying concept it intends to measure. It is imperative that each item used to compute a construct exhibits significant loading with its respective construct in comparison to other constructs (Al-Rahmi et al., 2018). Ensuring the validity of the research involves a systematic literature review in which the items employed are established and tested by prior scholars and researchers (Al-Rahmi et al., 2018). As indicated in Table 7, all items are appropriately aligned with their corresponding factors, displaying high loading in comparison to other constructs. Consequently, each item effectively loads on the factor it was intended to measure, affirming the overall validity of the measurement model.

Figure 8. Varimax with Kaiser normalization table
(IGI, 2024)

Rotated Factor Matrix[a]

	Factor				
	1	2	3	4	5
LM1	.885				
LM3	.818				
LM2	.783				
DC2		.857			
DC3		.738			
DC1		.736			
RC1			.751		
RC3			.693		
RC2			.580		
CC3				.898	
CC1				.743	
CC2				.555	
RA2					.766
RA1					.685
RA3					.576

Extraction Method: Principal Axis Factoring
Rotation Method: Varimax with Kaiser Normalization
a. Rotation converged in 5 iterations.

Bivariate Regression Analysis

Bivariate regression analysis is a method that elucidates the mathematical relationship expressed in an equation between a single metric dependent variable and a single metric independent variable. This analysis facilitates the determination of the simple correlation between these two variables (Malhotra & Birks, 2006). A significance value of $p < 0.05$ signifies acceptance of the hypothesis, while a value exceeding 0.05 indicates rejection. As depicted in Table 8, the relationship between cloud computing and cost reduction supports H1, with a significance value of 0.015, signifying a positive association in the higher education sector.

Figure 9. Anova for cloud computing: Cost reduction
(IGI, 2024)

ANOVA[a]

Model		Sum of Squares	df	Mean Square	F	Sig.
1	Regression	26.494	1	26.494	5.931	.015[b]
	Residual	1710.778	383	4.467		
	Total	1737.273	384			

a. Dependent Variable: RC
b. Predictors: (Constant), CC

However, Table 9 reveals that the relationship between cloud computing and resource availability does not support H2, as the significance value is 0.551, exceeding the threshold of $p < 0.05$, indicating no statistically significant relationship.

In Table 10, the significance value for the relationship between cloud computing and data confidentiality is 0.019, supporting H3 and establishing a negative correlation in the higher education sector.

Figure 10. Anova for cloud computing: Resource availability
(IGI, 2024)

ANOVA[a]

Model		Sum of Squares	df	Mean Square	F	Sig.
1	Regression	2.331	1	2.331	.355	.551[b]
	Residual	2513.009	383	6.561		
	Total	2515.340	384			

a. Dependent Variable: RA
b. Predictors: (Constant), CC

Figure 11. Anova for Cloud Computing: Data Confidentiality
(IGI, 2024)

ANOVA[a]

Model		Sum of Squares	df	Mean Square	F	Sig.
1	Regression	76.834	1	76.834	5.553	.019[b]
	Residual	5299.555	383	13.837		
	Total	5376.390	384			

a. Dependent Variable: DC
b. Predictors: (Constant), CC

Figure 12. Anova for Cloud Computing: Learning Motivation
(IGI, 2024)

ANOVA[a]

Model		Sum of Squares	df	Mean Square	F	Sig.
1	Regression	6.386	1	6.386	.369	.544[b]
	Residual	6636.591	383	17.328		
	Total	6642.977	384			

a. Dependent Variable: LM
b. Predictors: (Constant), CC

Finally, Table 11 illustrates the relationship between cloud computing and learning motivation, where H4 is rejected with a significance value of 0.544, indicating no significant association with the learning motivation of higher education students.

DISCUSSION

The impact of cloud computing on higher education has been examined through data analysis. In this context, hypotheses H1 and H3 have been supported, while H2 and H4 have been disproven. H1 suggests that cloud computing positively affects cost reduction. Interviews with 8 participants confirm this hypothesis, highlighting reduced expenses on physical educational materials and emphasizing the role of cloud computing in e-learning, which minimizes travel costs. These findings validate the positive influence of cloud computing on cost reduction in education. However, H2, proposing a positive impact on resource availability, is rejected based on significance values. Nonetheless, insights from participants stress the substantial improvement in resource accessibility through cloud computing, contradicting the statistical outcome. H3, proposing a negative impact on data confidentiality, is supported. Seven out of eight participants express concerns about storing sensitive data on cloud applications, citing potential risks like cybercrime and data leakage without robust security measures. Contrary to H4, suggesting a negative impact on learning motivation, the rejection of this hypothesis implies that cloud computing does not adversely affect learning motivation. Data from interviews reveal that four out of eight participants disagree, emphasizing that cloud computing facilitates the learning process and generates positive motivation without detriment to higher education students' motivation.

Figure 13. Variables and Cloud Applications
(IGI, 2024)

Variables	Cloud Applications	%	n
Reduced Cost	Google apps	59.0	227
	Microsoft 365	35.1	135
	Blackboard app	6.0	23
Resource Availability	Google apps	57.9	223
	Microsoft 365	31.2	120
	Blackboard app	10.9	42
Data Confidentiality	Google apps	50.1	193
	Microsoft 365	16.6	64
	Blackboard app	33.2	128
Learning Motivation	Google apps	24.2	93
	Microsoft 365	26.0	100
	Blackboard app	49.9	192

To gain further insights into this research topic, an examination of three prominent cloud applications which are the Google Apps, Microsoft 365, and Blackboard App were undertaken to discern their respective positive or negative impacts on students. Table 12 presents data derived from questionnaires, providing a comprehensive comparison of the perceived impacts of these cloud applications from the students' standpoint. As previously noted, Google Apps emerges as the most widely utilized cloud application, followed by Microsoft 365 and Blackboard App. Interviews reinforced this trend, with 6 out of 8 participants predominantly favoring Google Apps due to its simultaneous collaborative features, cost-effectiveness, and user-friendly interface. Conversely, 2 participants expressed a preference for Microsoft 365, citing its diverse array of features. From the data in Table 12, it is evident that 59% of respondents identified Google Apps as the most effective application for the cost reduction variable. The interview responses elucidated that Google Apps' convenience, allowing instant access to various Google applications, sets it apart from Microsoft 365, which entails a substantial subscription fee for accessing its complete features. Regarding resource availability, Google Apps garnered the highest preference, with 57.9% of respondents selecting it as the cloud application with the most abundant resources. Interview insights indicated that the free-of-charge nature of Google Apps fosters a willingness among users to share resources through this platform.

Concerning negative impacts on data confidentiality, most respondents (50.1%) expressed apprehensions about Google Apps, highlighting it as the cloud application raising the most significant concerns regarding data confidentiality.

Finally, Blackboard App was identified as having a negative impact on learning motivation. Despite the hypothesis rejection, interview responses revealed participant dissatisfaction with the app's non-interactive and inflexible interface, slow response system, and limited useful programs. Table 12 further supports these observations, indicating that Blackboard App has the lowest percentage for both positive impacts (6% for cost reduction and 10.9% for resource availability) among the three cloud applications. In conclusion, Google Apps emerges as the most effective cloud application in terms of cost reduction and resource availability, albeit with concerns about data confidentiality. Conversely, Blackboard App exhibits the least effectiveness among the three cloud applications.

IMPLICATION AND LIMITATIONS

Implication of Study

Cloud computing represents a noteworthy and beneficial advancement within Malaysia's education sector, particularly in the context of the ongoing pandemic. This research contributes significantly to the existing literature by delving into the adoption of cloud computing within higher education institutions in Malaysia. The study sheds light on which cloud applications prove more effective and exert a more substantial impact on institutions in the country. The findings underscore that numerous institutions and learners have benefited from simplified access to diverse applications and resources, all achieved at minimal cost. This research, by elucidating the effectiveness of various cloud applications, serves as a valuable resource for institutions contemplating the implementation of such technologies. It aids in identifying potential risks associated with cloud computing and their underlying causes. Consequently, this study advocates for the establishment of a secure cloud computing infrastructure within educational institutions, ensuring the efficient mitigation of issues that may arise during the implementation of cloud computing.

Limitations

Several limitations inherent in this research necessitate acknowledgment and consideration for future investigations. Primarily, the variables scrutinized in this study predominantly explore direct relationships, potentially overlooking the presence of moderators or mediators that could enrich the depth of understanding in this domain. Future research endeavours could delve into identifying and examining these moderating or mediating factors to enhance the intricacies of the topic. Moreover, the participants in this study were primarily bachelor's degree students, indicating a specific education level. Future research could benefit from a more diverse participant pool, encompassing various education levels. This approach would contribute to a more comprehensive and holistic exploration of the topic at hand.

FINDINGS

In conclusion, the importance of cloud computing in Malaysia's higher education system is evident, as demonstrated by the comprehensive examination of its positive and negative impacts in this study. The introduction of cloud computing services has proven to be a transformative and cost-effective solution for both educational institutions and learners. This technology provides expansive data storage capabilities and high computing power, eliminating the need for substantial capital investment in traditional hardware and physical machines. While the benefits of cloud computing in tertiary education are apparent, the study highlights critical issues, particularly in the realm of data security and confidentiality. The successful implementation of cloud computing relies on addressing these concerns and establishing a framework that is secure, scalable, and trustworthy. The study emphasizes the urgency of proposing and adopting models that can navigate the complexities of ensuring data security in the cloud computing landscape. Further exploration into the comparative analysis of three cloud applications which are the Google Apps, Microsoft 365, and Blackboard App provides nuanced insights into their respective impacts on higher education. Google Apps emerges as a positive force, demonstrating its effectiveness in enhancing the educational experience. Microsoft 365 showcases its diverse array of features, contributing positively to the higher education landscape. Conversely, Blackboard App appears to pose challenges for university students, prompting concerns regarding its compatibility and effectiveness within the higher education context. This comprehensive understanding of the implications of cloud computing in higher education positions stakeholders to make informed decisions, develop strategic plans, and explore potential areas for improvement. It underscores the need for continuous research and the development of adaptive solutions to optimize the advantages of cloud computing while effectively addressing the challenges that may arise in the ever-evolving landscape of higher education in Malaysia.

REFERENCES

Akhtar, N., Kerim, B., Perwej, Y., Tiwari, A., & Praveen, S. (2021). A Comprehensive Overview of Privacy and Data Security for Cloud Storage. *International Journal of Scientific Research in Science, Engineering and Technology*, 113–152. doi:10.32628/ IJSRSET21852

Al-Rahmi, W. M., Alias, N., Othman, M. S., Alzahrani, A. I., Alfarraj, O., Saged, A. A., & Rahman, N. S. A. (2018). Use of e-learning by university students in Malaysian higher educational institutions: A case in Universiti Teknologi Malaysia. *IEEE Access: Practical Innovations, Open Solutions*, 6, 14268–14276. doi:10.1109/ ACCESS.2018.2802325

Aldeen, Y. A. A. S., Salleh, M., & Razzaque, M. A. (2015). A survey paper on privacy issue in cloud computing. *Research Journal of Applied Sciences, Engineering and Technology*, 10(3), 328–337. doi:10.19026/rjaset.10.2495

Alghali, M., Najwa, H. M. A., & Roesnita, I. (2014). Challenges and benefits of implementing cloud based e-Learning in developing countries. *Proceeding of the Social Sciences Research ICSSR*, (pp. 9-10). IEEE.

Almaiah, M. A., Alfaisal, R., Salloum, S. A., Hajjej, F., Thabit, S., El-Qirem, F. A., Lutfi, A., Alrawad, M., Al Mulhem, A., Alkhdour, T., Awad, A. B., & Al-Maroof, R. S. (2022). Examining the impact of artificial intelligence and social and computer anxiety in e-learning settings: Students' perceptions at the university level. *Electronics (Basel), 11*(22), 3662. doi:10.3390/electronics11223662

Almajalid, R. (2017). *A survey on the adoption of cloud computing in education sector*. arXiv preprint arXiv:1706.01136.

Anuar, K., & Hajar, U. M. Z. (2024). Cloud computing scene in Malaysia. *The Malaysian Reserve*. https://themalaysianreserve.com/2023/07/27/cloud-computing-scene-in-malaysia/

Ashtari, S., & Eydgahi, A. (2015, October). Student perceptions of cloud computing effectiveness in higher education. In *2015 IEEE 18th International Conference on Computational Science and Engineering* (pp. 184-191). IEEE. 10.1109/CSE.2015.36

Aydin, H. (2021). A study of cloud computing adoption in universities as a guideline to cloud migration. Sage Open, 11(3).

Calixto, E. (2016). In E. Calixto (Ed.), *Human Reliability Analysis. Gas and Oil Reliability Engineering* (2nd ed., pp. 471–552). doi:10.1016/B978-0-12-805427-7.00005-1

Chan, Y. M. (2018). Self-directed learning readiness and online video use among digital animation students [Doctoral dissertation, Multimedia University (Malaysia)].

Cheah, P. K., Diong, F. W., & Yap, Y. O. (2018). Peer Assessment in Higher Education: Using Hofstede's Cultural Dimensions to Identify Perspectives of Malaysian Chinese Students. *Pertanika Journal of Social Science & Humanities, 26*(3).

Chung, E., Subramaniam, G., & Dass, L. C. (2020). Online learning readiness among university students in Malaysia amidst COVID-19. *Asian Journal of University Education, 16*(2), 45–58. doi:10.24191/ajue.v16i2.10294

Creswell, J. W. (2020). Educational research: Planning, conducting, and evaluating quantitative and qualitative research. Pearson Higher Ed.

Darus, P., Rasli, R. B., & Gaminan, N. Z. (2015). A review on cloud computing implementation in higher educational institutions. *International Journal of Scientific Engineering and Applied Science, 1*(8), 459–465.

Dawood, M., Tu, S., Xiao, C., Alasmary, H., Waqas, M., & Rehman, S. U. (2023). Cyberattacks and security of cloud computing: A complete guideline. *Symmetry, 15*(11), 1981. doi:10.3390/sym15111981

Dima, A., Bugheanu, A. M., Boghian, R., & Madsen, D. O. (2022). Mapping Knowledge Area Analysis in E-Learning Systems Based on Cloud Computing. *Electronics (Basel), 12*(1), 62. doi:10.3390/electronics12010062

Doyle, L., Brady, A. M., & Byrne, G. (2009). An overview of mixed methods research. *Journal of Research in Nursing, 14*(2), 175–185. doi:10.1177/1744987108093962

Dusek, G., Yurova, Y., & Ruppel, C. P. (2015). Using social media and targeted snowball sampling to survey a hard-to-reach population: A case study. *International Journal of Doctoral Studies, 10*, 279. doi:10.28945/2296

Hamed, P. K., & Preece, A. S. (2020). Google Cloud Platform Adoption for Teaching in HEIs: A Qualitative Approach. *OAlib, 7*(11), 1–23. doi:10.4236/oalib.1106819

Harfoushi, O. (2017). Influence of Cloud Based Mobile Learning Applications on User Experiences: A Review Study in the Context of Jordan. *International Journal of Interactive Mobile Technologies, 11*(4), 202. doi:10.3991/ijim.v11i4.6938

Hussein, L. A., & Hilmi, M. F. (2020). Cloud computing-based e-learning in Malaysian universities. *International Journal of Emerging Technologies in Learning (Online), 15*(8), 4. doi:10.3991/ijet.v15i08.11798

IBM. (2024). *What are Iaas, Paas and Saas?* IBM Newsroom. https://www.ibm.com/topics/iaas-paas-saas

Isa, W. W. M., Suhaimi, A. I. H., Noordin, N., Harun, A. F., Ismail, J., & Teh, R. A. (2019). Factors influencing cloud computing adoption in higher education institution. *Indonesian Journal of Electrical Engineering and Computer Science, 17*(1), 412–419.

Jaafar, J. A., Latiff, A. R. A., Daud, Z. M., & Osman, M. N. H. (2023). Does revenue diversification strategy affect the financial sustainability of Malaysian Public Universities? A panel data analysis. *Higher Education Policy, 36*(1), 116–143. doi:10.1057/s41307-021-00247-9

Jayabalan, J., Dorasamy, M., & Raman, M. (2021). Reshaping higher educational institutions through frugal open innovation. *Journal of Open Innovation*, 7(2), 145. doi:10.3390/joitmc7020145

Kaur, P., Stoltzfus, J., & Yellapu, V. (2018). Descriptive statistics. *International Journal of Academic Medicine*, 4(1), 60. doi:10.4103/IJAM.IJAM_7_18

Kumar, J. A., Bervell, B., & Osman, S. (2020). Google classroom: Insights from Malaysian higher education students' and instructors' experiences. *Education and Information Technologies*, 25(5), 4175–4195. doi:10.1007/s10639-020-10163-x

Kurelovic, E. K., Rako, S., & Tomljanovic, J. (2013). Cloud Computing in Education and Student's Needs. *Proceedings of 36th Internation Convention on Information and Communication Technology*, Opatija, Croatia.

Lam, L., Lau, N. S., & Ngan, L. C. (2013). An investigation of the factors influencing student learning motivation with the facilitation of cloud computing in higher education context of Hong Kong. *Hybrid learning: Theory, application and practice, 12*, 13.

Langshaw, S. J. (2017). *Relationship between the self-efficacy and self-directed learning of adults in undergraduate programs* [Doctoral dissertation, Capella University].

Lee, D. K., In, J., & Lee, S. (2015). Standard deviation and standard error of the mean. *Korean Journal of Anesthesiology*, 68(3), 220–223. doi:10.4097/kjae.2015.68.3.220 PMID:26045923

Majid, U. (2018). Research fundamentals: Study design, population, and sample size. *Undergraduate research in natural and clinical science and technology journal, 2*, 1-7.

Malhotra, N. K., Nunan, D., & Birks, D. F. (2017). *Marketing research: An applied approach*. Pearson.

Mampage, A., Karunasekera, S., & Buyya, R. (2022). A holistic view on resource management in serverless computing environments: Taxonomy and future directions. *ACM Computing Surveys*, 54(11s), 1–36. doi:10.1145/3510412

Mary, A. C., & Rose, P. J. (2020). The impact of graduate student's perceptions towards the usage of cloud computing in higher education sectors. *Univ. J. Educ. Res*, 8(11), 5463–5478. doi:10.13189/ujer.2020.081150

Mesbahi, M. R., Rahmani, A. M., & Hosseinzadeh, M. (2018). Reliability and high availability in cloud computing environments: A reference roadmap. *Human-centric Computing and Information Sciences*, 8(1), 1–31. doi:10.1186/s13673-018-0143-8

Mircea, M., & Andreescu, A. I. (2011). Using cloud computing in higher education: A strategy to improve agility in the current financial crisis. *Communications of the IBIMA*, 1–15. doi:10.5171/2011.875547

Mitchell, Á., & Cunningham, L. (2014, October). Impact of cloud computing in Ireland's institutes of higher education. In *eChallenges e-2014 Conference Proceedings* (pp. 1-11). IEEE.

Mohd Nordin, A. R., Mohd Fadzil, A. K., Syarilla Iryani, A. S., Syadiah Nor, W. S., & Jazurainifariza, J. (2017). The *Direction of Cloud Computing for Malaysian Education Sector in 21th Century*.

MOHE. (2019). Higher Education Statistics 2019. Ministry of Higher education, Putrajaya.

Nasri, N. M., & Mydin, F. (2017). Universiti students' view of self-directed learning in an online learning context. *Advances in Social Sciences Research Journal*, *4*(24).

Ogbonna, E., & Harris, L. C. (2000). Leadership style, organizational culture and performance: Empirical evidence from UK companies. international Journal of human resource management, 11(4), 766-788.

Qasem, Y. A., Abdullah, R., Jusoh, Y. Y., Atan, R., & Asadi, S. (2019). Cloud computing adoption in higher education institutions: A systematic review. *IEEE Access : Practical Innovations, Open Solutions*, *7*, 63722–63744. doi:10.1109/ACCESS.2019.2916234

Qasem, Y. A., Abdullah, R., Yaha, Y., & Atana, R. (2020). Continuance use of cloud computing in higher education institutions: A conceptual model. *Applied Sciences (Basel, Switzerland)*, *10*(19), 6628. doi:10.3390/app10196628

Rajesh, M. (2017). A systematic review of cloud security challenges in higher education. *The Online Journal of Distance Education and e-Learning : TOJDEL*, *5*(1).

Robinson, J. (2010). *Triandis' theory of interpersonal behaviour in understanding software piracy behaviour in the South African context* [Doctoral dissertation, University of the Witwatersrand].

Safdar, S., Ren, M., Chudhery, M. A. Z., Huo, J., Rehman, H. U., & Rafique, R. (2022). Using cloud-based virtual learning environments to mitigate increasing disparity in urban-rural academic competence. *Technological Forecasting and Social Change*, *176*, 121468. doi:10.1016/j.techfore.2021.121468

Sarstedt, M., & Mooi, E. (2014). A concise guide to market research. The Process. *Data*, 12.

Saunders, M. (2014). *Research Methods for Business Students* (6th ed.).

Sedgwick, P. (2014). Cross Sectional Studies: Advantages and Disadvantages. *BMJ (Clinical Research Ed.)*, (348), 1–2.

Sellke, T., Bayarri, M. J., & Berger, J. O. (2001). Calibration of ρ values for testing precise null hypotheses. *The American Statistician*, *55*(1), 62–71. doi:10.1198/000313001300339950

Shahzad, A., Golamdin, A. G., & Ismail, N. A. (2016). Opportunity and challenges using the cloud computing in the case of Malaysian higher education institutions. [IJMSIT]. *The International Journal of Management Science and Information Technology*, (20), 1–18.

Shahzad, A., Golamdin, A. G., & Ismail, N. A. (2016). Opportunity and challenges using the cloud computing in the case of Malaysian higher education institutions. [IJMSIT]. *The International Journal of Management Science and Information Technology*, (20), 1–18.

Shahzad, A., Hassan, R., Aremu, A. Y., Hussain, A., & Lodhi, R. N. (2021). Effects of COVID-19 in E-learning on higher education institution students: The group comparison between male and female. *Quality & Quantity*, *55*(3), 805–826. doi:10.1007/s11135-020-01028-z PMID:32836471

Shakeabubakor, A. A., Sundararajan, E., & Hamdan, A. R. (2015). Cloud computing services and applications to improve productivity of university researchers. *International Journal of Information and Electronics Engineering*, *5*(2), 153. doi:10.7763/IJIEE.2015.V5.521

Showkat, N., & Parveen, H. (2017). Non-Probability and Probability Sampling. *Media & Communication Studies*.

Sultan, N. (2010). Cloud computing for education: A new dawn? *International Journal of Information Management*, *30*(2), 109–116. doi:10.1016/j.ijinfomgt.2009.09.004

Taherdoost, H. (2016). *Validity and reliability of the research instrument; how to test the validation of a questionnaire/survey in a research. How to test the validation of a questionnaire/survey in a research (August 10, 2016).Tchifilionova* (Vol. 2011). Security and Privacy Implications of Cloud Computing-Lost in the Cloud.

Tehseen, S., Ramayah, T., & Sajilan, S. (2017). Testing and controlling for common method variance: A review of available methods. *Journal of management sciences, 4*(2), 142-168.

Yau, H. K., Cheng, A. L. F., & Ho, W. M. (2015). Identify the Motivational Factors to Affect the Higher Education Students to Learn Using Technology. *Turkish Online Journal of Educational Technology-TOJET*, *14*(2), 89–100.

Zhang, Y., Yang, M., Zheng, D., Lang, P., Wu, A., & Chen, C. (2018). Efficient and secure big data storage system with leakage resilience in cloud computing. *Soft Computing*, *22*(23), 7763–7772. doi:10.1007/s00500-018-3435-z

Chapter 6
Improving Teaching–Learning Through Smart Classes Using IoT

Saru Dhir
🆔 https://orcid.org/0000-0002-2381-2920
Amity University, India

Aditya Maheshwari
Amity University, India

Shanu Sharma
ABES Engineering College, India

ABSTRACT

This chapter explores the application of IoT in education, focusing on its potential to enhance learning experiences and automate processes. Smartphone-based remote appliance control and interactive learning are made possible by IoT integration in smart classrooms. IoT functions as a worldwide network, producing data to make our lives easier and safer while minimizing environmental effects. The report emphasizes better learning across disciplines as one of the revolutionary effects of IoT in higher education. Implementation problems are addressed. Additionally, it covers the effective use of big data analytics in education, performance prediction, and strategy adaptation. This study emphasizes the use of technology to enhance learning experiences in order to maximize the potential of IoT in education. Methods of collaborative learning are recognized as essential components in improving students' learning capacities. This research contributes to maximizing the potential of IoT in education and highlights the significance of leveraging technology for enriched learning experiences.

DOI: 10.4018/979-8-3693-2169-0.ch006

Copyright © 2024, IGI Global. Copying or distributing in print or electronic forms without written permission of IGI Global is prohibited.

INTRODUCTION

The phrase "Internet of Things" (IoT) refers to the worldwide interconnection of various physical items and gadgets. The education sector has embraced a cutting-edge approach known as smart classes, representing a novel vision in the field. Incorporating IoT into teaching and learning methods is an intelligent approach that involves the utilization of computers, internet connectivity, and projectors. This integration enhances the learning experience by offering a multitude of features for students. The effectiveness of this educational concept spans across all levels, from primary to higher education.

The use of technology in the classroom has been extremely important for educating and connecting students. It has had a significant influence on the field of education, not only transforming traditional teaching methods but also bringing about changes in the infrastructure of educational institutions.

It was also a major factor in bringing about the digital revolution. They encompass a wide range of technologies, from smart devices to high-speed internet, mobile applications, and cutting-edge research in emerging fields. These technologies are not only instrumental in fostering a competitive and inclusive information society but also in advancing all sectors of the economy, including education. Given this, it becomes imperative to transform the field of education to align with these priorities.

To improve employability and ensure that individuals are equipped with the necessary digital skills, significant changes need to be made in the education system. This entails adapting the way we train students, particularly to cater to the needs of the digital generation. As IOT becomes increasingly prevalent across various social and economic domains, including education, it has prompted substantial transformations in the way these areas operate. The teaching process in schools is no exception.

Modern education systems recognize classrooms as essential requirements. Numerous advancements in commonly used technologies have emerged, offering opportunities to enhance and optimize classroom environments. These developments aim to create better and more intelligent learning spaces.

Smart classrooms are lecture halls and classrooms that have been technologically improved to support cutting-edge teaching and learning techniques by integrating computer, multimedia, and network technologies. When it comes to intelligent virtual classrooms, the teaching and learning process greatly benefits from the use of the Internet of Things (IoT). It enhances the flexibility of educational delivery, enabling learners to access knowledge anytime and from anywhere.

Additionally, students benefit from educational programs and assignments that contribute to their learning outcomes. The acronym "SMART" encapsulates the key characteristics of these classrooms, namely: Showing, Manageable, Accessible, Real-time Interactive, and Testing.

The Internet of Things (IoT) is a major proponent of the idea of e-learning. Electronic tools and gadgets have taken the place of traditional methods requiring books and papers, providing a huge change for students and enhancing their interest in the method of education. Students can now engage in more interactive participation thanks to the integration of intelligence into learning. The introduction of new learning techniques can aid students who find the old pen-and-paper method monotonous by reducing their boredom and encouraging focus and attention. Students' attention levels have increased as a result of the use of technological devices in school. In order to ensure successful adoption, student-centered strategies like project-based learning encourage students to become active researchers while using technology as a tool.. Information and communication technology have revolutionized communication, enabling more efficient and effective presentation of ideas.

The Internet of Things (IoT) has found its application in numerous fields, including education. Over the years, technology in the education sector has undergone significant advancements, transitioning from conventional teaching approaches to the incorporation of interactive whiteboards and PowerPoint presentations. The IoT has emerged as a pivotal force propelling the educational sector towards a future-oriented direction.

In educational facilities, IoT technologies such as RFID readers can be implemented to enhance efficiency. Smart classrooms equipped with IoT can enable teachers to manage sessions using gestures, voice recognition, and facial recognition. They can also communicate with remote students easily and collect valuable feedback on teaching sessions. Data collected from sensors and analytics can provide insights into student behavior, interests, achievement and engagement.

From the standpoint of students, the Internet of Things (IoT) can enhance communication among peers, whether they are in close proximity or at a distance. It enables interactive discussions and the ability to annotate learning materials, while also granting access to remote learning resources. Additionally, IoT has the capability to personalize learning materials by taking into account contextual factors such as time, student engagement, and individual knowledge levels.

It is essential to prepare students for the demands of the contemporary technological landscape. Technical competence and computer literacy have become crucial skills. Therefore, introducing technology-rich environments and leveraging technology in education from an early age are necessary.

Numerous educational institutions have already integrated diverse technological tools, including computers, tablets, interactive whiteboards, multimedia resources, and projectors. In some cases, virtual and augmented reality devices have been embraced to cater to specialized subjects like science. By combining conventional and technology-enhanced teaching methods, schools can cultivate skills that are in line with the demands of contemporary society.

The influence of IoT on the education sector Is significant. It streamlines tasks, enhances education quality, and influences teaching and learning processes. It is particularly suited for real-world application in assessments.

Education is a powerful tool that drives social and technological changes. To ensure its accessibility and quality, continuous enhancements are necessary. The integration of IoT solutions in educational environments presents limitless opportunities to achieve these goals.

To address the challenges and maximize the benefits of technology in schools, a conceptual model is proposed. This model aims to create a smart classroom environment that optimizes the integration and utilization of technology tools. By implementing this model, schools can support effective teaching and learning processes, revolutionizing education and shaping a brighter future for students worldwide (M. Kassab, J. DeFranco & J. Voas, 2018).

LITERATURE REVIEW

Smart classes play a crucial role in enhancing education quality for students worldwide, particularly in terms of conceptual understanding, elaboration of concepts, and improvement of reading skills. Modern learning utilizes computer-based education systems, leading to the development of smart classrooms.

The author have described that cloud computing and edge computing also have significant roles in the field of IoT. Data processing in smart settings is made possible by the use of sensor devices and standalone devices that are physically connected to the outside world. However, the complex network interfaces and protocols of IoT pose challenges in the development and debugging of applications, necessitating rapid prototyping tools for network fragments and project-oriented training methods for developers (Rupashi B., Saru D., Nitasha H. & K. M. Soni., 2023).

The authors have developed an Electronic Information Desk System that employs an SMS-based approach in a unique manner. The system operates independently without requiring human operators. Whenever a student or employee requires information, they simply need to send an SMS to the system, which responds with the requested information. Various technical communities are actively engaged in researching topics that contribute to IoT.

The authors of this article give a brief overview of learning analytics, including how it is used in educational settings, what tools are accessible, and how student performance is tracked. The difficulties of using learning analytics in higher education are the main point of emphasis. The objective is to draw attention to the information that teachers can use to boost students' performance (J. Lagus, K. Longi, A. Klami & A. Hellas, 2018).

The authors have propose a comprehensive system consisting of smart sensors, actuators, and a module for controlling the classroom environment. This system can perform certain actions automatically, while also allowing the teacher to handle them based on the current circumstances. The educational resource module, managed by the teacher, provides the necessary learning materials. It communicates with the classroom environment module to create appropriate scenes, situations, ambiance, and backgrounds for ongoing lessons. This may involve incorporating audio and video effects, as well as adjusting air streams, to demonstrate various teaching material characteristics.

The presented smart classroom system utilizes IoT and employs sensors to observe audience activities, analyze voices and conversations, and track movements to determine the level of listener satisfaction with lecture quality. It classifies students' satisfaction based on parameters of the physical environment obtained using different smart devices.

Through analysis and study of theory and statistics, it becomes evident that the Internet of Things (IoT) has a significant and indispensable impact on the current education system. Digital learning and e-learning have become essential due to their ability to offer flexibility and opportunities for learning from any location and at any time (P. Srivastava, S. Dhir, N. Hasteer & K. M. Soni, 2023).

IOT – ENABLED LEARNING ENVIRONMENT

"Internet of Things" (IoT) technology must be incorporated into educational settings in order to improve learning outcomes. This is known as the adoption of an IoT-powered learning environment. Various IoT devices, including smart sensors, wearable devices, and connected classroom tools, can collect and analyze data in real-time, enabling personalized learning opportunities and providing valuable insights into student behavior, engagement, and performance. This data-driven approach empowers educators to make informed decisions and deliver tailored instruction to meet individual needs effectively (G. Caminero, M. Lopez-Martin & B. Carro, 2019).

In a connected learning environment, students have the ability to access educational resources and engage in collaborative activities with their peers, regardless of geographical barriers, fostering inclusive learning. Through the use of augmented reality (AR) and virtual reality (VR) applications, the integration of IoT-enabled devices offers new opportunities for interactive and immersive learning experiences. These technologies enhance student engagement and deepen their understanding of complex concepts. Additionally, teachers can leverage IoT technology to efficiently monitor and manage classroom resources, such as controlling smart whiteboards, managing digital content, and automating administrative tasks. Figure 1 represents the smart education architecture using IOT.

Reward learning has become a well-known method of protecting the Internet of Things (IoT) against hostile learning environments. The environment's behavior is integrated into the learning process concurrently through reinforcement learning. When several IoT devices produce significant amounts of bursty or continuous data streams, our special reinforcement learning function offers strong IoT security .

Figure 1. Smart education architecture using internet of things

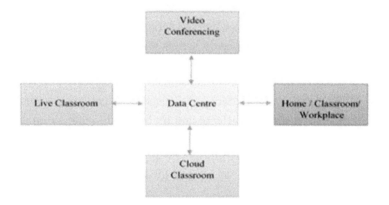

To protect the gathering and storage of student data, it is crucial to give security and privacy top priority in an IoT-powered learning environment. Adequate measures must be implemented to ensure data protection and prevent unauthorized access. Additionally, a resilient network infrastructure and reliable connectivity are essential to facilitate seamless operation and data transmission within IoT-enabled learning environments. Despite the fact that IoT use in education is still in its infancy, overcoming obstacles like cost, skill development, and system integration will be essential for broad acceptance.

REAL TIME COMMUNICATION AND COLLABORATION

Seamless and instantaneous communication and collaboration in teaching and learning are achieved through real-time utilization of IoT technology. In smart classrooms, enabled by IoT, teachers can deliver lectures, presentations, and interactive lessons using digital content that can be accessed simultaneously by students. This enables active participation, encourages questions, and facilitates immediate responses from teachers, promoting engagement and a deeper understanding of the subject matter.

IoT gadgets in smart classrooms dramatically improve collaborative learning. Students may work together on projects, share data and documents, and give one another real-time feedback thanks to these gadgets. Additionally, IoT technology allows teachers to remotely monitor and guide student progress, providing timely interventions and personalized support when required.

Real-time communication and collaboration in teaching and learning are not confined to the physical classroom alone. With IoT, students can connect with peers and teachers from different locations, creating virtual classrooms and opening up opportunities for remote learning. IoT-enabled smart classrooms foster interactive and inclusive learning environments by utilizing video conferencing, chat platforms, and online collaboration tools. The successful implementation of real-time communication and collaboration in teaching and learning relies on the presence of a dependable network infrastructure and robust connectivity to ensure seamless and uninterrupted communication. When deploying IoT devices in smart classrooms, it is also crucial to give privacy and security concerns top priority in order to protect student data and stop illegal access.

The implementation of real-time communication and collaboration in teaching and learning necessitates a strong network infrastructure and reliable connectivity. Connectivity plays a vital role in IoT solutions, and various communication protocols, such as Bluetooth, WiFi, Zigbee, and Z-Wave, can be employed depending on environmental constraints and specific IoT tasks. To address communication challenges, standardization organizations like IEEE and IETF have developed IoT-specific communication protocols .

Although there are challenges to overcome, such as initial setup costs and training requirements, the adoption of IoT for real-time communication and collaboration in teaching and learning holds the potential to revolutionize traditional educational practices and greatly enhance the learning experience for students.

ENHANCED STUDENT ENGAGEMENT

Multiple factors contribute to the improved engagement of students in smart classrooms. Among these factors, the strength of the student-teacher relationship is pivotal. Teachers who are perceived as knowledgeable, supportive, invested, and effective have a greater ability to foster student engagement. Additionally, the successful integration and application of technology in the classroom is greatly influenced by the instructors' level of confidence in their technological proficiency. In order to provide teachers with the technical know-how and abilities they need, continuous professional development is essential. This will successfully increase student engagement.

Providing regular, personalized, clear, and constructive feedback can also have a positive impact on engagement and student agency. Humor can be incorporated into online discussions to further enhance student engagement. However, access to technology is a concern as it can affect students' confidence and prior experience with technology, thus influencing their level of engagement.

IoT technology plays a significant role in enhancing student engagement in smart classes. Interactive whiteboards, tablets, and smart projectors create dynamic and immersive learning environments, capturing students' attention and encouraging active participation. Teachers can deliver interactive and multimedia-rich lessons that cater to diverse learning styles and preferences, making learning more engaging and enjoyable.

Real-time feedback and instant assessments provided by IoT devices enable students to monitor their progress and make necessary adjustments. Gamification elements, such as quizzes, competitions, and rewards, can be integrated to enhance interactivity and motivation. Personalized learning experiences are facilitated through IoT devices, adapting content and resources to individual students' needs.

Enriching students learning experiences involves providing them with access to a diverse array of educational resources, multimedia content, and interactive simulations. This approach ensures a more hands-on and experiential learning environment. Furthermore, collaborative learning is greatly enhanced as students collaborate on projects, exchange ideas, and offer feedback to one another, promoting the development of teamwork and communication skills.

Real-time communication between teachers and students through IoT devices allows for instant clarification of doubts, active participation, and meaningful discussions. However, the successful implementation of IoT in smart classes requires proper training and support for both teachers and students to effectively leverage the technology and maximize its potential for enhanced student engagement.

The combination of authentic learning and virtual learning using a variety of pedagogical tools has the ability to empower the future generation of digital citizens through enhanced and efficient learning experiences. Intelligent teaching systems (ITS) and story-based virtual worlds are two specific methods that help achieve this goal.

Intelligent tutoring systems aim to enhance or replace human instruction by sharing responsibility with instructors to guide the learning process. These systems analyze individual students' strengths and weaknesses and provide targeted assistance based on their specific needs. While ITSs have proven to be effective teaching tools, they often fall short in addressing student engagement issues. Student engagement remains a significant challenge in classrooms, hindering education regardless of students' intellectual abilities. To fully leverage the strengths of ITS, an additional structural layer is needed.

Narrative-driven virtual environments serve a crucial role in creating immersive and realistic situations for players to explore, enabling a combination of effective problem-solving and learning. By incorporating elements commonly found in commercial video games, such as motivating features and goal-oriented structures, these environments significantly enhance player engagement. The entertaining nature of narrative-based virtual environments offers a more captivating approach to presenting content and encourages students to solve domain-specific problems.

Extensive research demonstrates that integrating narrative-based virtual environments into educational settings provides an enjoyable and effective approach to learning. These environments not only capture students' attention but also foster practical problem-solving and open-ended exploration. The strengths of both intelligent tutoring systems and narrative-based virtual worlds can be used by educators to produce a dynamic and interactive learning environment that encourages student involvement and speeds up the acquisition of knowledge and skills.

SECURITY AND PRIVACY IN IOT-ENABLED CLASSROOMS

IoT devices gather vast amounts of user data to analyze and enhance platform performance, optimize device efficiency, and deliver personalized services based on user behavior. However, concerns arise regarding the sharing of personal data, leading to user hesitation. When data is stored in the cloud service of an IoT platform, users rely on the platform to safeguard the privacy of their information. Unfortunately, many platforms fail to adequately inform users about the specific types of data collected and the parties with whom it is shared.

To address these issues, it is crucial to establish a secure network infrastructure in the classroom. This includes implementing robust encryption protocols, secure Wi-Fi networks, and firewalls to prevent unauthorized access. Additionally, ensuring that IoT devices used in the classroom comply with production standards is essential. Thoroughly assessing manufacturers' security measures and selecting devices from reputable sources helps mitigate potential risks.

User knowledge and awareness play a critical role in effectively utilizing IoT devices, as their sophisticated functionalities require a solid understanding of associated threats and vulnerabilities. Users who lack knowledge in this domain are more vulnerable to social engineering attacks. However, it is important to acknowledge that IoT security and privacy concerns represent just a fraction of the potential attacks to which these devices may be exposed. Hence, it becomes imperative for users to maintain complete control over the devices they employ. Figure 2 represents how security and privacy interrelate.

Figure 2. Security and privacy

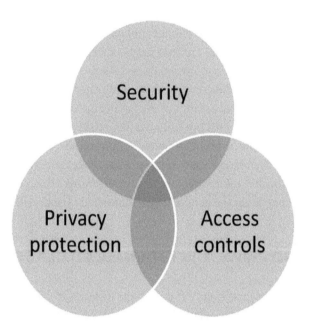

To safeguard sensitive information, data encryption emerges as a crucial measure. Strong algorithms like Advanced Encryption Standard (AES) can be employed to encrypt data transmitted between IoT devices and the network, effectively preventing eavesdropping and unauthorized access. Additionally, continuous monitoring and intrusion detection systems should be established to identify security incidents and suspicious activities promptly. Security analytics tools and "Security Information and Event Management" (SIEM) systems play a vital role in enabling timely responses to security threats.

"Security Information and Event Management" (SIEM) is a system designed to enhance the safety of computer systems within organizations. It combines security event management (SEM) and security information management (SIM), two crucial components. SIEM software delivers in-the-moment analysis and monitoring of network and computer-related events. It collects data from diverse sources, such as logs and records, facilitating the identification of security issues. SIEM also monitors user access, tracks changes in system settings, and aids in swift responses to security threats. Overall, SIEM serves as a powerful tool in maintaining the security of computer systems (H. Kamal, S. Dhir, N. Hasteer & K. M. Soni, 2023).

Security and privacy considerations hold significant importance in IoT-enabled classrooms, given the rapid proliferation of internet-connected devices. IoT security issues are brought on by the existence of various stakeholders, which could prevent IoT from being widely adopted. Addressing security aspects as fundamental requirements is vital to ensuring the trust and privacy of IoT systems.

Physical attacks represent a type of security threat that primarily targets the hardware components of IoT systems. These attacks necessitate the physical presence of the attacker and often involve substantial resources, making them difficult to execute. Node tempering is one form of physical attack, where attackers intentionally damage or replace sponsor nodes. In order to acquire unauthorized access and control over the flow of data, malicious node injection entails creating a new operating node among communication nodes. Attacks that cause physical damage directly affect the system, affecting service availability and quality. RF interference on RFID, malicious code injection, sleep deprivation, and social engineering are a few examples of physical attacks.

Software attacks exploit vulnerabilities within IoT systems through weaknesses in the software. These attacks encompass various malicious activities such as executing malicious scripts, conducting phishing attacks, spreading viruses, deploying spyware, initiating worms, and carrying out denial-of-service (DoS) attacks. Malicious scripts impede system availability and allow unauthorized access to sensitive data. Malicious software is injected into the system during a virus, spyware, or worm assault in order to gain unauthorized access.

Network attacks target the network infrastructure of IoT systems, which facilitates data transfer between devices. These threats include routing information assaults, sinkhole attacks, man-in-the-middle (MITM) attacks, RFID spoofing, illegal access, cloning, and traffic analysis. Encryption methods are used to secure communication channels, which are essential for integrating IoT devices with physical items. Attacks on the encryption used in IoT devices include side-channel attacks, MITM attacks, and cryptanalysis attacks. Their goal is to compromise the encryption mechanism.

Protecting the security and privacy of IoT-enabled classrooms requires the implementation of measures to mitigate various types of attacks. These measures may involve utilizing robust encryption algorithms, implementing access controls, regularly updating software and firmware, conducting security audits, and providing user awareness and training. By addressing security and privacy concerns, educators can establish a safe and secure learning environment that harnesses the benefits of IoT technology.

To effectively address security and privacy concerns in IoT-enabled classrooms, the following measures can be taken:

1. Access Controls:
   - Implement robust authentication mechanisms to ensure only authorized individuals can access IoT devices and systems.
   - Utilize role-based access control to assign privileges based on user roles and responsibilities.
   - Enforce secure password policies and encourage the use of strong, unique passwords for all IoT devices.

2. Encryption and Secure Communication:
   - Employ strong encryption algorithms, such as AES, to protect data transmission between IoT devices, ensuring confidentiality and integrity.
   - Implement secure communication protocols, like TLS/SSL, to establish encrypted connections and prevent eavesdropping or tampering.

3. Regular Software and Firmware Updates:
   - Keep up-to-date with the latest firmware and security patches provided by IoT device vendors.
   - Apply these updates regularly to address known vulnerabilities and ensure devices have the latest security enhancements.

4. Security Audits and Penetration Testing:
   - Conduct regular security audits to identify flaws in the IoT infrastructure and address potential vulnerabilities.
   - Engage external security specialists to perform comprehensive analyses and identify any security flaws that require remediation.

5. User Awareness and Training:
   - Educate teachers, administrators, and students about the importance of security and privacy in IoT-enabled classrooms.
   - Provide training on safe practices, such as recognizing phishing attempts, avoiding suspicious links and downloads, and promptly reporting security incidents or concerns.

6. Network Segmentation:
   - Implement network segmentation to isolate IoT devices from critical systems and sensitive information.
   - Establish separate network segments for IoT devices to prevent a compromise in one device from affecting the entire network.

7. Incident Response Plan:
   - Develop a comprehensive incident response strategy to address security or privacy incidents.
   - Establish communication channels, outline the necessary steps to take in the event of a security issue, and define roles and responsibilities for responding to incidents.

By implementing these measures, educational institutions can enhance the security and privacy of IoT-enabled classrooms, safeguarding sensitive data and ensuring a safe learning environment for students and faculty members.

While these measures address specific security concerns, it is important to recognize that IoT devices face various other potential attacks, such as malware vulnerabilities and social engineering. Users' awareness of IoT threats and vulnerabilities is crucial for their protection. By understanding the risks associated with IoT devices, users can exercise control and make informed decisions regarding their usage.

DATA AND LEARNING ANALYTICS

Data and learning analytics involve the collection, analysis, and reporting of important indicators related to students' academic performance. These insights are derived from various performance markers, but the challenge lies in managing and predicting temporal data about students at the start of a teaching session. To address this, there is a need for an efficient and user-friendly system that can gather data, predict students' performance, and present key indicators to help teachers enhance students' learning abilities.

Educational Data Mining (EDM) focuses on developing methodologies to explore unique data originating from educational environments. It specifically applies data mining (DM) techniques to datasets derived from educational settings to address significant educational inquiries.

On the other hand, Learning Analytics (LA) encompasses the dimension, collection, analysis, and reporting of data concerning learners and their surrounds. The objective is to comprehend and optimize learning processes and the environments in which they take place. This definition comprises three essential elements: data, analysis, and action, highlighting the importance of utilizing data to drive informed decision-making.

Learning analytics, commonly referred to as data analytics in education, is becoming more popular in sectors other than education administration. To improve the standard of instruction, it combines established teaching techniques with information and communication technology (ICT). Instructional activities in sizable institutions. By utilizing learning analytics, instructors may strengthen the value of their courses and improve student performance through an iterative process.

In educational institutions, learning analytics is crucial and is expected to become more significant in the years to come. It can help with decision-making to lessen student disengagement. The use of technology in educational contexts has grown significantly, and this has raised awareness of the significance of student participation. To increase stoner participation in literacy activities, such as the discussion of multimodal literacy analytics (MMLA), tracking and wearable technology are used. The goal of integrating wearable technology and the Internet of Things into education is to build a collaborative and interactive environment that boosts student engagement and learning.

The main goal of learning analytics Is to create a uniform framework for administrators and educational institutions to collect and analyze student data, enabling accurate evaluation of academic progress. This strategy is thought to be successful because it can

Forecast student success, improve future course results, boost retention rates, enhance the quality of instruction overall, and support improved decision-making.

Learning analytics can gather information from educational institutions or use questionnaires to gauge student progress early in the course to find factors affecting student achievement. With this knowledge, teachers can help difficult children more effectively by giving them timely interventions and additional support.

To support early intervention, learning analytics can give kids real-time feedback. Using an intelligent tutoring system, it can also analyze students' digital footprints, including demographics, behavioral logs, and facial expressions, to anticipate how well they will perform in class. This allows it to assess how well students retain information over the course of a semester.

Learning has been shown to be improved through collaborative learning, when students work and learn together in small communities. It is dependent on how teachers view collaborative learning and can be set up in a variety of ways, including teacher- or student-selected groups. Because teachers can construct groups with similar pupils to improve their learning capacities, teacher-selected groups frequently exhibit greater performance.

PERSONALIZED LEARNING

The implementation of personalized learning in education is facilitated by the utilization of IoT devices, enabling the gathering of valuable data regarding students' learning styles, progress, and areas of difficulty. This data serves as a foundation for developing personalized lesson plans and learning experiences tailored to the unique needs of each student. The advantages of personalized learning include:

1. Customized Instruction: IoT data empowers teachers to tailor their instruction to address the specific requirements of individual students. Students encountering difficulties with particular concepts can receive additional resources and support to enhance their understanding, while those excelling can be challenged with more advanced content.

2.   Improved Engagement: Personalized learning experiences that align with students' needs and interests are more likely to engage and motivate them. By making education relevant and meaningful, personalized learning fosters a sense of ownership and enthusiasm for learning.

However, delivering individualized instruction effectively poses challenges for traditional classroom structures. Students have diverse learning styles and require different instructional approaches. Guided learning methods have shown to benefit a larger number of students compared to discovery learning. Some students thrive in a guided and structured approach, while others prefer self-directed learning. Additionally, factors like motivation, prior knowledge, and individual capabilities influence the need for direct instruction or more independent learning.

To address these challenges and optimize personalized learning, it is crucial to integrate technology and innovative approaches. Intelligent tutoring systems (ITS) offer personalized guidance and support based on individual student strengths and weaknesses. Moreover, narrative-based virtual environments provide an immersive and entertaining way to present material and encourage effective problem-solving, thereby enhancing student engagement.

The integration of personalized learning with technology also involves the use of artificial education systems in narrative game environments. This approach leverages explanation-based concept learning, incorporating mental processes such as generalization, chunking, operationalization, and analogy to facilitate learning and understanding.

Furthermore, IoT devices can be utilized to incorporate the learner's affective state into personalized learning. Cameras, inertia sensors, and microphones can capture facial expressions and other indicators of the learner's emotional state, enabling adaptive learning experiences tailored to the learner's emotional needs.

Metacognition, or awareness of one's thinking process, plays a crucial role in learning. By fostering metacognitive interventions, students become more aware of their goals, dispositions, and attention, enabling them to take control of their learning. These interventions can be seamlessly integrated into personalized learning experiences to further enhance students' cognitive development.

The monitoring of the learner's emotional state is continuous, allowing tutors to intervene as needed. Personal preferences, including disabilities, are stored in user profiles to provide tailored support. The learner's emotional state informs adjustments to stimuli and learning activities. For instance, if a user is frustrated, they may:

1.   Receive assistance in resolving the issue causing frustration, opt for participation in a group learning activity, or access additional learning resources.

2.   The ultimate goal is to sustain the learner's engagement throughout the learning journey.

A fundamental aspect of human intelligence is learning, with research indicating that students who understand their cognitive processes have greater control over objectives, dispositions, and attention, thus enhancing learning capacity. This process of awareness and observation is known as metacognition. Accordingly, Gridlock incorporates various metacognitive interventions to support learners' cognitive development.

In conclusion, personalized learning facilitated by IoT devices and innovative approaches holds great potential for improving education. By leveraging data, technology, and metacognitive strategies, educators can create customized learning experiences that cater to individual needs, enhance engagement, and empower students to become active participants in their own education.

Figure 3. Benefits of smart classrooms

BENEFITS OF SMART CLASSROOMS

In the coming years, classrooms are undergoing a transformation into technologically advanced spaces, equipped with smart devices. When planning and designing these environments, it is crucial to consider both academic requirements and architectural elements. Smart classrooms should integrate the latest innovations, gadgets, and communication tools in mobile computing and information technology. They should be flexible and responsive to the changing needs of students within the learning environment. Additionally, sustainability and ergonomic design should also be prioritized to create comfortable and eco-friendly spaces for effective learning.

1. Tablets for Enhanced Learning Experience:
   ◦ Tablets like iPads offer opportunities for independent project achievement, particularly benefiting students with autism.
   ◦ Interactive tools foster student engagement, encourage collaboration, and create dynamic learning environments.
   ◦ Increased productivity and attention span are observed with the integration of interactive tools.
2. Technologically Advanced Whiteboards:
   ◦ Short-throw projectors can convert any surface into a smart board, eliminating the need for additional screens.
   ◦ Smart boards provide a cost-effective solution, allowing educators to switch between board layouts effortlessly.
   ◦ Teachers save time and resources by avoiding the use of traditional whiteboard supplies and the hassle of cleaning.
3. Accurate Feedback and Performance Improvement:
   ◦ Accurate feedback is essential for educators to assess content delivery and refine teaching methods.
   ◦ IoT technology analyzes voices, tracks movements, and observes behaviors to provide precise feedback on teacher performance and student engagement.
   ◦ Smart classrooms empower teachers to make timely improvements based on feedback received.
4. Integration of Devices for Enhanced Learning Experience:
   ◦ Seamless integration of various tools enhances the educational process, maximizing benefits for students and educators alike.
   ◦ Smart devices and technology effortlessly blend into the classroom environment, fostering effective learning experiences.

5.   Personalized Learning Paths:
   ◦   Smart classrooms allow for the customization of learning paths based on individual student needs, preferences, and learning styles.
   ◦   Adaptive learning software can tailor content delivery, pacing, and assessments to match each student's proficiency level and progress.
   ◦   Personalized learning paths promote student autonomy, engagement, and academic success by catering to their unique learning journeys.
6.   Collaboration Beyond Classroom Walls:
   ◦   Smart classrooms facilitate collaboration and communication beyond traditional classroom boundaries.
   ◦   Virtual collaboration tools enable students to connect with peers, experts, and resources worldwide, fostering global awareness and collaboration skills.
   ◦   Through virtual classrooms and online platforms, students can participate in collaborative projects, discussions, and learning activities regardless of geographical location.
7.   Real-time Data Analysis for Informed Decision-making:
   ◦   IoT-enabled sensors and analytics tools provide educators with real-time insights into student learning behaviors and performance.
   ◦   By analyzing data on student interactions, engagement levels, and learning outcomes, teachers can adjust instruction, interventions, and support strategies on the fly.
   ◦   Real-time data analysis empowers educators to make informed decisions that optimize teaching effectiveness, student engagement, and academic achievement.

Incorporating smart devices and IoT technology into classrooms enhances engagement, efficiency, and customization to meet the diverse needs of students and educators. These technologies promote collaboration, facilitate continuous improvement in teaching practices, and create dynamic learning environments that prepare students for success in the digital age.

CHALLENGES OF IOT IN EDUCATION

The integration of IoT in education offers substantial advantages; however, it also presents several obstacles that must be addressed. Here are some of the primary challenges encountered when deploying IoT in smart classrooms:

1. Financial and Legislative Challenges:
   - Educational institutions, including smart classrooms, face financial constraints in acquiring and maintaining IoT infrastructure.
   - Legislative issues and government efforts to incorporate smart classrooms still require further progress.
2. Security and Privacy Concerns:
   - The absence of effective and resilient security protocols and standards presents a notable hurdle in the implementation of IoT (S. Dhir & R. Dubey, 2021).
   - Nodes in IoT networks are considered vulnerabilities due to inadequate encryption, authentication, and authorization procedures.
   - Ensuring secure connections and protection against various exploits, such as sniffing attacks, remains a priority.
3. Competency and Resource Accessibility:
   - ICT incompetency and inadequate preparation of educators pose challenges in effectively utilizing IoT in classrooms.
   - Obstacles related to resource accessibility, such as inadequate availability of high-speed internet and telecommunications infrastructure, can impede the successful implementation of IoT-enabled classrooms.
4. Network Load and Infrastructure:
   - Applications for learning on mobile devices, such as tablets and e-books, require a high-speed internet connection, which may not be widely accessible in rural areas.
   - The network load from constant data transfer and multimedia demands can strain available connections and require sufficient Wi-Fi systems.
5. Security Risks and Privacy Concerns:
   - Security vulnerabilities in IoT can enable unauthorized activities, such as manipulating exam grades or unauthorized data gathering.
   - Privacy concerns arise from the extensive collection of GPS data and potential risks, such as kidnapping crimes.
6. Data Volume and Scalability:
   - IoT generates a large volume of sensor data, which presents challenges in analyzing and sorting relevant information and trends.
   - Scalability issues arise in managing and processing large amounts of data to extract meaningful insights.
7. Moral and Social Impact:
   - There are inquiries surrounding the ethical implications of IoT in human lives and concerns regarding individual autonomy and control.

○   The dehumanization of interactions between humans and machines is a valid concern, as IoT technologies may lead to a loss of the social element in traditional education settings.

8.   Quality and Ethics:

○   In recent years, there has been a lot of discussion about the rising cost of higher education as well as the quality of education, whether it is given on campus or online.

○   The IoT offers unique opportunities for delivering online courses. However, it also poses difficulties for assuring the caliber of instruction and assessing student work.

○   Tools and technologies are needed for IoT educational applications so that educators can improve the standard of their research and address ethical issues in higher education.

Addressing these challenges requires tackling security concerns, ensuring privacy protection, enhancing teacher competency, improving resource accessibility, strengthening infrastructure, and considering the moral and social impact of IoT technologies in education. By finding appropriate solutions, education institutions can harness the potential of IoT while mitigating associated risks (M. Kassab, J. DeFranco & P. Laplante, 2020).

THE FUTURE OF IOT

Affordability plays a critical role in the expansion of IoT, particularly concerning tracking, control mechanisms, and sensing devices. Securing funding for technological advancements can pose challenges, potentially impeding future developments. As the widespread adoption of billions of gadgets has the potential to have a substantial impact on society, it is imperative to address these issues and carefully consider any negative effects.

Future IoT development is anticipated to significantly alter a number of industries, including agriculture, healthcare, and education. Efforts are being made in these sectors to adapt and improve existing practices to fully utilize the potential of IoT technologies. This includes exploring innovative approaches and making necessary modifications to harness the benefits offered by IoT.

1.   Expansion of IoT Technologies:

○   The projected growth of IoT technologies will result in the connection of billions of devices.

○ Enabling technologies like semiconductor electronics, sensors, communication systems, and cloud networking play a vital role in ensuring the proper functioning of IoT devices.

2. Internet Speed and Connectivity:
   ○ High-speed wireless networks with extensive coverage are indispensable for the successful implementation of IoT technologies.
   ○ The speed and coverage of the internet are pivotal in establishing connections among IoT devices and enabling their seamless operations.

3. Affordability and Technological Updates:
   ○ The affordability of tracking and control mechanisms and sensing devices is vital for the widespread adoption of IoT.
   ○ Funding for technological updates can be a challenge, but it is important to invest in the necessary advancements for future developments.

4. Addressing Challenges:
   ○ With the rising number of IoT devices, it is imperative to tackle the challenges associated with security, privacy, and the implications for the population.
   ○ Analyzing potential drawbacks and finding solutions is essential for the responsible implementation of IoT technologies.

Over 125 billion linked devices will create smart environments across many different areas in the coming decade, according to predictions, which point to a significant growth in IoT technologies. In order to create these connections, high-speed internet and Wifi networks that work well. The ability to connect physical objects in various surroundings will be greatly aided by enabling technologies like semiconductor electronics, cellphones, sensors, and cloud networking.

Overall, the future potential of IoT in different sectors relies on addressing challenges, ensuring affordability, and continuously advancing enabling technologies to foster the creation of connected and smart environments.

The future of IoT in the field of education holds significant promise for universities and higher education institutions. These institutions recognize the transformative impact of technology in teaching, learning, and assessment. They understand the importance of technological disruption in attracting students, improving retention rates, and achieving desired educational outcomes.

Universities need strong academic leadership, access to high-quality curricula and content, and exposure to cutting-edge technologies to educate students for the workforce. Many institutes of higher learning are concentrating on IoT's applications and related technologies as a result of its growth. E-learning is now a standard practice, and the integration of the internet has permeated colleges and universities.

While not immediately apparent, education is one domain that can greatly benefit from IoT. Universities can leverage IoT technology in numerous ways, leading to significant implications. IoT has the potential to enhance operational efficiency in learning environments, improve classroom instruction, and provide better learning resources. It can also enhance learning methodologies, improve management efficiency, and reduce costs.

Devices like e-books offer engaging and interactive learning resources, but continuous advancements in technology are needed to support the learning process. In this scenario, high-speed wireless networks with enough capacity for streaming audio and video lectures are crucial.

Through the use of IoT, the teaching and learning process will be improved in the future. The convenience it offers will be advantageous to both students and teachers. Teachers will be better able to fulfill their duties, and students will benefit from improved learning opportunities. IoT tools are expected to transform education by providing a system that is more engaging, flexible, interactive, and measurable and can meet the various needs of a big student population.

The information highlights that students devote one-fifth of their time in the classroom to tasks that could easily be eliminated with the help of an IoT network. By leveraging IoT, teachers would have less administrative burden, allowing them to dedicate more time to working with students, monitoring their progress, helping them grasp complex concepts in shorter durations, automatically recording attendance, determining learner's cognitive brain activity using neuro sensors, and discreetly alerting students to refocus on their tasks through haptic vibrations transmitted to their wearables. Although the majority of schools have yet to adopt IoT programs, the realization of such a learning environment is not too distant.

In shaping the future IoT economy, experts and leaders in the higher education sector have a vital role to play. By educating students and fostering collaboration with businesses and industries, higher education institutions can drive technological innovation. Universities may set the pace by creating programs for business and technical leaders and supporting interdisciplinary research into innovative business practices utilizing IoT technologies.

By embracing the potential of IoT in education, universities can create a future that combines technology advancements with effective teaching and learning practices, empowering students and contributing to the growth of IoT-enabled economies.

CONCLUSION

In conclusion, the use of technology, particularly IoT, in education has provided new possibilities for enhancing the learning experience for both students and teachers. Research is actively exploring IoT-based teaching platforms, such as smart classrooms, labs, and campuses, as well as investigating the usefulness of smart learning applications. However, while IoT offers numerous advantages in education, privacy and security concerns must be addressed. It is anticipated that future advancements will help resolve these issues.

IoT integration in education is rapidly approaching reality and has the potential to completely change how we learn. Simply by interacting with things, students can access information, and mobile devices connected to PCs provide anytime, everywhere learning.

Positive outcomes from IoT-based classroom automation have allowed for efficient device control and freed up time for in-depth instruction. The logistics, transportation, security, energy, healthcare, and education sectors might all benefit greatly from the IoT. Cooperation is required to go past the initial stages of market development and fully capitalize on the opportunities offered by IoT.

Higher education institutions can benefit from the Internet of Things (IoT) if they are having issues with planning, campus safety, information access, or resource management. It has a lot of potential to engage and enthuse both students and professors, accelerating the pace of learning. The objective of this study was to assess the potential of IoT in higher education, identify its benefits, address its issues, and minimize its hazards. Future efforts to maximize the advantages of IoT will mostly be directed toward higher education.

Overall, the integration of IoT in education offers exciting prospects for transforming the learning environment and improving educational outcomes. By harnessing the potential of IoT and addressing associated challenges, we can create a more connected and effective educational system.

REFERENCES

Aksu, H., Babun, L., Conti, M., Tolomei, G., & Uluagac, A. S. (2018, November). Advertising in the IoT Era: Vision and Challenges. *IEEE Communications Magazine*, *56*(11), 138–144. doi:10.1109/MCOM.2017.1700871

Caminero, G., Lopez-Martin, M., & Carro, B. (2019). Adversarial environment reinforcement learning algorithm for intrusion detection. *Computer Networks*, *159*, 96–109. doi:10.1016/j.comnet.2019.05.013

Chango, W., Sánchez-Santillán, M., Cerezo, R., & Romero, C. (2020). Predicting Students' performance using emotion detection from face-recording video. IEDM Tech. Dig. pp. 1–3.

Dachyar, M., Zagloel, T. Y. M., & Saragih, L. R. (2019). Knowledge growth and development: Internet of things (IoT) research, 2006–2018. *Heliyon*, *5*(8), e02264. doi:10.1016/j.heliyon.2019.e02264 PMID:31517087

Darling-Hammond, L., Flook, L., Cook-Harvey, C., Barron, B., & Osher, D. (2020, April 02). Flook, C. Cook-Harvey, B. Barron, & Osher D. (2019). Implications for educational practice of the science of Learning and development. *Applied Developmental Science*, *24*(2), 97–140. doi:10.1080/10888691.2018.1537791

Dhir, S., & Dubey, R. (2012). Identification of Barriers To The Successful Integration of ICT in Teaching and Learning. [TOJQI]. *Turkish Online Journal of Qualitative Inquiry*, *12*(5), 4428–4440.

Felicia, A., Wong, W. K., Loh, W. N., & Juwono, F. H. (2021). Increasing Role of IoT in Education Sector: A Review of Internet of Educational Things (IoEdT). *International Conference on Green Energy, Computing and Sustainable Technology (GECOST)*. (pp. 1-6). IEEE. 10.1109/GECOST52368.2021.9538781

Frustaci, M., Pace, P., Aloi, G., & Fortino, G. (2017). Evaluating critical security issues of the IoT World: Present and future challenges. *IEEE Internet of Things Journal*, *5*(4), 2483–2495. doi:10.1109/JIOT.2017.2767291

Gligori N., Uzelac A. & Krco. S. (2023). *Smart Classroom: Real-Time Feedback on Lecture Quality*.

Gligoric, N., Uzelac, A., Krco, S., Kovacevic, I., & Nikodijevic, A. (2018). System for recognizing lecture quality based on analysis of physical parameters. Vol 35. Issue 3. June 2018.

Hlaing, H. K. T., Phyu, S. P., & Yi, M. T. S. (2018). Thida. Effective Classroom Management Information System to Improve Teaching and Learning Approach. *International Journal of Advanced Research in Computer Science and Software Engineering*, *8*(8).

Kamal, H., Dhir, S., Hasteer, N., & Soni, K. M. (2023). *Analysis of Barriers to ICT4D Interventions in Higher Education through Interpretive Structural Modeling*. 2022 4th International Conference on Advances in Computing, Communication Control and Networking (ICAC3N), Greater Noida, India. 10.1109/ICAC3N56670.2022.10074596

Kassab, M., DeFranco, J., & Laplante, P. (2020). A systematic literature Review on Internet of things in education: Benefits and challenges. *Journal of Computer Assisted Learning*, *36*(2), 115–127. doi:10.1111/jcal.12383

Kassab, M., DeFranco, J., & Voas, J. (2018, September/October). Smarter Education. *IT Professional*, *20*(5), 20–24. doi:10.1109/MITP.2018.053891333

Lagus, J., Longi, K., Klami, A., & Hellas, A. (2018). Transfer-learning methods In programming course outcome prediction. *ACM Trans. Comput. Educ.*, *18*(4), 1–18. doi:10.1145/3152714

J. C. Lester, E. Y. Ha, S. Y. Lee, B. W. Mott, J. P. Rowe & J. L. Sabourin (2017). Serious games get smart: Intelligent game-Based learning environments. *AI Mag.*, *34*(4).

Lester, J. C., Ha, E. Y., Lee, S. Y., Mott, B. W., Rowe, J. P., & Sabourin, J. L. (2017). Serious games get smart: Intelligent game-Based learning environments. *AI Magazine*, *34*(4), 31–45. doi:10.1609/aimag.v34i4.2488

Mohamad Noor, M. B., & Hassan, W. H. (2019). Current research on Internet of Things (IoT) security: A survey. *Computer Networks*, *148*, 283–294. doi:10.1016/j.comnet.2018.11.025

Nižetić, S., Šolić, P., López-de-Ipiña González-de-Artaza, D., & Patrono, L. (2020). Internet of Things (IoT): Opportunities, issues and Challenges towards a smart and sustainable future. *Journal of Cleaner Production*, *274*, 122877. doi:10.1016/j.jclepro.2020.122877 PMID:32834567

Patwa, N., Seetharaman, A., Sreekumar, K., & Phani, S. (2018). Learning Analytics: Enhancing the quality of higher education. *Res. J. Econ.*, *2*(2), 13–29.

Rupashi, B., Saru, D., Nitasha, H., & Soni, K. M. (2023). [IJIET.]. *Analysis of Barriers in Conduct of Lab Based Courses in Remote Teaching Learning Paradigm.*, *13*(3), 475–481.

Soni, V. D. (2019). Security issues in using iot enabled devices and their Impact. *Int. Eng. J. Res. Dev.*, *4*(2), 7.

Srivastava, P., Dhir, S., Hasteer, N., & Soni, K. M. (2023). *Examining Parameters that Influence the Choice of Learners in Selecting Massive Open Online Courses.* 2023 2nd Edition of IEEE Delhi Section Flagship Conference (DELCON). Rajpura. India. 10.1109/DELCON57910.2023.10127325

Vicente, L. C. (2020). Elena de la G., Teresa O., M Julia F. & Luis O.-B. *IEEE Transactions on Learning Technologies*, *13*(4), 704–717.

Chapter 7

Gamification in Teacher Education:
Teacher Educators and Trainee Teachers' Perspectives in India

G. S. Prakasha
https://orcid.org/0000-0002-1287-7606
Christ University, India

Sanskriti Rawat
https://orcid.org/0000-0002-6042-9074
Christ University, India

Ishani Basak
Christ University, India

Sebastian Mathai
https://orcid.org/0000-0002-1795-7349
Christ University, India

ABSTRACT

Gamification emerged as a teaching-learning pedagogy in recent years. Its usage increased during the Covid-19 lockdown and continued post-pandemic time. Its usage ranges from online to offline tools; teachers lack its awareness as a pedagogy. The present study aimed to understand perspectives of teacher educators and teacher trainees on inclusion of gamification pedagogical training in teacher preparation programmes. The study employed a mixed-method approach and included qual-quant sequential explanatory research design. Researchers conducted semi-structured interviews with six teacher educators and six trainee teachers and collected the

DOI: 10.4018/979-8-3693-2169-0.ch007

Copyright © 2024, IGI Global. Copying or distributing in print or electronic forms without written permission of IGI Global is prohibited.

opinion of 200 teacher educators and trainee teachers. The study employed inductive thematic analysis and Chi-square analysis for qualitative and quantitative data respectively. Findings revealed six main themes and twelve sub-themes. Chi-square revealed a gender science-stereotype amid association between teacher educators and teacher trainees' opinion. Senior teacher educators did not believe in the importance of gamification inclusion in teacher preparation.

INTRODUCTION

Gamification is an innovative pedagogical strategy with researchers working on its application all across the world. Students playing computer games conceptualized this approach. Researchers saw the potential of gaming in learning (Ishak et. al., 2023). It first showed its application among engineering and business management courses, although gradually, a proper framework invaded the educational space (Bhatia et. al., 2023). Gamification is a widely used pedagogical strategy for various educational programmes (Begosso, 2018) for enhanced learner engagement.

Studies pertaining gamification in school education have their focus towards 21st century. Digital games have achieved increased motivation and learner engagement in the last decade. Recent research studies showed 'Game' as a method for educational delivery (Sailer & Homner, 2020). Gamification is an effective way to increase motivation of students towards learning and it has led to better academic achievement (Zainuddin et. al., 2020). Thus, the theories and application of this innovative learning strategy are slowly coming into use (Xi & Hamari, 2019). 21st century education emphasises teamwork, group discussion, technology enabled learning, problem solving, task immersion with reward cycles, and gamification in teaching and learning (Md. Khambari, 2019).Studies have found that gamified tools lead to more student interaction with the exercises and assessments(Ramirez et al.,2023). Around 11.30% of teachers in the higher education sector use gamification on a regular basis in class whereas others want to know more and possess a positive perception about this. Studies reveal that gamification is more prominent as a pedagogical strategy in private universities than public universities (Martí-Parreño et al., 2016). Learning by doing, a Dewey's notion, supports this and thus learning management tools like gamification for learning management systems (GLMS) help to create gamified innovation (Handayani et al., 2021). Researchers study various types of game design structures like rewards, leader-boards, levels or stage, progress-bars, storyline, and feedback-designs in order to discover an innovative learning practice through fun (Bitrián et. al., 2021). The fun learning with 99% participation of learners with a fulfilled learning objective thus shows that teachers should be trained about gamification or game-education (Siemon & Eckardt, 2017). Application of gamification in learning noted a statistically positive significance. Moreover, the level of educational interest, creativity and motivation boosted (Dehghanzadeh et. al., 2021). Additionally, student achievement is higher in this type of application (Yildirim, 2017). Empirical researches prove that gamification is not limited to engineering curriculum but in a lot more disciplines (Mangla et. al., 2022).

Different types of free, open, and virtual platforms show a significant positive and encouraging atmosphere (Alahmari et. al., 2023). Gamified uses of science education have a noteworthy effect on students as per research (Hursen & Bas, 2019).Students generally like the integration of game elements in their daily lessons that provides multidimensional framework enhancing more student engagement and motivation(Zourmpakis et al.,2023).Ease of learning, motivation, interactivity and interest are some of the necessary variables of gamification. Unfortunately, they are not accessible due to lack of resources, teacher's consciousness and student proneness (Sánchez-Mena & Martí-Parreño, 2017). Moodle platforms with contents containing multimedia games show the level of increased motivation in students (Kaya & Ercag, 2023). The high learning effect as a result of gamification is therefore a bright sunshine for STEM programmes (Ortiz-Rojas et al., 2019).

Gamification in Teacher Training

Many case studies reveal that a proper gamification training is crucial for teachers for subject specific diverse applications (Pektaş, & Kepceoğlu, 2019). However, to make this structure effective, the competency of teachers is important to add integrity with professionalism (Nousiainen et al., 2018). Gamification offers a better teaching learning environment (Ariffin et al., 2022). But still many trainee teachers are not sufficiently conscious about the process (Özdener, 2018). Still, many pre-service and in-service teachers feel that it may affect the students negatively (Alabbasi, 2018). The preschool children are enjoying this gamified learning resulting in minimum attention deficit (Wang, 2023). The primary teachers are now trained with gamification strategies in order to conduct blended learning. The teachers are interested and intrigued to apply the techniques and are reporting positive results (Gómez-Carrasco et al., 2020). Thus, the emergence of gamified education is the need of the hour in teacher education for a better professional scenario. (Al-Dosakee & Ozdamli, 2021). It has a vast impact on teaching and learning (Lampropoulos et. al., 2022). Further research is needed to narrow down the gap of gamified learning as a theory and practical pedagogical approach (Sajinčič et al., 2022). Teachers do not have sufficient training on the usage and utilization of gamification as a pedagogical tool. Hence, lack of ICT training and limited knowledge is the drawback of gamifying lessons (Araújo, 2017). Gamification has the potential to create a more active and engaging classroom. The mechanics and aesthetical outlook of gamified education is opening the door of dynamic learning (Kusuma et al., 2018). The gamified taxonomy provides an in-depth effective learning (Toda et al., 2019). Massive open online courses (MOOC), blended learning, and e-learning use gamified approaches for increasing retention of attention (Mohamad et al., 2018). Different types of workshops help in the implementation of gamification in the educational sector (Putz et al., 2020). Moreover, the perception of students about the approach of gamification was positive (Reyes & Gálvez, 2021). Hence, gamification is a promising disruption of technology in education.

Theory dominated undergraduate classrooms are now in need of a gamified approach (Gressick & Langston, 2017). The e-learning platforms are discovering the increasing competencies on the basis of social values by creating the atmosphere of real life through gamification (Osipovskaya & Miakotnikova, 2020). Diversified organisation of various activities in interdisciplinary areas are creating enjoyment and better potency of achieving good results (Moseikina et al., 2022). The number of students attempting through gamified modes are solving the challenges of learning (Flores, et al., 2020). In the recent times, this type of learning is creating a superior learning environment which is surpassing the traditional platforms (Escamez & Tapia, 2021). The students' preferred role as a player with a real life like environment is thus adding to their professional value in future (López Carrillo, 2019). Frameworks of transference, motivation and collaboration are actively present in the gamification and action research that prove that a proper transformative learning happens through this (Flores-Aguilar et al., 2023). Various social platforms or virtual learning platforms like Edmodo use gamification as an active method for teaching learning and it is recorded that the pupil activity is high (Montiel-Ruiz et al., 2023)

Research shows that the gamification elements like leaderboard, badge, points and level are powerful for learning (Saleem et al., 2022). Many stakeholders of education have a positive outlook on applications like Quizizz as it is helping them to interact better (Kristiani & Usodo, 2022). Through various experimental studies, researchers believe that the basic reason for the popularity of GameEd is fun learning and enjoyment. In the case of teachers, it is a way to upgrade their portfolio, and make narratives interesting (Fernandez-Rio et al., 2020). Thus, online 3D arrangements are a color changer for inquiry-based learning (Chung & Lin, 2022). The game hubs of Ukraine are already working on merging gaming sites with educational instructions to induce better effect. Gamification adds a competitive spirit and enjoyable learning (Gdowska et al., 2018). One of the popular online gamification platforms is Kahoot. There was a thought that remote learning is very difficult to hold back the attention and motivation of students. However, research proved that Kahoot increased the interest of learning among students. Moreover, its effect improved student performance (Martín-Sómer et al., 2021). Many students find it difficult to understand the lesson delivered through lectures. They find the deficit of real-world applications in those lectures. Thus, AI videos and various platforms like Kahoot, Quizziz help them understand concepts better and retain them (Chaturvedi et al., 2023). Recent studies proved that 65% students had better academic results using Kahoot as a mode for their practice. It helps in betterment of interest, assimilation of educational contents and motivation (Cortés-Pérez et al., 2023). Practice based assignments using gamification based augmented reality elements increase the readiness of learners (Petrovych et al., 2023). Research proves that the engagement of students and satisfaction about the course increases with application of both digitized and non-digitized gamification approaches (Qiao et al., 2023).

Theoretical Framework

Vygotsky's social development theory guided the present study. The teacher educators and pre-service teachers may understand that, school students could learn better through social interaction and gamification pedagogy provides that opportunity (Vygotsky & Cole, 1978). Further, present study seeks the support of self-determination theory to explain the intrinsic and extrinsic motivation that induces critical thinking skills in gamification pedagogy (Deci et al., 2012). In addition, the reinforces applied in the gamification classes such as leader boards, badges, points, rewards, etc., lead to intrinsic motivation among learners (Skinner, 1971). Further, Fogg behaviour model supports the learning through gamification as the students' ability, motivation, and timely prompts in gamification pedagogy results in behavioural change (Fogg, 2019).

Context of the Study

In the recent era, the world revolved around technology and there is a need to seep it into education as well. Educators all over the world face the challenge of accepting and using any new technology in their teaching-learning process. However, best utilization of such technologies lead to a better classroom in terms of engagement, motivation and academic achievement. Gamification is the emerging pedagogical approach aimed at school education across the world and promotes joyful learning. It adds a healthy competitive spirit among students (Gdowska et al., 2018). Learning through gamification strategy motivates students in facing various challenges while learning the subject content knowledge (Flores et al., 2020). Numerous competency development workshops organized across the globe train the teachers on integrating gamifying elements in their teaching methods (Putz et al., 2020). Gamification, if introduced as a pedagogical strategy in teacher training, will train pre-service teachers handling such pedagogy with ease and confidence (Wu et al., 2023). Further, enables them to use it easily when they begin their teaching profession after completing the teaching license programme (Zourmpakis et al., 2022). Gamification stimulates various types of thinking and problem-solving skills among school students. It increases the classroom interaction, learner engagement, learning attention, interest, and breaks the learning boredom (Kabilan & Chuah, 2023). Thus, educators across the globe started embracing gamified pedagogy in school education. However, in countries of developing economies, there is a gender science-stereotype towards its implementation and lack of awareness on its benefits. Thus, investigating its inclusion in teacher training programme especially in countries of developing economies gains importance. Therefore, present study aims to investigate the inclusion of gamified pedagogical-training in teacher education curriculum through the perspectives of teacher educators and pre-service teachers.

Significance of the Study

The present study aims to ensure that teacher education programmes align with the preferences and needs of educators in training. Additionally, the perceptions of teacher educators and trainee teachers help identify potential barriers or concerns, enabling the development of targeted strategies to address any challenges in implementing gamification. Hence, it is crucial to know the valuable insights of teacher educators and trainee teachers regarding the acceptance and effectiveness of gamification approach.

Research Objectives

1. To explore the perception of Teacher Educators and pre-service teachers on inclusion of gamification in teacher education
2. To determine the perception of Teacher Educators on inclusion of gamification in teacher education based on their gender and teaching experience.
3. To determine is gender stereotype affecting the inclusion of gamification in teacher education.

Research Questions

1. 1. What are the perceptions of teacher educators and trainee teachers regarding gamification as a part of teacher education?
2. Are there any differences between the perceptions of teacher educators and trainee teachers regarding gamification based on their gender and teaching experience?

3.   Does gender stereotyping affect the perception of teacher educators and trainee teachers about gamification?

Method

The present research followed a mixed-method approach and included qualitative-quantitative sequential explanatory research design to obtain a holistic understanding on the integration of gamification in teacher education. Researchers selected six teacher educators and six trainee teachers through purposive sampling to devote more time to each participant and collect richer data on their perception about gamification as a pedagogical tool. Table 1 shows the demographic details of the interview participants. The researchers developed interview items and subjected the items for face and content validity with a panel of experts from the field to check whether the questions are relevant, comprehensive and appropriately framed. Table 2 shows the items considered for the semi-structured interview. Corresponding author with 20 years of experience in the relevant field and holds a PhD degree conducted the interview. Researcher conducted the interviews in person and recorded the conversation with the permission from the participants. Each interview began with signing of consent forms and an introduction about the purpose of the interview. This facilitated to elicit in-depth responses and researcher could ask many on-spot questions in sequel to the responses provided by the participants to obtain detailed information. Researchers employed inductive thematic analysis for the qualitative data collected in the study as themes evolve by the collected data than any preconceived ideas. Thus, researchers followed the systematic procedure as below:

•   Researchers read and re-read the interview transcripts several times to get themselves familiar with the data
•   Organised the data into meaningful chunks to generated the initial codes based on the perspectives shared
•   Developed themes based on the significant pattern observed in the transcripts
•   Re-visited the themes and organised them distinctly and identified sub-themes within each theme
•   Defined each them and sub-themes with narrative excerpts and describe the results in detail.

To obtain a broader perspective upon the acceptance of gamification among teacher educators and trainee teachers teaching Bachelors in Education (B.Ed) programme, a teaching license programme at secondary school level, researchers selected 200 participants through convenience sampling. Researchers contacted them through social media platforms such as LinkedIn, WhatsApp groups, etc. Sample had an equal representation of men and women teacher educators and male and female teacher trainees. Researchers collected the opinion from teacher educators and trainee teachers on inclusion of gamification in teacher preparation programme. The respondents responded either Yes or No to the opinion statement. Researchers subjected the data to chi-square test of association to determine the association between the opinions provided by teacher educators and trainee teachers. Result section presents the results of chi-square statistical analysis through SPSS programme.

Ethical Considerations

The researchers took permission from the research-conduct-ethics-committee of the institution for approval of the present study. Researchers sought informed consent form signed by all the participants at the beginning of each interview. The researchers assured the participants about their data privacy and security. The researchers allowed the participants to leave at any point in the middle of the interview if they find themselves uncomfortable responding to the questions. Researchers transcribed the recorded interviews and stored the data in a password-protected file. The data is accessible only to the researchers. To ensure privacy, researchers assigned pseudonyms to each participant while narrating the results.

Table 1. Demographic details of participants

Pseudonym	Age	Gender	Teacher Trainee/Educator	Educational qualification
TE1	47	M	Teacher Educator	MA. Med, MPhil
TE2	42	F	Teacher Educator	M.Sc. MEd, PhD
TE3	37	M	Teacher Educator	B.Sc. MEd, PhD
TE4	50	M	Teacher Educator	MA. MEd, PhD
TE5	46	F	Teacher Educator	M.Sc. MEd, PhD
TE6	34	F	Teacher Educator	M.A. MEd, PhD
TT1	30	M	Trainee Teacher	M.Com. (B.Ed)
TT2	27	M	Trainee Teacher	MA. (B.Ed)
TT3	37	F	Trainee Teacher	BSc. (B.Ed)
TT4	29	F	Trainee Teacher	MA. (B.Ed)
TT5	32	M	Trainee Teacher	BA. (B.Ed)
TT6	26	F	Trainee Teacher	MSc. (B.Ed)

Table 2. Semi structured interview items

For Teacher Educators • What do you know about Gamification? • Do you think teacher training must include training on gamification? Elaborate • Why is gamification a need for school education? Give Reasons
For Trainee Teachers • What do you know about Gamification? • Do you think teacher training must include training on gamification? Elaborate • Why is gamification a need for school education? Give Reasons

RESULTS AND DISCUSSION

The interview of teacher educators and trainee teachers gave us the perspectives, concepts and awareness of the samples about gamification. The following Table 3 is presenting the themes and subthemes noted from the analysis of transcripts.

Table 3. Presenting themes and sub-themes of inductive analysis

Interview participants	Theme type	Theme and subtheme titles
Teacher educators	Main Theme 1 Subtheme Subtheme Main Theme 2 Subtheme Subtheme Main Theme 3 Subtheme Subtheme	**Learning Platform** 1. Online Quizzes 2. Pedagogical tools **Gamification is the need of the hour** 1.21st century learning skills 2. Interactive **Future is Technology** 1. ICT Training 2. Gadgets
Trainee teachers	Main Theme 1 Subtheme Subtheme Main Theme 2 Subtheme Subtheme Main Theme 3 Subtheme Subtheme	**Technology enabled learning** 1. Technological knowledge 2. Online tools for non- game contexts **Students like gamification** 1. Child friendly 2. Play Way Method **Joyful learning** 1.Enthusiasm 2. Colourful

Main Theme One: Learning Platform

Most of the teacher educators agree that various learning platforms make learning innovative. They are aware about Kahoot and Quizziz. They agreed that gamification catalyses the thinking ability of a student and helps the problem-solving approaches too. It helps the learner to feel intrinsically motivated in order to be engaged with the learning process. Research proves that although participants do not believe in the advantages of video games for learning, it is clear that application of gaming elements causes higher degree of activity with increased level of thinking and motivation. The level of interest increased the academic performance too (Kaya & Ercag, 2023).

TE6: Gamification will be useful as they will have more problem solving and critical understanding kind of thing.

TE2: Day by day we need to train teachers with gamification to move forward. It is relevant in teacher education. The approaches of gamification must be known to add more varieties in teaching learning process for more engaging, point to be noted, more engaging the student in the learning environment.

TE3: A step by step process from simple to complex maintaining the enthusiasm of the learner and rewarded for each step.

Subtheme: Online Quizzes

The teacher educators agreed that the problem-solving approach is the need of the hour in the 21st century. The collaborative approach with game -based learning designs increase retention among students. The instant feedback and reinforcements with rewards, points, badges, and leader boards helps them become motivated, which in turn helps in fulfilling the learning objectives. Post-pandemic, teachers noted that offline face-to-face interactions were not enhancing the attention level of students. Kahoot and other platforms improves the situation by enabling fun-filled learning (Martín-Sómer et al., 2021).

TE6: Kahoot, Quizziz and tons of fun learning platforms ... the students are encouraged to learn from simple to complex steps.

Sub Theme: Pedagogical Tools

According to the teacher educators, gamification encourages trainee teachers to learn technology enabled designs. This removes their mindset from rote learning. They try to understand the practical implications of game-based classes that enhance their cognitive growth. School education will receive a proper growth if trainee teachers arrange activity-based learning with proper rewards or reinforcements. The students learn team approach, problem solving and critical thinking through gamification. The teacher-training curriculum should consist of various strategies applying gamification. Research proves that the gamified platforms improve the achievement level of students in various subjects. A university showed improved performance and engagement among its students using Kahoot (Ares et al., 2018).

T1E: To make learning interesting, to improve learner retention, to enhance learning experiences provision of instant feedback and reinforcement is made. That is why this feature is needed.

TE3: Psychology of learning and teaching, application of operant conditioning, through games children are encouraged to learn from simple to complex. Example: Kahoot

Main Theme Two: Gamification is the Need of the Hour

Many teacher educators agreed upon the issue of lack of training and awareness about a gamified environment in schools. They highlighted the digital ignorance among the teachers of government schools. According to national education policy (NEP) 2020, classrooms should be interactive and the students should be intrinsically motivated to learn. The 21st century learning paradigm shows how rote learning is outdated. As the teacher educators mentioned, after the prolonged lockdown, students are deviating their attention from listening, which demands new methods of teaching learning. The promotion of various digital tools will increase the active engagement and involvement of students (Correia & Santos, 2017).

TE2: The learning environment, the teacher training and teaching learning curriculum constantly changing in order to improve the quality of students. However, I am doubtful about including gamification as a part of teacher training

TE1: In general, in government schools the teachers the teachers themselves are not that much exposed to newer.

TE3: Teacher education is somewhat stagnant and usually the lecture method is followed. Throughout Karnataka a great disparity in training colleges. Teacher educators not trained properly to train the trainees as the prospective teachers when they go to school they should be equipped. Instead of learning it as a job requirement in the school it will be better if they learn it as a part of strategy. A student already in these days know many information and thus these approaches may be used for active learning and not just sit and learn.

Sub Theme: 21ˢᵗ Century Learning Skills

The 21ˢᵗ century learning skills demand an interactive session with application of game -based elements in non-game contexts. The teacher educators believe that gamification works well both in online and offline mode. Whilst the students should learn through collaboration with healthy competitive spirits. Quizzes constructed with instant feedback motivate students to perform better. Challenging tasks help students brainstorm by giving them reinforcement badges and points. Points, badges, leaderboards. Progress boards, levels help a student become confident and motivated. An effective instruction with a game-based approach checks the traits, behaviours, shortcomings of every student (Oliveira et. al., 2022).

TE5: I like to give them some badges or smileys. I gave them stars on leaderboards. Students feel more motivated and becomes the problem solver.

TE5: When we use gamification, students feel more motivated. So, gamification needs to be included in the teacher education strategy.

TE3: Practically speaking the teachers are not trained adequately. Most of the time to them b.ed is just a teacher training course. They just read the chapter and deliver and students are mostly passive learners. Students will lose interest. So gamified strategy aroused enthusiasm and more involvement in learning.

Sub Theme: Interactive

The teacher educators agree that the interactive mode of classroom will be successful in retaining the learning objectives in the mind of students. Gaming strategy increases the habit of collaborating, critically thinking and solving challenges. This lands in better instruction (Oliveira et. al., 2022).

TE6: Traditional assessment can be boring and classrooms can be made more engaging and interactive.

*TE5: I give them some challenges and task. When they perform, I give them some points for the accomplishment or execution of the tasks. I have decided some levels and give motivational badges. I made a leaderboard and accordingly I reward them and accordingly rank all students. As I have told you earlier, we have the **game-based** elements in **non-game** contexts students become motivated and learn easily.*

Main Theme Three: Future is Technology

Teacher educators emphasised the use of technology in the teacher training in order to make the teachers aware about different strategies of learning. They mentioned national initiative for school heads' and teachers' holistic advancement (NISHTHA) and study webs of active learning for young aspiring minds (SWAYAM) platforms that enhance the thinking process of trainee teachers in order to spread 21st century learning skills in the classroom (Araújo, 2017).

TE3: We have to embrace change and understand the niche of the learner. We should try to remove digital ignorance. Teachers are not equipped with these approaches and the administrators may say that it is not a requirement because they are only concentrating on completing syllabus. The cognitive development of individuals is needed and thus gamification is needed. Seniors and junior teachers are having competition and seniors are doubting the change. The only way is continuous practice through workshops.

TE4: It is already there like Nishtha, Swayam. Activity based training programs needed for trainee teachers.

TE5: Boys may like it, but I seriously doubt its acceptance by woman teacher educators

Sub Theme: ICT Training

Instant feedback is the core attraction of game-based learning as it motivates the student to work more for attaining the goal. The teacher educators believed in applying this in a trainee teacher's classroom with aid of technology where gamification acts as a method of learning how to teach. The motivation of rewards, badges help them brainstorm various ways to make learning interactive. With aid of ICT training, they use various google forms, levels which excite the children. In order to effectively apply this the teachers should be properly trained (Flores et. al., 2023).

TE6: It will also help with the rewarding kind of thing.

TE5: Game thinking approach must be introduced in pedagogical approach.

TE4: It is the age of technology and pedagogical changes are proposed for application of 21ˢᵗ century learning skills. This technology, if learned can reach each and every child.

Sub Theme: Gadgets

Many schools are introducing robotics and learning tabs. The teacher educators are trying to evolve both effective online and offline ways of gamified approaches as various private schools are extracting money in the name of these facilities. If teachers spread game-based awareness across all types of schools, then children from all the sections of society will enjoy learning and it will help them cognitively. A smart classroom contributes to interdisciplinary knowledge of students (Kaur et al., 2022). Spreading awareness about gamification will be possible through a proper training of teachers. Additionally, many teachers think that gamification works well offline and manually, with a properly planned lesson.

TE1: Role play, puppet show may help. We will be making teaching more effective for student satisfaction.

TE3: Some private schools have introduced robotics but only **upper-class** *people will get the facilities and competition can arise. So, more training is needed to integrate it in learning system and not syllabus coverage only. The main thing is resistance to change.*

Main Theme Four: Technology Enabled Learning

Many trainee teachers **believe** that after the pandemic, the students are more prone to use tablets, laptops and mobiles. In order to channelise the learning and grab their attention, gamification is an effective approach. Many use the platforms like Kahoot and Quizziz for formative assessments. The instant feedback of points in these platforms help the students to become motivated. Moreover, it helps them to be aware of the technology enabled learning world (Özdener, 2018).

TT1: I feel that students are more interested in Minecraft and not interested in listening to what the teacher is telling so gamification is one way of doing that.

TT5: It can be used for formative assignments. It is effective for science and maths. These types of tools make the learning memorable. Gamifying it may make it interesting and the concept can be effectively relevant.

TT3: Though future is technology, I don't know a thing about gamification, I am not sure will all students like it in school...

Sub Theme: Technological Knowledge

The students are less prone to listening so these **game-based** approaches help them to solve problems, think critically and brainstorm. The growing interest helps them to attain the basic comprehending power which was lessening due to lockdown and screen addiction. The deviating attention of students enhances if active use of colourful activities is used in a learning environment with proper game-like platforms for assessments. The invention of AI and smart classrooms help increasing the cooperative spirit of children (Demkah & Bhargava, 2019).

TT1: Students have access to all information in this age through Google and Wikipedia

TT3: It is necessary to introduce gamification in the teacher training curriculum. There is a theoretical based syllabus and in a modern technological world a trainee teacher must learn to make learning fun. As a teacher we must know how to implement it.

Sub Theme: Online Tools for Non-Game Contexts

The virtual learning environment transformed into blended learning classrooms. The teachers use these to increase excitement among students. Moreover, real life applications are possible through gamified environments which make students think in an innovative way (Saleem et al., 2022).

TT1: Gamifying course contents. If we know it will be easier for us to apply in school

TT3: It is helpful for certain contents so that the monotonous rote learning can be cut down. Along with the regular classrooms it should go hand in hand.

Main Theme Five: Students Like Gamification

Students like the gaming approach, as according to the trainee teachers, they love the energy and enthusiasm of activity. They rack their brains to think about what they are learning and for them, badges and points seem exciting. Revision classes conducted through various gamified platforms like Kahoot, Quizziz and the instant feedback create a joyful and competitive spirit among the students (Martín-Sómer et al., 2021).

TT2: Make it a fun experience for child

TT5: It can be used for formative assignments. It is effective for science and maths. These types of tools make the learning memorable. Gamifying it may make it interesting and the concept can be effectively relevant.

Sub Theme: Child Friendly

The monotonous listening days are over as colourful gamified elements are more friendly and near to a child's mind in order to create a vibrant environment. It helps to retain the attention of a child. The application of this in various researches proved that it increases active engagement (Semartiana, 2022).

TT5: Interesting things for children, unique and interesting.

TT3: Making learning fun, playing as well learning.

TT1: It is more feasible for teachers. It is user friendly and the interaction is child friendly.

Sub Theme: Play Way Method

Rousseau's play way method is a catalyst in the gamification of learning classrooms. Here, the children learn through the way they like. These methods help in creating a feel-good thing among students. The interfaces are feasible and easier for teachers to use in class. These approaches help in quicker cognitive growth of a child. The sound effects, colours excite the specially gifted children as well as all others which make a teaming engagement happen (Cristiano et al., 2019).

TT4: Making learn fun and attractive to students so that they can enjoy

TT4: in order to grab the attention of students to teach concepts I can make students play a game. Intrinsic motivation can take place

*TT3: In order to grab the attention of students one needs to make learning attractive. Playway method is needed. To teach a concept we can use **these** strategies*

Main Theme Six: Joyful Learning

The trainee teachers think that it is useful for grabbing the attention of students. Out from the monotonous environment, this brings back animation concepts and video games as a new and effective way of learning (Correia & Santos, 2017).

TT5: Kahoot, quiz platforms, teachers who are going to class may know how to create.

TT3: The students will not learn for just the sake of learning. Content is easier and the teacher will not be burdened as like the flipped classroom teacher will be aware that the student is already aware of the concept and through revisions it will be clearer.

TT1: Using quizzes may be teaching curriculum will be more interesting. The trainee teachers must have the idea about how to teach in a gamified approach.

Sub Theme: Enthusiasm

The trainee teachers with many of them having school experience are expressing their excitement on seeing a colourful classroom. They **believe** that hands-on experience is happening through this unique method (Correia & Santos, 2017).

TT2: some kind of teaching experience, some comes without. It is good to introduce gamification so that teachers can understand and interact.

TT5: Gamification is basically what curriculum you are teaching; it must be through fun learning and not monotonous. There are online platforms and through quizzes or fun games. It is technologically oriented.

Sub Theme: Colourful

Teachers use google forms in a colourful manner with pictures and videos that appeal to the kids. The students answer by brainstorming them. Moreover, this enhances their motivation and engages them. Teachers create innovative projects in order to enhance team learning approach (Cristiano et al., 2019).

TT2: Fun games in class, enjoyment

TT1: Gamification is interesting for children. I feel rather than the usual worksheets, it is unique and colourful for them.

Chi-Square Test of Association

To determine the presence of association between inclusion of gamification in teacher education between senior and junior teacher educators and between male and female teacher educator and between male and female teacher trainees, which are the two dichotomous variables. study employed Chi-square tests. Table 4, Table

5, and figure 1 below presents the result of Chi-square test for dichotomous variable inclusion of gamification among senior and beginner teacher educators.

From cross-tabulation table 4, it is clear that there are more senior teacher educators who are not for inclusion of gamification. Similarly, there are more beginner teacher educators, who wish to include gamification in teacher preparation programme.

*Table 4. Teacher educator * inclusion of gamification cross-tabulation*

			Inclusion of Gamification		Total
			Yes	No	
Teacher Educator	Senior Teacher Educators	Count	65	35	100
		Expected Count	72.5	27.5	100
	Beginner Teacher Educators	Count	80	20	100
		Expected Count	72.5	27.5	100

*Table 5. Showing the chi-square test for teacher educator * inclusion of gamification*

	Value	df	Asymp. Sig. (2-sided)	Exact Sig. (2-sided)	Exact Sig. (1-sided)
Pearson Chi-Square	5.643[a]	1	.018		
Continuity Correction[b]	4.915	1	.027		
Likelihood Ratio	5.698	1	.017		
Fisher's Exact Test				.026	.013
Linear-by-Linear Association	5.614	1	.018		
N of Valid Cases	200				

a. 0 cells (0.0%) have expected count less than 5. The minimum expected count is 27.50.

b. Computed only for a 2x2 table

Table 5 above shows that, there is a significant association between the teacher educators (seniors and beginners) and their opinion (Yes or No) on inclusion of gamification in teacher preparation programme ($\chi^2 = 5.643$, $p = 0.018$).

From cross-tabulation table 6, it is clear that there are more male teacher educators agreeing to include gamification in teacher preparation than their female counterparts. Similarly, there are more female teacher educators, who do not wish to include gamification in teacher preparation programme.

Table 7 above shows that, there is a significant association between the teacher educators (male and female) and their opinion (Yes or No) on inclusion of gamification in teacher preparation programme ($\chi^2 = 7.091$, $p = 0.008$).

Table 6. Teacher educator * inclusion of gamification cross-tabulation

| | | | Inclusion of Gamification | | Total |
			Yes	No	
Teacher Educator	Male Teacher Educators	Count	80	20	100
		Expected Count	71.5	28.5	100.0
	Female Teacher Educators	Count	63	37	100
		Expected Count	71.5	28.5	100.0

Table 7.Showing the chi-square test for teacher educator (gender) * inclusion of gamification

	Value	df	Asymp. Sig. (2-sided)	Exact Sig. (2-sided)	Exact Sig. (1-sided)
Pearson Chi-Square	7.091[a]	1	.008		
Continuity Correction[b]	6.281	1	.012		
Likelihood Ratio	7.174	1	.007		
Fisher's Exact Test				.012	.006
Linear-by-Linear Association	7.056	1	.008		
N of Valid Cases	200				

a. 0 cells (0.0%) have expected count less than 5. The minimum expected count is 28.50.
b. Computed only for a 2x2 table

Table 8 Teacher trainees * inclusion of gamification cross-tabulation

| | | | Inclusion of Gamification | | Total |
			Yes	No	
Teacher Trainees	Male Teacher Trainees	Count	94	6	100
		Expected Count	57.0	43.0	100.0
	Female Teacher Trainees	Count	20	80	100
		Expected Count	57.0	43.0	100.0

From cross-tabulation table 8, it is clear that there are more male teacher trainees agreeing to include gamification in teacher preparation than their female counterparts. Similarly, there are more female teacher trainees, who do not wish to have training in gamification at teacher preparation programmes.

*Table 9. Showing the Chi-square test for teacher trainees (gender) * inclusion of gamification*

	Value	df	Asymp. Sig. (2-sided)	Exact Sig. (2-sided)	Exact Sig. (1-sided)
Pearson Chi-Square	111.710[a]	1	.000		
Continuity Correction[b]	108.711	1	.000		
Likelihood Ratio	127.852	1	.000		
Fisher's Exact Test				.000	.000
Linear-by-Linear Association	111.151	1	.000		
N of Valid Cases	200				

a. 0 cells (0.0%) have expected count less than 5. The minimum expected count is 43.00.
b. Computed only for a 2x2 table

Table 9 above shows that, there is a significant association between the teacher trainees (male and female) and their opinion (Yes or No) on inclusion of gamification in teacher preparation programme ($\chi^2 = 111.710$, $p = 0.000$).

DISCUSSION

The mixed method approach confirms that there is more inclination towards inclusion of gamification in teacher education programme and future teachers are looking forward to its pedagogical deliberations in the school education (Schnitzler et. al., 2020). Both qualitative and quantitative analysis showed a positive response towards inclusion of gamified elements in teacher training programme. However, study found gender science stereotypic attitude from both teacher educators and trainee teachers. Further, senior teacher educators were apprehensive about its inclusion in teacher training programme. Senior and female teacher educators expressed the lack of awareness about the application of gamification in both digitized and offline ways in non-game contexts.

Teacher educators and trainee teachers expressed that prior to pandemic, students were passive listeners and mostly were rote learning in classes (Santos-Villalba et. al., 2020). Post pandemic, school students are more familiar to technology and it is challenging to grab their attention to the lessons (Marinensi et. al, 2023). Therefore, teachers in general tried various strategies to grab their attention. Majority of the teachers failed to understand students like games and capitalising it for teaching learning might be beneficial. Many teacher educators are of the view that learning to gamify the lesson plans is an art and trying to grasp it as per job requirement is more difficult. Thus, it will be better if gamification is a pedagogical strategy to be embedded as part of teacher education curriculum. Knowing gamified pedagogy will enable teachers to be future ready with 21st century learning skills (Araújo, 2017). However, traditionally trained teachers are not ready for this paradigm shift in organising teaching learning with a gamified approach. There is a need for teachers' capacity building programme on gamified teaching and learning. Already platforms like NISHTHA and SWAYAM attempt to make the teachers understand the effectiveness of active learning. Moreover, a recent study confirms that, gamified elements enhance active learning and gamification is a good strategy, whether used offline or online (Qiao et al., 2023). Another study revealed that, providing students with various levels of learning from simple to complex with reinforcements like badges and rewards amid gamification pedagogy enhances learning engagement (Saleem et al., 2022). Themes from qualitative analysis such as leaning platform, future is technology, technology enabled learning, and students liking and enjoying gamification are all showing positive inclination towards embracing it as a pedagogical discourse and need for more professional training to practice it. A recent study clearly identifies various platforms like Kahoot, Quizziz etc., helps in classroom discussion, assessment, and reinforcement by providing badges and rewards (Martín-Sómer et al., 2021).

Quantitative analysis results after qualitative further confirmed the presence of strong association between the opinion of teacher educators and trainee teachers with respect their experience and gender. There is a gender science stereotype among female teacher educators and trainee teachers by expressing their negation towards inclusion of gamification practices in the teacher preparation programme. Senior teacher educators were not confident in how to go about its inclusion. However, beginner teacher educators and male teacher trainees had strong inclination towards including gamification in teacher education and need for gamified pedagogical training. Owing to the opinions expressed by teacher educators and teacher trainees in qualitative interviews and further quantitative results confirming association between their opinion on inclusion of gamification training in teacher education programme, study recommends future researchers to explore more in-depth understanding on this topic.

LIMITATIONS

The present research is based only on the teacher educators and trainee teachers. The study is done based on teacher educators and trainee teachers from India. The interviews of the teacher educators and trainee teachers are taken through purposive sampling. A survey is done on 200 teacher educators and trainee teachers across

India through convenience sampling. Collection of their opinion is analysed through Chi square analysis.

Implications for Further Research

The teacher educators and trainee teachers need more practical hands-on training about incorporating gamified elements in classrooms across disciplines. The present study yields far-reaching implications for educational practices, teacher educators, and trainee teachers. The study's findings can help enhance curriculum design by identifying areas where gamification aligns with educational goals, ensuring that teacher education programs remain relevant and effective. Moreover, the study's insights can inform targeted professional development initiatives for teacher educators, addressing potential gaps in knowledge and fostering innovation in instructional approaches. Moreover, the study offers valuable input for resource allocation, ensuring that institutions invest in developing effective gamified educational materials and tools. This approach contributes to a dynamic learning environment that resonates with trainee teachers, ultimately enhancing their engagement and preparation for future roles. Therefore, the study has implications for the evolution of teacher education practices in response to changing perceptions and outcomes in the unique context of India.

CONCLUSION

Gamification in teacher education promotes successful skill acquisition and pedagogic innovation by increasing engagement, encouraging active involvement and creating a dynamic learning environment. The present research explored the perspectives of teacher educators and trainee teachers on inclusion of gamification in teacher education. The study revealed a positive inclination towards its inclusion in teacher preparation programme. Integrating gamification in teacher -education courses yield several benefits. Firstly, it increases participation among learners by adding interactive elements that enhance and personalise the learning process. Secondly, it encourages teacher educators and trainee teachers to collaborate, exchange ideas, and solve problems as a group. Finally, through encouraging active engagement and real time feedback, gamification improves instructional skills among educators, thus guaranteeing a more productive learning environment. However, quantitative analysis revealed the existence of gender science-stereotype among teacher educators and trainee teachers. Further, senior teacher educators failed to understand the benefits of embedding it in teacher training. The views of teacher educators and trainee teachers expressed in the study increased the chance of productivity of application of gamification as a pedagogical strategy in teacher education curriculum. Thus, there is a need for qualitative and quantitative studies further expose this matter to make stakeholders in the countries of developing economies to understand the situation and take necessary action. Study included only the opinion of teacher educator and trainee teachers. Opinion from stakeholders might be more feasible. Study recommends future researchers to take detailed stock of the situation to improve the understanding of including gamification training and its benefits in teaching learning.

Conflict of Interest

The authors of the present study have no competing interest to declare.

ACKNOWLEDGEMENT

Sincere thanks to all the interview participants for their cooperation. Our sincere thanks to the University for supporting to conduct the present research.

REFERENCES

Al-Dosakee, K., & Ozdamli, F. (2021). Gamification in teaching and learning languages: A systematic literature review. *Revista Romaneasca Pentru Educatie Multidimensionala, 13*(2), 559–577. doi:10.18662/rrem/13.2/436

Alabbasi, D. (2018). Exploring teachers' perspectives towards using gamification techniques in online learning. *Turkish Online Journal of Educational Technology-TOJET, 17*(2), 34-45. https://eric.ed.gov/?id=EJ1176165

Alahmari, M., Jdaitawi, M. T., Rasheed, A., Abduljawad, R., Hussein, E., Alzahrani, M., & Awad, N. (2023). Trends and gaps in empirical research on gamification in science education: A systematic review of the literature. *Contemporary Educational Technology, 15*(3), ep431. doi:10.30935/cedtech/13177

Araújo, I., & Carvalho, A. A. (2017). Empowering teachers to apply gamification. *2017 International Symposium on Computers in Education (SIIE),* (pp. 1–5). IEEE. 10.1109/SIIE.2017.8259668

Ares, A. M., Bernal, J., Nozal, M. J., Sánchez, F. J., & Bernal, J. (2018). Results of the use of Kahoot! gamification tool in a course of Chemistry. In *4th international conference on higher education advances (HEAD'18)* (pp. 1215-1222). Editorial Universitat Politècnica de València. 10.4995/HEAD18.2018.8179

Ariffin, N. A. N., Ramli, N., Badrul, N. M. F. H. N., Yusof, Y., & Suparlan, A. (2022). Effectiveness of gamification in teaching and learning mathematics. *Journal on Mathematics Education*, *13*(1), 173–190. doi:10.22342/jme.v13i1.pp173-190

Begosso, L. R., & Begosso, L. C. Da Cunha, D. S., Pinto, J. V., Lemos, L., & Nunes, M. (2018). The use of gamification for teaching algorithms. In FedCSIS (Communication Papers) (pp. 225-231). doi:10.15439/2018F165

Bhatia, M., Manani, P., Garg, A., Bhatia, S., & Adlakha, R. (2023). Mapping Mindset about Gamification: Teaching Learning Perspective in UAE Education System and Indian Education System. *Revue d'Intelligence Artificielle*, *37*(1), 47–52. doi:10.18280/ria.370107

Bitrián, P., Buil, I., & Catalán, S. (2021). Enhancing user engagement: The role of gamification in mobile apps. *Journal of Business Research*, *132*, 170–185. doi:10.1016/j.jbusres.2021.04.028

Braun, V., & Clarke, V. (2006). Using thematic analysis in psychology. *Qualitative Research in Psychology*, *3*(2), 77–101. doi:10.1191/1478088706qp063oa

Brull, S., & Finlayson, S. (2016). Importance of gamification in increasing learning. *Journal of Continuing Education in Nursing*, *47*(8), 372–375. doi:10.3928/00220124-20160715-09 PMID:27467313

Chaturvedi, I., Cambria, E., & Welsch, R. E. (2023). Teaching Simulations Supported by Artificial Intelligence in the Real World. *Education Sciences*, *13*(2), 2. Advance online publication. doi:10.3390/educsci13020187

Chung, C. H., & Lin, Y. Y. (2022). Online 3D gamification for teaching a human resource development course. *Journal of Computer Assisted Learning*, *38*(3), 692–706. doi:10.1111/jcal.12641

Correia, M., & Santos, R. (2017). *game-based learning: the use of kahoot in teacher education*. *International Symposium on Computers in Education (SIIE)*, Lisbon, Portugal. 10.1109/SIIE.2017.8259670

Cortés-Pérez, I., Zagalaz-Anula, N., López-Ruiz, M. C., Díaz-Fernández, Á., Obrero-Gaitán, E., & Osuna-Pérez, M. C. (2023). Study based on gamification of tests through *kahoot!*™ and reward game cards as an innovative tool in physiotherapy students: A preliminary study. *Health Care, 11*(4), 578. doi:10.3390/healthcare11040578 PMID:36833112

Cristiano, J., Rahmani, M., Helland, K., & Puig, D. (2019). Gable–gamification for a better life. *Opportunities and challenges for European Projects, 1*, 2017-18. doi:10.5220/0008862401240132

Dehghanzadeh, H., Fardanesh, H., Hatami, J., Talaee, E., & Noroozi, O. (2021). Using gamification to support learning English as a second language: A systematic review. *Computer Assisted Language Learning, 34*(7), 934–957. doi:10.1080/095 88221.2019.1648298

Demkah, M., & Bhargava, D. (2019). *Gamification in education: a cognitive psychology approach to cooperative and fun learning. Amity International Conference on Artificial Intelligence (AICAI)*, Dubai, United Arab Emirates. /10.1109/AICAI.2019.8701264

Flores, E. G. R., Mena, J., Montoya, M. S. R., & Velarde, R. R. (2020). The use of gamification in xMOOCs about energy: Effects and predictive models for participants' learning. *Australasian Journal of Educational Technology, 36*(2), 43–59. doi:10.14742/ajet.4818

Flores-Aguilar, G., Prat-Grau, M., Fernández-Gavira, J., & Muñoz-Llerena, A. (2023). I learned more because I became more involved": Teacher's and students' voice on gamification in physical education teacher education. *International Journal of Environmental Research and Public Health, 20*(4), 3038. doi:10.3390/ijerph20043038 PMID:36833730

Fogg, B. J. (2019). Fogg behavior model. *Behavior Design.* https://behaviordesign.stanford.edu/resources/fogg-behavior-model

Gdowska, K., Gaweł, B., Dziabenko, O., & Blazhko, O. (2018). Gamification in teaching humanities – „GameHub" project. *Zeszyty Naukowe Wydziału Elektrotechniki i Automatyki Politechniki Gdańskiej, 58*, 27–32. 19.04-20.04.2018

Gómez-Carrasco, C. J., Monteagudo-Fernández, J., Moreno-Vera, J. R., & Sainz-Gómez, M. (2020). Evaluation of a gamification and flipped-classroom program used in teacher training: Perception of learning and outcome. *PLoS One, 15*(7), e0236083. doi:10.1371/journal.pone.0236083 PMID:32673373

Gressick, J., & Langston, J. B. (2017). The gilded classroom: Using gamification to engage and motivate undergraduates. *The Journal of Scholarship of Teaching and Learning*, *17*(3), 109–123. doi:10.14434/v17i3.22119

Handayani, P. W., Raharjo, S. R., & Putra, P. H. (2021). Active Student Learning through Gamification in a Learning Management System. *Electronic Journal of e-Learning*, *19*(6), 601–613. doi:10.34190/ejel.19.6.2089

Hursen, C., & Bas, C. (2019). Use of gamification applications in science education. *International Journal of Emerging Technologies in Learning*, *14*(1), 4. doi:10.3991/ijet.v14i01.8894

Ishak, S. A., Hasran, U. A., & Din, R. (2023). Ishak,Hasran UA, Din R. Media Education through Digital Games: A Review on Design and Factors Influencing Learning Performance. *Education Sciences*, *13*(2), 102. doi:10.3390/educsci13020102

Kabilan, M. K., Annamalai, N., & Chuah, K. M. (2023). Practices, purposes and challenges in integrating gamification using technology: A mixed-methods study on university academics. *Education and Information Technologies*, *28*(11), 14249–14281. doi:10.1007/s10639-023-11723-7 PMID:37361777

Kaur, A., Bhatia, M., & Stea, G. (2022). A survey of smart classroom literature. *Education Sciences*, *12*(2), 86. doi:10.3390/educsci12020086

Kaya, O. S., & Ercag, E. (2023). The impact of applying challenge-based gamification program on students' learning outcomes: Academic achievement, motivation and flow. *Education and Information Technologies*, *28*(8), 1–26. doi:10.1007/s10639-023-11585-z PMID:36691635

Kristiani, T., & Usodo, B. (2022). Exploration of the use of quizizz gamification application: Teacher perspective. *International Journal of Elementary Education*, *6*(2). doi:10.23887/ijee.v6i2.43481

Kusuma, G. P., Wigati, E. K., Utomo, Y., & Suryapranata, L. K. P. (2018). Analysis of gamification models in education using MDA framework. *Procedia Computer Science*, *135*, 385–392. doi:10.1016/j.procs.2018.08.187

Lampropoulos, G., Keramopoulos, E., Diamantaras, K., & Evangelidis, G. (2022). Augmented Reality and Gamification in Education: A Systematic Literature Review of Research, Applications, and Empirical Studies. *Applied Sciences (Basel, Switzerland)*, *12*(13), 6809. doi:10.3390/app12136809

López Carrillo, D., Calonge García, A., Rodríguez Laguna, T., Ros Magán, G., & Lebrón Moreno, J. A. (2019). Using gamification in a teaching innovation project at the university of alcalá: A new approach to experimental science practices. *Electronic Journal of e-Learning, 17*(2), 93–106. doi:10.34190/JEL.17.2.03

Mangla, A. S., Bhatia, M., Bhatia, S., & Kumar, P. (2022). Current State of Engineering Education in India: Student Teacher Scenario in Online Mode. Rising Threats in Expert Applications and Solutions. *Lecture Notes in Networks and Systems, 434*, 465–476. doi:10.1007/978-981-19-1122-4_49

Marinensi, G., Di Lallo, M., & Botte, B. (2023). Gamification as a strategy to increase student engagement in Higher Education: exploring teachers' perspective. In S. Capogna, G. Makrides, & V. Stylianakis (Eds.), *The European Higher Education Area facing the Digital Challenge.*

Martí-Parreño, J., Seguí-Mas, D., & Seguí-Mas, E. (2016). Teachers' attitude towards and actual use of gamification. *Procedia: Social and Behavioral Sciences, 228*, 682–688. doi:10.1016/j.sbspro.2016.07.104

Martín-Sómer, M., Moreira, J., Cintia Casado. (2021). *Use of kahoot! to keep students' motivation during online classes in the lockdown period caused by covid 19, education for chemical engineers.* IEEE. doi:10.1016/j.ece.2021.05.005

Md. Khambari, M. N. (2019). Instilling innovativeness, building character, and enforcing camaraderie through interest-driven challenge-based learning approach. *Research and Practice in Technology Enhanced Learning, 14*(1), 19. doi:10.1186/s41039-019-0115-2

Mohamad, S. N. M., Sazali, N. S. S., & Salleh, M. A. M. (2018). Gamification approach in education to increase learning engagement. *International Journal of Humanities. Arts and Social Sciences, 4*(1), 22–32. doi:10.20469/ijhss.4.10003-1

Montiel-Ruiz, F. J., & Solano-Fernández, I. M. (2023). Social networks and gamification in physical education: A case study. *Contemporary Educational Technology, 15*(1), ep401. doi:10.30935/cedtech/12660

Moseikina, M., Toktamysov, S., & Danshina, S. (2022). Modern technologies and gamification in historical education. *Simulation & Gaming, 53*(2), 135–156. doi:10.1177/10468781221075965

Nieto-Escamez, F. A., & Roldán-Tapia, M. D. (2021). Gamification as online teaching strategy during COVID-19: A mini-review. *Frontiers in Psychology, 12*, 648552. doi:10.3389/fpsyg.2021.648552 PMID:34093334

Nousiainen, T., Kangas, M., Rikala, J., & Vesisenaho, M. (2018). Teacher competencies in game- based pedagogy. *Teaching and Teacher Education, 74*, 85–97. doi:10.1016/j.tate.2018.04.012

Oliveira, W., Hamari, J., Shi, L., Toda, A. M., Rodrigues, L., Palomino, P. T., & Isotani, S. (2022). Tailored gamification in education: A literature review and future agenda. *Education and Information Technologies, 28*(1), 373–406. doi:10.1007/s10639-022-11122-4

Ortiz-Rojas, M., Chiluiza, K., & Valcke, M. (2019). Gamification through leaderboards: An empirical study in engineering education. *Computer Applications in Engineering Education, 27*(4), 777–788. doi:10.1002/cae.12116

Osipovskaya, E., & Miakotnikova, S. (2020). Using gamification in teaching public relations students. Auer, M., Tsiatsos, T. (eds) the challenges of the digital t ransformation in education. icl 2018. Advances in Intelligent Systems and Computing, (vol 916). Springer, Cham. doi:10.1007/978-3-030-11932-4_64

Özdener, N. (2018). Gamification for enhancing Web 2.0 based educational activities: The case of pre-service grade school teachers using educational Wiki pages. *Telematics and Informatics, 35*(3), 564–578. doi:10.1016/j.tele.2017.04.003

Pektaş, M., & Kepceoğlu, İ. (2019). What do prospective teachers think about educational gamification? *Science education international, 30*(1). doi:10.33828/sei.v30.i1.8

Petrovych, O., Zavalniuk, I., Bohatko, V., Poliarush, N., & Petrovych, S. (2023). Motivational readiness of future teachers-philologists to use the gamification with elements of augmented reality in education. *International Journal of Emerging Technologies in Learning, 18*(3), 4–21. doi:10.3991/ijet.v18i03.36017

Putz, L. M., Hofbauer, F., & Treiblmaier, H. (2020). Can gamification help to improve education? Findings from a longitudinal study. *Computers in Human Behavior, 110*, 106392. doi:10.1016/j.chb.2020.106392

Qiao, S., Yeung, S., Zainuddin, Z., Ng, D. T. K., & Chu, S. K. W. (2023). Examining the effects of mixed and non-digital gamification on students' learning performance, cognitive engagement and course satisfaction. *British Journal of Educational Technology, 54*(1), 394–413. doi:10.1111/bjet.13249

Quast, K. (2020). Gamification, foreign language teaching and teacher education. *Revista Brasileira de Lingüística Aplicada, 20*, 787–820. doi:10.1590/1984-6398202016398

Ramírez-Donoso, L., Pérez-Sanagustín, M., Neyem, A., Alario-Hoyos, C., Hilliger, I., & Rojos, F. (2023). Fostering the use of online learning resources: Results of using a mobile collaboration tool based on gamification in a blended course. *Interactive Learning Environments, 31*(3), 1564–1578. doi:10.1080/10494820.2020.1855202

Reyes, E., Gálvez, J. C., & Enfedaque, A. (2021). Learning course: Application of gamification in teaching construction and building materials subjects. *Education Sciences, 11*(6), 287. doi:10.3390/educsci11060287

Ryan, R. M., & Deci, E. L. (2000). Self-Determination Theory and the Facilitation of Intrinsic Motivation, Social Development, and Well-Being. *The American Psychologist, 55*(1), 68–78. doi:10.1037/0003-066X.55.1.68 PMID:11392867

Sailer, M., & Homner, L. (2020). The gamification of learning: A meta-analysis. *Educational Psychology Review, 32*(1), 77–112. doi:10.1007/s10648-019-09498-w

Sajinčič, N., Sandak, A., & Istenič, A. (2022). Pre-service and in-service teachers' views on gamification. *International Journal of Emerging Technologies in Learning (IJET), 17*(3). doi:10.3991/ijet.v17i03.26761

Saleem, A. N., Noori, N. M., & Ozdamli, F. (2022). Gamification applications in e-learning: A literature review. *Tech Know Learn, 27*(1), 139–159. doi:10.1007/s10758-020-09487-x

Saleem, A. N., Noori, N. M., & Ozdamli, F. (2022). Gamification applications in e-learning: A literature review. *Tech Know Learn, 27*(1), 139–159. doi:10.1007/s10758-020-09487-x

Sánchez-Mena, A., & Martí-Parreño, J. (2017). Drivers and barriers to adopting gamification: Teachers' perspectives. *Electronic Journal of e-Learning, 15*(5), 434–443. https://eric.ed.gov/?id=EJ1157970

Santos-Villalba, M. J., Olivencia, J. J. L., Navas-Parejo, M. R., & Benítez-Márquez, M. D. (2020). Higher education students' assessments towards gamification and sustainability: A case study. *Sustainability (Basel), 12*(20), 1–20. doi:10.3390/su12208513

Schnitzler, K., Holzberger, D., & Seidel, T. (2020). All better than being disengaged: Student engagement patterns and their relations to academic self-concept and achievement. *European Journal of Psychology of Education.* doi:10.1007/s10212-020-00500-6

Semartiana, N., Putri, A., & Rosmansyah, Y. (2022). A systematic literature review of gamification for children: game elements, purposes, and technologies. In *International Conference on Information Science and Technology Innovation (ICoSTEC)* (Vol. 1, No. 1, pp. 72-76). IEEE. 10.35842/icostec.v1i1.12

Siemon, D., & Eckardt, L. (2017). Gamification of teaching in higher education. In S. Stieglitz, C. Lattemann, S. Robra-Bissantz, R. Zarnekow, & T. Brockmann (Eds.), *Gamification. Progress in IS*. Springer. doi:10.1007/978-3-319-45557-0_11

Skinner, B. F. (1971). Operant conditioning. *The encyclopedia of education, 7*, 29-33.

Stott, A., & Neustaedter, C. (2013). Analysis of gamification in education. *Surrey, BC, Canada, 8*(1), 36. http://clab.iat.sfu.ca/pubs/Stott-Gamification.pdf

Toda, A. M., Klock, A. C. T., Oliveira, W., Palomino, P. T., Rodrigues, L., Shi, L., Bittencourt, I., Gasparini, I., Isotani, S., & Cristea, A. I. (2019). Analysing gamification elements in educational environments using an existing gamification taxonomy. *Smart Learn. Environ., 6*(1), 16. doi:10.1186/s40561-019-0106-1

Wang, Y. H. (2023). Can gamification assist learning? A study to design and explore the uses of educational music games for adults and young learners. *Journal of Educational Computing Research, 60*(8), 2015–2035. doi:10.1177/07356331221098148

Wu, M. L., Zhou, Y., & Li, L. (2023). The effects of a gamified online course on pre-service teachers' confidence, intention, and motivation in integrating technology into teaching. *Education and Information Technologies, 28*(10), 12903–12918. doi:10.1007/s10639-023-11727-3 PMID:37361757

Xi, N., & Hamari, J. (2019). Does gamification satisfy needs? A study on the relationship between gamification features and intrinsic need satisfaction. *International Journal of Information Management, 46*, 210–221. doi:10.1016/j.ijinfomgt.2018.12.002

Yildirim, I. (2017). The effects of gamification-based teaching practices on student achievement and students' attitudes toward lessons. *The Internet and Higher Education, 33*, 86–92. doi:10.1016/j.iheduc.2017.02.002

Yildiz, İ., Topçu, E., & Kaymakci, S. (2021). The effect of gamification on motivation in the education of pre-service social studies teachers. *Thinking Skills and Creativity, 42*, 100907. doi:10.1016/j.tsc.2021.100907

Zainuddin, Z., Chu, S. K. W., Shujahat, M., & Perera, C. J. (2020). The impact of gamification on learning and instruction: A systematic review of empirical evidence. *Educational Research Review, 30*, 100326. doi:10.1016/j.edurev.2020.100326

Zourmpakis, A. I., Kalogiannakis, M., & Papadakis, S. (2023). Adaptive gamification in science education: An analysis of the impact of implementation and adapted game elements on students' motivation. *Computers*, *12*(7), 143. doi:10.3390/computers12070143

Zourmpakis, A. I., Papadakis, S., & Kalogiannakis, M. (2022). Education of preschool and elementary teachers on the use of adaptive gamification in science education. *International Journal of Technology Enhanced Learning*, *14*(1), 1–16. doi:10.1504/IJTEL.2022.120556

KEY TERMS AND DEFINITIONS

Gamification: The practice of incorporating game like features into non -gaming contexts to promote engagement.

Teacher educator: Anyone who works in colleges or universities and is professionally involved in the preliminary and continuing education of future teachers.

Trainee Teacher: A student engaged in a teacher preparation program who, in order to receive a teaching license, must satisfactorily fulfil degree requirements, including coursework and field experience.

Chapter 8

Gamification in an EFL Classroom and the Use of Games for Learning English:
Spanish Technical Engineering Degree

Isabel María García Conesa
iD https://orcid.org/0000-0001-7005-2509
Centro Universitario de la Defensa de San Javier, Spain

ABSTRACT

In recent years, the use of ICTs has increased in the education field and many different types of contents have been created. One of them are educational games. However, very little research has been done to date if games are as effective as they try to be. The aim of this study was to collect information related to ICTs and games in relation to L2 learning in a technical engineering degree and create some questionnaires which would be analysed and compared with the data previously mentioned. Results show how little teachers know of the methodological applications of ICTs and videogames, the benefits that they can provide to the bilingual classroom, such as how students who use games usually have a generally positive view of English learning. These results suggest that information and professional preparation regarding ICTs and games have not been shared and are not mandatory, which leads to the incorrect and insufficient use of the resources. What we are using currently it will become obsolete and new methodologies will have to be created in consequence

DOI: 10.4018/979-8-3693-2169-0.ch008

Copyright © 2024, IGI Global. Copying or distributing in print or electronic forms without written permission of IGI Global is prohibited.

INTRODUCTION

This study will investigate the use of games in an engineering classroom, the different types that are currently available, to show whether those games could be used to learn or reinforce a new language, and if they are truly effective. Current times require current actions, and teaching needs to be updated. There have been several improvements in the last few decades that allow students to participate in their learning and, most recently, in the use of Information and Communication Technologies (ICTs hereafter) inside the classroom.

This brings new opportunities to teachers, as this technology grants them the opportunity to teach a subject in a more interactive manner that will catch students' attention and make their learning more meaningful. The digital transformation of society requires education professionals to develop dynamic actions that favour digital development in future generations through innovative and active methodologies that address the changing pace of learning technologies.

Games have been used inside the classroom for a long time to reinforce content or to introduce a new topic, as they are entertaining for students. With the introduction of ICTs, the quality and quantity of games that can be brought to the class have increased. There are a lot of games and resources that can be found on the Internet for different topics, but are all of them useful? Which are effective, and where can one find them? What is the difference between game-based learning and gamification? This chapter attempts to address these questions.

Digital games have been identified as having the potential to enhance language learning (Párraga et al., 2022), because they offer the possibility of representing virtual worlds and presenting objects and scenes in a multimedia context. However, for learners who find it difficult to move into such contexts, game-based learning is a beneficial alternative that allows them to meaningfully integrate the knowledge and skills needed to learn a second language. Digital games can simulate concrete learning contexts and examples, where acquired second language knowledge and skills can be applied in a technology-mediated situation.

The main objective of this chapter is to demonstrate whether game-based learning would improve students' learning and motivation in the Technical English subject, as current classrooms possess materials to allow this type of learning. These materials include tablets, smartboards, computers, and Internet connections. The secondary objectives are to study the gamification process and its application inside the classroom using different tools, and to show the knowledge that teachers have of ICTs and their uses inside the class.

THEORETICAL FRAMEWORK

In the current era, everything is constantly changing, from basic things such as transportation to how we can communicate, thanks to the use of technology. Each day is different from the previous day and affects society. Teaching methods must be constantly updated to avoid becoming obsolete. Traditional classes where the teacher only gives information, and the students copy it, are not the only way students can learn. They can also benefit from other tools, such as audios, videos, and games, owing to the possibility that ICTs bring.

This section will focus on different literature based on games and technology (ICTs) that are used in the classroom, their advantages, and disadvantages, how they can affect a lesson, their motivational factors, and the difference between game-based learning and gamification.

ICTs

ICTs are abbreviations for Information and Communication Technologies. ICTs have played an important role in the field of education since the 1980s. The use of these tools began in the 1980s in countries such as the United States, Mexico, England, and France, and constitutes an important innovative function in higher education.

Although George (2021) stated that ICTs were all media that arose as a result of the development of microelectronics, fundamentally video, computer, and telecommunications systems, they can range from simple calculators to the latest generation of computers, peripherals, multimedia resources, cameras, audio, and visual devices.

Álvarez and González (2022) mentioned that ICTs are a fundamental part of our daily lives and have made them easier. They allow the acquisition of information in an easy and fast manner where neither books nor specialised libraries are needed to obtain what the user needs. It also allows for faster communication between distant places, creating a more connected world.

Bottino (2020) indicated that ICTs are technological instruments that focus on information and discovery. The main characteristics of ICTs are immateriality, interactivity, the ability to interconnect, the quality of the information found there (including photographs and audios), constant innovation, speed, and diversity.

Moreira and Cedeño (2023) shared the same opinion in relation to ICTs, a more actualized opinion compared to previous ones. These include hypertext, multimedia, virtual reality, the Internet, and satellite television. They also mentioned how, thanks to the new technology, ICT allows users to express themselves in different ways, such as visually or auditorily, and not only in written form (López & González, 2021).

Venegas and Proaño (2021) mentioned how teachers' roles in the classroom change with the integration of ICTs. Now, the student is the protagonist in the class, while the teacher provides the best resources and conditions for the student to learn through their own means. The teacher shows the students how to use ICTs so that they can learn at their own rhythm, investigate, and create new knowledge to which they can relate. However, the current classroom is not as perfect, as previously mentioned. As Salado et al. (2019) alluded to, our current schools and education laws are more prepared to face 20th century rather than 21st century problems. Moreover, there is not enough data to prove whether they are truly efficient or just a support inside the class as teachers continue teaching with the same methods as in the last century, where the teacher imparts knowledge while the students absorb it (Poveda & Cifuentes, 2020).

When ICTs were introduced in universities, to constitute additional means that favour a better teaching and learning process, different denominations appeared to qualify the learning environments with this quality (Contreras et al., 2022). Hypermedia environments strengthened teaching tasks and enriched them personally by providing them with practical knowledge; for students, on the one hand, it facilitates individual work and, on the other, team and group work, which is highly necessary; in the student-content relationship, the use of computer tools helps with the understanding and assessment of content; in terms of content, it strengthens it because new resources are incorporated into it; between teacher-content, it facilitates their work and its transmission (George, 2020).

Parallel teacher training is, therefore, necessary, which should focus on the acquisition of competencies that allow for the full integration of ICT resources into their teaching processes, which is in line with the contextual needs of their reality. The teaching and learning processes in ICT-influenced environments must seek the realisation of general and specific competencies that build meaningful learning for education and life (George, 2021).

These new strategic forms of innovation loaded with ICT resources should include good teaching practices that can be implemented in the classroom. For this purpose, the four principles of good teaching practices proposed by Contreras et al. (2022) provide a good basis:

- Computers do not generate improvements in teaching and learning; however, the planned didactic dynamic is crucial.
- ICTs should be used for the organisation and development of learning processes of a socio-constructivist nature, extracting the message of learning through problematic activities and collaborative work, and seeking the reconstruction of meanings.

- Computer technology, unlike print or audio-visual media, allows for the manipulation, storage, distribution, and retrieval of large volumes of information easily and quickly, such as digital literacy, which can be interpreted as hypermedia or hypertext.
- Digital technologies are powerful resources for communication between subjects, students and teachers, who are geographically distant or do not coincide in time. ICTs make it possible to work collaboratively and within the framework of all the other strategies mentioned above, without any kind of spatial or temporal barriers.

According to Araya and Majano (2022), there are several advantages to ICTs use in higher education:

- It enables learning anytime, anywhere. This characteristic, known as ubiquity, is the ability to conduct a large number of activities, turning any place into a potential learning environment, as long as there is an Internet connection and appropriate application.
- This provides space for a greater number of synchronous and asynchronous interactions. Thus, through an application that allows conversations and live or pre-recorded conferences, spaces for teacher-student exchanges are promoted that go beyond the classroom. In addition, the student has the possibility of interacting, in the same way, with his or her classmates at the time he or she considers appropriate for this purpose.
- This enhances student-centred learning. According to the characteristics of the learners, they can progress as their understanding of the concepts increases. Moreover, they control the use of the application and, therefore, their progress. This is undoubtedly one of the main advantages over traditional education.
- This favours collaborative learning. Collaboration can be formally understood as part of the training methodology; however, it can also be part of the work culture of students and teachers. Mobile applications facilitate the creation of groups in social networks, collaborative blogs, and shared documents.
- This allows for immediate evaluation of educational content. As the student completes the proposed tasks, the teacher has the facility to correct, using the same application, when it is a questionnaire-type assessment, or can correct the work done by the student.
- The time spent in the classroom was productively used. By improving interaction with the teacher, classroom time is put to good use. The student, in a certain way, has the need to study, and when the class is given, there is

a greater possibility that he/she will have doubts, and so the improvement in teaching would be evident.

- Support for learners with disabilities. Undoubtedly, inclusion is one of the tasks that becomes a priority for formal education, in order to guarantee equal rights as stipulated in the Universal Declaration of Human Rights, and mobile applications become a true ally in this aspect because of the aforementioned ease of promoting individual learning.

However, according to Del Padre et al. (2022), there are some disadvantages that are interesting to analyse:

- The cost of mobile device applications often makes it difficult for students to access them. Owing to the speed at which technology advances, purchased equipment often becomes obsolete in a short time. Certain applications or operating systems that, although it is true that they are usually acquired free of charge, sometimes the cost of using the platform must be borne either by the student or by higher education institutions.
- It should also be borne in mind that it an Internet connection is indispensable for accessing the applications, so this involves an additional cost at the time of additional cost at the time of use. Therefore, and in a variable way, it is important to consider applications that do not have very high requirements to adapt to students' possibilities.
- Other limitations include the physical characteristics of mobile devices. Mobile devices are restricted in terms of screen size, processing power, and power availability, which often affects access to the information available in the application and can lead to difficulties in the learning process for students.

ICTs are still used as support instead of innovating and using them inside the class as a main resource. One of the things necessary for this to change is the way of teaching, the pedagogy used in the centres. It is outdated, with a focus on the materials in the book (Padilla & Ayala, 2021). To efficiently apply ICTs, a study of the social and cultural framework is needed, together with the organisational framework of the place where it is going to be implemented. According to Pardo et al. (2021), teachers need to change their methodology and start mixing new content with ICTs, encouraging participation, and collaborating with each other or even between schools.

The Use of Videogames to Teach English

The development of technology in the 21st century has revolutionised people's lives in all aspects and areas. Some of the keys to this digital revolution are the development of mobile devices with the same working capacity as computers, remote Internet connection services, and the emerging software industry in the form of computer programmes, including video games. Currently, more opportunities are gradually becoming available globally to turn videogames into teaching and learning tools for issues related to peace, sustainability, culture, social issues, gender, education, and global citizenship (Barrera & Morales, 2023).

Although videogames have been in use since before the 1980s, it was at this time that two major companies broke into the console world: Nintendo and Sega. Subsequently, Sony and Microsoft joined the two market leaders and continue to develop the market to the present day. It has also been shown that many videogames, whose initial purpose was purely recreational, have served to educate players in many areas of knowledge. These areas include history, geography, mathematics, physics, music, and language. In the field of language teaching, we find several authors who have written about the benefits of using conventional or commercial videogames. Some examples are Chen et al. (2021), Casañ et al. (2022), or Briones et al. (2023), to mention just a few.

Videogames can facilitate language learning, whether through the narration of the story, the dialogues between characters, game instructions, or chats - by written message or by voice - that allows communication between players from different parts of the world. However, it is possible to deal with almost any subject using video games. Educational video games serve to diversify classroom teaching and make learning more enjoyable for students, according to Gómez and Urraco (2022).

With regard to foreign language teaching-learning processes, Donoso et al. (2023) understood that success depends on a good pedagogical model, which should be based on the principles of active, collaborative, and autonomous learning, varied interactivity options, synchronous and asynchronous communication, relevant and creative activities or tasks, and continuous assessment and feedback.

It is worth noting that in recent years, the offer of educational videogames, which are presented as purchasing alternatives to violent videogames, has increased significantly. One of the offerings of these educational games is the musical games of chance, logic, adventure, interactivity and strategy. Videogames can facilitate language learning through subtitles, stories, narrations, music soundtracks in English, written messages, and voices. To test their effectiveness, Garay and Ávila (2021) analysed different tools for learning English through videogames, breaking down both their advantages and disadvantages:

The advantages are as follows: video games are new tools for learning a new language while learners play; audiovisual activities are more practical for some learners while learning and playing; students invest extra time outside of school to play games including learning other languages; students get even more subconscious learning from learning a second language; free choice of second language to learn in a video game; second language learning in video games is unconscious.

Among the disadvantages, we can include the following: high levels of distraction; excessive hours of investment in video games; video games with no or little second language dialogue; gameplay with no linguistic and cultural input; low ability of learners to understand a second language without subtitles; free choice of language of video games to be implemented in their native language; gamers do not always choose a foreign language; discomfort when playing the game.

In reference to research on videogames and language teaching, it is unquestionable that there is currently a need to assess the influence of videogame use on learners in their teaching and learning processes. In this sense, Casañ (2017) compiled several studies conducted in the field of education that have assessed the learning and acquisition of foreign languages focusing on communicative skills and/or grammar and vocabulary as well as the acquisition of non-linguistic content, or the influence of the motivation to learn by playing video games.

Table 1. Examples of videogames to develop different skills in foreign language learning

Skill	Videogames
Oral comprehension	The Conference Interpreter
	Lyrics Training
Oral expression	Second Life
	Minecraft
Written comprehension	Neverwinter Nights
	Rayman Raving Rabbids
Written expression	The Mad City Mystery
	Uncharted 2: Among Thieves
Vocabulary and Grammar	Pokemon Go
	Parappa the Rapper 2
Non-linguistic contents	Tactical Levantine Arabic
	Robotic Surgery
Motivation	Ever Quest 2
	Club Penguin

Note. Own elaboration from Casañ (2017, p. 29)

Game-Based Learning

Following the definition given by Al-Karawi (2020, p. 15), game-based learning is "borrowing certain gaming principles and applying them to real-life settings to engage users". This means using different aspects such as live points, ability points, menu options, competition, etc., in the classroom to help students improve.

Figure 1. Model of game-based learning
Note. Belda & Calvo (2022, p. 8)

Chen et al. (2021) mentioned that 2003 was the year when game-based learning started to arise as it was an era of new discoveries, where the Internet started having an increased impact on research on new information and social media, such as Facebook, which started in that year. It was also the year that the term "*digital native*" began to be used.

Games can be used as constructivist tools because knowledge is fully created and elaborated through practical social experiences, using previous knowledge to develop new knowledge (Ghazy et al., 2021). However, it is up to the teacher to create favourable experiences that are best linked to the way their students learn and not to collect content created without considering the characteristics of the students.

Foreign language learning has become an increasingly prominent issue. Given its importance, it is an area in which many researchers are working to find more effective and motivating ways of teaching learners (Rodríguez et al., 2020). Technology combined with these pedagogical innovations can help make language teaching more effective and reach more people through a more accessible and motivating process.

One possible method to achieve this is to use games. The act of playing and providing pleasure is a means of developing reasoning and cognitive skills by stimulating attention (Silalahi, 2019). Games act as resources capable of motivating people and are presented as efficient alternatives in the process of knowledge generation. in the knowledge generation (Vélez et al., 2020).

Donoso et al. (2023) listed several characteristics that digital natives have while learning: they get unlimited information at the same time very quickly; they can perform several tasks at the same time in a parallel manner; they learn in a dynamic and active way; they work with ICTs constantly; they can access new information whenever and wherever they want randomly and instantaneously; they receive immediate feedback on how they do something; and they are constantly interacting with others using social networks.

This type of student needs interactive and dynamic learning so that they remain focused and interested in new content and can create meaningful information for themselves. If not, they become bored easily, and it is harder for them to focus on the lesson. Dimitra et al. (2023) compiled the different types of games used for learning:

- **Motivational Games** engage students and motivate them to learn new content. This type of game requires an essential aspect, that is, the fun element that videogames provide, which helps students maintain their interest in what they are learning. It also helps motivate them, as it can integrate aspects such as competition and the capacity to learn individually in their classes.
- **Drill and Practice Games** use repetition to practice certain topics or to reinforce something. They are usually used after the theory is given by the teacher, so drill and practice games can be considered an add-on to traditional books.
- **Content Mastery Games** help students master the information that they already have. It can be done with the help of simulations with game features. They propose a challenge to the students, where they must apply their knowledge to solve problems in an interesting and interactive way.
- **21st Century Competency Games** are those that unlike drill and practice games, are focused on HOTS and social skills, integrating collaboration between students in their games. These situate players in an authentic context with genuine problems, which helps the student create a meaningful idea of the abstract skills they are trying to improve.
- **Scavenger Hunts** are games in which students must fulfil the required task on a topic given by the teacher. It is like the table game "Trivia" where the player must answer several questions, but in this case related to a topic. This type of game-based learning also encourages cooperative work, as students can help each other with their questions.

The practice of a game in class must be of quality, as it attracts the interest of the learner to the elements of the work. To check that a game is well designed,

González and Álvarez (2022) proposed a number of ideas and features that can be adapted to 21st century games.

- Interactive problem solving. That is, encouraging interaction between the player and the medium used, in this case, between the game and user.
- Specific goals and rules. All games should have a goal that serves as the final objective, as well as a set of rules to avoid possible shortcuts.
- Adaptive challenges. This point focuses on sequencing tasks, from simpler to more complex ones. This ensures that learners are not frustrated and can perform more advanced tasks with great success.
- Control. The management of any kind of digital game requires control of the game, so that it can be modified according to the interests of the players.
- Instant feedback. The use of digital games promotes immediate feedback, as learners will naturally be able to predict whether they have succeeded or are making mistakes.
- Uncertainty. A game must contain elements of surprise for the player because the player must be constantly surprised by the tasks to be developed.
- Stimulating symptoms. This feature is fully implemented in digital games, as these resources are covered with "live" elements such as audios or animated images that stimulate both the player's emotions and meaningful learning.

According to Johnson et al., game-based learning methodology is "an innovative methodology that takes advantage of the educational potential offered by games in general and serious games in particular to boost training processes, thus making it easier for users to achieve motivated learning" (2020, p. 891). In other words, it is a methodology that takes advantage of the potential offered by games and serious games to enhance teaching and promote learning in a more motivating way (Roca & Véliz, 2022).

Game-based language learning methodology facilitates language acquisition because of intrinsic motivation, abundant textual input, and the interactive and immersive experience offered by games, which encourages learners to have a positive attitude, engage in meaningful language use, increase interactions, and reduce anxiety. It also promotes the acquisition of new terms and forms of language through the development of mind maps in which learners associate symbols, references, and referents (Masadeh, 2022).

The nature of this methodology means that learning is learner-centred, which facilitates the transfer of linguistic constructs to other contexts. According to Ortega and Vásquez (2021), the transfer of knowledge, skills, and attitudes from games to both school and real-life activities is vital for effective teaching through games.

Furthermore, the development of autonomy in language learning is crucial, and games facilitate this, as learners control their learning.

Gamification

Gamification started gaining popularity around 2010, when big companies such as Microsoft started creating game elements in their software and were successful (Alonso et al., 2021). One educational approach that promises effectiveness and innovation in the classroom is gamification. Gamification in education is an innovative methodology that uses the elements and mechanics of games to enhance student learning, creating a motivating and participatory environment to promote the development of skills, such as problem solving, decision making, and teamwork, offering a creative and effective way to engage students (Santos, 2023).

In the classroom, gamification is a pedagogical strategy that uses game elements to motivate students in the learning process. By integrating elements, such as challenges, rewards, and levels, it creates a playful and participatory environment that fosters collaboration, healthy competition, and enthusiasm for knowledge acquisition. According to Pérez & Gertrudis, "gamification in the classroom favours the development of different areas of the individual, encourages discovery, the acquisition of content, the development of skills, abilities and competences, social interaction, the expression of emotions, and the desire to learn" (2021, p 221).

Gamification is an effective educational tool that combines elements of gamification and motivation to foster learning and teamwork in the classroom. By implementing gamified strategies, students are immersed in fun and challenging experiences that motivate them to actively participate in their learning process. By facing challenges, solving problems, and achieving goals, students develop key skills, such as problem solving, decision making, and team collaboration (Zhan et al., 2022).

Parra González et al. described the most relevant findings obtained in their research, among which they highlight that "students mostly feel involved during the teaching-learning process; this is an essential element for learning, since when students are active, they become the main protagonists who construct their own learning, the results also indicate that participants have increased their levels of activation when they are immersed in the development of the experience, and no significant differences were found across the board" (2020, p. 287).

Caraballo (2023, p. 1824) defined gamification as a "discipline in which the main objective is to analyse the components that make videogames entertaining as they are and applying them to other places not related to games, such as colleges". This definition can change but the main components of gamification are "using game-based mechanics, aesthetics and game thinking to engage people, motivate action, promote learning and solve problems" (Cerezo, 2021, p. 276).

Nowadays, there is a generational gap between students and teachers, as students are those known as "digital natives" while the teachers are not. These new students have different experiences from those their teachers might have from their past, as they have been born with technology. They require different pedagogy because they have different learning styles, and those previously used are not sufficient to maintain their motivation (Infante, 2023).

The main difference between game-based learning and gamification is that gamification is "a system in which learners, players, consumers, and employees engage in an abstract challenge defined by rules, interactivity, and feedback that results in a quantifiable outcome ideally eliciting an emotional reaction" (Kim & Castelli, 2021, p. 9) whereas game-based learning is when games are used or created fully to review or teach new content. Gamification can be used in any place that considers it correct, such as programs, classes, or companies, whereas game-based learning is used exclusively in the classroom.

Gamification has proven to be an effective strategy for teaching and learning English. Integrating game elements into the educational process captures the attention and interests of students, encouraging their motivation and active participation. By using games, challenges, and rewards, students can practice and improve their language skills in a fun and playful manner. Solis and Marquina (2022) stated that their results were positive, demonstrating its usefulness in learning English as a foreign language.

According to García et al. (2019), through the design and implementation of an intervention programme based on gamification, they generated significant improvements in English language learning while increasing students' motivation towards this subject. Therefore, they concluded that the use of gamification as a learning tool stands out because of its ability to increase motivation and improve students' language proficiency.

Similarly, Molina et al. stated that "gamification has become a valuable tool to implement game-based teaching strategies to create favourable environments for the educational process to be carried out effectively and thus achieve the development of language skills, so necessary for the mastery of English" (2021, p. 729). This means that gamification is an effective strategy that promotes the mastery of English language skills and enhances learning through play.

Gamified educational applications have also been applied in non-academic areas such as language teaching (Duolingo has 300 million active users) and software usage (Microsoft's Ribbon Hero). Other popular gamified applications include Kahoot and Quizizz, which can be easily set up and used in various subjects, bringing game elements into the classroom without any special effort (García & Rodríguez, 2022). Although gamification has an important role in education, both inside and outside higher education institutions, there is still little effective guidance on how to combine different gamification features to improve learning performance in different educational contexts (Caravaca & Sáez, 2021).

METHODOLOGY

Type of Investigation

This investigation will have an argumentative nature, where the author will collect data from other authors and use that information to create their own materials and analyse them to compare them with the previous data collected. There has been an investigation using documents, books, and articles from different authors, based on the topic of gamification, students' motivation, and the use of ICTs inside the classroom. These data will then be used as the theoretical foundation for the hypothesis discussed in this chapter.

To verify whether the teachers know the advantages and disadvantages of the use of ICTs inside the classroom and to confirm whether the use of gamification increases students' motivation, a questionnaire will be created and given to several teachers currently working at the technical university. Some of them used gamification in their classes, whereas others did not.

Hypothesis

This investigation aimed to prove that gamification as a learning tool for English is currently useful and its effects on students and teachers. These must not only prepare the subject materials, but also understand and use the ICTs correctly and know which games are more beneficial for what they want to achieve in class. It will also prove whether students' motivation increases when using a more interactive method to which they can relate.

This investigation shows whether the gamification method is truly effective or not, not to prove if this method is "perfect" as it can also have some disadvantages. We present a different method in which technical engineering students can learn English using games as a motivational tool and show the advantages and disadvantages of this method.

Participants

The participants in the questionnaire were divided into two groups: teachers and students. In the teacher party, a total of five teachers working in the technical university centre completed the questionnaire. Four of them were men between the ages of 35 and 45 years, while the last teacher was a 40-year-old woman. One of them was the youngest, only 35 years old, and had one-year experience, while the others were 37, 42, and 45 years old. The one with the most experience was the oldest, with nearly twenty years of teaching technical students, followed by the 37-year-old one with six years of experience, and finally the youngest with only one.

Different technical engineering classrooms were chosen for the students. There were 125 students in different classrooms with an average English level, two of whom had special needs. One of them had dyslexia, whereas the other had trouble learning; therefore, the content was adapted. Due to the situation we were in (Covid-19), the data collected from them might not be the most accurate, but it will be considered when analysing the data.

Instruments Used

The tools used to collect the data previously mentioned were:

- Questionnaire on ICT knowledge for teachers. In this questionnaire, the teacher had to answer several questions on a Likert scale ranging from 1 (disagree) to 5 (totally agree) about their knowledge of ICTs, going from basics like searching for something on the Internet, to creating their own materials using several programs.
- Questionnaire on gamification knowledge for teachers. In this questionnaire, they had to answer several questions, grading them again from 1 (nothing) to 5 (a lot) regarding their knowledge of the gamification method. They also had to write their answers to questions about where they were asked if they would implement it and how.
- Questionnaire to students about games, what kind of games they usually use in class, and which ones they think are better. Similar to the previous ones, they were given several questions and had to write their answers.

Data Analysis

The questionnaires were analysed in Microsoft Excel, a statistical data processing software offered by Microsoft. The procedure followed was to prepare an Excel spreadsheet, enter the data from each teacher, and then statistically process the data using the JASP statistical software to analyse the inferential data obtained from the interviews.

For this purpose, we used the Kolmogorov-Smirnov and the Ryan Joiner normality tests. The calculated Kolmogorov-Smirnov value was 0.1774, whereas the Kolmogorov-Smirnov table value was 0.2734, with a p-value of 0.2538. These data were corroborated using the Ryan-Joiner test. With a p-value of 0.3059, the calculated Ryan Joiner value was 1.0023, and the Ryan Joiner table value was 0.9104.

Table 2. Kolmogorov-Smirnov and Ryan-Joiner tests

Value	t-value	p-value	Test
0.1774	0.2734	0.2538	Kolmogorov-Smirnov
1.0023	0.9104	0.3059	Ryan-Joiner

FINDINGS

This chapter aimed to study the gamification process and its applications in the Technical English classroom, its pros and cons, the importance of motivation in the learning process, and teachers' knowledge of ICTs and gamification. In this framework, several topics related to the aforementioned objectives were investigated. Once sufficient knowledge was collected, several tools were created to collect data. These tools were three types of questionnaires, two of which were developed for teachers and the third for students.

In the following section, there is a description of the teachers and students who took the questionnaire, their definitions, and an analysis of the data collected, which will then be compared with the information previously collected, explaining why the results might be similar.

Descriptive Analysis and Main Findings in the ICT Questionnaire

This questionnaire was administered only to teachers. The questionnaire consisted of 20 statements to which participants crossed the number they considered the most correct. One would completely disagree, whereas five would completely agree. The statements used in this questionnaire were centred on the previous knowledge of ICTs, the technical and didactic knowledge of it, the interest and motivation to use it, how the centre uses ICTs, and the overall rating that they would give to it. The main findings of this study are as follows:

- All five teachers heard and used ICTs at some point in their careers.
- They all used ICTs in their classrooms, although one teacher added that they were outdated.

- Three of the five teachers had a great interest in learning more about ICTs and how to implement them in the classroom, while the other two were neutral.
- Three of the five teachers did not have sufficient technical knowledge of ICTs. One of them was not interested in keeping updated, or in adding software or hardware, and was not interested in learning how to. Another was aware of the importance of updating with technology but did not consider it very important. The other three agreed that keeping up to date in technology and how to use it correctly was an essential step in applying ICTs correctly.
- Two teachers commented that the ICT tools proportionated by the university were outdated, and because of that, they were unable to use them to their full extent.
- Overall, all the teachers agreed that ICTs were used to learn a new second language.

Several statements were given similar answers, such as the use of ICTs for L2 learning while others, such as creating new material through programs like H5P, were very dissimilar. Only one of them mentioned that she was fully capable of doing it, while the others were capable but not sure.

A very important topic in this questionnaire was the outdated tools in technical centres. This specific concept appeared previously in the disadvantages of ICTs, as ICT tools such as computers, laptops, smartboards, and tablets are expensive, and technology is constantly upgrading. Therefore, a digital tool that has 5 or more years is outdated and needs an upgrade.

Main Findings in the Gamification Questionnaire

Unlike the previous questionnaire, this was composed of different questions: in the first five, the participants chose the correct answer, the next was to cross the number that they considered applied in each situation, and finally, the participants answered the questions in a precise and short way. The questionnaire was administered to the same teachers as the previous one.

For the data collected with this gamification questionnaire, the author wanted to know the teachers' previous knowledge about gamification and game-based learning, its pedagogical uses, the frequency with which they used game or technology elements, and their opinions in relation to the use of games in a classroom.

Question 1: "Have you heard about the term gamification before? And game-based learning?"

For the first question, most of them chose the second option (four votes), they had heard about it but did not know in depth, while a minority (one vote) had heard and knew about it. Game-based learning is more well-known than gamification, with three choosing the first option and the other two marking the second. This may be because gamification is more recent than game-based learning is.

Question 2: "Would you be able to distinguish both terms?"

Once we address the second question, it is easy to see the data from the previous question reflected in this question. Two of the teachers could not differentiate between the two terms, whereas the other two could but were not certain and only one could easily differentiate between these two terms. The same subject was aware of the two previous terms.

Question 3: "Do you think that the use of games inside the classroom facilitates the L2 learning?"

The third question received mostly positive responses, with three out of five agreeing that games help learn a new language by a lot, and the other two thinking that, yes, it helps but not that much.

Question 4: "What do you think gamification can be used for?

In question four, there was a mix of answers. Only four of the eight answers were chosen by all participants. There was no limit to the number of answers they could choose. One teacher chose every option for the activity. That one would be the correct one because games can be used for everything mentioned. In general, they think that games are significant in promoting critical thinking, feedback, reward effort, and participation because of the motivation they bring to the class. These are the answers that most people would give without knowing much about games and their pedagogical use.

Question 5: "Have you used a game in class recently? If so, how?"

Returning to choosing the best option in question five, all of them have recently used a game in their classroom. Two used it to teach new content, while the other three used it to review and reinforce previous knowledge. This last option is the most commonly used among teachers, as it is easier to find and is an addition to the classroom, not its main point. Giving games a relevant part of the lesson is not something that is commonly used yet; however, with the increase in the use of games in the classroom, this will probably change in the future.

Question 6: "Do you use gamification in your classes?"

Question six shows how one of the teachers used gamification daily in their classes, as they used experience points and other game content daily in their classrooms. This can be an effective way to increase students' motivation without using real-life rewards. It also mentions the problem mentioned earlier, how most of them (three out of five) do not use games to present new content, while the other two use it more than once for each term.

Question 7: "What advantages and disadvantages does gamification have inside the classroom?"

In question 7, the advantages that the five teachers shared were similar to those of activity 4, as they might have been influenced by it. This improves critical thinking and problem solving, rewards effort used in problem solving, encourages participation in class, gives feedback, increases motivation in students, and is fun to use in class. Other advantages that are mentioned are their ability to adapt and how they can allow students with learning difficulties to learn in a different way but were not included in the list as only some teachers mentioned them.

However, this method also has several disadvantages. The disadvantages that they mentioned were time cost (many of them do not have enough free time to prepare games as they need to); need to use ICTs (they consider that ICTs are not completely reliable, and they might fail); distractions (the students may focus more on the game than on the lesson); game addiction (some teachers fear that a constant use of games inside and outside the classroom might cause game addiction to the students).

Question 8: "Do you think gamification can be used daily in class?"

In question 8, the reliability of ICTs returns. Four of the five teachers considered that ICTs in their centres were not reliable enough to focus on the entire lesson around them. The last one, while thinking that they could be and can be used daily in class, admits that on several occasions there were some technology problems that made impossible to use them and had to change the lesson and do "Plan B"

Question 9: "What games do you use or can be used in class?"

Question 9 was also interesting. In this one, the teachers had to write about what kinds of games they knew about or used in their classrooms. Several of these are more commonly known, but others are not easy to see. The games cited were: Kahoot, Class Dojo, Moodle, Socrative, Quizizz, EducaPlay, and Hot Potatoes.

None of them used real games, but educational games were specifically created for classroom use. This makes it easier for the teacher to use, but it can also bring monotony and boredom to the students, as they think it is only another activity in a different format, not a game.

Main Findings in the Questionnaire About Games in Class

A questionnaire was administered to 125 technical engineering degree students. It consists of five questions in which the students developed their answers. It was created in Spanish to facilitate this activity. The questionnaire asked about the degree they were studying. All of them were studying for the same degree at the technical university: 80 students were male while the other 45 were female, a noticeable difference between the two genres, which is not surprising considering the technical nature of the degree.

Question 1: "Do you like videogames? Write down your favourite videogame."

In this question, students had to answer their favourite videogames. All the students answered affirmatively to the first question, they liked videogames, which is usual for students of their age. Currently, there are several different answers for their favourite games, but some appear several times. Those were:

- Fortnite: A shooter game that has been increasing its popularity since its launching day
- Minecraft: A crafting game where you craft objects, fight monsters, and create your own world. It is quite old, so it is surprising that it remains popular among this generation.
- Pokémon: A classic RPG where the player collects monsters called Pokémon and fights with other trainers to strengthen them.
- Among Us: Game online, where the player, together with other players, must discover who the impostor is without dying. The player can be a crewmate or impostor.

Some of the reasons that they gave when asked why those games were interesting are the following: you can play with friends, you love the story in the game, the design of the monster is "cool". As we can see, several of these are what make a game interesting: they are motivating, entertaining, foment group work and have a story that can captivate the audience.

Question 2: "Where do you usually play videogames?"

Most students used computers to play videogames, followed by Play Stations with half of the computer players, then Switch and finally Smartphones. The vast use of computers to play videogames might be due to the reason that almost every house currently has a computer, may that be their parents' or the students', but a great deal of houses has one, which can be used to get information from the news, use social networks, watch a movie, or as mentioned in the beginning, play videogames.

Play Station is the next option because it has a large repertoire of videogames, for children, and for adults, so parents can play with it too as a play station is expensive. Switch and Smartphones are close to each other in terms of the number of users. This might be because the switch has less capacity or it does not have as many interesting games as the previous two options, the same as the smartphone, where the games on it have less quality.

Question 3: "Have you ever played a game in class? If so, which one?"

In question 3, it was easy to see what the general consensus was. Yes, they have recently played games in English. Kahoot was used to reinforce the knowledge provided the lesson and as a cool-down activity. Some students added the score they received, indicating the competitive aspect of the game itself. An educational game was used, which can be adapted to whatever subject or lesson the teacher is trying to do, as they are the ones who created the game.

Question 4: *"Do you like the subject of English? How are classes usually given?"*

This question is important, as it shows the motivation that students had with regard to learning English, which will affect how involved they are in their learning and how much effort they put into overcoming the challenges that the technical degree carries.

The graphic shows how more than half of the classes want to learn and use English; they have intrinsic motivation, while the others choose sometimes, or no extrinsic motivation, depending on how the class is conducted. Fortunately, it seems that this balance favours the affirmative. This might be due to the preparation and work done by the teachers who, with the correct use of scaffolding, resources, and motivation, make a hard lesson easier to understand.

Question 5: "Do you think English lessons would be more interesting of games were used in class?"

This question clashed with the previous one, as they had already been using educational games in the classroom. For this question, the students answered that they had already used them. Some of them would write that it would be cool to use Minecraft.

CONCLUSION

Technological advances have increased in the last two decades. Computers have started to be used in classrooms together with other materials such as smartboards, projectors, Internet connections, and tablets, which are also known as ICTs. Thanks to this increase in ICTs, possibilities that were not possible before were possible; for example, videos in the classroom to explain something or audios to listen to songs. Another aspect that also appeared with the widespread use of computers is the creation of educational videogames that were created specifically so that they are used inside the classroom.

The purpose of this chapter was to determine the effectiveness of technical engineering degree of videogames as well as ICTs, and how it can affect students and teachers. To do this, information was collected, and several questionnaires were created that were given to teachers and students and analysed to compare the collected data. The results of the questionnaires are as follows:

- The sample of teachers who took the questionnaire had a variety of opinions regarding ICTs and videogames.
- More than half of the teachers did not have sufficient technical knowledge of ICTs or were not interested in improving their technological abilities.
- The ICT tools provided by the centres are soon outdated owing to the fast release of new technological content and improvements.
- They used ICTs in class daily in the form of projections, videos, or games.
- Teachers were unaware of the different definitions of gamification and game-based learning.
- They also did not use games in their full pedagogical capacity and were unaware of their other uses.

- Most of them do not want to use ICTs or games as a main component of the lesson, as it requires a long time to prepare and can fail due to bad Internet connections.
- The games that teachers mainly use in the lessons are educational games.
- Students feel motivated when learning L2 with the help of games, scaffolding, and correct lesson difficulty.
- Students mainly use computers to play videogames, which can lead to side tracking when working in other projects such as investigations, or presentations.

Something to emphasize after collecting data about ICTs and videogames is how little it is known about them. There are many ways in which a videogame can be implemented in the classroom, and studies have been conducted to show what type of game should be better, depending on what the teacher wants to use. Even so, almost no one knew how to effectively implement real videogames in lessons, as they did not seem to fit with anything. It is also not widely known how videogames can have a positive effect on students.

REFERENCES

Al-Karawi, M. (2020). English Language Learning Through Games. *Educational Challenges*, *25*(1), 9–20. doi:10.34142/2709-7986.2020.25.1.01

Alonso García, S., Martínez-Domingo, J. A., Berral Ortiz, B., & De la Cruz Campos, J. C. (2021). Gamificación en educación superior. Revisión de experiencias realizadas en España en los últimos años. *Hachetetepé. Revista Científica de Educación y Comunicación*, *23*(23), 1–21. doi:10.25267/Hachetetepe.2021.i23.2205

Álvarez Cadavid, G., & González Manosalva, C. (2022). Apropiación de TIC en docentes de la educación superior: Una mirada desde los contenidos digitales. *Praxis Educativa (Santa Rosa)*, *26*(1), 1–25. doi:10.19137/praxiseducativa-2022-260104

Araya Muñoz, I., & Majano Benavides, J. (2022). Didáctica universitaria en entornos virtuales. Experiencia en ciencias sociales. *Educare (San José)*, *26*(3), 511–529. doi:10.15359/ree.26-3.28

Barrera López, E. H., & Morales Vázquez, E. (2023). Aplicación de videojuegos, en aulas virtuales ¿Es buena para aprender otro idioma? *Ciencia Latina Revista Científica Multidisciplinar*, *7*(4), 2544–2576. doi:10.37811/cl_rcm.v7i4.7072

Belda Medina, J., & Calvo Ferrer, J. (2022). Preservice Teachers' Knowledge and Attitudes toward Digital-Game-Based Language Learning. *Education Sciences*, *12*(3), 1–16. doi:10.3390/educsci12030182

Bottino, R. (2020). Schools and the digital challenge: Evolution and perspectives. *Education and Information Technologies*, *25*(3), 2241–2259. doi:10.1007/s10639-019-10061-x

Briones, D., Pallaroso, C., & Cangas, E. (2023). El impacto de los videojuegos de aventura en el aprendizaje de lenguas extranjeras y las percepciones de los alumnos. *MQRInvestigar*, *7*(2), 188–203. doi:10.56048/MQR20225.7.2.2023.188-203

Caraballo Padilla, Y. Y. (2023). Gamificación educativa y su impacto en la enseñanza y aprendizaje del idioma inglés: Un análisis de la literatura científica. *Ciencia Latina. Revista Científica Multidisciplinar*, *7*(4), 1813–1830. doi:10.37811/cl_rcm.v7i4.7011

Caravaca Llamas, C., & Sáez Olmos, J. (2021). Gamificación en la enseñanza superior: Descripción de los principales recursos para su utilización. *Edutech Review*, *8*(2), 165–177. doi:10.37467/gkarevedutech.v8.3039

Casañ Pitarch, R. (2017). Enseñanza de lenguas extranjeras a través de videojuegos: revisión de caso experimentales y prácticos. In *Estudios de Lingüística Aplicada* (pp. 27–35). Servicio de Publicaciones de la Universidad Politécnica de Valencia.

Casañ Pitarch, R., Girón García, C., & Holgado Sáez, C. (2022). Desarrollo de un videojuego para la enseñanza del inglés como lengua extranjera para fines específicos y el fomento de conocimientos en Educación para el Desarrollo y Ciudadanía Global en Ingeniería Industrial. *Tabanque: Revista pedagógica, 34*, 68-87. doi:10.24197/trp.1.2022.68-87

Cerezo Cortijo, I. (2021). La gamificación como metodología innovadora en el ámbito educativo. In *Avances y Desafíos para la Transformación Educativa* (pp. 272–280). Servicio de Publicaciones de la Universidad de Oviedo.

Chen, H. J. H., Hsu, H. L., Chen, Z. H., & Todd, A. G. (2021). Investigating the Impact of Integrating Vocabulary Exercises into an Adventure Videogame on Second Vocabulary Learning. *Journal of Educational Computing Research*, *59*(2), 318–341. doi:10.1177/0735633120963750

Contreras, J. L. G., Torres, C. A. B., & Ojeda, Y. C. E. (2022). Using of ICT in higher education: A bibliometric analysis. *Revista Complutense de Educación*, *33*(3), 601–613. doi:10.5209/rced.73922

Del Padre, L., González, A., & Benítez Ayala, D. A. (2022). Uso de las TIC para el proceso enseñanza aprendizaje en la educación superior. *LATAM Revista Latinoamericana de Ciencias Sociales y Humanidades*, *3*(2), 1393–1411. doi:10.56712/latam.v3i2.191

Dimitra, K., Kousaris, K., & Zafeiriou, C. (2023). Types of Game-Based Learning in Education: A Brief State of the Art and the Implementation in Greece. *European Educational Researcher*, *3*(2), 87–100. doi:10.31757/euer.324

Donoso Cedeño, M. M., Echeverría Zurita, L. O., Moreira Pérez, R. W., & Ponce Anchundia, L. S. (2023). Innovación en la enseñanza del inglés en la educación superior: Desafíos, oportunidades y buenas prácticas. *Revista Científica Arbitrada Multidisciplinaria PENTACIENCIAS*, *5*(7), 165–174. doi:10.59169/pentaciencias. v5i7.924

Garay, J., & Ávila, C. (2021). Videojuegos y su influencia en el rendimiento académico. *Episteme Koinonía*, *4*(8), 1–10. doi:10.35381/e.k.v4i8.1343

García, C., Martín Peña, M. L., & Díaz Garrido, E. (2019). Gamificar una asignatura sin tecnología avanzada. *Working Papers on Operations Management, 10*(2), 20-35. doi:10.4995/wpom.v10i2.12662

García Intriago, S. S., & Rodríguez Zambrano, A. D. (2022). *Revisión de estudios sobre el uso de la gamificación en educación especial*. Mawil Publicaciones Impresas y Digitales.

George Reyes, C. E. (2020). Uso de las TIC en la Educación Superior: Incorporación en el modelo educativo de la Universidad Autónoma del Estado de Hidalgo. *Debates en Evaluación y Currículum*, *5*, 1–13.

George Reyes, C. E. (2021). Incorporación de las TIC en la educación. Recomendaciones de organismos de cooperación internacional 1972-2018. *Revista Caribeña de Investigación Educativa*, *5*(1), 101–115. doi:10.32541/recie.2021. v5i1.pp101-115

Ghazy, A., Wajdi, M., Sada, C., & Ikhsanudin, I. (2021). The use of game-based learning in English class. *Journal of Applied Studies in Language*, *5*(1), 67–78. doi:10.31940/jasl.v5i1.2400

Gómez García, L., & Urraco Solanilla, M. (2022). Relación entre los videojuegos y las aplicaciones y la adquisición de vocabulario en inglés como lengua extranjera. *Revista Iberoamericana de Tecnología en Educación y Educación en Tecnología*, *31*(31), 60–68. doi:10.24215/18509959.31.e6

González Pérez, A., & Álvarez Serrano, A. (2022). Aprendizaje basado en juegos para aprender una segunda lengua en educación superior. *International Journal of Technology and Educational Innovation, 8*(2), 114–128. doi:10.24310/innoeduca.2022.v8i2.13858

Infante Plaza, A. A. (2023). La gamificación como una herramienta necesaria en el aprendizaje de los estudiantes. *Espíritu Emprendedor TES, 7*(4), 74–91. doi:10.33970/eetes.v7.n4.2023.360

Johnson, E., Larner, A., Merritt, D., Vitanova, G., & Sousa, S. (2020). Assessing the impact of game modalities in second language acquisition. *Journal of Universal Computer Science, 26*(8), 880–903. doi:10.3897/jucs.2020.048

Kim, J., & Castelli, D. (2021). Effects of Gamification on Behavioral Change in Education: A Meta-Analysis. *International Journal of Environmental Research and Public Health, 18*(7), 1–14. doi:10.3390/ijerph18073550 PMID:33805530

López Espinosa, J. R., González Bello, E. O. (2021). Educación superior, innovación y docencia: alcances y limitaciones de la virtualidad como estrategia institucional. *Revista Iberoamericana para la investigación y el desarrollo educativo, 12*(23), 1-34. doi:10.23913/ride.v12i23.1051

Masadeh, T. S. (2022). Teaching English as a Foreign language and the Use of Educational Games. *Asian Journal of Education and Social Studies, 30*(3), 26–34. https://doi.org/. doi:10.9734/ajess/2022/v30i330721

Molina García, P. F., Molina García, A. R., & Gentry Jones, J. (2021). La gamificación como estrategia didáctica para el aprendizaje del idioma inglés. *Dominio de las Ciencias, 7*(1), 722–730. doi:10.23857/dc.v7i1.1672

Moreira Santos, M.G. & Cedeño Zambrano, E.G. (2023). El uso de las tecnologías de la información y comunicación (TIC) como estrategia en la enseñanza y aprendizaje en la educación superior. *RECIAMUC, 7*(2), 101-109. https://doi.org/. (2).abril.2023.101-109 doi:10.26820/reciamuc/7

Ortega, F., & Vásquez, C. (2021). Análisis del impacto de la enseñanza basada en juegos en el compromiso de los estudiantes en la clase de inglés. *Ingenio Libre, 9*(19), 66–88.

Padilla Escobedo, J. C., & Ayala Jiménez, G. G. (2021). Competencias digitales en profesores de educación superior de Iberoamérica: una revisión sistemática. *Revista Iberoamericana para la investigación y el desarrollo educativo, 12*(23), 1-19. doi:10.23913/ride.v12i23.1096

Pardo Cueva, M., Chamba Rueda, L. M., Higuerey Gómez, Á., & Jaramillo Campoverde, B. G. (2021). Las TIC y rendimiento académico en la educación superior: Una relación potenciada por el uso del Padlet. *Revista Ibérica de Sistemas e Tecnologias de Informação, 28*, 934–944.

Parra González, M. E., Segura Robles, A., Vázquez Cano, E., & López Meneses, E. (2020). Gamificación para fomentar la activación del alumnado en su aprendizaje. *Revista Linguagem e Tecnologia, 13*(3), 278–293. doi:10.35699/1983-3652.2020.25846

Párraga Solórzano, R.J., Vargas Serrano, J.V., Solórzano Alcivar, E.A. & Gómez Rivas, I.B. (2022). Recursos didácticos digitales en la enseñanza del idioma inglés. *Universidad, Ciencia y Tecnología, 26*(116), 84-92). doi:10.47460/uct.v26i116.647

Pérez, E., & Gertrudis, F. (2021). Ventajas de la gamificación en el ámbito de la educación formal en España. Una revisión bibliográfica en el periodo de 2015-2020. *Contextos Educativos. Review of Education, 28*(28), 203–227. doi:10.18172/con.4741

Poveda Pineda, D. F., & Cifuentes Medina, J. E. (2020). Incorporación de las tecnologías de información y comunicación (TIC) durante el proceso de aprendizaje en la educación superior. *Formación Universitaria, 13*(6), 95–104. doi:10.4067/S0718-50062020000600095

Roca Castro, Y. D., & Véliz Robles, F. M. (2022). Innovación en la Enseñanza del Idioma Inglés a Nivel de Educación Superior en Postpandemia. *Domino de las Ciencias, 8*(2), 361–377. doi:10.23857/dc.v8i2.2759

Rodríguez Cajamarca, L. P., García Herrera, D. G., Guevara Vizcaíno, C. F., & Erazo Álvarez, J. C. (2020). Alianza entre aprendizaje y juego: Gamificación como estrategia metodológica que motiva el aprendizaje del Inglés. *Revista Arbitrada Interdisciplinaria KOINONIA, 5*(1), 370–391. doi:10.35381/r.k.v5i1.788

Salado, L., Amavisca, S., Richart, R., & Rodríguez, R. (2019). Alfabetización digital de estudiantes universitarios en las modalidades presencial y virtual. *Revista Electrónica de Investigación e Innovación Educativa, 5*(1), 30–47. doi:10.6018/red.444751

Santos González, D. C. (2023). La gamificación en el aprendizaje de segundas lenguas extranjeras: FLE y su aprendizaje en la enseñanza pública de España. *Revista Educación. Investigación. Innovación y Transferencia, 1*(1), 68–91. doi:10.26754/ ojs_reiit/eiit.202318813

Silalahi, M. (2019). Improving students' interest in learning English by using games. *International Journal of Theory and Application in Elementary and Secondary School Education, 1*(1), 50–56. doi:10.31098/ijtaese.v1i1.24

Solís Castillo, J. C., & Marquina Lujan, R. J. (2022). Gamificación como alternativa metodológica en la educación superior. *Revista ConCiencia EPG, 7*(1), 66–83. doi:10.32654/CONCIENCIAEPG.7-1.5

Vélez, K. G. C., Cedeño, M. A. P., & Ponce, G. V. B. (2020). Enseñanza de inglés como lengua extranjera (EFL) en el desarrollo de la destreza speaking a través de clases virtuales en la educación superior. *Revista Cognosis, 5*, 167–178. doi:10.33936/ cognosis.v5i0.2785

Venegas Álvarez, G. S., & Proaño Rodríguez, C. E. (2021). Las TIC y la formación del docente de educación superior. *Dominio de las Ciencias, 7*(1), 575–592. doi:10.23857/dc.v7i1.1662

Zhan, Z., He, L., Tong, Y., Liang, X., Guo, S., & Lan, X. (2022). The effectiveness of gamification programming education: Evidence from a meta-analysis. *Computers and Education: Artificial Intelligence, 3*(1), 1–11. doi:10.1016/j.caeai.2022.100096

KEY TERMS AND DEFINITIONS

Game-Based Learning: Game-based learning brings about strategies, rules, and social experiences of playing games in the classroom. The game-based learning model allows teachers to target certain activities that benefit the real-world application of concepts.

Games: All types of games may be used in an educational environment; however, educational games are designed to help people learn about certain subjects, expand concepts, reinforce development, understand a historical event, or culture, or assist them in learning a skill as they play.

Gamification: Gamification is a strategic attempt to enhance systems, services, organizations, and activities by creating experiences similar to those experienced when playing games to motivate and engage users.

ICTs: ICTs, or information and communications technologies, refer to the infrastructure and components that enable modern computing. Among the goals of technologies, tools and systems aim to improve the way humans create, process, and share data or information with each other.

Videogames: Any of the various interactive games played using a specialized electronic gaming device, computer, or mobile device and a television or other display screen, along with a means of controlling graphic images.

Chapter 9
Employing Online Video Platforms in English Language Teaching:
Opportunities and Challenges

Challa Srinivas Rao
Sreenidhi Institute of Science and Technology, India

Karayil Suresh Babu
Vasireddy Venkatadri Institute of Technology, India

ABSTRACT

The Covid-19 pandemic introduced substantial challenges and unique opportunities in education, especially in English language teaching. Loss of instruction time and a decline in learning outcomes emerged as significant problems in engineering education. Amidst these difficulties, the surge in internet-based learning emerges as a promising solution. This chapter conducts an analytical study on the crisis's impact on language learning, the efficacy of online learning in bridging gaps, and the future implications for English language teaching. The methodology involves a questionnaire survey among engineering students and teachers. Students exhibit a passive attitude towards online learning, attributing it to limited interaction during virtual classes. They stress the necessity of on-campus classes for certain concepts like writing and speaking skills. Teachers identify vocabulary learning, reading comprehension, and error spotting as suitable for online teaching. Both groups unanimously support blended learning for the future.

DOI: 10.4018/979-8-3693-2169-0.ch009

Copyright © 2024, IGI Global. Copying or distributing in print or electronic forms without written permission of IGI Global is prohibited.

INTRODUCTION

English language teaching in India has undergone many changes in teaching methods, especially in recent decades, resulting in the development of a variety of innovative approaches and methods. Switching over to a completely online mode of teaching during the COVID-19 pandemic opened opportunities and an equal number of risks for both students and teachers.

The situation created by the COVID-19 pandemic prompted institutions to switch to an online instruction format in a very short span of time. This threw challenges for both the teachers and students. The opportunities created by online teaching were also significant. The current work intends to record both the challenges and opportunities faced by the teachers and the students. These new opportunities required teachers to adapt themselves to a different kind of teaching methodology and assessment.

Research Questions

The current work focuses primarily on the opportunities and challenges faced by students and teachers in the process of online English Language Teaching and Learning. The following research questions have been framed to extract appropriate insights.

1. In what ways did the pandemic affect the English language learning of Engineering students?
2. To what extent has the online mode bridged the gap in language learning?
3. What are the futuristic implications of using the online mode of learning in the field of English Language Teaching?

LITERATURE SURVEY

A considerable amount of research was done in this area during the COVID-19 pandemic period. The work has to be reviewed. Some studies have explored these challenges in specific contexts. For example, Sepulveda-Escobar and Morrison's (2020) study showed that Chilean teacher candidates suffered from teacher–student online interactions and from distractions and limitations caused by working from home. According to nine English teachers from London who participated in Evans et al (2020) study, there are a number of difficulties with online instructions. They include students' inability to afford the necessary technological devices, limited interaction, mental and emotional issues, and assessment of students' learning. A few other studies have examined these issues from a cross-cultural perspective. For instance, MacIntyre, Gregersen, and Mercer (2020) looked at the difficulties faced by language teachers in Asia, Europe, North America, South America, and the Middle East when teaching remotely during the COVID-19 issue. The following COVID-19-related online teaching challenges were mentioned by respondents in three comprehensive cross-cultural reports published by the British Council (2020 a, b, c): performance assessment, technology access and device availability, learner demotivation, online learning content and delivery, teacher support, teacher technology illiteracy, and parental support and communication. The idea of MOOCS began a decade ago, institutionalised online learning; most of the time, it has been self-learning modules which students can choose according to their convenience. But during the pandemic, the entire teaching switched to online mode, thus opening the doors for many challenges and, indeed, a few opportunities.

Methodology

The methodology is based on a questionnaire survey, which was conducted among engineering students. The students belonged to different branches of engineering. The survey hosted using an online form (MS Forms) was shared among students and teachers from five different Engineering Colleges via mail and WhatsApp. The questionnaire used for the students was a semi-structured one, which had 14 items, including a demographic profile. The questionnaire used for the teachers included details of the teacher's attitude towards online learning. The responses from both students and teachers were collected and analysed for insights.

Population

Students and instructors from engineering colleges were taken into consideration for the current study. The following are the justifications for picking engineering colleges. Most engineering colleges adopted an online teaching style during the pandemic in order to maximise the use of class time, finish the degree on time, and be prepared for employment or further study. A complete semester's worth of instruction was delivered online. Since both researchers are employed by engineering institutions, they have direct access to both staff and students. The researchers assumed that there would be plenty of opportunities to obtain important information that would help them undertake meaningful study.

Sample

A total of four autonomous engineering colleges were considered for this study. Two colleges each from the states of Andhra Pradesh and Telangana were part of this study. Students who are currently in their 3rd, 5th and 7th semesters were selected as samples. These were the students who attended online classes during the COVID-19 pandemic period. All the teachers working in these four engineering colleges who conducted online classes were part of the sample.

Survey

Two independent questionnaires, one each for the students and teachers were used in this study. The questionnaire included questions related to the students' and teachers' attitudes towards challenges posed by online learning besides crucial details about the online teaching and learning process. The students and teachers were asked to share their suggestions to improve online learning.

Questionnaire for Students

The questionnaire for students has 22 questions which were aimed at collecting details like the year of study, college, English language topics taught online, duration and frequency of online classes etc., Eight yes/no type questions, four multiple answer questions, four multiple choice questions, and four questions that require specific answers were included in the questionnaire besides a Likert question and a question that require a descriptive answer. This questionnaire was hosted on an MS Form and the link was shared among the students. Following is the link to the student questionnaire. https://forms.office.com/r/Jq18jrkgx5.

Two yes/no questions were used to ascertain if the students had attended any online classes in general and English language classes in particular. The remaining yes/no questions were intended to understand if the students were given an opportunity to interact during the online sessions and whether any quizzes or polls were conducted during the online classes. A question was included to know if the students felt a need to have a follow-up class. Multiple-answer questions were used to collect information pertaining to the modules that were taught, the topics students felt were ideal for online classes, the topics that required face-to-face interaction, and the problems they faced while attending online classes. Multiple choice questions were included to collect details like the number of classes held per week, the mode of instruction they preferred, the year of study and the name of the college they study.

Questionnaire for Teachers

The questionnaire for teachers has 21 questions which were aimed at collecting details like the college, English language topics taught online, duration and frequency of online classes, problems faced while conducting online etc., Seven yes/no type questions, five multiple answer questions, five multiple choice questions, and a question that requires specific answer were included in the questionnaire besides a question that requires a descriptive answer. The teacher's email ID was also collected for future communication. This questionnaire was hosted on an MS Form, and the following link https://forms.office.com/r/jmN40jMjz3 was shared among the teachers.

Two yes/no questions were used to confirm if the teachers have conducted online classes to teach English Language. The remaining yes/no questions were intended to understand if the teachers allowed the students to interact during the online sessions. The same type of questions were used to know if any quizzes or polls were conducted during the online classes. A question was included to know if the teachers felt a need to conduct a follow-up class to clarify the doubts. A yes/no question is also used to determine whether the teacher had used any application that aids teaching during the online classes. Multiple answer questions were used to collect information pertaining to the modules that were taught; the topics teachers felt ideal for online classes, the topics which require face-to-face interaction and the problems they faced while conducting online classes. Multiple choice questions were included to collect details like the number of classes held per week, the mode of instruction they preferred, and the name of the college they worked in.

Responses From Student's Questionnaire

After eliminating inconsistent data, the responses submitted by 301 students have been considered for this study. Students belong to four Autonomous Engineering Colleges, two each from the states of Andhra Pradesh and Telangana. Vasireddy Venkatadri Institute of Technology, Guntur and Lakireddy Balireddy College of Engineering, Mylavaram, were the two colleges from Andhra Pradesh, whereas Sreenidhi Institute of Science and Technology, Hyderabad and ACE Engineering College, Hyderabad, were the two colleges from the state of Telangana considered for this study. All these students claim to have attended online English language classes. Fundamental details like i) the size of the class, ii) the duration of the class, and iii) the screen presence of the teacher were collected. Table 1 and Table 2 present the summary of the responses collected for the above three questions.

The chart in Figure 1 represents the semester-wise breakup of the students who responded to the survey. The IV B.Tech students were in their seventh semester, the III years were in their fifth semester and the II years were in their third semester while attempting this survey.

The students were asked five questions about the activities and interactions they had during the online classes. The students were asked to confirm if any polls, quizzes and group activities were conducted during the online classes. They were also asked if they were allowed to interact with the teachers during the online classes. One more question was asked to ascertain if the teachers were using any other applications, like PPTs, whiteboards, etc, while teaching online. All the responses given by the students are summarised in Table 3 given below.

A question was asked about the modules taught during the Online English language classes. This question allowed students to give multiple answers. The responses collected are presented in Figure 2. The student response helps us to understand that teachers gave importance to Vocabulary lessons, Reading Comprehension lessons and Grammar lessons while teaching online.

Table 1. Size of the class

Class Size	Response	%
<= 30	28	9.3
31 to 90	177	58.8
91 to 180	52	17.3
> 181	44	14.6

Table 2. Duration and screen presence of the teacher

Duration	Max	Min	Average
What was the duration of the class? (In minutes)	120	30	55
How long was the teacher available on the screen? (In minutes)	40	10	30

Figure 1. Year of study

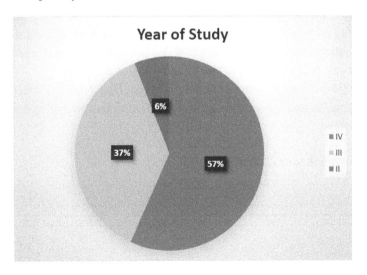

Table 3. Interaction

Questions	Total	Yes		No	
		Num	%	Num	%
Were the students allowed to speak?	301	99	32.9	203	67.4
Were any polls conducted during the online sessions?	301	53	17.6	249	82.7
Were any activities like discussion, pair work, and texting used during the classes?	301	67	22.3	235	78.1
Were any quizzes conducted as part of each class?	301	104	34.6	198	65.8
Were any online applications used during the class? (PPT, Online Whiteboard, etc.)	301	169	56.1	133	44.2

Figure 2. Modules taught

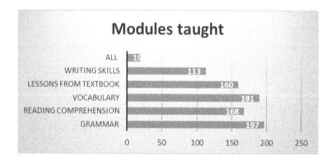

Students' opinions about the topics they prefer to listen to online and the topics they believe need a follow-up class are collected. Their responses are summarised and presented in Figure 3 and Figure 4. These two questions also allowed students to give more than one answer. A basic reading of the summary of the responses given by the students reveals that the students are very clear in their opinions.

Table 4 depicts the students' opinions about the number of classes they wish to have every week. Students wish to have 2 to 3 classes a week.

As depicted in Figure 5, the students, in unequivocal terms, stated that they needed a follow-up class. A yes/no question is used to extract their opinion.

Table 4. Ideal number of classes per week

Duration	Max	Min	Avg
How many classes per week for English Language Teaching is ideal, according to you?	6	2	3

Figure 3. Topics ideal for online teaching

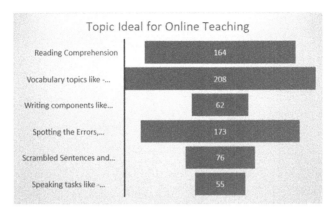

Figure 4. Topics ideal for face-to-face instruction

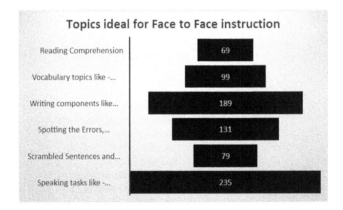

Responses were also collected from the students about the reasons they felt had restrained their interest in online classes. A Likert question is also included in the questionnaire to understand their overall interest in the online classes they attended. Their responses are presented in Table 5. The data in Table 5 is presented in the form of a frequency table.

A question to guess the mode of teaching they prefer in future is included in the questionnaire. This question helps to reinforce the opinion the students hold about online classes.

Figure 5. Need for a follow-up class

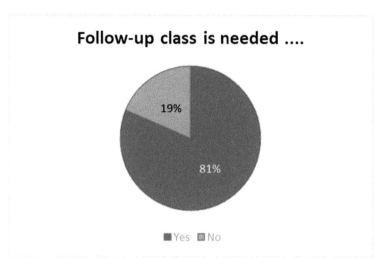

Figure 6. Problems faced during online classes

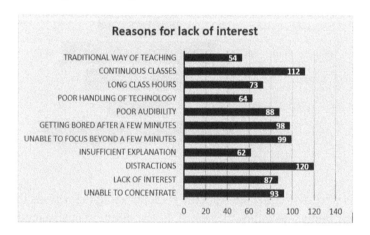

Responses From Teacher's Questionnaire

The teachers were also asked to respond to questions like the size of the class, duration of the class and the number of classes taken per week. It is noted that there is a correlation between the teachers' and the students' responses. Table 6 below presents the details.

Table 5. Rating given by students

Grade	Responses	%
10	10	3.3
9	19	6.3
8	35	11.7
7	38	12.7
6	48	16.0
5	39	13.0
4	32	10.7
3	28	9.3
2	38	12.7
1	14	4.7

Figure 7. Future preference-students

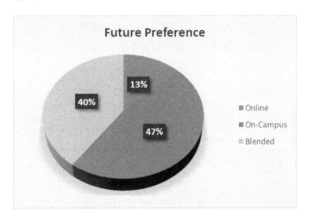

Table 6. Teacher Responses on Class Details

Duration	Max	Min	Average
What was the size of the class?	500	6	150
What was the duration of the class? (in minutes)	120	45	60
How many classes were taken per week?	6	2	4

There is a slight mismatch between what the students said the teachers claimed on points like i) allowing students to speak, ii) polls conducted, iii) quizzes conducted, iv) pair work activities, v) online application used, and vi) needing a follow-up class. It can be observed from the data presented in Table 7 that the majority of the teachers have answered in affirmation to the questions asked.

It is evident from the data in Table 8 that all the teachers were using the most popular Online Teaching (Meeting) platforms like Cisco Webex, MS Teams, Google Meet and Zoom. The important point to be noted here is that the teachers will be using a platform bought by the college. So, there is not much choice for the teachers to use different platforms.

The teachers were also asked questions about the modules they taught during the Online English language classes. This question allowed teachers to give multiple answers. The responses collected are presented in Figure 8. These responses help us to understand that teachers conducted classes for almost every module, like Vocabulary lessons, Reading Comprehension lessons and Grammar lessons, while teaching online.

But when the teachers were asked for their opinion about the ideal topic or module for online teaching, as shown in Figure 9, they gave importance to Teaching Vocabulary and Spotting errors.

Table 7. Polls, quizzes, and activities conducted

Questions	Total	Yes		No	
		Number	%	Number	%
Were the students allowed to speak?	15	11	73.3	4	26.7
Were any polls conducted during the online sessions?	15	7	46.7	8	53.3
Were any activities like discussion, pair work, and texting used during the classes?	15	11	73.3	4	26.7
Were any quizzes conducted as part of each class?	15	10	66.7	5	33.3
Were any online applications used during the class? (PPT, Online Whiteboard, etc.)	15	15	100.0	0	0.0
Do you think a follow-up class for the online content delivered is required?	15	12	80.0	3	20.0

Table 8. Platforms Used

Platform	
Cisco Webex	**5**
MS Teams	5
Google Meet	2
Zoom	3

Figure 8. Modules taught-teachers

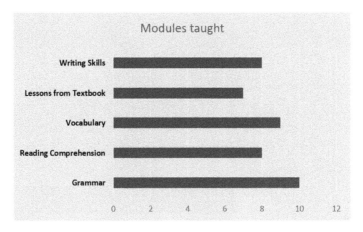

Figure 9. Topics ideal for online teaching

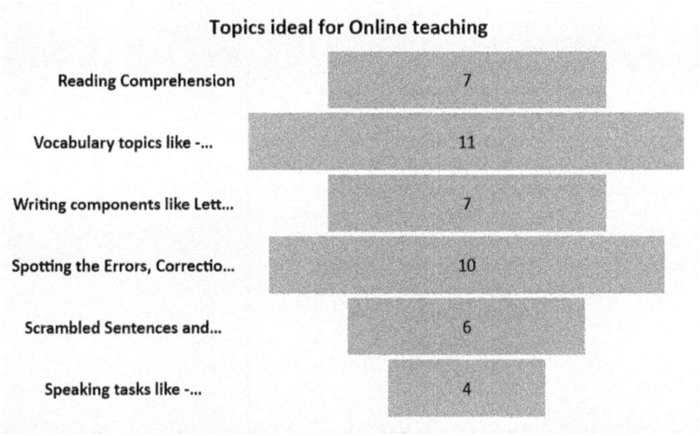

The same thought resonated in the responses they gave to the question, "The topic or module ideal for Face-to-Face Teaching". According to the teachers' speaking activities and writing, activities require face-to-face interaction. They were also very clear about the number of classes to be allotted for English in online mode. 90% of them opined that there should not be more than two classes a week and the class size should not exceed 60 students.

Figure 10 depicts the topics that are ideal for Face-to-face instruction. The problems the teachers faced while conducting the classes, i) non-responsiveness of the students, ii) students leaving the class in the middle, and iii) inability to conduct descriptive tests, are considered major problems. Figure 11 also lists a few more problems highlighted by the teachers, which also require attention.

Figure 10. Topics ideal for face-to-face instruction

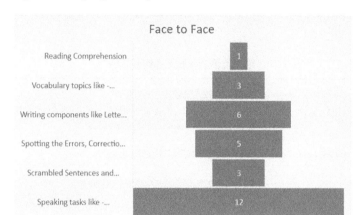

Figure 11. Problems faced by teachers

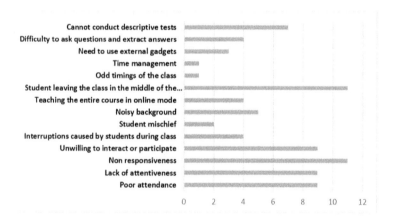

Another area of concern for teachers is the technology. The teachers were inquired about the technical hassles they faced while conducting online classes. All the hassles the teachers mentioned deserved to be addressed. Figure 12 depicts the responses given by the teachers.

DISCUSSION

Clearly, the crux of this study is evaluating the opportunities and challenges of using online video platforms while Teaching the English Language. The opportunities and challenges are further assessed from the perspectives of the students and the teachers.

Figure 12. Technical hassles

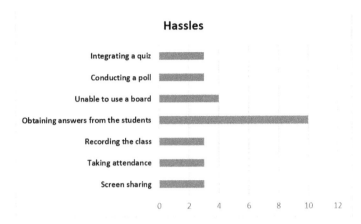

Student Perspective: Prima Facie, the students exhibited a passive attitude towards online learning. The reason for their attitude can be guessed from the responses they gave. The summary of the responses depicted in Table 3 justifies our claim. According to the majority of the students who participated in this survey, they did not get many chances to interact during the classes. It can also be understood from the data that in most of the instances, the teachers were not using any polls or quizzes as part of the online learning. Moreover, it can be observed that a significant 81.7% of students wanted to have a follow-up class after an online class. From the above observations, it can be surmised that there is a concerted effect of the factors mentioned above in creating a passive attitude among students about online learning.

Furthermore, the details presented in Figure 6 provide insight into why students do not show interest towards online learning. Two important reasons they mentioned are distractions and traditional ways of teaching. For a question about the mode they prefer, the students have unequivocally stated that they prefer on-campus classes or a blended mode of teaching to complete online classes. The data pertaining to this question is presented in Figure 7.

But from the responses they gave about the topics they like to learn through online mode, it can be understood that they are not totally turning down the option to learn online. Figure 3 clearly states that the students are willing to attend sessions on vocabulary, reading comprehension, and error identification through online mode. According to them, face-to-face, on-campus classes are required for learning concepts like writing skills and speaking skills (Figure 4). So, this can be seen as an opportunity to design lessons for a few concepts through online mode and blend them into the course structure.

Teacher Perspective: The data collected and analysed suggest that the teachers' attitudes have largely been positive towards online learning. If the problems they mentioned in Figure 11 can be addressed, there is scope for the teachers to use the online mode of teaching more effectively. Both the teachers and students agreed upon the topics or concepts ideal for online learning. Teachers have considered vocabulary learning, reading comprehension, and spotting errors as ideal topics for online teaching. As the students opined, teachers were also of the opinion that speaking and writing skills required face-to-face, on-campus teaching. All the teachers who participated in this survey unanimously considered blended learning as the ideal mode for the future.

CONCLUSION

If the learning experience is enjoyable, the students will be motivated to learn through online mode. Suppose the teachers focus on mastering the technology of using online platforms, learning to use applications like whiteboard, embedding quizzes and polls into the lesson plan, and choosing content appropriate to be delivered online. In that case, there are immense chances that students will welcome the option of online learning. Students do not like an overdose of anything. They expect different experiences of learning over online. So, the onus lies on the teachers to make online learning effective. If online learning can be embedded into the regular course, it will undoubtedly help reinforce the students' learning. A short training programme will help the teachers equipped with the necessary skills to become conversant with online teaching. More parametric research is required to establish the exact skill or concept that is ideal to be taught online.

REFERENCES

British Council. (2020a). *English Language Teaching and Covid-19: A Global Snapshot of Ministries of Education Responses in the State Primary and Secondary Sector*. British Council. [Google Scholar]

British Council. (2020b). *English Language Teaching and Covid-19: A Survey of Teacher and Teacher Educator Needs During the Covid-19 Pandemic April–May 2020*. British Council. [Google Scholar]

British Council. (2020c). *English Language Teaching and Covid-19: A Global Snapshot of Ministries of Education Responses During the Period of School Reopening, in the State Primary and Secondary Sector*. British Council. [Google Scholar]

Evans, C., O'Connor, C., Graves, T., Kemp, F., Kennedy, A., Allen, P., Bonnar, G., Reza, A., & Aya, U. (2020). Teaching Under Lockdown: The Experiences of London English Teachers. [Google Scholar]. *Changing English*, *27*(3), 244–254. doi:10.1080/1358684X.2020.1779030

MacIntyre, P. D., Gregersen, T., & Mercer, S. (2020). 'Language Teachers' Coping Strategies During the Covid-19 Conversion to Online Teaching: Correlations with Stress, Wellbeing and Negative Emotions.' [Google Scholar]. *System*, *94*, 1–13. doi:10.1016/j.system.2020.102352

Sepulveda-Escobar, P., & Morrison, A. (2020). Online Teaching Placement During the COVID-19 Pandemic in Chile: Challenges and Opportunities. [Google Scholar]. *European Journal of Teacher Education*, *43*(4), 587–607. doi:10.1080/02619768 .2020.1820981

Chapter 10
Enriching EFL Teaching Through Multimodal Integration of QR Codes:
A Stepwise Guide for Foreign Language Teachers

Gülin Zeybek

https://orcid.org/0000-0002-6863-7169

Isparta University of Applied Sciences, Turkey

ABSTRACT

The purpose of this in-depth chapter is to present the multimodal integration of quick response (QR) codes in the field of foreign language education, with a particular emphasis on English language skills. This chapter presents practical applications and ideas for introducing QR codes into teaching practices in a seamless manner, which will improve the experiences of language learners. All aspects of language abilities, including listening, speaking, reading, and writing, are included in the scope of this analysis. The chapter also notes that there are challenges associated with the incorporation of QR codes. In conclusion, the chapter suggests that the use of QR codes into language instruction might be a paradigm change in terms of pedagogical approach. The presentation of QR code integration in this chapter is framed within a multimodal approach, which acknowledges the value of mixing many modes of communication, such as verbal, visual, auditory, gestural, and spatial modes, in order to produce an experience that is both comprehensive and immersive for language acquisition.

DOI: 10.4018/979-8-3693-2169-0.ch010

Copyright © 2024, IGI Global. Copying or distributing in print or electronic forms without written permission of IGI Global is prohibited.

INTRODUCTION

A Quick Response (QR) code is a 2D barcode and has been widely used for many purposes for a long time. QR codes have the capacity to hold a substantial quantity of information such as alphanumeric letters, binary data, and URLs. QR codes are comprised of black squares organised on a white square grid. They can be easily scanned and interpreted by camera-equipped devices like smartphones and tablets. Users commonly utilise the camera on their smartphone or a specialised QR code scanner application to engage with a QR code. The gadget reads the data included in the QR code and enables its' users to retrieve the encoded material. QR codes are able to encode a wide range of information such as text, URLs, contact information, and other forms of data. The data capacity of a QR code is contingent upon its dimensions and the encoding method employed. QR codes are specifically designed for rapid identification. The systematic arrangement of contrasting black and white squares enables devices to quickly interpret the code, enabling them well-suited for applications that need high speed. QR codes have a wide range of uses in our daily lives. They are often employed for marketing, mobile transactions, event tickets, product details, website hyperlinks, Wi-Fi network configuration, and other applications. The widespread use of smartphones equipped with integrated cameras has had a significant effect in the widespread use of QR codes (Perwitasari & Hendrawan, 2023). QR codes may be effortlessly scanned by users using the camera on their smartphone, and this provides a useful way of obtaining information. QR codes became more popular during the COVID-19 outbreak because to their ability to facilitate contactless interactions (Damodharan, 2022). Amidst the COVID-19 epidemic, QR codes gained significant prominence for the purpose of contact tracking, accessing menus in eateries, and facilitating various forms of touchless interactions (Davies et al, 2023).

The beginning of QR codes dates back to 1994 when Denso Wave, a subsidiary of Toyota, pioneered their creation (Davies et al, 2023). Their idea was primarily intended to monitor automobile parts during the production process. However, the global popularity of QR codes has been significantly boosted by the widespread utilisation of smartphones equipped with integrated cameras and QR code scanning functionalities (Perwitasari & Hendrawan, 2023). This increased the use of QR codes and eliminated the need for supplementary equipment. Consequently, QR codes are now employed in various domains, including educational purposes.

QR codes have transitioned from their initial use in industrial tracking to become a widely accepted technology worldwide. Their adaptability has created new opportunities for innovation in several fields and QR codes have been significantly utilised in the field of education, namely in the teaching of foreign languages (Chee & Tan, 2021). The evolution from their historical origins to their incorporation into language teaching exemplifies a wider transformation in the utilisation of technology to augment educational experiences. QR codes provide educators with a versatile tool in foreign language education and enable them to actively involve students (Celik, 2023), provide immediate access to language materials, and promote interactive and personalised learning (Christopoulos et al, 2021). The use of QR codes into language instruction is in line with the changing digital world and emphasises the importance of developing engaging and efficient language learning environments for language learners.

Using QR codes in foreign language teaching improve the learning process for both students and instructors by enabling interactive educational activities (Chee & Tan, 2021). Teachers can generate QR codes that connect to other forms of multimedia, such as films, audio samples, or interactive tasks. This interactive feature helps language teachers actively involve their students and creates a more dynamic language learning environment. QR codes offer a helpful and efficient method for students to reach various language learning materials. Through the utilisation of a QR code, language learners can reach resources such as vocabulary lists, grammatical explanations, and language activities. Thus, this immediate access facilitates ongoing education outside the borders of a conventional classroom environment (Chiappe et al, 2020; Rikala & Kankaanranta, 2012). Furthermore, the use of QR codes can enhance the effectiveness of foreign language teaching by increasing the advantages of mobility and ubiquity (Kukulska-Hulme et al., 2017). In other words, students can use their smartphones or tablets to scan codes and conveniently access language materials while on the move. Consequently, this enhances the flexibility and adaptability of their learning experience to suit their specific needs and learning paths (Christopoulos et al, 2021). It makes it possible for language teachers to generate codes that connect to resources specifically designed for the individual student's skill level, thereby offering customised educational experiences.

QR codes have the ability to connect to genuine linguistic material such as articles, blogs, or social media postings in the target language. Exposing language learners to this authentic language usage improves their comprehension of cultural intelligence, idiomatic phrases, and current language patterns (Kuru Gönen & Zeybek, 2022a). Moreover, QR codes can be included into language learning exercises that are designed to be interactive and engaging (Law & So, 2010). For instance, language teachers can design a scavenger hunt activity in which students use QR codes to uncover hints or engage in language-based tasks. Introducing this aspect of enjoyment to the educational journey stimulates students' engagement and encourages their active involvement. Additionally, through these activities, QR codes can enhance the process of collaborative learning (Akçayır & Akçayır, 2017; Crompton, 2013; Hsu, 2017). These collaborative activities can necessitate students to collaborate in order to scan codes and accomplish language-related assignments.

This cooperative work promotes effective communication and collaboration, which are vital abilities for acquiring a foreign language.

QR codes can also be used by language teachers in order to implement formative assessment in their classes (Law & So, 2010). By associating codes with quizzes, surveys, or assessments, educators can immediately assess their students' comprehension of language skills and adapt their language teaching methods accordingly. Additionally, instead of distributing worksheets or textbooks, language teachers can generate QR codes that direct to the digital resources. Therefore, they can minimize the need for printed materials and promote an eco-friendly learning environment (Law & So, 2010). Integrating QR codes brings foreign language instruction in line with contemporary technology developments. This integration not only enhances the level of student engagement in learning, but also equips them with the necessary skills to navigate a digital world where technology plays a vital role in communicating and accessing information.

UNDERSTANDING MULTIMODALITY IN LANGUAGE EDUCATION

The concept of multimodality emerged in the early 2000s, as evidenced by the works of Jewitt (2009), Kress and van Leeuwen (2001), Kress et al. (2001, 2005), and van Leeuwen (2005). According to Kress and van Leeuwen (2001), multimodality refers to the utilisation of multiple semiotic modes in the creation of a semiotic product or event. These modes can be combined in various ways, such as reinforcing each other, fulfilling complementary roles, or being hierarchically ordered. The concept of multimodality was derived from Michael Halliday's theories on language as a social semiotic system. He asserts that speaking and writing have distinct purposes in various circumstances to convey meaning. Thus, they facilitate the emergence of diverse epistemologies and subsequently diverse approaches to acquiring knowledge (Halliday, 1985). With the emergence of the telephone and the growing popularity of television, spoken language, which had been previously overlooked, started to gain recognition (Halliday, 1985). Furthermore, advancements in technology have diminished the prominence of writing since it now faces competition from visual and spoken language.

Kress and van Leeuwen (2001) have expanded upon Halliday's concepts of meaning-making. According to them, language is a complex system composed of several 'modalities' such as written, spoken, visual, and bodily resources (see Figure 1). Each of these 'modalities' has its own materialities and affordances for creating meaning. Language consists of several separate systems that contribute to the creation of a single, yet intricate, integrated and differentiated text-message

(Kress, 2000b). According to the source mentioned, modes refer to collections of socially and culturally influenced tools for creating meaning, namely 'channels' for representation or communication (Kress & van Leeuwen, 2001). The term "materiality" describes how social actors shape tangible objects into cultural resources and symbols. Semiotic resources encompass the relationship between many forms of representation (such as physical, societal, and cultural resources) and the actions individuals undertake using these resources (Jewitt, 2013). Furthermore, affordance refers to the limitations and possibilities of various modes, meaning "what can be easily expressed, represented, or communicated using the resources of a mode, and what is more complex or even impossible to do so" (Kress, 2010).

Figure 1. Modes of communication

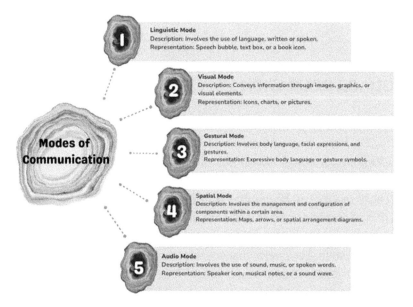

In the present day, individuals have more opportunities to engage with a wider range of media options and utilise different methods to create meaning, referred to as 'orchestration of meaning' by Kress et al. (2001). They are acknowledged as actors who create significance and generate texts, while continuously modifying the representational resources in the process. Put simply, as creators of written content, they manipulate, alter, adjust, and revise all of the components employed (Kress, 2000a). Furthermore, mobile gadgets serve as evident illustrations that facilitate these activities.

Incorporating mobile devices into the learning process offers learners the opportunity to engage in multimodal activities, facilitating the construction of meaning (Kukulska-Hulme et al., 2017). This is a crucial aspect in the field of English language education. Levitt (2017) states that multimodal MALL tools facilitate EFL learning by engaging many sensory channels and delivering information through voice, video, images, colour display, text, touchscreen, and interactive elements. The advancements in mobile technology, such as smartphones and tablets, have facilitated the incorporation of many sensors into conversational interfaces, allowing for multimodal interactions (Griol & Molina, 2016). Hence, the incorporation of several modes in these mobile technologies enables learners to discover settings that are more easily accessible and user-friendly. This flexibility takes into account the cognitive capabilities and constraints of the learners (Magal-Royo et al., 2011). In addition, the integration of several technologies in mobile devices enables learners to utilise speech, stylus, or keyboard interchangeably, depending on their communication requirements (Magal-Royo et al., 2011). The functionalities of gadgets facilitate EFL learners to engage in multimodal communication, cooperation, and language rehearsal (Chua et al., 2020).

Chanier and Lamy (2017) state that individuals utilise both linguistic and non-linguistic methods to communicate messages in written media. In computer-mediated interactive language learning, the range of these resources available to learners expands. Mobile technologies, akin to computer technologies, allow users to achieve language learning goals by utilising these platforms that are essentially computerised and portable. Chanier and Lamy (2017) assert that modality is the amalgamation of three facets of communication. Table 2.1 demonstrates that technology instruments provide language learners several strategies for meaning-making through distinct characteristics. Nevertheless, the mere existence of these tools and modalities is insufficient to constitute multimodal language activities. If the presentation techniques are customised to match the capabilities of mobile technologies and the cognitive ability of learners, the multimedia content provided to learners can lead to multimodal learning (Milutinovic et al., 2015). Hence, the integration of multimodal technologies in EFL learning is crucial for enhancing the learning process and yielding favourable consequences for learners.

RECENT RESEARCH ON QR CODE USE IN EFL TEACHING

The research on QR code use in foreign language teaching have revealed various several benefits. For example, their use has been found to be helpful in improving social and content interaction among language learners by promoting collaborative learning (Akçayır & Akçayır, 2017; Crompton, 2013; Hsu, 2017). Moreover, they enable just-in-time learning by providing various methods for the comprehension of course content (De Pietro & Frontera, 2012; Le & Dinh, 2020). QR codes provide self-assessment by helping students in specific activities (Law & So, 2010) and enhance diverse learning styles (Chen et al., 2010). Furthermore, they enhance autonomous learning, drive motivation, and alleviate stress (Chen et al., 2020; Garzón & Acevedo, 2019; Hwang et al., 2011; McCabe & Tedesco, 2012; Nadolny, 2017), providing learners with the ability to quickly access material ubiquitously, regardless of time or location (Law & So, 2010).

QR codes have been found to be advantageous in EFL settings as they effectively enhance motivation in foreign language learning (Bakla, 2018) and enhance learners' self-esteem (Balintag & Wilang, 2020). Their contribution leads to enhanced learning outcomes and increased context-awareness (Liu et al., 2008). In terms of time management, Vigil (2017) asserts that QR codes offer a convenient way to save time and facilitate innovative learning experiences for both educators and English as a Foreign Language (EFL) students.

Research examining the viewpoints of English as a Foreign Language (EFL) learners about the utilisation of QR codes demonstrates favourable views towards the enhancement of language skills. Learners highlight the advantageous features of QR codes in terms of accessing language learning resources and fostering engagement (Amanah & Yunus, 2018). QR codes are highly preferred for English as a Foreign Language (EFL) listening skills because they offer practicality and quick access to hearing resources (Azizza, 2020). Similarly, according to Bakla (2018), QR codes are more suited for teaching receptive skills like listening and reading, but they present difficulties when it comes to teaching writing and speaking.

In their study, Yunus et al. (2020) found out that the use of QR codes enabled learners to independently control their speed in the foreign language learning process. This, in turn, enhanced their confidence and self-esteem. The study conducted by Balingtag and Wilang (2020) found out that participants expressed a preference for QR codes since they promoted both autonomous and collaborative learning settings. This method was favoured above traditional approaches that rely on memory. The results emphasise the varied and beneficial influence of QR codes on language acquisition in English as a Foreign Language (EFL) environments.

In their research, Kuru Gönen and Zeybek (2022) investigated a group of 28 students who were studying English as a Foreign Language (EFL) and were enrolled in a British culture course at a Turkish university. In order to facilitate learners' understanding of culture-specific concepts that are challenging to comprehend through dictionary definitions, QR code augmented authentic reading texts were created for the research. The results emphasise the potential for using augmented reality (AR) technology, such as QR codes, into language teaching to enhance learning outcomes. Additionally, they underscore the need of ensuring technological access to enable all students to take advantage of the widespread presence of technology.

Apart from the numerous advantages mentioned in the literature review, Yelland's (2018) study emphasises the use of QR codes in delivering multimodality in education. This highlights the active function of QR codes in enhancing language teaching experiences by integrating different forms of communication. Given the comprehensive exploration of QR code usage in EFL teaching in the literature study, it is important to also examine the concept of multimodality in language instruction.

MULTIMODAL INTEGRATION OF QR CODES IN LANGUAGE SKILLS

This section specifically examines the practical applications of integrating Quick Response (QR) codes into teaching English language skills. Teachers may get important insights and practices relevant to each language skill by exploring implementations for speaking, writing, listening, and reading. The guide below offers a focused examination of the various ways in which QR codes can enhance the language learning experience. It includes examples such as incorporating interactive QR code features into listening exercises, promoting collaboration in speaking activities, enhancing reading tasks, and innovating writing assignments. The parts that follow provide practical and useful approaches that enable EFL teachers to effortlessly incorporate QR codes into their classroom activities, resulting in dynamic and student-centered language learning settings.

Integrating QR Codes for Listening

1.*Audiobook Access:* EFL teachers can create QR codes that link to online audiobooks or audio versions of literature, allowing their students to listen to authentic English language content. This exposes them to various accents, intonations, and styles.
  Steps:

1. Curate a thoughtfully selected list of audiobooks or audio versions of literature that align with the language proficiency and interests of your EFL students. The emphasis is on offering a diverse range of genres, spanning fiction, non-fiction, classic literature, contemporary works, and various cultural perspectives.
2. Create QR codes for each audiobook using a reliable generator, ensuring clear and scannable codes.

3. In the classroom, introduce the concept of audiobooks and set up QR code stations with descriptions, and facilitate active engagement by assigning tasks related to the content.
4. As follow up activities, encourage group discussions and reflective writing to deepen your students' understanding and connection with diverse accents.
5. As homework, you can create a library of QR code-linked audiobooks for ongoing exploration.

Some elements of multimodality in this context:

1. *Linguistic Mode:* The process of choosing and organising audiobooks involves the use of written and spoken words, focusing on the linguistic aspect. Group conversations and reflective writing projects foster active student participation with the subject matter via both oral and written means.
2. *Visual Mode:* QR codes are visual components that students scan in order to retrieve the audiobooks, so introducing a visual aspect to the learning process. The descriptions accompanying the QR code stations serve to give further visual information, so complementing the visual mode.
3. *Auditory Mode:* The main emphasis is on the auditory mode as students engage in listening to genuine English language material via audiobooks. This improves their ability to comprehend spoken language and increases their familiarity with different accents and intonations.
4. *Gestural Mode:* Although the main emphasis is on verbal, visual, and auditory modes, students may also employ gestural interactions with their devices, such as scanning QR codes. Scanning, being a physical action, introduces a nuanced gestural component to the process of acquiring knowledge.
5. *Spatial Mode:* The spatial mode refers to the physical layout of QR code stations in the classroom and the positioning of students as they interact with the information.

2. *Interactive Worksheets:* Teachers can design worksheets with QR codes that link to audio prompts or conversations. EFL students can scan the codes to listen to instructions or dialogues, making the learning process more interactive and dynamic.
Steps:

1. Curate audio content such as prompts or dialogues that align with the lesson's objectives, ensuring they cater to the language proficiency level of the students.
2. Generate QR codes and embed them into the worksheets, each code corresponding to a specific audio prompt.

3.   Students, equipped with smartphones or tablets, can effortlessly scan these QR codes to access the audio content, providing an auditory dimension to their learning experience.

Some elements of multimodality in this context:

1.   *Linguistic Mode:* The worksheet is designed to accommodate the linguistic mode, since it presents written instructions and prompts for students to read and comprehend. QR codes can be accompanied by written material, which offers more language input.
2.   *Visual Mode:* QR codes function as visual components that students scan in order to retrieve the auditory prompts. The use of visual interactivity introduces a dynamic and technology-focused element to the conventional worksheet structure. Incorporating images or pictures onto the worksheet can augment the visual aspect.
3.   *Auditory Mode:* The main emphasis is on the auditory mode as students engage in listening to audio cues or discussions accessed via QR codes. This improves their ability to comprehend spoken language and increases their exposure to it.
4.   *Gestural Mode:* Although the main emphasis is on verbal, visual, and auditory modes, students may also utilise gestural interactions with their devices, such as tapping to scan the QR code. The act of scanning introduces a nuanced gestural component to the process of acquiring knowledge.
5.   *Spatial Mode:* Students strategically position themselves in physical space to utilise their smartphones or tablets for the purpose of scanning QR codes, therefore engaging in the spatial mode. The configuration of content on the worksheet, encompassing the positioning of QR codes, might impact the manner in which students browse and engage with the material.

3. *Interactive Quizzes:* EFL teachers can create QR codes for listening comprehension quizzes. Students can scan the codes to access questions and respond, providing instant feedback on their understanding of the audio material.
Steps:

1.   Design quizzes that align with the language proficiency level and learning objectives of the students.
2.   Generate QR codes for each quiz linking directly to the corresponding questions.
3.   When students scan the codes using their smartphones or tablets, they gain immediate access to the quiz, allowing them to respond to questions and receive instant feedback on their comprehension of the audio material.

Some elements of multimodality in this context:

1. *Linguistic mode:* quiz questions and answer options are provided in written format, necessitating pupils to comprehend and analyse textual material. This is designed for the linguistic or alphabetic mode.
2. *Visual Mode:* QR codes are visual components that students scan in order to retrieve the quiz questions. The incorporation of visual elements into the coding experience enhances the learning process by introducing a visual component.
3. *Aural Mode:* The main emphasis is on the auditory mode as students engage in listening to the audio content that is connected to the quiz questions. This improves their ability to listen and understand spoken language.
4. *Gestural Mode:* Although the main emphasis is on linguistic and auditory modes, students may incorporate gestural activities with their devices (such as tapping to scan the QR code), so introducing a modest gestural component to the process.
5. *Spatial Mode:* Spatial factors may influence students' physical positioning when they utilise their smartphones or tablets to scan QR codes. The configuration of students in the classroom can also impact collaborative interactions throughout the quiz.

Integrating QR Codes into Speaking

1. ***Pronunciation Guides:*** EFL teachers can create QR codes linked to pronunciation guides or tutorials. Students can scan the codes to access audio examples and practice pronouncing challenging words or sounds.
Steps:

1. Curate a selection of challenging words or sounds that align with the specific pronunciation goals of your lesson.
2. Generate QR codes, each linked to audio examples or tutorials corresponding to the chosen words or sounds. These QR codes can be strategically incorporated into educational materials, handouts, or posted within the classroom.
3. When students scan the codes using their smartphones or tablets, they gain immediate access to the pronunciation guide, allowing them to listen to audio examples and practice challenging phonetics.
4. As a follow up activity, each student can take turns pronouncing the words/ sounds they practiced using the QR codes.
5. As homework, ask students to keep an online pronunciation notebook in which they record the QR codes of words/sounds that they find difficult.

Some elements of multimodality in this context:

1. *Linguistic Mode:* The process of selecting difficult words or sounds incorporates linguistic factors when pupils engage with written and spoken language. The online pronunciation notebook for homework enhances the linguistic mode by prompting students to record their discoveries in writing format.
2. *Visual Mode:* QR codes function as visual components that students scan in order to access the pronunciation guides, so enhancing the learning process with a visual aspect. Integrating QR codes into instructional materials or handouts enhances the visual aspect.
3. *Auditory Mode:* The main emphasis is on the auditory mode, where students engage in listening to audio samples and engage in practicing complex phonetics. This improves their ability to comprehend and get familiar with spoken communication.
4. *Gestural Mode:* Although the main emphasis is on verbal, visual, and auditory modes, students may also utilise gestural interactions with their devices, such as tapping to scan the QR code. The act of scanning introduces a nuanced gestural component to the process of acquiring knowledge.
5. *Spatial Mode:* The spatial configuration of QR codes inside the classroom and the placement of students as they interact with the content are factors that influence the spatial mode. The arrangement of an online pronunciation notebook requires careful spatial planning as students organise and position their recorded data.

2. ***Role-Play Scenarios:*** Teachers can develop QR codes that lead to different role-play scenarios. Each code can provide students with a specific role or situation, encouraging them to engage in spontaneous conversations and apply language in real-life contexts.

Steps:

1. Design a variety of role-play scenarios that align with language proficiency levels and learning objectives.
2. Generate QR codes, with each code linked to a specific role or situation. These QR codes can be distributed on worksheets, displayed in the classroom, or incorporated into lesson materials.
3. When students scan the codes using their smartphones or tablets, they are instantly assigned a role-play scenario, prompting them to engage in spontaneous conversations using the target language.
4. Following the role-play situations, arrange a session for peer feedback and reflection. Arrange students into pairs or form small groups to engage

in discussions and offer constructive criticism on one another's role-play performances.

5. For homework assignment, allocate students the task of producing a role-play reflection diary. Within the diary, students are required to select a single role-play scenario that they felt to be especially demanding or captivating.

Some elements of multimodality in this context:

1. *Linguistic Mode:* The creation of role-play scenarios entails the use of written and spoken language, specifically targeting the linguistic mode.
2. *Visual Mode:* The design and visual presentation of role-play worksheets or materials enhance the visual aspect.
3. *Aural Mode:* The main emphasis is on the auditory mode as students participate in impromptu discussions utilising the language being learned. Peer feedback sessions entail the exchange of spoken information, so adding to the auditory method of communication.
4. *Gestural Mode:* Students participate in gestural exchanges during role-play situations, utilising movement, emotion, and body language.
5. *Spatial Mode:* The spatial configuration of QR codes within the classroom and the placement of students during role-play activities contribute to the spatial mode.

3. Interactive Games: EFL teachers can design interactive games with QR codes that prompt speaking. For example, a QR code could link to a task like describing an image, answering a question, or participating in a quick speaking challenge.
Steps:

1. Conceptualize a range of speaking tasks suitable for their students, such as describing an image, answering questions, or participating in quick speaking challenges.
2. Generate QR codes, with each code linked to a specific speaking task. These QR codes can be incorporated into game materials, worksheets, or displayed around the classroom.
3. When students scan the codes using their smartphones or tablets, they are presented with a speaking prompt that encourages them to express themselves verbally.
4. Assign students an extensive oral task as an assignment. Furnish a collection of fresh QR codes, each associated with a more intricate speaking assignment or subject. Students utilise their smartphones or tablets to scan the QR codes

from their homes and engage in the speaking challenges by submitting recorded audio or video responses.

Some elements of multimodality in this context:

1. *Linguistic Mode:* The formulation of speaking assignments entails linguistic factors as students participate in oral communication. The QR codes, which function as cues for describing visuals, responding to queries, or engaging in speaking tasks, enhance the language aspect.
2. *Visual Mode:* The design and visual presentation of gaming materials or worksheets add to the visual aspect.
3. *Aural Mode:* The main emphasis is on the aural mode as students are encouraged to communicate vocally in reaction to the speaking challenges.
4. *Gestural Mode:* Students also participate in gestural exchanges during speaking difficulties. This can encompass non-verbal gestures as a means to augment communication.
5. *Spatial Mode:* The spatial configuration of QR codes within the classroom or on gaming materials, as well as the location of students as they interact with the verbal prompts, contribute to the spatial mode.

Integrating QR Codes into Reading

1. **Vocabulary Expansion:** Language teachers can create QR codes for specific vocabulary words in a reading passage. When scanned, these codes can provide definitions, synonyms, or example sentences, aiding comprehension and expanding students' vocabulary.

Steps:

1. Identify pivotal vocabulary words within a chosen passage.
2. Create QR codes that link to definitions, synonyms, or example sentences for each term.
3. Place these QR codes within or alongside the reading material.
4. When students encounter an unfamiliar word, the use of their smartphones or tablets to scan the corresponding QR code instantly provides them with supplemental information, facilitating an immediate understanding of the word's meaning, usage, and context.
5. For homework, direct learners to keep a vocabulary diary to record words encountered in the current reading text. Students should document the definition acquired from the QR code and write a phrase utilising the given term within a context that is similar to the reading section.

Some elements of multimodality in this context:

1. *Linguistic Mode:* The linguistic mode includes activities that use written and spoken words, such as identifying important vocabulary terms, generating QR codes, and keeping a vocabulary journal.
2. *Visual Mode:* The positioning of QR codes within or alongside the reading content enhances the visual aspect.
3. *Aural Mode:* Students have the option to engage in the aural mode by listening to pronunciation examples or phrase use through the QR codes.
4. *Gestural Mode:* The act of scanning QR codes with smartphones or tablets requires physical gestures, which are part of the gestural mode.
5. *Spatial Mode:* The spatial mode refers to the arrangement of QR codes within or alongside the reading material and the positioning of pupils as they interact with the information. Maintaining a vocabulary journal requires students to carefully arrange and order their collected material, taking into account spatial factors.

2. **Grammar and Syntax Focus**: EFL teachers can generate QR codes linked to grammar or syntax explanations related to the reading passage. Students can scan the codes to access additional information, reinforcing their understanding of language structures.

Steps:

1. Identify key grammar or syntax concepts within the reading material and embed QR codes that provide detailed explanations, examples, or additional resources.
2. Place these QR codes alongside or within the reading passage.
3. When students encounter challenging grammatical or syntactical elements, a quick scan of the corresponding QR code using their smartphones or tablets instantly provides them with supplementary information, offering clarification and reinforcement of the specific language structure.
4. As a follow up activity, Organise a grammar exploration workshop in the classroom, where students work together to analyse and debate the grammar or syntactic topics presented via QR codes.

Some elements of multimodality in this context:

1. *Linguistic Mode:* The linguistic mode encompasses activities such as identifying fundamental grammar or syntax principles, generating QR codes, and participating in a workshop that delves into grammar inquiry.

2. *Visual Mode:* The positioning of QR codes within or beside the reading passage, as well as the utilisation of visual aids during the grammar exploration session, enhance the visual aspect.
3. *Auditory Mode:* Although the main emphasis is on linguistic and visual modes, students have the opportunity to listen to explanations or participate in verbal conversations during the grammar discovery workshop, thereby activating the auditory mode.
4. *Gestural Mode:* During the grammar exploration session, participants may utilise gestures and facial expressions to enhance their collaborative efforts.
5. *Spatial Mode:* The spatial configuration of QR codes within or alongside the reading material and the placement of students during the grammar discovery workshop contribute to the spatial mode.

3. *Author Interviews and Background:* Teachers can create QR codes that link to interviews, biographies, or background information about the author. This enriches students' understanding of the context in which the text was written.

Steps:

1. Identify EFL reading materials according to the levels of your students.
2. Find additional content for these reading materials where authors discuss their inspirations, motivations, or writing processes, as well as biographical information providing insights into their lives.
3. Create QR codes associated with specific these specific contents
4. Before reading the assigned materials, allow students to access additional content by scanning the codes with their smartphones or tablets.
5. After the reading activity, hold discussion sessions in which learners can associate the information they obtained from QR codes with the reading content.

Some elements of multimodality in this context:

1. *Linguistic Mode:* The linguistic mode encompasses activities such as identifying reading materials, generating QR codes, and producing author interviews and biographies, all of which revolve around written and spoken language. Post-reading discussion sessions enable students to articulate their comprehension vocally, so actively including the language aspect.
2. *Visual Mode:* QR codes can incorporate visual components like photographs or graphics to enhance the visual aspect.
3. *Aural Mode:* The material associated with QR codes may have auditory components, such as author interviews or spoken biographies, stimulating the

sense of hearing. Discussion sessions may entail actively listening to peers' viewpoints and actively participating in spoken communication.

4. *Gestural Mode:* The act of scanning QR codes with smartphones or tablets requires physical gestures, which are part of the gestural mode. During discussion sessions, students may utilise gestures and expressions to effectively communicate and demonstrate their comprehension.

5. *Spatial Mode:* The spatial configuration of QR codes in close proximity to reading materials or across the classroom influences the spatial mode. The spatial mode is engaged through group configurations during discussion sessions and the physical act of interacting with materials.

Integrating QR Codes Into Writing

1. Digital Writing Prompts: Language teachers use QR codes for digital writing prompts that lead to multimedia content, such as images, videos, or audio clips. This approach sparks creativity and encourages students to write in response to various stimuli.

Steps:

1. Find various multimedia content such as images, videos, or audio clips which can be used as writing prompts according to your students' language levels.

2. Generate QR codes associated with specific writing prompts, each code leading to multimedia content.

3. Distribute these codes to the students or stick them on your classroom walls.

4. Ask students scan these QR codes using their smartphones or tablets.

5. Encourage your students to respond to visual, auditory, or audio-visual prompts and complete their writing task (e.g. describing a picture, writing a poem for a given sound, etc.)

6. As a follow up activity, after collecting and mixing the students' writings, distribute them back to the students in a mixed manner and ask them to match each writing with the one prompt.

7. Conduct a discussion session to explore the students' decisions and prompt them to provide explanations for their choices.

Some elements of multimodality in this context:

1. *Linguistic Mode:* The production of QR codes, dissemination of prompts, and the written replies from pupils encompass the use of written and spoken language, specifically catering to the linguistic mode.

2. *Visual Mode:* QR codes function as visual components that students scan in order to retrieve multimedia material, so enhancing the learning process with a visual aspect. The placement of QR codes throughout the classroom and the reactions of the pupils to visual cues add to the visual mode.

3. *Aural Mode:* Multimedia information associated with QR codes may incorporate audio samples, stimulating the auditory mode. The follow-up activity's discussion sessions may entail spoken communication, so adding to the aural mode.

4. *Gestural Mode:* The process of scanning QR codes with smartphones or tablets requires physical gestures, which are part of the gestural mode. During the discussion session, students may utilise expressions and gestures to effectively communicate and elucidate their selections.

5. *Spatial Mode:* The spatial configuration of QR codes across the classroom adds to the spatial mode.

    2. Research Resources: Teachers can create QR codes that link to online research resources. Students can scan the codes to access articles, websites, or videos relevant to their writing topics, enriching the content of their compositions.

Steps:

1. Assign your students a writing subject.
2. Curate a comprehensive selection of pertinent internet research materials, including articles, websites, and videos, that are directly connected to the writing themes.
3. Create QR codes for each research resource.
4. Position the QR codes conspicuously and conveniently inside the classroom or distribute a personalised set of QR codes to each student, corresponding to their respective writing subjects.
5. Designate a certain period of time for students to utilise their smartphones or tablets to scan the QR codes.
6. Encourage students to engage in resource exploration by utilising the online research resources connected to the QR codes. This will enable them to obtain vital knowledge to enhance their writing works.
7. Ask students to engage in the process of note-taking and start the initial stages of composing their written works, integrating ideas and information acquired from the research resources.
8. Encourage students to engage in collaborative activities and discussions to share and exchange ideas on the materials they have examined.
9. Provide students with guidance on correctly referencing and integrating material from their studied sources into their writing.

10. After the writing process, facilitate a classroom dialogue or reflective session in which students explore their experiences with the research process, emphasising significant insights gained and difficulties encountered.

Some elements of multimodality in this context:

1. *Linguistic Mode:* The linguistic mode encompasses tasks such as selecting writing topics, organising research materials, and engaging in verbal and written debates.
2. *Visual Mode:* The positioning of QR codes in the classroom enhances the visual aspect.
3. *Auditory Mode:* Although the main emphasis is on linguistic and visual modes, students have the opportunity to participate in debates and engage in vocal communication during collaborative activities, therefore utilising the auditory mode.
4. *Gestural Mode:* Collaborative activities sometimes entail the use of gestures and emotions when students engage in communication and exchange ideas.
5. *Spatial Mode:* The spatial configuration of QR codes in the classroom and the physical allocation of customised groups of QR codes stimulate the spatial mode. Classroom conversations and collaborative activities are influenced by the physical layout and closeness of individuals, which contributes to the spatial aspect.

CHALLENGES AND STRATEGIES FOR QR CODE INTEGRATION

Incorporating QR codes into educational processes, such as language acquisition, might provide many advantages, but it also comes with a set of challenges for both language teachers and learners. An obstacle can arise from the disparity in technological access among language learners. In other words, some students may lack smartphones or devices with the ability to scan QR codes, which can hinder their participation to the language activities (Castells, 2002; Eastin et al., 2015). In order to solve this issue, it is possible to offer alternative methods for accessing material, such as classroom gadgets or collaborative use of smartphones. Furthermore, technical difficulties, such as malfunctions, network disruptions, or incompatibility with devices can cause problems in successfully implementing QR codes into language activities (Rikala & Kankaanranta, 2012). In order to solve this problem, language teachers can perform technology checks before implementing activities. Furthermore, curating high-quality information that is relevant and contributing to the overall learning experience is important while linking language materials to QR codes. Considering accessibility factors, such as incorporating appropriate text size and contrast in QR code activities can help language learners with visual impairments (Thornton & Hauser, 2002).

Another problem may arise from digital illiteracy. There may be students who are unfamiliar with QR codes or lack the necessary abilities in digital literacy (Scheerder et al., 2017). For example, in Zeybek (2020)'s research the findings revealed that the EFL learners' first encounter with mobile technologies hindered their success in the activities and as they have become more familiar with the technology they did better in such tasks. Moreover, in this study the instructors of these learners helped learners use the multimodal mobile technologies at their hands during the activities. Thus, offering instructional sessions, tutorials, or materials on the use of QR codes may help in closing this divide, and a step-by-step introduction with explicit guidance and assistance can cultivate assurance. Additionally, some students may not want to participate in these activities because of data security, especially when utilising QR code generators provided by third-party sources or establishing connections to external websites (Wong & Looi, 2010). To overcome these challenges, language teachers can use reliable QR code generators and guarantee the security of the material. Restricted internet access for students may provide challenges (Castells, 2002), especially when accessing online information is necessary. Offering downloadable tools or alternate information can help students who have restricted internet connectivity. Also, teachers can share their internet with these students during these activities.

Some language teachers can be resistant to change their present teaching methods and may prefer conventional teaching techniques. By using a step-by-step approach, emphasising the advantages of incorporating QR code integration, and offering comprehensive training and assistance (Kuru Gönen & Zeybek, 2022b), language teachers and learners may develop a sense of ease and assurance. In order to achieve a successful incorporation of QR codes into language learning, instructors can use a range of strategies. With the help of precise directions, language teachers can proficiently convey the procedure of integrating QR codes into teaching foreign languages (Kuru Gönen & Zeybek, 2022b). Training events and workshops may help instructors and students get more familiar with QR code technology and its uses, therefore improving their digital literacy abilities. Additionally, the cooperation among language teacher can enable the exchange of exemplary methods and inventive approaches in using QR codes by building a supportive and cooperative educational community (Zeybek, 2020).

CONCLUSION

The multimodal use of QR codes into language learning represents a significant change in the field of educational technology, bringing in a period of innovation and increased involvement. This technical instrument not only provides a means for acquiring language, but more significantly, it enhances the teaching methods in the digital era. As we explore the wide-ranging use of QR codes in foreign language learning, it is significant to further examine the complex obstacles and complex strategies that come with this new language teaching method. An important concern is the unequal access to technology among language learners, which requires careful solutions. Offering various access methods, such as classroom gadgets and collaborative learning, is crucial to promote inclusion and accommodate the varying technology preferences of learners.

Moreover, the issue of disparities in digital literacy becomes prominent, emphasising the necessity for focused endeavours in foreign language learning. Workshops and training sessions are essential for instructors and students who have problems in implementing the QR code technology. These can serve to both close the gap in digital literacy and enable educators and learners to fully understand the potential of QR codes. Another factor to consider is how to effectively include QR codes into regular teaching methods. Of course it is important to keep in mind the dangers of over dependence on technology. However, adopting a balanced approach by seeing QR codes as supplementary tools can help language teachers. The various activities in this chapter provide a balanced and cooperative way of using QR codes in advantageous ways in foreign language teaching.

The quality of the language teaching content connected to QR codes serves as a keystone in the success of this integration. The selection of materials should go beyond just being relevant and should aim providing significant value to the learning process. By selecting and organising material that supports language learning goals can meet the various needs of learners. In this way, QR codes can be used as interactive tools enhancing comprehension and active involvement. Furthermore, the success of using QR codes in language teaching relies on constant monitoring and evaluation. Feedback from both language teachers and learners can enable an effective implementation. Also, collaboration among educators is essential for effectively integrating QR codes into language teaching. The exchange of best methods, understandings, and problem-solving approaches helps in building a dynamic and encouraging educational community. By working together, language teachers can contribute to the continuous development of QR code integration, creating an atmosphere that promotes shared learning and progress.

To summarise, the multimodal use of QR codes into language acquisition represents more than just a technological enhancement; it signifies a significant pedagogical shift. The prudent use of QR codes in foreign language teaching, as offered in many activities proposed in this chapter, can serve as s catalytic force for language teachers. They aim to light up ideas for creative integration of QR codes and effective use in order to fully unlock the capabilities of technology in language learning. This empowers foreign language teachers and learners and facilitates their progress in the ever-changing digital world, while also creating a harmonious blend of technology and teaching methods for the future.

REFERENCES

Akçayir, M., & Akçayir, G. (2016). Üniversite Öğrencilerinin Yabancı Dil Eğitiminde Artırılmış Gerçeklik Teknolojisi Kullanımına Yönelik Görüşleri. *Erzincan Üniversitesi Eğitim Fakültesi Dergisi*, *18*(2), 1169–1186. doi:10.17556/jef.86406

Amanah, F. S., & Yunus, M. M. (2018). QR codes in ESL classroom learning. *International Journal of Innovative Research and Creative Technology*, *4*(3), 74–77.

Aziza, P. K. (2020). The Implementation of using quick response Codes in listening comprehension for senior high school. *Retain*, *8*(1), 125–131.

Bakla, A. (2018). Quick response codes in foreign language instruction: Practical ideas and strategies, Inonu University. *Journal of the Faculty of Education*, *19*(3), 749–762. doi:10.17679/inuefd.475262

Balintag, C. M., & Wilang, J. D. (2020). QR codes utilization in EFL classroom: Affective language learning attributes in writing. *Script Journal: Journal of Linguistics and English Teaching*, *5*(1), 1–13. doi:10.24903/sj.v5i1.425

Castells, M. (2002). *The Internet galaxy: Reflections on the Internet, business, and society*. Oxford University Press. doi:10.1093/acprof:oso/9780199255771.001.0001

Castells, M. (2002). *The Internet galaxy: Reflections on the Internet, business, and society*. Oxford University Press. doi:10.1093/acprof:oso/9780199255771.001.0001

Celik, B. (2023). EFL learners' perceptions on QR code enriched instruction in developing macro-skills. *International Journal of Social Sciences & Educational Studies*, *10*(3).

Chanier, T., & Lamy, M. N. (2017). Researching Technology-mediated Multimodal Interaction. The handbook of technology and second language teaching and learning, 428-443.

Chee, K. M., & Tan, K. H. (2021). QR Codes as a Potential Tool in Teaching and Learning Pronunciation: A Critical Review. *Higher Education and Oriental Studies, 1*(1).

Chen, N. S., Teng, D. C. E., & Lee, C. H. (2010). Augmenting paper-based reading activities with mobile technology to enhance reading comprehension. In *2010 6th IEEE international conference on wireless, Mobile, and ubiquitous technologies in education* (pp. 201–203). IEEE. 10.1109/WMUTE.2010.39

Cheng, S. C., Hwang, W. Y., Wu, S. Y., Shadiev, R., & Xie, C.-H. (2010). A mobile device and online system with contextual familiarity and its effects on English learning on Campus. *Journal of Educational Technology & Society, 13*(3), 93–109.

Chiappe, A., Amado, N., & Leguizamón, L. (2020). Educommunication in digital environments: An interaction´s perspective inside and beyond the classroom. *Innoeduca. International Journal of Technology and Educational Innovation, 6*(1), 34–41. doi:10.24310/innoeduca.2020.v6i1.4959

Christopoulos, A., Mystakidis, S., Pellas, N., & Laakso, M. J. (2021). ARLEAN: An augmented reality learning analytics ethical framework. *Computers, 10*(8), 92. doi:10.3390/computers10080092

Crompton, H. (2013). A historical overview of m-learning; Toward learner-centered education. In Z. Berge & L. Y. Muilenburg (Eds.), *Handbook of mobile learning* (pp. 3–14). Routledge.

Damodharan, V. S. (2022). Antecedents of QR code acceptance during Covid-19: Towards sustainability. *Transnational Marketing Journal, 10*(1).

Davies, H., Hjorth, L., Andrejevic, M., Richardson, I., & DeSouza, R. (2023). QR codes during the pandemic: Seamful quotidian placemaking. *Convergence,* 13548565231160623.

De Pietro, O., & Fronter, G. (2012). *Mobile tutoring for situated learning and collaborative learning in AIML application using QR-Code.* In The sixth international conference on complex, intelligent, and software systems (CISIS-2012), Palermo, Italy.

Eastin, M. S., Cicchirillo, V., & Mabry, A. (2015). Extending the digital divide conversation: Examining the knowledge gap through media expectancies. *Journal of Broadcasting & Electronic Media, 59*(3), 416–437. doi:10.1080/08838151.2015.1054994

Garzón, J., & Acevedo, J. (2019). Meta-analysis of the impact of augmented reality on students' learning gains. *Educational Research Review*, *27*, 244–260. doi:10.1016/j.edurev.2019.04.001

Griol, D., & Molina, J. M. (2016). From VoiceXML to multimodal mobile Apps: Development of practical conversational interfaces. *Advances in Distributed Computing and Artificial Intelligence Journal*, *3*(5), 43–53. doi:10.14201/ADCAIJ2016534353

Halliday, M. A. K. (1985). *Spoken and written language*. Deakin University Press.

Hsu, T. C. (2017). Learning English with augmented reality: Do learning styles matter? *Computers & Education*, *106*, 137–149. doi:10.1016/j.compedu.2016.12.007

Hwang, G. J., Wu, C. H., Tseng, J. C. R., & Huang, I. (2011). Development of a ubiquitous learning platform based on a real-time help-seeking mechanism. *British Journal of Educational Technology*, *42*(6), 992–1002. doi:10.1111/j.1467-8535.2010.01123.x

Jewitt, C. (2009). *The Routledge Handbook of Multimodal Analysis*. Routledge.

Kress, G. (2000a). Design and transformation: New theories of meaning. In B. Cope & M. Kalantzis (Eds.), *Multiliteracies: Literacy learning and the design of social futures* (pp. 153–161). Routledge.

Kress, G. (2000b). Multimodality. In B. Cope & M. Kalantzis (Eds.), *Multiliteracies: Literacy learning and the design of social futures* (pp. 182–202). Routledge.

Kress, G. (2010). *Multimodality: A social semiotic approach to contemporary communication*. Routledge.

Kress, G., Jewitt, C., Bourne, J., Franks, A., Hardcastle, J., Jones, K., & Reid, E. (2005). *English in Urban Classrooms: A Multimodal Perspective on Teaching and Learning*. Routledge.

Kress, G., Jewitt, C., Ogborn, J., & Tsatsarelis, C. (2001). *Multimodal teaching and learning*. Continuum Press.

Kress, G. R., & van Leeuwen, T. (2001). *Multimodal Discourse: the modes and media of contemporary communication*. Edward Arnold.

Kukulska-Hulme, A., Lee, H., & Norris, L. (2017). Mobile learning revolution: Implications for language pedagogy. In The handbook of technology and second language teaching and learning, 217-233.

Kuru Gönen, S. İ., & Zeybek, G. (2022a). Using QR code enhanced authentic texts in EFL extensive reading: A qualitative study on student perceptions. *Education and Information Technologies, 27*(2), 2039–2057. doi:10.1007/s10639-021-10695-w

Kuru Gönen, S. İ., & Zeybek, G. (2022b). Training on multimodal mobile-assisted language learning: A suggested model for pre-service EFL teachers. *Computer Assisted Language Learning*, 1–22. doi:10.1080/09588221.2022.2157016

Law, C., & So, S. (2010). QR codes in education. *Journal of Educational Technology Development and Exchange, 3*(1), 85–100. doi:10.18785/jetde.0301.07

Law, C. Y., & So, S. (2010). QR codes in education. [JETDE]. *Journal of Educational Technology Development and Exchange, 3*(1), 7. doi:10.18785/jetde.0301.07

Le, N., & Dinh, H. (2020). Augmented reality: A brief introduction, its potentials, and implications in language education. In J. Perren, K. Kelch, J. Byun, S. Cervantes, & S. Safavi (Eds.), *Applications of CALL theory in ESL and EFL environments* (pp. 291–352). IGI Global.

Liu, T. Y., Tan, T. H., & Chu, Y. L. (2008). QR code and augmented reality-supported mobile English learning system. In Workshop of mobile multmedia processing (pp. 37–52). Heidelberg.

Magal-Royo, T., Giménez-López, J. L., Pairy, B., García-Laborda, J., & Gonzalez-del Rio, J. (2011). Multimodal application for foreign language teaching. In *Interactive Collaborative Learning (ICL), 2011 14th International Conference on* (pp. 145-148). IEEE. 10.1109/ICL.2011.6059564

McCabe, M., & Tedesco, S. (2012). Using QR codes and mobile devices to foster a learning environment for mathematics education. *International Journal of Technology Inclusive and Inclusive Education, 1*(6), 37–43. doi:10.20533/ijtie.2047.0533.2012.0006

Milutinović, M., Labus, A., Stojiljković, V., Bogdanović, Z., & Despotović-Zrakić, M. (2015). Designing a mobile language learning system based on lightweight learning objects. *Multimedia Tools and Applications, 74*(3), 903–935. doi:10.1007/s11042-013-1704-5

Nadolny, L. (2017). Interactive print: The design of cognitive tasks in blended augmented reality and print documents. *British Journal of Educational Technology, 48*(3), 814–823. doi:10.1111/bjet.12462

Perwitasari, I. D., & Hendrawan, J. (2023). Design of a library book lending information system using qr code technology. *Prosiding Universitas Dharmawangsa, 3*(1), 577–584.

Rikala, J., & Kankaanranta, M. (2012). The use of quick response codes in the classroom. In M. Specht, M. Sharples, & J. Multisilta (Eds.), *Proceedings of the 11th Conference on Mobile and Contextual Learning* (pp. 148–155)., Retrieved from https://ceur-ws.org/Vol-955/papers/paper_40.pdf

Scheerder, A., van Deursen, A., & van Dijk, J. (2017). Determinants of Internet skills, uses and outcomes: A systematic review of the second-and third-level digital divide. *Telematics and Informatics, 34*(8), 1607–1624. doi:10.1016/j.tele.2017.07.007

Thornton, P., & Houser, C. (2002). M-learning: Learning in transit. In P. Lewis (Ed.), *The changing face of CALL: A Japanese perspective* (pp. 229–243). Swets & Zeitlinger.

van Leeuwen, T. (2005). *Introducing Social Semiotics*. Routlegde.

Vigil, K. M. (2017). *Quick response (QR) codes for audio support in foreign language learning.* [Doctoral dissertation, Boston University].

Wong, L.-H., & Looi, C.-J. (2010). Vocabulary learning by mobile-assisted content creation and social meaning-making: Two case studies. *Journal of Computer Assisted Learning, 26*(5), 421–433. doi:10.1111/j.1365-2729.2010.00357.x

Yelland, N. J. (2018). A pedagogy of multiliteracies: Young children and multimodal learning with tablets. *British Journal of Educational Technology, 49*(5), 847–858. doi:10.1111/bjet.12635

Yunus, M., Lau, E. Y. Y., Khair, A. H. M., & Yusof, N. M. (2020). Acquisition of vocabulary in primary schools via GoPic with QR code. *International Journal of English Language and Literature Studies, 9*(3), 121–131. doi:10.18488/journal.23.2020.93.121.131

Zeybek, G. (2020). Multimodal mobile-assisted language learning classroom applications: A study in pre-service teacher education. [Doctoral Dissertation, Anadolu University, Eskişehir].

Chapter 11

Revolutionizing Language Learning Beyond Tradition in Business Education 4.0:
Artificial Intelligence–Driven Language Learning Towards English Proficiency

Mohammad Rashed Hasan Polas
Sonargaon University, Bangladesh

Asghar Afshar Jahanshahi
 https://orcid.org/0000-0003-2241-9913
IPADE Business School, Mexico

Siti Aida Samikon
Limkokwing University of Creative Technology, Malaysia

Tahmina Akter
University of Dhaka, Bangladesh

Md. Arif Hosseon Roky
Universiti Putra Malaysia, Malaysia

ABSTRACT

This study investigates the interplay of attitude, learning environment, motivation, technological adaptability, and self-confidence with English language proficiency, leveraging artificial intelligence (AI) tools within the context of the Business Education 4.0 era among university students in Bangladesh. Methodologically, a quantitative approach was employed, embracing positivism. A stratified random

DOI: 10.4018/979-8-3693-2169-0.ch011

Copyright © 2024, IGI Global. Copying or distributing in print or electronic forms without written permission of IGI Global is prohibited.

sampling technique was applied, yielding a sample of 433 university students from five universities who are currently studying at the Department of Business Administration in Dhaka, Bangladesh. Structured surveys were used to collect data from the respondents. To analyze the data, SPSS V.25 was used. Findings reveal a significant positive association between a learning environment and English language proficiency. Technological adaptability, facilitated by AI, positively influences language skills. Self-confidence plays a crucial role, aligning with Bandura's Social Cognitive Theory.

INTRODUCTION

In the dynamic landscape of higher education, the importance of English proficiency has become increasingly pivotal for university students, particularly those enrolled in business administration programs, as emphasized by Neumann et al. (2019) and Zhai (2023). The interconnection of global economies, the rise in multinational corporations, and the advent of Education 4.0, characterized by the integration of advanced technologies, underscore the necessity of a robust command of the English language for aspiring professionals, as noted by Zou et al. (2020). This investigation explores the intricate relationship between English proficiency, Artificial Intelligence (AI), and key determinants such as the learning environment, motivation, technological adaptability, and self-confidence among undergraduate students pursuing business administration within the context of Bangladesh, as outlined by Liu et al. (2023).

Global business demands effective cross-cultural communication, with English serving as the essential lingua franca (Ibrahim et al., 2023). Mastery of English is crucial for business students navigating international interactions, providing access to academic and professional resources (Khasawneh & Jadallah Abed Khasawneh, 2023). Proficiency is vital for staying updated on industry trends and engaging with cutting-edge knowledge. In today's business landscape, multinational corporations prioritize candidates with strong academic backgrounds and excellent English communication skills, influencing employability and career trajectories (Rose et al., 2020). English proficiency is a key differentiator in recruitment, shaping business graduates' success in forums, conferences, and global initiatives (Alhassan et al., 2021).

The emergence of Education 4.0, marked by the integration of Artificial Intelligence (AI) and advanced technologies into the educational landscape, underscores the heightened significance of English proficiency, as highlighted by Han (2021) and Chen et al. (2022). As educational paradigms pivot towards digitally-driven modes of instruction, communication, and collaboration, students excelling in English gain a competitive edge in fully leveraging the potential of these technological advancements. Proficiency in the English language emerges as a crucial determinant for success in a world characterized by rapid evolution, interconnectedness, and shaped by the forces of globalization, as posited by Ebadi and Amini (2022). The context of Bangladesh, with its growing role on the global stage, accentuates the paramount importance of effective English communication skills for university students (Khasawneh & Jadallah Abed Khasawneh, 2023). This study embarks on a comprehensive exploration of the intricate factors influencing English language proficiency within the context of the Education 4.0 era, with a particular focus on the interconnected dynamics of attitudes, learning environments, motivation, technological adaptability, and self-confidence among university students in Bangladesh, as outlined by Farley et al. (2020).

As Bangladesh becomes more integrated into the global community, the ability of its university students to navigate academic and professional realms in English becomes pivotal. English serves as the lingua franca of international academia, with many leading educational institutions and scholarly publications utilizing it as the primary medium of communication (Malik et al., 2023). Proficiency in English is, therefore, a crucial determinant of Bangladeshi students' ability to access and contribute to global academic discourse, fostering participation in collaborative research projects, academic conferences, and international knowledge exchange (Madhavi et al., 2023).

In today's global job market, English proficiency is a prized skill, sought by multinational corporations, NGOs, and international entities (Srivani et al., 2022). For Bangladeshi university students, mastering English enhances employability and unlocks diverse career opportunities locally and globally (Han, 2021). The study addresses the pivotal role of English proficiency in the evolving global role of Bangladesh, examining the intricate relationships between individual attitudes, learning environments, motivation, technological adaptability, and self-confidence (Avello et al., 2019; Nguyen & Vo, 2021). The integration of technology into academia and professional life requires high technological adaptability, often intertwined with English proficiency (AbdAlgane & Jabir Othman, 2023). Given that digital platforms predominantly operate in English, proficiency becomes essential for navigating the digital landscape and leveraging tools for academic and professional success (Melvina & Julia, 2021; Khoo & Kang, 2022). Beyond functional communication, English proficiency facilitates cultural exchange, fostering a global mindset (Kang, 2022). Moreover, it cultivates collaboration, presentation, and persuasion skills vital for success in the interconnected global environment. Motivation and self-confidence are crucial elements in language acquisition, emphasizing the need for effective language programs and interventions (Sun et al., 2023).

This study explores the nexus between English proficiency, Artificial Intelligence integration, and critical factors like learning environment, motivation, technological adaptability, and self-confidence among business administration undergraduates in Bangladesh. The study aims to provide insights for educational policies, curriculum design, and pedagogical approaches tailored to the Education 4.0 era. It specifically delves into the intricate relationships influencing English proficiency, offering guidance for formulating policies, curriculum development, and support mechanisms. The impact of learning environments, both in-classroom and extracurricular, on language acquisition is dissected, scrutinizing institutional structures, teaching methods, and societal perceptions affecting English proficiency advancement.

In the subsequent segments, we will explore the distinct facets of our research, meticulously scrutinizing each variable to furnish a thorough comprehension of the intricate dynamics shaping the proficiency in the English language among university students in Bangladesh within the context of the Education 4.0 era.

The study was proposed to answer the following research questions:

Research Question 1 (RQ1): What factors, capable of yielding both positive and negative outcomes, may impact the involvement of university students in the acquisition of English language skills through the integration of artificial intelligence?

Research Question 2 (RQ2): To what degree can artificial intelligence be employed to facilitate the development of English language proficiency at the university level?

Research Question 3 (RQ3): What obstacles exist in the implementation of artificial intelligence for enhancing English language proficiency among university students?

The findings of this research bear potential implications for educational policies, curriculum design, and pedagogical approaches aimed at enhancing English language proficiency among Bangladeshi university students. By comprehensively examining the interplay between attitudes, learning environments, motivation, technological adaptability, and self-confidence, this study aspires to contribute valuable insights that can inform targeted interventions, ultimately empowering students to navigate the globalized world with linguistic dexterity. In essence, the investigation into the current scenario of English proficiency among Bangladeshi university students is a critical endeavor with far-reaching consequences for the academic, professional, and personal trajectories of the nation's future leaders and global participants.

LITERATURE REVIEW AND HYPOTHESES DEVELOPMENT

Theoretical Foundations

This study delves into exploring positive and significant associations among attitude, learning environment, motivation, technological adaptability, self-confidence, and

English language proficiency among university students. To enrich the context of these relationships, it is imperative to expand the literature review by incorporating recent studies at the crossover of AI, adaptive learning technology, and English language proficiency building (Mujahidah & Yusdiana, 2023). Insights from the last three years focusing on the innovative use of AI in enhancing various aspects of English proficiency would offer a contemporary perspective to the existing theories (Ryan & Deci, 2022; Goldfarb et al., 2023).

Moreover, the background section could be broadened to highlight the specifics of the Education 4.0 paradigm, shedding light on its inherent issues, complexities, and opportunities (Tudge et al., 2022; Navarro & Tudge, 2023). Emphasizing the challenges and prospects associated with the integration of AI in advancing English proficiency education within the context of Education 4.0 would provide a more comprehensive understanding (Tudge et al., 2022; Navarro & Tudge, 2023). This expansion would not only align the study with cutting-edge developments but also address the reviewer's suggestion to scrutinize the specific complexities and opportunities presented by the evolving educational landscape (Zhang, 2023). By integrating recent literature and elucidating the intricacies of Education 4.0, the study can present a more nuanced exploration of the interconnected realms of AI-driven language learning and English proficiency (Rumjaun & Narod, 2020; Navarro & Tudge, 2023).

Self-Determination Theory posits that individuals are motivated when their basic psychological needs for autonomy, competence, and relatedness are fulfilled (Ryan & Deci, 2022; Goldfarb et al., 2023). In the context of this study, students experiencing a sense of autonomy and competence in their language learning, coupled with a supportive and connected learning environment, may demonstrate higher motivation, thereby contributing to the enhancement of English language proficiency (Ryan & Deci, 2017; Goldfarb et al., 2023). Bronfenbrenner's theory directs attention to the myriad environmental systems shaping an individual's development (Tudge et al., 2022; Navarro & Tudge, 2023). Your research aligns with this theory as it examines how diverse ecological factors, including the university learning environment, socio-cultural influences, and technological factors, interact to influence English language proficiency (Rosa & Tudge, 2013; Navarro & Tudge, 2023).

The Technology Acceptance Model delves into the process by which users accept and adopt technology (Aburbeian et al., 2022). In the context of your study, technological adaptability may be shaped by factors such as perceived ease of use and perceived usefulness. Students perceiving technology as accessible and advantageous are likely to exhibit heightened technological adaptability, thereby positively influencing their proficiency in the English language (Vélez-Agosto et al., 2017; Wang et al., 2023). Krashen's Affective Filter hypothesis posits that emotional factors, such as motivation and anxiety, can impact the effectiveness of language acquisition. In your study, positive attitudes, motivation, and self-confidence may serve as facilitators, reducing the affective filter and fostering a more conducive environment for language learning (Lin et al., 2015; Zhang, 2023). Vygotsky's theory underscores the significance of social interaction and scaffolding in the learning process (Zhang, 2023). Within your study, the learning environment and interactions with peers or instructors may function as a 'zone of proximal development,' where students receive support in their language proficiency development through social engagement and collaborative learning (Topçiu & Myftiu, 2015; Kiruthiga & Christopher, 2022).

The Expectancy-Value Theory centers on individuals' beliefs about their ability (expectancy) and the significance they attribute to a task. In your study, self-confidence may align with expectancy, while motivation may be influenced by the perceived value of English language proficiency for the students' academic and career goals (Lee & Song, 2022; Shang et al., 2023). Bronfenbrenner's theory directs attention to the myriad environmental systems shaping an individual's development. Your research aligns with this theory as it examines how diverse ecological factors, including the university learning environment, socio-cultural influences, and technological factors, interact to influence English language proficiency (Rosa & Tudge, 2013; Wang & Xue, 2022; French et al., 2023). The Technology Acceptance Model delves into the process by which users accept and adopt technology. In the context of your study, technological adaptability may be shaped by factors such as perceived ease of use and perceived usefulness (French et al., 2023). Students perceiving technology as accessible and advantageous are likely to exhibit heightened technological adaptability, thereby positively influencing their proficiency in the English language (Vélez-Agosto et al., 2017; Goldma et al., 2022; French et al., 2023).

Student's Attitude and Intention for English Proficiency

The notion of attitude has been a focal point of interest for researchers in both first and second language acquisition (Studer & Konstantinidou, 2015; Chen et al., 2022; Chueh & Huang, 2023). A multitude of studies has consistently underscored the crucial role of students' attitudes in the learning process, asserting that it ought to be an integral component of pedagogy in the instruction of second or foreign languages (Bagheri & Andi, 2015; Sardegna et al., 2018; Boonsuk & Fang, 2022; Liu & Ma, 2023). Investigating students' attitudes toward language learning holds paramount importance for several reasons. Primarily, attitudes are believed to exert a substantial influence on various behaviors, such as the selection and reading of books, as well as the willingness to engage in conversations in a foreign language (Alfadda & Mahdi, 2021; Lee, 2022). Furthermore, a distinct correlation between attitudes and academic success or achievement has been established. Getie (2020) posits that there is compelling evidence supporting the idea that attitudes play a causative role in influencing achievement, rather than the reverse. The underlying rationale for this connection lies in the assertion that attitudes not only shape behaviors but also impact one's internal disposition and, consequently, the learning process (Sun & Gao, 2020; Lai et al., 2022; Liu & Ma, 2023). It is evident that a reciprocal relationship exists between language learning and the environmental components that shape a student's upbringing. Both negative and positive attitudes wield considerable influence over the trajectory and success of language acquisition. This intricate interplay emphasizes the need for a nuanced understanding of the role of attitudes in the language learning journey (Sari & Wahyudin, 2019; Huang et al., 2020; Liu & Ma, 2023).

The association between students' attitudes and their intention to attain proficiency in English has been a central focus in educational research, illuminating the intricate interplay between psychological factors and language acquisition (Zhu et al., 2020; Noviana & Oktaviani, 2022; Liu & Ma, 2023). Numerous investigations have delved into the dynamic nature of attitudes and their influence on language learning outcomes. Notably, the research on the Attitude-Motivation Test Battery underscores the significance of attitudes in second language acquisition, with findings suggesting that positive attitudes toward the target language enhance motivation and contribute to elevated language proficiency (Din, 2020; Noviana & Oktaviani, 2022; Liu et al., 2023). Subsequent studies have extended this framework, underscoring the pivotal role of attitude in shaping learners' intentions and efforts (Galloway & Ruegg, 2020; Noviana & Oktaviani, 2022; Liu et al., 2023). Additionally, research grounded in the Theory of Planned Behavior (Ajzen, 1991) has highlighted the predictive power of attitudes in determining behavioral intentions. Within the realm of language learning, studies such as those conducted by Chen et al. (2022) demonstrated that positive attitudes toward English positively influence students' intentions to engage in language learning activities, ultimately impacting their language proficiency (Liu et al., 2023).

The socio-cultural dimension of attitudes has been explored by studies like Alfadda and Mahdi (2021), which found that societal attitudes toward English influenced individual learners' attitudes. This highlights the interconnectedness of societal perceptions and personal attitudes, shaping students' intentions for English proficiency. Technological advancements have introduced new dimensions to attitudes (Liu & Ma, 2023). A study conducted by Huang et al. (2020) investigated the influence of computer-assisted language learning on attitudes and identified a positive correlation with language proficiency. This implies that incorporating technology into language learning environments may impact students' attitudes and, subsequently, their intention to achieve proficiency in English (Din, 2020; Liu et al., 2023). This research endeavors to augment the current body of literature by empirically examining the nature and strength of the connection between attitudes and the intention for English proficiency, offering valuable insights for educators, policymakers, and researchers dedicated to enhancing language learning environments.

Building upon the insights from existing research, we formulate the following hypothesis:

H1: There is a positive and significant relationship between students' attitude for English learning and their intention for English proficiency.

This hypothesis is grounded in the notion that a favorable attitude toward the English language is likely to stimulate motivation and a proactive intention to achieve proficiency. Drawing from the theoretical foundations of the Attitude-Motivation Test Battery, the Theory of Planned Behavior, and socio-cultural perspectives, we anticipate that students who harbor positive attitudes toward English will demonstrate a heightened intention to engage in language learning activities, leading to enhanced English language proficiency.

Learning Environment and Intention for English Proficiency

The examination of the association between students' learning environment and their intention to achieve proficiency in English constitutes a pivotal exploration in the domain of language education (Akhmedov & Shuhkrat, 2020; Getie, 2020; Wang et al., 2021; Chen et al., 2022; Barrett et al., 2023). A scrutiny of existing literature reveals a nuanced interrelation between the learning environment and students' aspirations in language learning. Chen et al.'s (2021) research underscores the importance of a positive and supportive language learning environment in nurturing motivation and proficiency (Barrett et al., 2023). The study highlights that an environment fostering student autonomy, delivering ample language input, and cultivating a sense of belonging positively impacts learners' intention to participate in language learning activities (Akhmedov & Shuhkrat, 2020; Öztürk & Çakıroğlu, 2021; Chen et al., 2022; Barrett et al., 2023).

Furthermore, the ecological perspective proposed by Chen and Hsu (2020) accentuates the dynamic relationship between learners and their environment. This theoretical framework suggests that the learning environment is not merely a physical space but an intricate system of interactions (Gutiérrez-Colón et al., 2023). Studies such as those by Cardullo et al. (2021) have extended this perspective to language learning, emphasizing the need for a supportive, learner-centered environment that aligns with individual preferences and goals (Closs et al., 2022; Manegre, M., & Gutiérrez-Colón, 2023; Gutiérrez-Colón et al., 2023). Incorporating socio-cultural dimensions, Noviana & Oktaviani (2022) posits that the learning environment plays a central role in facilitating language development. Collaborative interactions within the learning environment, according to this theory, provide opportunities for scaffolding, where more knowledgeable peers or instructors support learners in reaching higher levels of proficiency. Moreover, research by Niemiec et al. (2010) within the framework of Self-Determination Theory underscores the importance of autonomy-supportive environments. The study indicates that environments fostering autonomy, competence, and relatedness positively impact learners' motivation, ultimately influencing their intention for language proficiency (Law et al., 2019; Akhmedov & Shuhkrat, 2020; Wang et al., 2021; Closs et al., 2022; Manegre, M., & Gutiérrez-Colón, 2023).

Building upon the insights from the literature, we propose the following hypothesis:

H2: There is a positive and significant relationship between students' perception of their learning environment and their intention for English proficiency.

This hypothesis posits that an environment characterized by support, autonomy, and opportunities for collaborative learning will contribute positively to students' intention to achieve English proficiency (Law et al., 2019; Akhmedov & Shuhkrat, 2020; Wang et al., 2021; Closs et al., 2022; Manegre, M., & Gutiérrez-Colón, 2023). Drawing on the ecological perspective, ZPD, and Self-Determination Theory, we anticipate that learners who perceive their language learning environment as conducive and supportive will exhibit a heightened intention to actively engage in language learning activities, fostering a positive trajectory toward enhanced English language proficiency. This study seeks to deepen our understanding of the complex dynamics between the learning environment and students' language learning intentions, providing valuable insights for educators, curriculum designers, and policymakers aiming to optimize language learning contexts (Closs et al., 2022; Manegre, M., & Gutiérrez-Colón, 2023).

Motivation and Intention for English Proficiency

The connection between students' motivation and their intention to attain proficiency in English has been a central focus in language acquisition research, revealing the intricate interplay between psychological factors and language learning outcomes (Cocca & Cocca, 2019; Chen et al., 2022; Zhou & Thompson, 2023). Deci et al.'s Self-Determination Theory (1994) has played a crucial role in elucidating the motivational dynamics in language learning. According to this theory, individuals experience motivation when their fundamental psychological needs for autonomy, competence, and relatedness are fulfilled (Xia et al., 2023). Research conducted by Ghanea et al. (2011), Shih and Reynolds (2018), and Chen et al. (2022) has demonstrated that autonomous motivation is significantly correlated with language proficiency and a positive attitude toward language learning (Almusharaf et al., 2023). Additionally, Gardner's Socio-Educational Model introduced the concept of integrative motivation, emphasizing the desire to learn a language as a means of integrating into a specific community or culture (Lovato & Junior, 2011; Zhang et al., 2020). Studies have underscored the positive impact of integrative motivation on language learning outcomes, predicting higher levels of intention to attain language proficiency (Rasool & Winke, 2019; Liu, 2020; Balouchi & Samad, 2021; Chen, 2023).

Moreover, Dörnyei's conceptualization of motivation introduced the concept of the L2 Motivational Self System, emphasizing the significance of the ideal self, the ought-to self, and the L2 learning experience in shaping motivation (Dörnyei & Chan, 2013; Yu et al., 2023). Investigations by Rasool and Winke (2019), Lamb and Arisandy (2020), and Kim & Kim (2021) have affirmed the impact of these motivational components on learners' intentions to attain language proficiency (Almusharaf et al., 2023). Within the framework of the Theory of Planned Behavior (Ajzen, 1991), research conducted by Kim et al. (2011) demonstrated that motivation plays a substantial role in the formation of behavioral intentions. In the context of language learning, studies by Jiang et al. (2019) further illustrated that motivation positively influences learners' intentions to participate in language learning activities, subsequently affecting their language proficiency (Ni & Cheung, 2023).

Building upon the insights from existing research, we propose the following hypothesis:

H3: There is a positive and significant relationship between students' motivation for English language learning and their intention for English proficiency.

This hypothesis is rooted in the premise that a high level of motivation will lead to a more proactive intention to achieve English proficiency. Grounded in Self-Determination Theory, the Socio-Educational Model, and the Theory of Planned Behavior, we anticipate that students who are intrinsically motivated, exhibit integrative motivation, and align their language learning goals with their ideal selves will demonstrate a heightened intention to engage in language learning activities, ultimately leading to enhanced English language proficiency (Dörnyei & Chan, 2013; Yu et al., 2023).

This research endeavors to provide empirical evidence to augment the current body of literature, aiming to offer valuable insights into the intricate relationship between motivation and the intention to achieve proficiency in English. Such insights hold significance for educators, policymakers, and researchers dedicated to improving language learning motivation and outcomes among students (Almusharaf et al., 2023).

Technological Adaptability and Intention for English Proficiency

The exploration of the relationship between students' technological adaptability and their intention for English proficiency delves into the evolving landscape of language education, where technology plays an increasingly integral role (Ginaya et al., 2018; Alfadda & Mahdi, 2021; Bag et al., 2022; Jie & Sunze, 2023). Research by Huang et al. (2020) paved the way for understanding the impact of technology on language learning. Their study demonstrated that technology integration positively influenced learners' motivation and language proficiency (Habib et al., 2021; Zhao & Lai, 2023). This finding aligns with the Technological Acceptance Model (Davis, 1989), which posits that perceived ease of use and perceived usefulness significantly impact users' acceptance of technology. Recent studies Xu et al. (2019) and Alfadda andMahdi (2021) have highlighted the role of mobile technologies in language learning. These technologies offer learners flexibility, enabling them to engage with English language materials beyond the confines of traditional classrooms. The positive correlation observed between learners' technological adaptability and their language proficiency suggests a dynamic interplay between technology and language learning intentions (Rafiee & Abbasian-Naghneh, 2021; Zhao & Lai, 2023).

Furthermore, the technological dimensions of Augmented Reality (AR) and Virtual Reality (VR) have been the subject of investigation. Research conducted by Shafie et al. (2019) and Muñoz et al. (2022) has shown that AR and VR applications enhance language learning experiences, positively influencing learners' motivation and intention to achieve language proficiency. The Community of Inquiry framework (Chen et al., 2019; Chen et al., 2022; Zhao & Lai, 2023) further underscores the significance of technology in establishing a collaborative and engaging learning environment. Asynchronous and synchronous online platforms facilitate interaction, fostering a sense of community among learners. Studies by Qureshi et al. (2021), Huang et al. (2022), and Lee and Hwang (2022) indicate a positive correlation between online interaction, technological adaptability, and language learning outcomes.

Building upon the insights from existing research, we propose the following hypothesis:

H4: There is a positive and significant relationship between students' technological adaptability and their intention for English proficiency.

This hypothesis is grounded in the belief that students who are technologically adaptable are more likely to embrace and utilize technology for language learning, leading to a heightened intention to achieve English proficiency. Drawing from the Technological Acceptance Model, mobile technology research, and the Community of Inquiry framework, we anticipate that students with high technological adaptability will exhibit an increased intention to engage in language learning activities facilitated by technology, ultimately contributing to enhanced English language proficiency (Chen et al., 2019; Chen et al., 2022; Zhao & Lai, 2023).

This research endeavor aspires to enrich the ongoing discussion surrounding technology-assisted language learning by furnishing empirical evidence pertaining to the correlation between technological adaptability and intentions for language learning. The insights gleaned from this study bear implications for educators and policymakers striving to adeptly harness technology within language education programs (Chen et al., 2022; Zhao & Lai, 2023).

Self-Confidence and Intention for English Proficiency

The examination of the association between students' self-confidence and their intention to achieve English proficiency represents a noteworthy avenue within the realm of language acquisition research (Maftuna, 2020; Waluyo & Rofiah, 2021; Aziz & Asih, 2023). Self-confidence assumes a pivotal role in shaping learners' attitudes, motivation, and overall language learning outcomes. Research conducted by Darasawang and Reinders (2021) underscored the significance of self-efficacy, a constituent of self-confidence, in predicting academic performance. In the context of language learning, self-efficacy pertains to learners' beliefs in their capability to effectively execute language tasks (Gojkov-Rajić et al., 2023). Studies, such as those conducted by Ghasemi et al. (2020) and Sagita (2021), have demonstrated a positive correlation between learners' self-efficacy and their intention to participate in language learning activities (Ozdemir & Papi, 2022; Briones et al., 2023).

Moreover, the socio-affective dimensions of language learning have been explored by Gardner (2010) within the framework of the Socio-Educational Model. This model posits that learners' beliefs about their language learning abilities, including self-confidence, influence their motivation and intention for language proficiency (Jindapitak et al., 2022; Rosmayanti et al., 2023). Research by Aoyama & Takahashi (2020) and Waluyo and Rofiah (2021) substantiated this viewpoint, indicating that learners with heightened levels of self-confidence are more prone to manifest a positive intention toward language proficiency (Sato, 2023). The concept of the affective filter further accentuates the significance of alleviating anxiety and fostering self-confidence in language learning (Darasawang & Reinders, 2021). Studies conducted by Sagita (2021) and Ozdemir and Papi (2022) demonstrated that learners with elevated levels of self-confidence encountered reduced levels of language learning anxiety, thereby contributing to a more favorable language learning environment (Siani & Harris, 2023).

Building upon the insights from existing research, we propose the following hypothesis:

H5: There is a positive and significant relationship between students' self-confidence in English language learning and their intention for English proficiency.

This hypothesis is grounded in the idea that students with higher levels of self-confidence will exhibit a more positive intention to engage in language learning activities, ultimately contributing to enhanced English language proficiency. Drawing from Bandura's self-efficacy theory, Gardner's Socio-Educational Model, and the affective filter hypothesis, we anticipate that learners who possess greater self-confidence in their language learning abilities will approach language learning tasks with a heightened intention to succeed, positively influencing their language proficiency outcomes (Jindapitak et al., 2022; Rosmayanti et al., 2023).

This study aims to contribute empirical evidence to the existing body of literature, shedding light on the nuanced relationship between self-confidence and language learning intentions. Insights from this research can inform educators and policymakers in developing strategies to nurture learners' self-confidence and optimize language learning environments (Siani & Harris, 2023).

Figure 1. The framework of the study

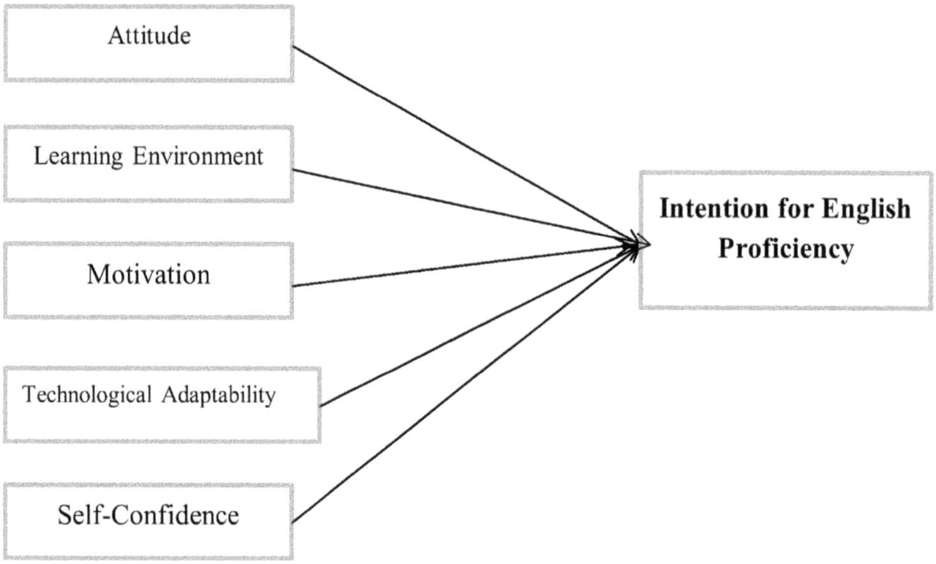

As illustrated in Figure 1, every factor within the conceptual framework, namely attitude, learning environment, motivation, technological adaptability, and self-confidence, exerts an influence on the intention to achieve proficiency in the English language.

METHODOLOGY OF THE STUDY

Research Design

Adopting a quantitative research design firmly grounded in positivism, this study delves into the intricate connections among learning environment, motivation, technological adaptability, self-confidence, and English language proficiency, harnessing the power of Artificial Intelligence (AI). The comprehensive design ensures a systematic exploration of variables within a meticulously structured framework, enabling objective analysis and interpretation (Polas & Raju, 2021). By employing AI, this research transcends traditional boundaries, embracing cutting-edge technology to offer a nuanced understanding of the interplay between these factors. The structured framework guarantees not only a thorough examination of relationships but also facilitates the extraction of meaningful insights, contributing to the advancement of knowledge in this field.

Sampling Technique

In implementing a meticulous research approach, a stratified random sampling method is employed to carefully select 433 undergraduate students specializing in business from five prominent universities situated in Dhaka, Bangladesh. This methodical choice ensures a strategic focus on the business administration department, aligning the sample selection with both academic and professional contexts. By specifically targeting this department, the research aims to enhance relevance, thereby contributing to a participant pool that is not only representative but also diverse. This thoughtful sampling technique seeks to capture a broad spectrum of experiences, enriching the study's findings with comprehensive insights into the intricate dynamics of business education in the local context.

Data Collection

To comprehensively evaluate English language proficiency while ensuring a standardized assessment, a meticulously crafted structured survey instrument was employed. This instrument gathered data on participants' perceptions of the learning environment, motivation, technological adaptability, and self-confidence. The questionnaire, adapted from prior research and literature, employed a five-point Likert scale, ranging from 1 (Strongly Disagree) to 5 (Strongly Agree). This method aimed to provide a nuanced understanding of various factors, including attitude, learning environment, motivation, technological adaptability, and self-confidence, within the context of achieving proficiency in English.

In an effort to boost participant engagement and response rates, a creative incentive was introduced: respondents were offered the prospect of receiving ice cream. This innovative incentive was strategically designed to not only encourage a positive response but also to cultivate a collaborative and interactive research environment. By incorporating such a lighthearted reward, the research sought to create a more enjoyable experience for participants, potentially fostering a positive attitude toward the survey and, by extension, contributing to the reliability and authenticity of the gathered data. The incentive not only added an element of enjoyment to the research process but also aimed to build a sense of camaraderie between the researchers and participants, fostering a conducive atmosphere for open and candid responses.

To thoroughly assess potential non-response bias, a detailed time-trend extrapolation analysis was conducted. This meticulous examination sought to discern any disparities between non-responsive late respondents and two distinct groups: early late respondents, constituting the initial 25%, and the broader category of overall late respondents, comprising the final 25%. The objective was to ensure the robustness and validity of our findings in the face of potential biases.

The outcomes of these comprehensive assessments provided reassuring evidence of the resilience of our findings against non-response bias, aligning with the guidelines established by Armstrong and Overton (1977). By specifically scrutinizing different segments of late respondents, we aimed to identify any patterns or variations that could indicate biases in the data. The findings, however, affirmed the consistency and reliability of our results, reinforcing the credibility of the study. This meticulous analysis not only contributes to the internal validity of our research but also underscores our commitment to methodological rigor, strengthening the overall trustworthiness of the study's conclusions.

The demographic profile of the participants reveals a diverse composition. Among the respondents, 66.56% identified as male, reflecting a notable gender distribution. In terms of age, 35.42% fell within the 20 to 22 bracket, highlighting a concentration within this age range. The majority of participants, constituting 95.56%, reported being single, indicating a predominant marital status among the sampled population.

Regarding academic progression, 26.65% were in their fourth year of university, showcasing a range of educational stages within the sample. In terms of technology usage patterns, 39.34% reported daily smartphone usage, underscoring the integration of mobile technology into the daily lives of a significant portion of the participants. Furthermore, a substantial 59.32% possessed advanced-level computer skills, emphasizing the high proficiency levels in computer literacy within the surveyed group.

This multifaceted demographic overview provides a nuanced understanding of the participants, capturing key aspects such as gender distribution, age representation, marital status, academic progression, and technological proficiency. Such insights enrich the interpretation of research findings, offering a contextualized perspective on how these demographic variables may influence or interact with the measured constructs in the study.

Questionnaire Design

In the final survey, comprising 25 questions (excluding seven demographic queries), a total of six variables were incorporated. Our 25-item survey aligns with the minimal criteria for a robust instrument, as outlined by Hair et al. (2017). The assessment of the attitude construct involved the utilization of four items from Bagheri & Andi (2015). Subsequently, Jung (2015)'s four items were employed to quantify the learning environment, while four questions from Bagherzadeh & Azizi (2012) to measure motivation. Technological adaptability was measured using four items from Tawafak et al. (2023). Four items adopted from Tridinanti (2018) to measure the Self-confidence construct. Five items used to measure the intention for English proficiency adopted from Jung (2015).

Data Analysis

To unravel intricate patterns and relationships among variables, advanced statistical techniques such as correlation and regression analyses are employed in data analysis, utilizing SPSS V.25. The selection of these methods is deliberate, as they offer a powerful toolkit for discerning nuanced connections within the dataset. Correlation analysis unveils the strength and direction of relationships, while regression analysis delves deeper into predicting outcomes based on identified patterns. By leveraging these statistical tools, the study aims to extract meaningful insights, fostering a comprehensive understanding of the interplay between various factors and contributing to the validity and reliability of the research findings.

Ethical Considerations

Ethical considerations hold utmost significance in this study. A rigorous process is employed to obtain informed consent from all participants, affirming a dedication to confidentiality and voluntary involvement. The research strictly adheres to ethical standards, emphasizing the protection of the well-being and rights of the participants throughout the entirety of the research process.

Summary of Hypotheses

Table 1. Summary of hypotheses

Hypothesis	Statement
H1	There is a positive and significant relationship between students' attitude for English learning and their intention for English proficiency.
H2	There is a positive and significant relationship between students' perception of their learning environment and their intention for English proficiency.
H3	There is a positive and significant relationship between students' motivation for English language learning and their intention for English proficiency.
H4	There is a positive and significant relationship between students' technological adaptability and their intention for English proficiency.
H5	There is a positive and significant relationship between students' self-confidence in English language learning and their intention for English proficiency.

FINDINGS AND DISCUSSION

In investigating descriptive correlations, this study utilized the Pearson-Correlation method through SPSS software (Version 25) to examine the relationships among variables. The outcomes, summarized in **Table 2**, incorporate both descriptive statistics and correlation coefficients. Within this analytical framework, a statistically significant and positive correlation emerges between the independent and dependent variables. It is crucial to highlight that the strength of correlation varies among the independent variables concerning the dependent variable. The correlation analysis involved a total of twelve variables, encompassing five independent variables and one dependent variable. Notably, the dependent variable is the "Intention for English Proficiency," while the independent variables consist of attitude, learning environment, motivation, technological adaptability, and self-confidence.

Upon scrutinizing **Table 2**, it is evident that there exists a perceptible association between the independent variables (IVs) and the dependent variable (DVs). Notably, each independent variable demonstrates a statistically significant connection with the dependent variables. To delve into the particulars, the initial independent variable, namely 'gender,' is particularly intriguing as it reveals a noteworthy association with the 'Intention for English proficiency' at a significance level of 0.163^*. Furthermore, age is significantly correlated with the technological adaptability and self-confidence at the significance level of 0.581^{***} and 0.432^{**}. Moreover, Teacher Parents has a significant correlated with the learning environment, motivation, technological adaptability, self-confidence and Intention for English proficiency at the significance

Table 2. Descriptive correlations

SL. NO.	Variables	Mean	STD.	1	2	3	4	5	6	7	8	9	10	11	12
1	Gender	1.56	0.81	1											
2	Age	21.4	2.54	0.143	1										
3	Marital status	1.67	0.61	0.147	0.087	1									
4	Department	2.23	0.54	0.059	0.143	0.254*	1								
5	Teacher Parents	1.23	1.34	0.098	0.092	0.571	0.145	1							
6	Monthly Family Income	4.3	1.47	0.091	0.069	0.071	.468**	0.137	1						
7	Attitude	3.47	1.53	0.168	0.093	0.073	0.068	0.068	0.047	1					
8	Learning Environment	3.23	1.39	0.078	0.078	0.257*	0.078	0.357**	0.08	0.255**	1				
9	Motivation	3.67	0.55	0.167	0.075	0.079	0.469	0.567***	.379*	0.358***	.478**	1			
10	Technological Adaptability	3.39	1.39	0.156	0.581***	0.159	0.275	0.476**	0.167	0.198*	.584**	.583**	1		
11	Self-Confidence	3.98	0.59	0.157	0.432**	0.056	0.045	0.588***	.278*	0.457	.467**	.551**	.469**	1	
12	English Proficiency	3.38	1.79	0.163*	0.071	0.258**	0.456**	0.556***	0.479	0.456***	.474**	.485**	.389**	.383**	1

Notes: **Correlation is significant at the 0.01 level (2-tailed).

*Correlation is significant at the 0.05 level (2-tailed).

level of 0.357**, 0.567***, 0.476**, 0.588***, and 0.556***. This initial variable serves as a foundational point for data interpretation. Similarly, the second independent variable, 'Attitude', significantly correlates with the subsequent independent variable, 'learning environment', at a higher significance level of 0.255**.

Furthermore, substantial connections emerge between the third independent variable, 'Motivation', with 'technological adaptability', 'self-confidence' and 'intention for English proficiency'. The significance levels of 583**, .551**, and .485** accentuate the robustness of these relationships. Additionally, the independent variable 'Self-Confidence' exhibits a noteworthy link with 'intention for English Proficiency' at a significance level of 0.383**. In essence, this comprehensive correlation analysis unveils intricate relationships among variables, elucidating the nuanced interplay within the research framework. Each variable is intricately connected with others, offering a multifaceted perspective on the dynamics at play. The significance levels provide a nuanced understanding of the strength and directionality of these correlations, contributing valuable insights to the overarching narrative of the research.

Table 3. Relationships between IVs and DV

Name of Variables	English Proficiency	t value	p-value	VIF
Gender	0.138*	2.122	0.045	1.987
Age	0.211	2.456	0.032	1.872
Marital status	−0.029	-1.543	0.066	1.879
Department	0.278*	2.783	0.023	2.563
Teacher Parents	0.342**	3.456	0.004	2.876
Monthly Family Income	0.232*	2.323	0.041	3.772
Attitude	0.089	`1.211	0.067	2.887
Learning Environment	0.594***	5.043	0.000	2.678
Motivation	0.486***	4.087	0.000	2.876
Technological Adaptability	0.454***	3.267	0.014	2.678
Self-Confidence	0.367**	2.576	0.005	2.234
R2	0.658			
Adj. R2	0.545			
F	6.356***			

Note: *p<0.05, **p<0.01, ***p<0.001

Table 3 provides a comprehensive illustration of the direct relationships between independent variables and the dependent variable in our study. In alignment with the hypothesized framework, a systematic compilation of all elements was meticulously conducted to evaluate the congruence of the collected data with the research objectives. The robustness of the data is substantiated by a Kaiser Meyer Olkin (KMO) value of 0.867 and a Bartlett's test result of 0.000, affirming the adequacy of our sample for analysis. In the pursuit of convergent validity, confirmatory factor analysis (CFA) was implemented, following the established guidelines outlined by Anderson and Gerbing (1988). This analytical approach aimed to determine whether the items utilized in the study exhibited acceptable factor loadings on the associated theoretical constructs at a statistically significant level. Through this meticulous process, the methodological rigor of our study was ensured, and the appropriateness of our chosen constructs was validated.

The proposed framework, delineated through H1, H2, H3, H4, and H5, suggested positive and substantial associations among university students' attitude, learning environment, motivation, technological adaptability, self-confidence, and their intention to achieve English proficiency through the utilization of artificial intelligence within the context of Education 4.0. Nonetheless, our inquiry unveiled nuanced findings that enrich the comprehension of these interconnected dynamics.

Hypothesis 1 proposed a positive link between students' attitude and their intention for English Proficiency. Surprisingly, our analysis did not substantiate this assertion ($\beta = 0.089$, $p > 0.05$; see Table 3). Consequently, Hypothesis 1 was not accepted, diverging from the findings of Studer & Konstantinidou (2015), Zulfikar et al. (2019), and Jalbani et al. (2023). This implies that fluctuations in university students' attitude do not correspondingly impact their intention for English proficiency, challenging the anticipated connection.

Contrastingly, Hypothesis 2 posited a positive and significant relationship between students' learning environment and their intention for English Proficiency. Our findings validated this hypothesis ($\beta = 0.594^{***}$, $p < 0.001$, Table 3), aligning with studies by Jung (2015), Balouchi & Samad (2021), and Wut et al. (2022). This suggests that alterations in the university students' learning environment with the help of artificial intelligence directly influence their intention for English proficiency, substantiating the importance of a conducive academic milieu.

Hypothesis 3 suggested a positive and significant association between students' motivation and their intention for English Proficiency. Our results supported this hypothesis ($\beta = 0.486^{***}$, $p < 0.001$, see Table 3), corroborating findings from studies by Shih & Reynolds (2018), Septiani et al. (2021), and Peng and Patterson (2022). Evidently, fluctuations in university students' motivation with the help of artificial intelligence are mirrored in their intention for English proficiency, emphasizing the motivational factor in language learning.

Similarly, Hypothesis 4 postulated a positive and significant relationship between students' technological adaptability and their intention for English Proficiency, a notion substantiated by our analysis ($\beta = 0.454^{***}$, $p < 0.05$, see Table 3). This finding aligns with the studies of Yang and Pu (2022), Farsawang and Songkram (2023), and Li et al. (2023), emphasizing the pivotal role of technological adaptability in fostering language proficiency in the context of Education 4.0 with the help of artificial intelligence.

Furthermore, Hypothesis 5 suggested a positive and significant link between students' self-confidence and their intention for English Proficiency. Our analysis supported this hypothesis ($\beta = 0.367^{**}$, $p < 0.001$, see Table 3), echoing findings from Riasati (2018), Su (2021), Alberth (2023). This underscores the influential role of self-confidence in shaping students' intention for English proficiency with the help of artificial intelligence, highlighting the interconnectedness of psychological factors in language acquisition.

Intricacies within these relationships unravel the nuanced dynamics shaping university students' language proficiency intentions with the help of artificial intelligence. While some variables exhibit the anticipated connections, others challenge conventional assumptions, emphasizing the multifaceted nature of language learning in the era of Education 4.0. This empirical exploration contributes substantively to the existing body of literature, offering valuable insights for educators, policymakers, and researchers invested in enhancing language education strategies.

CONCLUSION

Our study embarked on a comprehensive exploration of the intricate factors shaping English language proficiency within the cohort of business administration university students in Bangladesh, harnessing the transformative capabilities of Artificial Intelligence (AI). By undertaking an in-depth analysis of the interconnected dynamics among the learning environment, motivation, technological adaptability, self-confidence, and English language proficiency, our research adds substantial value to the current literature and theories in the domains of language acquisition and education, particularly within the unique context of Bangladesh. The integration of AI as a facilitator amplifies the relevance of our findings, signifying a pioneering approach to language learning. This study not only expands the understanding of how these factors interplay but also addresses the evolving landscape of education, where technology becomes an indispensable ally. The implications extend beyond conventional methodologies, offering insights into the innovative use of AI for enhancing language proficiency, thus contributing to the ongoing discourse on the intersection of technology and education. The contextual significance of our research lies in its potential to inform educational practices and policies in Bangladesh and potentially beyond, as the global landscape increasingly embraces AI-driven interventions in pursuit of educational excellence.

The findings of our study underscore the pivotal role of the learning environment in shaping English language proficiency among business administration university students, with a focus on the integration of AI. A conducive learning environment, marked by interactive classrooms, easy access to resources, and a supportive network of peers, emerged as a crucial predictor of language proficiency. This observation aligns seamlessly with Vygotsky's sociocultural theory, emphasizing the significance of social interactions and environmental influences in language development. Importantly, our study expands upon this understanding by acknowledging the role of AI in creating adaptive and personalized learning environments, fostering a more efficient and tailored language acquisition process.

Motivation, a perennially significant factor in language learning, revealed a strong positive correlation with English language proficiency, supported by the integration of AI. This aligns with well-established motivational theories such as Deci and Ryan's Self-Determination Theory, emphasizing intrinsic and extrinsic factors driving individuals to engage in language learning. In the context of AI, our findings suggest that the incorporation of AI-driven tools and applications can serve as motivational stimuli, providing interactive and engaging experiences that sustain students' interest in language acquisition.

The capacity for technological adaptability has emerged as a noteworthy factor influencing English language proficiency among undergraduate students in business universities in Bangladesh, particularly in conjunction with artificial intelligence (AI) facilitation. The incorporation of AI into language learning environments has demonstrated a positive influence on students' language skills, aligning with modern educational theories that underscore technology's significance in language acquisition. The dynamic attributes of AI afford adaptive and personalized learning experiences, catering to individual learning styles and preferences. Our study underscores the importance for universities to invest in AI-infused technological infrastructure, thereby integrating innovative tools and platforms to enrich language learning experiences.

Self-confidence, identified as a robust positive correlate with English language proficiency, gains new dimensions when considering AI's role. Students with higher levels of self-confidence demonstrated greater proficiency in English, aligning with Bandura's Social Cognitive Theory, which underscores the role of self-efficacy in skill development. The incorporation of AI, with its ability to provide instant feedback, personalized learning pathways, and targeted support, contributes to fostering a sense of self-confidence among students. This aspect is crucial in optimizing language proficiency outcomes.

The amalgamation of these factors emphasizes the interconnected nature of elements influencing English language proficiency among business administration university students in Bangladesh, especially when considering the impact of AI. Our study not only provides empirical evidence of these relationships within the specific context of Bangladesh but also presents a framework for understanding the symbiotic relationship between traditional factors and emerging technological influences.

The study, propelled by the integration of AI, advances the understanding of the factors influencing English language proficiency and provides practical implications for educational institutions. The role of AI in creating adaptive, personalized, and technologically advanced learning environments cannot be overstated. These findings offer valuable insights for educators, policymakers, and researchers, guiding the development of effective strategies to enhance English language proficiency among university students, taking full advantage of the opportunities presented by AI.

In the future, further investigation can improve upon these discoveries through the exploration of additional factors, examination of longitudinal perspectives, and evaluation of the lasting effects of AI-driven interventions designed to enhance language proficiency among university students in Bangladesh. The changing terrain of education and technology necessitates continuous exploration to guarantee that language learning encounters stay vibrant, efficient, and customized to meet the evolving needs of students in an increasingly interconnected global environment.

IMPLICATIONS OF THE STUDY

Embarking on an exploration of the intricate connections between the learning environment, motivation, technological adaptability, self-confidence, and English language proficiency among university students specializing in business and management in Bangladesh, our study unravels practical and theoretical implications with substantial ramifications. The integration of Artificial Intelligence (AI) into this intricate web of factors heralds a paradigm shift in language acquisition and education. Our findings not only offer practical insights into enhancing English proficiency among business students but also contribute to the theoretical underpinnings of educational research. The fusion of traditional educational elements with cutting-edge AI technologies represents more than a mere augmentation; it signifies a transformative potential. As we navigate the nexus of AI and language proficiency, our study points towards innovative methodologies that could revolutionize language education. Beyond its immediate application in Bangladesh, our research offers a broader perspective on how the synergy of traditional and modern educational approaches, empowered by AI, can redefine language learning paradigms globally.

This transformative potential extends beyond the confines of business education, resonating with a broader educational landscape that increasingly seeks to harness the power of technology for more effective and personalized learning experiences.

The practical implications of our findings underscore the importance of creating tailored learning environments. Educational institutions in Bangladesh can leverage AI technologies to customize learning experiences, considering individual preferences, pace, and proficiency levels. Implementing AI-driven adaptive learning platforms can ensure that students receive personalized support, leading to enhanced English language proficiency. Cultivating and sustaining motivation is a practical challenge in language learning. Our study suggests that AI can serve as a motivational catalyst. Educational practitioners can incorporate AI-driven interactive tools, gamified learning platforms, and real-time feedback mechanisms to keep students engaged and motivated. This approach aligns with the theoretical underpinnings of Deci and Ryan's Self-Determination Theory, emphasizing autonomy, competence, and relatedness.

The study highlights the need for universities in Bangladesh to invest in technological infrastructure, incorporating AI to optimize language learning experiences. Integrating AI-powered tools into classrooms can facilitate a seamless combination of traditional teaching methods with innovative technological solutions. This approach caters to the diverse learning styles of students, fostering a technologically rich and immersive language learning environment. Fostering self-confidence is crucial for language proficiency. Educational institutions can employ AI to provide targeted support and constructive feedback. AI-driven language assessment tools, coupled with personalized learning plans, contribute to students' sense of self-efficacy. Initiatives focused on enhancing self-confidence align with Bandura's Social Cognitive Theory, emphasizing the role of belief in one's capabilities.

Recognizing the impact of technological adaptability on language proficiency, educators and administrators should invest in continuous professional development. Training programs that familiarize faculty with AI tools and methodologies can enhance their ability to create dynamic, technology-infused learning environments. This ensures that educators are well-equipped to harness the full potential of AI for language education. Vygotsky's sociocultural theory posits that social interactions and environmental influences shape language development. Our study extends this theory by incorporating AI into the socio-cultural context. The integration of AI into the learning environment becomes an additional layer of influence, enabling students to engage with intelligent technologies that adapt to their individual needs, thereby influencing language development.

The study reinforces Deci and Ryan's Self-Determination Theory, highlighting the intrinsic and extrinsic factors that drive language learning motivation. By recognizing AI as a motivational catalyst, the theoretical framework can be expanded to include technology-driven motivational strategies. The integration of AI aligns with the theory's emphasis on autonomy, competence, and relatedness, providing new avenues for motivational interventions.

Our findings contribute to contemporary educational theories emphasizing the role of technology in language acquisition. The study suggests that technological adaptability, especially with the integration of AI, positively impacts language skills. This aligns with the broader theoretical discourse on the transformative role of technology in education, extending its application to language proficiency enhancement.

Bandura's Social Cognitive Theory highlights the role of self-efficacy in skill development. The study extends this theory by recognizing AI as a tool for building self-efficacy in language learning. AI-driven assessments, personalized feedback, and adaptive learning experiences contribute to students' confidence in their language abilities, aligning with the theory's emphasis on self-belief as a precursor to skill development.

Overall, the study's practical implications offer actionable insights for educational stakeholders in Bangladesh, providing a roadmap for the integration of AI into language learning environments. These interventions not only address the specific context of English language proficiency but also contribute to the broader discourse on leveraging technology for educational enhancement. The theoretical implications extend established frameworks, recognizing AI as a dynamic element in shaping language acquisition processes. As technology continues to evolve, the synergies between traditional educational elements and AI present a promising pathway for optimizing language education in the 21st century.

LIMITATIONS AND FUTURE DIRECTIONS

While our investigation yields valuable insights into the associations among attitude, learning environment, motivation, technological adaptability, self-confidence, and English language proficiency within the university student population in Bangladesh, it is essential to acknowledge several limitations. Firstly, the cross-sectional design constrains our ability to establish causality, underscoring the necessity for longitudinal studies to unravel temporal relationships. The study's exclusive focus on university students in Bangladesh may restrict the generalizability of our findings to diverse contexts. Future research endeavors should encompass a more extensive and varied sample, including participants from various academic levels and cultural backgrounds, to enhance the external validity of the results. Although quantitative measures provide statistical rigor, they may fall short in capturing the nuances of qualitative experiences. The integration of qualitative methods could offer a more comprehensive understanding of students' perceptions and experiences in language learning.

Furthermore, the utilization of self-reported data in the study introduces potential biases. Subsequent research efforts could adopt mixed-methods approaches, amalgamating quantitative data with qualitative insights, to present a more holistic comprehension of the determinants influencing English language proficiency. In the dynamic technological landscape, the investigation prioritized technological adaptability; nonetheless, future research could delve more deeply into specific technological tools and interventions, exploring their nuanced impact on language proficiency. Acknowledging these limitations, future research initiatives should embrace a diversified approach, integrating longitudinal designs, mixed-methods analyses, and broader participant samples to advance our understanding of the intricate dynamics influencing English language proficiency among university students.

REFERENCES

Abd Algane, M., & Jabir Othman, K. A. (2023). Utilizing artificial intelligence technologies in Saudi EFL tertiary level classrooms. *Journal of Intercultural Communication*, *23*(1), 92–99.

Ajzen, I. (1991). The theory of planned behavior. *Organizational Behavior and Human Decision Processes*, *50*(2), 179–211. doi:10.1016/0749-5978(91)90020-T

Akhmedov, B., & Shuhkrat, K. (2020). Cluster methods of learning english using information technology. *Science Progress*, *1*(2), 40–43.

Alberth, A. (2023). How Important Is Communicating with Native English Speakers to EFL Learners' Self-Confidence in their English Language Proficiency? *Journey: Journal of English Language and Pedagogy*, *6*(2), 380–393. doi:10.33503/journey. v6i2.3169

Alfadda, H. A., & Mahdi, H. S. (2021). Measuring students' use of zoom application in language course based on the technology acceptance model (TAM). *Journal of Psycholinguistic Research*, *50*(4), 883–900. doi:10.1007/s10936-020-09752-1 PMID:33398606

Alhassan, A., Ali, N. A., & Ali, H. I. H. (2021). EFL students' challenges in English-medium business programmes: Perspectives from students and content teachers. *Cogent Education*, *8*(1), 1–15. doi:10.1080/2331186X.2021.1888671

Aoyama, T., & Takahashi, T. (2020). International students' willingness to communicate in English as a second language: The effects of l2 self-confidence, acculturation, and motivational types. *Journal of International Students*, *10*(3), 703–723. doi:10.32674/jis.v10i3.730

Armstrong, J. S., & Overton, T. S. (1977). Estimating nonresponse bias in mail surveys. *JMR, Journal of Marketing Research*, *14*(3), 396–402. doi:10.1177/002224377701400320

Avello, M., Camacho-Miñano, M. D. M., Urquia-Grande, E., & del Campo, C. (2019). "Do You Use English in Your Daily Life?" Undergraduate Students' Perceptions of Their Extramural Use of English. *Journal of Teaching in International Business*, *30*(1), 77–94. doi:10.1080/08975930.2019.1627978

Bagheri, M., & Andi, T. (2015). The relationship between medical students' attitude towards English language learning and their English language proficiency. *ICT & Innovations in Education—International Electronic Journal, 3*(1), 7-19.

Bagheri, M., & Andi, T. (2015). The relationship between medical students' attitude towards English language learning and their English language proficiency. *ICT & Innovations in Education—International Electronic Journal, 3*(1), 7-19.

Bagherzadeh, H., & Azizi, Z. (2012). Learners' Beliefs about English Language Learning: Examining the Impact of English Proficiency Level on the Motivation of Students among Non-English Major EFL Students. *Theory and Practice in Language Studies*, *2*(10), 1987–1992. doi:10.4304/tpls.2.10.2096-2102

Balouchi, S., & Samad, A. A. (2021). No more excuses, learn English for free: Factors affecting L2 learners intention to use online technology for informal English learning. *Education and Information Technologies*, *26*(1), 1111–1132. doi:10.1007/s10639-020-10307-z

Cardullo, V., Wang, C. H., Burton, M., & Dong, J. (2021). K-12 teachers' remote teaching self-efficacy during the pandemic. *Journal of research in innovative teaching & learning, 14*(1), 32-45.

Chen, C. H., Hung, H. T., & Yeh, H. C. (2021). Virtual reality in problem-based learning contexts: Effects on the problem-solving performance, vocabulary acquisition and motivation of English language learners. *Journal of Computer Assisted Learning*, *37*(3), 851–860. doi:10.1111/jcal.12528

Chen, H. Y., Das, A., & Ivanov, D. (2019). Building resilience and managing post-disruption supply chain recovery: Lessons from the information and communication technology industry. *International Journal of Information Management*, *49*, 330–342. doi:10.1016/j.ijinfomgt.2019.06.002

Chen, J., Lai, P., Chan, A., Man, V., & Chan, C. H. (2022). AI-assisted enhancement of student presentation skills: Challenges and opportunities. *Sustainability (Basel)*, *15*(1), 196. doi:10.3390/su15010196

Chen, M. P., Wang, L. C., Zou, D., Lin, S. Y., Xie, H., & Tsai, C. C. (2022). Effects of captions and English proficiency on learning effectiveness, motivation and attitude in augmented-reality-enhanced theme-based contextualized EFL learning. *Computer Assisted Language Learning*, *35*(3), 381–411. doi:10.1080/09588221.2019.1704787

Chen, M. P., Wang, L. C., Zou, D., Lin, S. Y., Xie, H., & Tsai, C. C. (2022). Effects of captions and English proficiency on learning effectiveness, motivation and attitude in augmented-reality-enhanced theme-based contextualized EFL learning. *Computer Assisted Language Learning*, *35*(3), 381–411. doi:10.1080/09588221.2019.1704787

Chen, Y. L., & Hsu, C. C. (2020). Self-regulated mobile game-based English learning in a virtual reality environment. *Computers & Education*, *154*, 103910. doi:10.1016/j.compedu.2020.103910

Cocca, M., & Cocca, A. (2019). Affective Variables and Motivation as Predictors of Proficiency in English as a Foreign Language. *Journal on Efficiency and Responsibility in Education and Science*, *12*(3), 75–83. doi:10.7160/eriesj.2019.120302

Darasawang, P., & Reinders, H. (2021). Willingness to communicate and second language proficiency: A correlational study. *Education Sciences*, *11*(9), 517. doi:10.3390/educsci11090517

Davis, F. D. (1989). Perceived usefulness, perceived ease of use and user acceptance of information technology. *Management Information Systems Quarterly*, *13*(3), 319–339. doi:10.2307/249008

Deci, E. L., Eghrari, H., Patrick, B. C., & Leone, D. R. (1994). Facilitating internalization: The self-determination theory perspective. *Journal of Personality*, *62*(1), 119–142. doi:10.1111/j.1467-6494.1994.tb00797.x PMID:8169757

Din, M. (2020). Evaluating university students' critical thinking ability as reflected in their critical reading skill: A study at bachelor level in Pakistan. *Thinking Skills and Creativity*, *35*, 100627. doi:10.1016/j.tsc.2020.100627

Dörnyei, Z., & Chan, L. (2013). Motivation and vision: An analysis of future L2 self images, sensory styles, and imagery capacity across two target languages. *Language Learning*, *63*(3), 437–462. doi:10.1111/lang.12005

Ebadi, S., & Amini, A. (2022). Examining the roles of social presence and human-likeness on Iranian EFL learners' motivation using artificial intelligence technology: A case of CSIEC chatbot. *Interactive Learning Environments*, ●●●, 1–19. doi:10.1 080/10494820.2022.2096638

Farley, A., Yang, H. H., Min, L., & Ma, S. (2020). Comparison of Chinese and Western English language proficiency measures in transnational business degrees. *Language, Culture and Curriculum*, *33*(3), 319–334. doi:10.1080/07908318.2019 .1630423

Farsawang, P., & Songkram, N. (2023). Fostering technology integration and adaptability in higher education: Insights from the COVID-19 pandemic. *Contemporary Educational Technology*, *15*(4), ep456. doi:10.30935/cedtech/13513

Galloway, N., & Ruegg, R. (2020). The provision of student support on English Medium Instruction programmes in Japan and China. *Journal of English for Academic Purposes*, *45*, 100846. doi:10.1016/j.jeap.2020.100846

Gardner, R. C. (2010). *Motivation and second language acquisition: The socio-educational model* (Vol. 10). Peter Lang.

Getie, A. S. (2020). Factors affecting the attitudes of students towards learning English as a foreign language. *Cogent Education*, *7*(1), 1738184. doi:10.1080/233 1186X.2020.1738184

Ghanea, M., Pisheh, H. R. Z., & Ghanea, M. H. (2011). The relationship between learners-motivation (integrative and instrumental) and English proficiency among Iranian EFL learners. *International Journal of Educational and Pedagogical Sciences*, *5*(11), 1368–1374.

Ghasemi, A. A., Ahmadian, M., Yazdani, H., & Amerian, M. (2020). Towards a model of intercultural communicative competence in Iranian EFL context: Testing the role of international posture, ideal L2 self, L2 self-confidence, and metacognitive strategies. *Journal of Intercultural Communication Research*, *49*(1), 41–60. doi:1 0.1080/17475759.2019.1705877

Ginaya, G., Rejeki, I. N. M., & Astuti, N. N. S. (2018). The effects of blended learning to students' speaking ability: A study of utilizing technology to strengthen the conventional instruction. *International journal of linguistics, literature and culture*, *4*(3), 1-14.

Habib, M. N., Jamal, W., Khalil, U., & Khan, Z. (2021). Transforming universities in interactive digital platform: Case of city university of science and information technology. *Education and Information Technologies*, *26*(1), 517–541. doi:10.1007/s10639-020-10237-w PMID:32837236

Han, D. (2021). An Analysis of Korean EFL Learners' Experience on English Classes Using AI Chatbot. *Robotics & AI Ethics*, *6*(3), 1–9. doi:10.22471/ai.2021.6.3.01

Huang, F., Teo, T., & Zhou, M. (2020). Chinese students' intentions to use the Internet-based technology for learning. *Educational Technology Research and Development*, *68*(1), 575–591. doi:10.1007/s11423-019-09695-y

Huang, W., Hew, K. F., & Fryer, L. K. (2022). Chatbots for language learning—Are they really useful? A systematic review of chatbot-supported language learning. *Journal of Computer Assisted Learning*, *38*(1), 237–257. doi:10.1111/jcal.12610

Ibrahim, H., Liu, F., Asim, R., Battu, B., Benabderrahmane, S., Alhafni, B., Adnan, W., Alhanai, T., AlShebli, B., Baghdadi, R., Bélanger, J. J., Beretta, E., Celik, K., Chaqfeh, M., Daqaq, M. F., Bernoussi, Z. E., Fougnie, D., Garcia de Soto, B., Gandolfi, A., & Zaki, Y. (2023). Perception, performance, and detectability of conversational artificial intelligence across 32 university courses. *Scientific Reports*, *13*(1), 12187. doi:10.1038/s41598-023-38964-3 PMID:37620342

Jalbani, A. N., Ahmad, A., & Maitlo, S. K. (2023). A Comparative Study to Evaluate ESL Learners' Proficiency and Attitudes towards English Language. *Global Language Review*, *VIII*(II), 446–455. doi:10.31703/glr.2023(VIII-II).36

Jiang, L., Zhang, L. J., & May, S. (2019). Implementing English-medium instruction (EMI) in China: Teachers' practices and perceptions, and students' learning motivation and needs. *International Journal of Bilingual Education and Bilingualism*, *22*(2), 107–119. doi:10.1080/13670050.2016.1231166

Jung, H. J. (2015). Fostering an English teaching environment: Factors influencing English as a foreign language teachers' adoption of mobile learning. *Informatics in Education-An International Journal*, *14*(2), 219–241. doi:10.15388/infedu.2015.13

Kang, H. (2022). Effects of Artificial Intelligence (AI) and native speaker interlocutors on ESL learners' speaking ability and affective aspects. *Multimedia-Assisted Language Learning*, *25*(2), 9–43.

Khasawneh, M. A. S., & Jadallah Abed Khasawneh, Y. (2023). The potentials of artificial intelligence in stimulating motivation and improving performance of undergraduates in foreign languages. *Journal of Namibian Studies: History Politics Culture*, *34*, 7059–7077.

Khoo, E., & Kang, S. (2022). Proactive learner empowerment: Towards a transformative academic integrity approach for English language learners. *International Journal for Educational Integrity, 18*(1), 1–24. doi:10.1007/s40979-022-00111-2

Kim, J. Y., Shim, J. P., & Ahn, K. M. (2011). Social networking service: Motivation, pleasure, and behavioral intention to use. *Journal of Computer Information Systems, 51*(4), 92.

Kim, T. Y., & Kim, Y. (2021). Structural relationship between L2 learning motivation and resilience and their impact on motivated behavior and L2 proficiency. *Journal of Psycholinguistic Research, 50*(2), 417–436. doi:10.1007/s10936-020-09721-8 PMID:32691245

Lamb, M., & Arisandy, F. E. (2020). The impact of online use of English on motivation to learn. *Computer Assisted Language Learning, 33*(1-2), 85–108. doi:10.1080/09588221.2018.1545670

Law, K. M., Geng, S., & Li, T. (2019). Student enrollment, motivation and learning performance in a blended learning environment: The mediating effects of social, teaching, and cognitive presence. *Computers & Education, 136*, 1–12. doi:10.1016/j.compedu.2019.02.021

Lee, H., & Hwang, Y. (2022). Technology-enhanced education through VR-making and metaverse-linking to foster teacher readiness and sustainable learning. *Sustainability (Basel), 14*(8), 4786. doi:10.3390/su14084786

Li, Z., Lou, X., Chen, M., Li, S., Lv, C., Song, S., & Li, L. (2023). Students' online learning adaptability and their continuous usage intention across different disciplines. *Humanities & Social Sciences Communications, 10*(1), 1–10. doi:10.1057/s41599-023-02376-5

Lin, H. C. K., Chao, C. J., & Huang, T. C. (2015). From a perspective on foreign language learning anxiety to develop an affective tutoring system. *Educational Technology Research and Development, 63*(5), 727–747. doi:10.1007/s11423-015-9385-6

Liu, C., Hou, J., Tu, Y. F., Wang, Y., & Hwang, G. J. (2023). Incorporating a reflective thinking promoting mechanism into artificial intelligence-supported English writing environments. *Interactive Learning Environments, 31*(9), 5614–5632. doi:10.1080/10494820.2021.2012812

Liu, H., Zhang, X., & Fang, F. (2023). Young English learners' attitudes towards China English: Unpacking their identity construction with implications for secondary level language education in China. *Asia Pacific Journal of Education, 43*(1), 283–298. doi:10.1080/02188791.2021.1908228

Liu, I. F. (2020). The impact of extrinsic motivation, intrinsic motivation, and social self-efficacy on English competition participation intentions of pre-college learners: Differences between high school and vocational students in Taiwan. *Learning and Motivation, 72*, 101675. doi:10.1016/j.lmot.2020.101675

Liu, X., Zhu, Y., You, H., & Hong, J. C. (2023). The relationships among metacognitive strategies, acculturation, learning attitude, perceived value, and continuance intention to use YouTube to learn English. *Computer Assisted Language Learning*, 1–21. doi:10.1080/09588221.2023.2297037

Lovato, C., & Junior, O. S. (2011). Motivation in Second Language Acquisition-Gardners Socio-Educational Model. In *9th Symposium on Graduate Education. Piracicaba, Br.* IEEE.

Madhavi, E., Sivapurapu, L., Koppula, V., Rani, P. E., & Sreehari, V. (2023). Developing Learners' English-Speaking Skills using ICT and AI Tools. *Journal of Advanced Research in Applied Sciences and Engineering Technology, 32*(2), 142–153. doi:10.37934/araset.32.2.142153

Maftuna, A. (2020). Self-confidence in oral performance. *Бюллетень науки и практики, 6*(4), 444-452.

Malik, A. R., Pratiwi, Y., Andajani, K., Numertayasa, I. W., Suharti, S., Darwis, A., & Marzuki. (2023). Exploring Artificial Intelligence in Academic Essay: Higher Education Student's Perspective. *International Journal of Educational Research Open, 5*, 100296. doi:10.1016/j.ijedro.2023.100296

Manegre, M., & Gutiérrez-Colón, M. (2023). Foreign language learning through collaborative writing in knowledge building forums. *Interactive Learning Environments, 31*(3), 1364–1376. doi:10.1080/10494820.2020.1836499

Melvina, M., & Julia, J. (2021). Learner Autonomy and English Proficiency of Indonesian Undergraduate Students. *Cypriot Journal of Educational Sciences, 16*(2), 803–818. doi:10.18844/cjes.v16i2.5677

Mujahidah, N., & Yusdiana, Y. (2023). Application of Albert Bandura's Social-Cognitive Theories in Teaching and Learning. *Edukasi Islami: Jurnal Pendidikan Islam, 12*(02).

Muñoz, J. L. R., Ojeda, F. M., Jurado, D. L. A., Peña, P. F. P., Carranza, C. P. M., Berríos, H. Q., & Vasquez-Pauca, M. J. (2022). Systematic review of adaptive learning technology for learning in higher education. *Eurasian Journal of Educational Research*, *98*(98), 221–233.

Navarro, J. L., & Tudge, J. R. (2023). Technologizing Bronfenbrenner: Neo-ecological theory. *Current Psychology (New Brunswick, N.J.)*, *42*(22), 19338–19354. doi:10.1007/s12144-022-02738-3 PMID:35095241

Neumann, H., Padden, N., & McDonough, K. (2019). Beyond English language proficiency scores: Understanding the academic performance of international undergraduate students during the first year of study. *Higher Education Research & Development*, *38*(2), 324–338. doi:10.1080/07294360.2018.1522621

Nguyen, T. N. Q., & Vo, N. T. T. (2021). The need of applying English learning apps to help Van Lang University students improve their spoken English performance. *AsiaCALL Online Journal*, *12*(2), 72–86.

Ni, A., & Cheung, A. (2023). Understanding secondary students' continuance intention to adopt AI-powered intelligent tutoring system for English learning. *Education and Information Technologies*, *28*(3), 3191–3216. doi:10.1007/s10639-022-11305-z PMID:36119127

Niemiec, C. P., Ryan, R. M., & Deci, E. L. (2010). Self-determination theory and the relation of autonomy to self-regulatory processes and personality development. Handbook of personality and self-regulation, 169-191.

Noviana, N., & Oktaviani, L. (2022). The correlation between college student personality types and English proficiency ability at Universitas Teknokrat Indonesia. *Journal of English Language Teaching and Learning*, *3*(1), 54–60. doi:10.33365/jeltl.v3i1.1709

Ozdemir, E., & Papi, M. (2022). Mindsets as sources of L2 speaking anxiety and self-confidence: The case of international teaching assistants in the US. *Innovation in Language Learning and Teaching*, *16*(3), 234–248. doi:10.1080/17501229.2021.1907750

Öztürk, M., & Çakıroğlu, Ü. (2021). Flipped learning design in EFL classrooms: Implementing self-regulated learning strategies to develop language skills. *Smart Learning Environments*, *8*(1), 2. doi:10.1186/s40561-021-00146-x

Peng, A., & Patterson, M. M. (2022). Relations among cultural identity, motivation for language learning, and perceived English language proficiency for international students in the United States. *Language, Culture and Curriculum, 35*(1), 67–82. doi:10.1080/07908318.2021.1938106

Polas, M. R. H., & Raju, V. (2021). Technology and entrepreneurial marketing decisions during COVID-19. *Global Journal of Flexible Systems Managment, 22*(2), 95–112. doi:10.1007/s40171-021-00262-0

Qureshi, M. I., Khan, N., Raza, H., Imran, A., & Ismail, F. (2021). *Digital technologies in education 4.0. Does it enhance the effectiveness of learning?*

Rafiee, M., & Abbasian-Naghneh, S. (2021). E-learning: Development of a model to assess the acceptance and readiness of technology among language learners. *Computer Assisted Language Learning, 34*(5-6), 730–750. doi:10.1080/09588221.2019.1640255

Rasool, G., & Winke, P. (2019). Undergraduate students' motivation to learn and attitudes towards English in multilingual Pakistan: A look at shifts in English as a world language. *System, 82*, 50–62. doi:10.1016/j.system.2019.02.015

Riasati, M. J. (2018). Willingness to speak English among foreign language learners: A causal model. *Cogent Education, 5*(1), 1455332. doi:10.1080/2331186X.2018.1455332

Rosa, E. M., & Tudge, J. (2013). Urie Bronfenbrenner's theory of human development: Its evolution from ecology to bioecology. *Journal of Family Theory & Review, 5*(4), 243–258. doi:10.1111/jftr.12022

Rose, H., Curle, S., Aizawa, I., & Thompson, G. (2020). What drives success in English medium taught courses? The interplay between language proficiency, academic skills, and motivation. *Studies in Higher Education, 45*(11), 2149–2161. doi:10.1080/03075079.2019.1590690

Rosmayanti, V., Ramli, R., & Rafiqa, R. (2023). Building beginners' self-confidence in speaking at private high school in Makassar. *EduLite: Journal of English Education. Literature and Culture, 8*(1), 192–208.

Rumjaun, A., & Narod, F. (2020). Social Learning Theory—Albert Bandura. *Science education in theory and practice: An introductory guide to learning theory*, 85-99.

Ryan, R. M., & Deci, E. L. (2017). Self-determination theory: Basic psychological needs in motivation. Development, and Wellness. Guilford Press, 10(978.14625), 28806.

Ryan, R. M., & Deci, E. L. (2022). Self-determination theory. In *Encyclopedia of quality of life and well-being research* (pp. 1–7). Springer International Publishing. doi:10.1007/978-3-319-69909-7_2630-2

Sagita, I. K. (2021). Applying Conversation Method and Self-Confidence and Its Effect to Learning Achievement. *Journal Corner of Education, Linguistics, and Literature, 1*(2), 122–131. doi:10.54012/jcell.v1i2.11

Sardegna, V. G., Lee, J., & Kusey, C. (2018). Self-efficacy, attitudes, and choice of strategies for English pronunciation learning. *Language Learning, 68*(1), 83–114. doi:10.1111/lang.12263

Sari, F. M., & Wahyudin, A. Y. (2019). Undergraduate Students' Perceptions Toward Blended Learning through Instagram in English for Business Class. *International Journal of Language Education, 3*(1), 64–73. doi:10.26858/ijole.v1i1.7064

Sato, R. (2023). Examining fluctuations in the WTC of Japanese EFL speakers: Language proficiency, affective and conditional factors. *Language Teaching Research, 27*(4), 974–994. doi:10.1177/1362168820977825

Septiani, E., Petrus, I., & Mirizon, S. (2021). The Correlations Among Teachers' Competences, Students' Learning Motivation, and Students' English Proficiency. *Eralingua: Jurnal Pendidikan Bahasa Asing Dan Sastra, 5*(1), 143. doi:10.26858/eralingua.v5i1.14316

Shafie, H., Majid, F. A., & Ismail, I. S. (2019). Technological pedagogical content knowledge (TPACK) in teaching 21st century skills in the 21st century classroom. *Asian Journal of University Education, 15*(3), 24–33. doi:10.24191/ajue.v15i3.7818

Shang, C., Moss, A. C., & Chen, A. (2023). The expectancy-value theory: A meta-analysis of its application in physical education. *Journal of Sport and Health Science, 12*(1), 52–64. doi:10.1016/j.jshs.2022.01.003 PMID:35051641

Shih, Y. C., & Reynolds, B. L. (2018). The effects of integrating goal setting and reading strategy instruction on English reading proficiency and learning motivation: A quasi-experimental study. *Applied Linguistics Review, 9*(1), 35–62. doi:10.1515/applirev-2016-1022

Siani, A., & Harris, J. (2023). Self-Confidence and STEM Career Propensity: Lessons from an All-Girls Secondary School. *Open Education Studies, 5*(1), 20220180. doi:10.1515/edu-2022-0180

Srivani, V., Hariharasudan, A., Nawaz, N., & Ratajczak, S. (2022). Impact of Education 4.0 among engineering students for learning English language. *PLoS One*, *17*(2), e0261717. doi:10.1371/journal.pone.0261717 PMID:35108282

Studer, P., & Konstantinidou, L. (2015). Language attitudes and language proficiency of undergraduate students in English-medium instruction. *Revue Tranel (Travaux neuchâtelois de linguistique)*, 215-231.

Su, Y. C. (2021). College Students' Oral Communication Strategy Use, Self-perceived English Proficiency and Confidence, and Communication Anxiety in Taiwan's EFL Learning. *Educational Studies (Ames)*, *57*(6), 650–669. doi:10.1080/00131946.2021.1919677

Sun, L., Asmawi, A., Dong, H., & Zhang, X. (2023). Empowering Chinese undergraduates' business english writing: Unveiling the efficacy of DingTalk-Aided Problem-based language learning during Covid-19 period. *Education and Information Technologies*, 1–33.

Sun, Y., & Gao, F. (2020). An investigation of the influence of intrinsic motivation on students' intention to use mobile devices in language learning. *Educational Technology Research and Development*, *68*(3), 1181–1198. doi:10.1007/s11423-019-09733-9

Tawafak, R. M., Al-Obaydi, L. H., Klimova, B., & Pikhart, M. (2023). Technology integration of using digital gameplay for enhancing EFL college students' behavior intention. *Contemporary Educational Technology*, *15*(4), ep452. doi:10.30935/cedtech/13454

Topçiu, M., & Myftiu, J. (2015). Vygotsky theory on social interaction and its influence on the development of pre-school children. *European Journal of Social Science Education and Research*, *2*(3), 172–179. doi:10.26417/ejser.v4i1.p172-179

Tridinanti, G. (2018). The correlation between speaking anxiety, self-confidence, and speaking achievement of Undergraduate EFL students of private university in Palembang. *International Journal of Education and Literacy Studies*, *6*(4), 35–39. doi:10.7575/aiac.ijels.v.6n.4p.35

Tudge, J. R., Merçon-Vargas, E. A., Liang, Y., & Payir, A. (2022). The importance of Urie Bronfenbrenner's bioecological theory for early childhood education. In *Theories of early childhood education* (pp. 50–61). Routledge. doi:10.4324/9781003288077-5

Vélez-Agosto, N. M., Soto-Crespo, J. G., Vizcarrondo-Oppenheimer, M., Vega-Molina, S., & García Coll, C. (2017). Bronfenbrenner's bioecological theory revision: Moving culture from the macro into the micro. *Perspectives on Psychological Science*, *12*(5), 900–910. doi:10.1177/1745691617704397 PMID:28972838

Waluyo, B., & Rofiah, N. L. (2021). Developing Students' English Oral Presentation Skills: Do Self-Confidence, Teacher Feedback, and English Proficiency Matter? *Mextesol Journal*, *45*(3), n3.

Wang, C., Ahmad, S. F., Ayassrah, A. Y. B. A., Awwad, E. M., Irshad, M., Ali, Y. A., & Han, H. (2023). An empirical evaluation of technology acceptance model for Artificial Intelligence in E-commerce. *Heliyon*, *9*(8), e18349. doi:10.1016/j.heliyon.2023.e18349 PMID:37520947

Wang, N., Chen, J., Tai, M., & Zhang, J. (2021). Blended learning for Chinese university EFL learners: Learning environment and learner perceptions. *Computer Assisted Language Learning*, *34*(3), 297–323. doi:10.1080/09588221.2019.1607881

Wang, Q., & Xue, M. (2022). The implications of expectancy-value theory of motivation in language education. *Frontiers in Psychology*, *13*, 992372. doi:10.3389/fpsyg.2022.992372 PMID:36425822

Wut, T. M., Xu, J., Lee, S. W., & Lee, D. (2022). University student readiness and its effect on intention to participate in the flipped classroom setting of hybrid learning. *Education Sciences*, *12*(7), 442. doi:10.3390/educsci12070442

Xia, Q., Chiu, T. K., Chai, C. S., & Xie, K. (2023). The mediating effects of needs satisfaction on the relationships between prior knowledge and self-regulated learning through artificial intelligence chatbot. *British Journal of Educational Technology*, *54*(4), 967–986. doi:10.1111/bjet.13305

Xu, Z., Banerjee, M., Ramirez, G., Zhu, G., & Wijekumar, K. (2019). The effectiveness of educational technology applications on adult English language learners' writing quality: A meta-analysis. *Computer Assisted Language Learning*, *32*(1-2), 132–162. doi:10.1080/09588221.2018.1501069

Yang, S., & Pu, R. (2022). The effects of contextual factors, self-efficacy and motivation on learners' adaptability to blended learning in college english: A structural equation modeling approach. *Frontiers in Psychology*, *13*, 847342. doi:10.3389/fpsyg.2022.847342 PMID:35465522

Yu, Z., Xu, W., & Sukjairungwattana, P. (2023). Motivation, learning strategies, and outcomes in mobile English language learning. *The Asia-Pacific Education Researcher*, *32*(4), 545–560. doi:10.1007/s40299-022-00675-0

Zhai, C., & Wibowo, S. (2023). A systematic review on artificial intelligence dialogue systems for enhancing English as foreign language students' interactional competence in the university. *Computers and Education: Artificial Intelligence, 100134*, 100134. doi:10.1016/j.caeai.2023.100134

Zhang, H., Dai, Y., & Wang, Y. (2020). Motivation and second foreign language proficiency: The mediating role of foreign language enjoyment. *Sustainability (Basel), 12*(4), 1302. doi:10.3390/su12041302

Zhang, Y. (2023). Teaching Strategies of College English Listening based on Affective Filter Hypothesis. *The Educational Review, USA, 7*(1), 26–30. doi:10.26855/er.2023.01.007

Zhao, Y., & Lai, C. (2023). Technology and second language learning: Promises and problems. In *Technology-mediated learning environments for young English learners* (pp. 167–206). Routledge. doi:10.4324/9781003418009-8

Zhou, S., & Thompson, G. (2023). Exploring role of English proficiency, self-efficacy, and motivation in listening for learners transitioning to an English-medium transnational university in China. *System, 113*, 102998. doi:10.1016/j.system.2023.102998

Zhu, Y., Zhang, J. H., Au, W., & Yates, G. (2020). University students' online learning attitudes and continuous intention to undertake online courses: A self-regulated learning perspective. *Educational Technology Research and Development, 68*(3), 1485–1519. doi:10.1007/s11423-020-09753-w

Zou, B., Liviero, S., Hao, M., & Wei, C. (2020). Artificial intelligence technology for EAP speaking skills: Student perceptions of opportunities and challenges. *Technology and the psychology of second language learners and users*, 433-463. doi:10.1007/978-3-030-34212-8_17

Zulfikar, T., Dahliana, S., & Sari, R. A. (2019). An Exploration of English Students' Attitude towards English Learning. *English Language Teaching Educational Journal, 2*(1), 1–12. doi:10.12928/eltej.v2i1.947

Chapter 12
Expanding Literacy and Textual Work With Comics and Digital Instruction

Jason D. DeHart
The University of Tennessee, Knoxville, USA

ABSTRACT

This chapter examines the nexus of comics and digital work in the context of both secondary and post-secondary instruction with adolescents. The chapter draws upon the qualitative and self-study centered approach of the author as teacher and as reader, with implications related to the future possibilities for instruction. In this case, the context is centered in literacy as the author has worked with students over the course of approximately seventeen years to foster deeper connections to reading, writing, and composing.

INTRODUCTION

It is with curiosity and with hope that this author explores the connections between philosophical development, instructional possibilities, and the centrality of literacy history across types of media in a descriptive analysis of teaching methods in literacy/English courses over a seventeen-year period. This work is toward an effort of beginning to imagine a speculative form of literacy education, imagining a future beginning to be realized now. This exploration occurs both in terms of comic book readership and participation as a member of the philosophical and educational community, rooted in the Appalachian region in which the author's work as an educator and researcher has been situated.

DOI: 10.4018/979-8-3693-2169-0.ch012

Copyright © 2024, IGI Global. Copying or distributing in print or electronic forms without written permission of IGI Global is prohibited.

This tracing of educational journey draws upon a critical qualitative approach, with an emphasis on narrative (Polkinghorne, 1995) as classroom practitioner and with emphasis on future pedagogical directions through self-study methods (Pinnegar & Hamilton, 2009), including journaling, returning to personal photographs and autographa, and reflection on instructional and reading practices.

Through the consideration of a number of sources, the author traces their journey in reflection/response to the interactions of adolescent readers in secondary and post-secondary contexts, including the links between and among affinities with particular forms of media.

POSITIONALITY

The author is an educator with an interest in the possible, including speculative notions of what could be accomplished and encouraged in education, as well as an interest in the mythic from a background as a comics reader, film viewer, and member of religious community. At the same time, the author draws on his own history in academia and formal education as one who has experienced his own disconnection from school life and practices, having at one time been a high school dropout and, at present, is serving as a high school English teacher who has a Ph.D. in literacy. The author is also a constant reader of the comics and visual form, given the use of transmedial texts that are endemic to his age/generation. The author's actions in the classroom world are centered around teaching, storytelling, and finding ways to merge beliefs with everyday interactions. This network of interactions with texts that occur not by prescriptive means but with a sense of agency and choice on the part of the reader are a central component of Street's (2006) conceptualization of the dimensions along which engagement with literacy practices occur. Though the school space and home space are not always clearly delineated, with some interactions and practices spilling over, there is space in this conceptualization for asking about conceptions of power and autonomy for students, including the ways in which students take up secret spaces and practices in classrooms, as when a student disengages with the intended curriculum and engages in some spontaneous and even subversive sense of creating.

The author is a reader, thinker, believer, teacher, and student, all at the same time – and, moreover in terms of spirituality, the author is a devoted seeker of truth who wants to help others on their journey. This lens as a thinker and practitioner is often influenced by personal beliefs. It with a careful sensibility that the author attempts to mitigate any sense of bias that the author brings along with this background, embracing and honoring a variety of worldviews. The author embarks on this journey each day from the framework of a scholar who is invested in finding pathways for reading and writing experiences for others.

Essentially, the author's identity as a person and as a scholar is rooted in an intertextual array of experiences and concepts. His interest in religion led him to earn a Bachelor's degree in a religion-based field in the early 2000s, and his love of graphic novels and visual literacy led to a development of a reading-focused dissertation, culminating in a PhD. The author teaches about reading, but the elements of what the author believes about God and universe serve as a set of ethical praxes for instructional life and inform a sensibility of comics reading and film viewing that draws upon a distinct set of interpretive and experiential tools.

Media in Education

Comics in education and comics studies have roots in decades past, with attention to the ways the medium of comics can be used linking to Chase et al. (2014), including attention the modeling reading processes in the form rather than assuming a comfort and familiarity with the form for all readers. Writing as a contemporary, Jacobs (2014) discovered that a majority of adolescents had not encountered comics in traditional form outside of newspaper strips at the time, but were regularly engaging with web comics. Years later, Wallner (2019) noted the continued advancement of the mingling of web-based tools and comics storytelling.

A description of literacy practices among secondary and post-secondary students conceptually involves both a resistance to traditional texts and an almost feverish engagement with alternative forms of literacy navigation, including film, web-based games, and digital comics. Students often position themselves with statements like, "I don't read." This statement indicates that it is not a lack of ability but an active choice to be engaged with other forms of storytelling.

To trace a journey as a reader of the word, and, to borrow and reconfigure Freire's phrase, a reader of the comics world, involves the screen in an authentic report from the field of literacy education across contexts. This chapter is about personal development, but it is about trends in the classroom. In this view of literacy, students are actively reading all the time as they consume stories and ideas across forms.

The mingling of mythology and realistic narrative, whether in rural or urban landscapes, speaks to both the speculative nature of comics, as well as a textual space for exploring what is possible in lived experiences (Teampau, 2015). An accurate exploration of literacy development includes personal reflections, memories of the books (and now digital stories) which have been part of history and development, and acknowledgement of philosophical questions that persist across forms of storytelling. The existence of the realistic or supranatural across forms reaches to notions of myth and revolves around the narratology that is pervasive across cultures. In the current context of writing this chapter, Artificial Intelligence (AI) is a growing reality in educational practices, issuing into questions of what it means to teaching voice and creativity in the context of technological advancements.

The personal and professional interaction which exists at the heart of this chapter centers around the developing understanding of the importance of visual storytelling, including the filmic, digital, and comics-oriented. The author's work is situated within comics studies and fandom, notions which transcend regional boundaries, given the prevalence of media across geographical spaces. Coupled with this, the author positions from this work from an action-oriented stance with an interest in social practices that are encapsulated in a broader framework of how texts contribute to who people are, and how they navigate the written and spoken word (Gee, 2013). It seems that the stories that people, including youth, tell and retell are important for a variety of reasons, and these stories reach to cultural understandings and undergird the ways in which both the tellers and listeners view the world. These ways of being issue into our ways of doing, and into the decisions that people make in their lives and work, including how individuals define themselves in relationship to text and storytelling.

Linking Texts and Lived Experiences

There are a curious number of themes and tenets that align between philosophical ideas and comic book lore, although there are also differences. The journey of a hero in a traditional superhero narrative might be traced the archetypes that are found for these types of stories across time – yet, comics a medium and not a genre. The medium allows for a range of storytelling practices, from memoir to mythic, along with a mingling of the two. What draws a particular reader to a movement in visual literacy is a matter of some variance, depending on the reader's age, interests, and willingness to disclose such interests in adolescence.

The words narrative, narratology, and storytelling might refer to the printed and digital pages of comics panels or prose novels; however, there are additional textual connections that take place outside those boundaries of textual definition. From a pedagogical foundation, the practice of teaching itself might be related to narratology, or the passing on a story that is composed and co-constructed in a shared space, including the resonant themes that become part of a classroom environment. Anyon (1981), for example, noted the ways in which schools can be spaces for the reconstituting of troublesome social norms. On the other hand, hooks (1996) imagined and approached schools as transformational and liberatory spaces, linking to the work of Freire, as well as the more recent contributions of Parker (2022). This reflection on the school space is not only about the descriptive narrative of what is visible, but the speculative nature of what is not yet seen. In philosophical and theological terms, there is a trajectory of what is already, as well as what is not yet – but could be (Moltmann, 1993). This view of the classroom, and of textual interactions, does not necessarily rely on a particular spiritual framework, but is more ecumenical and universal than such limitations preclude.

Bakhtin's notions of narratology, and the driving forces that unite stories across disparate times and contexts. Superhero stories are a large of part of this consideration, but reading in comics and graphic novels extends beyond these narrative tropes to include a range of genres.

Subversive and Sophisticated

Such work is subversive and yet sophisticated at times, and it is this sense of agency and the political power of the individual student which acts as a pivot for rethinking what is possible in schooling, including moments when educators intentionally make space and avenues for agency, as well as moments in which this sense of agency occurs in the place of a curricular intention. The idea of joining the throng of creativity and embracing of multiple ways of engaging text might lead to a sort of surrender mindset, and yet the author does not position this move as a choice that undermines the teacher. In this instance, authors like Pilkey (2023) have pointed to the ways that images and reflections in creativity sometimes rail against the conformity of traditional schooling approaches. This is seen in Pilkey's sharing of his story as a student who was removed from the classroom, and who was constantly creating images.

Recalling his interactions with text, the author notes the few occasions that comics and superhero-based narratives were part of the prescribed and regulated school spaces. While such texts were not available in the author's schooling experiences in many instances, the few examples (as when the author discovered a graphic novel/ comic form in the school library, or the example of locating a superhero-themed book in the school bookfair) were resonant. In response, the author's understanding of reading motivation and engagement with materials has issued into a diverse classroom library both in terms of author identity/identities, and in terms of types of texts, from classics to comics. When a text is seen in the school library space or school book sale space, there is a sense of importance or approval that carries with the text.

In essence, the author has wished for and continues to practice an evolving sense of what education can mean, expanding on the ways in which reading and composing occur in classrooms. School, in effect, was not the most positive experience for the author. As a teacher, he now brings this sensibility both to research and practice.

At the same time, images from personal life and spirituality can be traced in comics, from salvific figures to a range of experiences with religion/religious communities of varying types. This linking of spirituality and comics is not without precedence (Fronk, 2016).

Narrative Practices and Trends

There is a narrative practice that is central to comics and fandom, as noted earlier in this chapter. This sense of storytelling revolves around the notion of witnessing humanity or human experiences in some form (DeHart, 2020). The act of storytelling across media is focused on sharing experiences of community, as well as investment in hope. In recent years, there has been a resurgence of interest in romantic fiction among the author's students, from the work of Colleen Hoover to Ibi Zoboi's *Pride* (2019). There is a hopefulness in many stories, as well as a movement toward the modern sensibility of the less positive dénouement, as well as the postmodern conceptualization that madness and a lack of order punctuates lived experiences.

From dystopian works to fantasy/mythic comics, a number of titles and trends have proven to be popular choices through classroom readings in the past two decades, as noted in the author's experiences. There has been a recurring motif of the statement "I am not a reader" among students in the author's charge; this is an ironic statement, given the prolific engagement with texts across types of media with which students engage. The prevalence of the superhero film in recent years has now been replaced, in many cases, by a range of streaming media, and the presence of one-to-one technology in classrooms makes these visual stories readily available for students.

In a turn to the self, there is a sense of hope and optimism that punctuates the author's classroom practices. In all stories that the author centers there is either a critique of interactions, as in classic choices like F. Scott Fitzgerald's work, as well as through the work of J.D. Salinger. This trend can also be located in the more contemporary choices the author centers, including the work of Jason Reynolds. In terms of comics texts, the presence of a heroic character acting as change agent is a recurring element across story examples.

Students are living in an increasingly visual world (Author, 2020), and a range of visual texts are now available at finger's length. This appreciation for ways of storytelling stems from the author's identity as a member of fandom, and as a reader who recognizes the powerful juxtaposition of words and images. Sometimes students might find words difficult, but an image can convey a range of thoughts and emotions. The use of images, then, is a means of conceptualizing what communication means, embracing a range of tools that have been increasing in availability over the past few decades, from the rise of the personal computer to the more recent emphasis on instantly-accessible streaming media.

Exploring the Use of Symbols and Imagery

In addition to the heroic mythic that punctuates the author's experiences as a reader and teacher, the presence of the religious and spiritual has been a key feature of teaching in Appalachian spaces.

The author has seen this intersection of spiritual identity and heroic myth, as well as the influence of Appalachian culture, first-hand as a classroom teacher and as an educational researcher, but also in reflections on personal growth as a reader and belief whose early experiences with spirituality stemmed from religion-informed picture books and the occasional Christian or Biblically-centered comic book, not discounting the Chick tracts that have been circulated for generations. These texts provided a unique merging of the visual and religiously iconographic to create a broadened appreciation of pictorial/image-based reading materials early on in the author's life, and students that are enrolled in the author's college and high school classes continue to point to the Bible as an authoritative text in their lives. The degree to which students engage with a traditional or visual Bible is a matter of some variance, as some students choose to read Biblical text for self-selection, while others note awareness and even affiliation with such texts without making their reading practices visible in the space of the classroom. The tendency to link text with belief systems, as has been evident in the author's literacy journey, brings to mind the range of stories that can be told in the comics medium – across genres and intentions. Alongside this growth as a reader, the author's sense of criticality which is illustrated in his teaching also draws upon and builds in a spiritual sense of welcoming community and religious diversity (DeHart, 2023).

When readers engage with a story most, their minds bring that story to life through visualization (Lefèvre, 2009). Both comics and film do some of this work to a degree, providing some of the visuals and allowing the reader/viewer to take in new dimensions of the story, building inferences and further cognitive work related to the interactions of characters and the movement of the story. However, when considering transmedial storytelling, the trajectory of thinking continues. As a young reader and view, the author continued the stories found in various types of media, and even retold them through a variety of methods, including play and drawing. This included the practice of simulating film work with action figures and cassette tape soundtracks, as well as creating original stories in notebooks that drew on popular characters.

Returning to spirituality, a focus from the space of religion is hardly devoid of myth and supernatural elements, so often found in superhero narratives. Where else does the ringing of a bell symbolize a transformation from one state to another, unless attention focuses back on high school class changes? It is from comics design features that the author first locates theoretical connections for scholarship, and to which the author so often turns. There is further ideological work of personhood to explore in graphica, including the ways in which one may draw one's self and one's world. The merging of realism and the mythic takes place as imagined characters with expansive powers enter landscapes that mirror reality and contend with conflicts that sometimes reflect real life, albeit with different stakes and a range of counters that might not exist for ordinary beings in daily lived experiences. Readers find meaning in magazine images, the flickering celluloid of film, and even in the frames and narrative boxes that we can panels in the pages of graphica, seeing themselves and also peering into the lives of others (Bishop, 1990).

Sometimes readers see themselves reflected back in characters who are like them, and sometimes an element of humanity is discovered in a character who comes from a different perspective. This, too, is a spiritually-inform work for this author, or is at least an ethical and human-centered one of noting the threads of the human story that can located in literature and emphasized as part of instruction. The human being expressed through text is at center here and, pivoting from prioritized standards, an educator might first ask themselves the primary question of what a text offers in terms of a view to humanity.

Returning to and reapplying Moltmann, readers find what they are and want to be, and they look for others with whom they can identify, in much the same way that they recognize a sense of what is happening in the present alongside the promise of progression, linking to the long-held notion of reading communities (Pawley, 2002). In the best of ways, reading then is an exercise in empathy and exploring the lives of others, as well as developing a keen awareness and understanding of one's self (McCreary & Marchant, 2017).

Expanding on these notions of self, literacy can lead to identity-based work, including the notion of the identity kit that is advanced by Gee (2013). The ways in which individuals interact with one another and form community, as well as the ways that storytelling occurs across media, can inform that methods by which readers and viewers advance their positionalities and political identifications in social spaces. These practices are, in fact, inextricable from writing and other daily practices, from the ways students subvert and add humor to activities and the ways students comply or refuse to comply with particular assignment structures. Along with this activity of agency, young people are reading and engaging with a textual world, even if this textual universe is post-print and, in some cases, post-typographic. Such a shift to the digital and multimodal is nothing new. An accurate portrayal of this author's readership timeline would include a variety of comic books and graphic novels, works from the late 1980s, 1990s, and 2000s that depicted popular characters and, increasingly, a range of representation and experiences, as well as religious texts.

Through the course of developing an understanding of self through this study, particular texts have been mile markers to revisit and reconsider. Some of these textual encounters are the first reunions with these books that the author has had in decades. It may seem surprising to read such an anthropomorphic description of reading a book, but these texts served as friends in times of loneliness and even miraculous adventures when processing difficult events. They were voices that echoed in childhood in between the other voices the author found among family, teachers, and friends. There are also filmic texts that occur as part of this exploration of self, with the author's first interest comics arriving at about the same time as the 1989 *Batman* film by Tim Burton. The Batman character served as a dark and gothic example of revenge and trauma, while the lighter aspects of superheroic exploits were made popular in the Christopher Reeves *Superman* films.

In the past few decades, the mainstream focus on biographical, autobiographical, and fact-based graphic novels only seems to have grown and has expanded the way the author considers the comics medium. If authors take up the world through words and artist represent experiences through images, comics have a dual prong set of possibilities in uniting these features into unique ways to tell stories and convey ideas, taking up narrative as well as the visual. The religious texts that informed experiences, including books that have been considered to be sacred over time, including the Bible in its many translations, as well as the Koran, the Bhagavad-Gita, and a range of commentaries on spiritual life and development, as well as one or two comic book adaptations of Bible stories. At the time, all of these books were part of a reading agenda as the author attempted to understand the many religions that are in the world, and the themes that seem to connect them all. For the author, here is something of being a reader at the heart of being spiritual, as well as something of the composer in assembling understandings.

It was in attempting to shape an ethical behavior and sense of cosmology that the author first took a course in New Testament Greek, exploring a new set of symbols for constructing meaning and rediscovering particular elements of native language. Whether spiritual or mythic concepts are born across the textual surface of Hebrew, Greek, or ancient English, or else modernized into updated visual and written translations, the substance of an idea is still contained within what we know as text, including the image or word. It is often in translation and interpretation that the most difficult (and sometimes divisive) work begins. It is the translation then of the mythic to ethical and communal that might serve as a nexus point for enacting theory and practice. Literacy is about the ways that words and other meaning systems can be applied for communicative purposes; the direction of that purpose underscores the value of the communicator, and this sense of the essential human nature of storytelling is a dominant pedagogical thread.

In practice, the communicator takes an idea and wraps words around it so that the idea can pass on to others. Sometimes, the communication includes character or pictures. In those words and pictures, there is a part of who the communicator is or wishes to be, issuing in a kind of speculative and even self-directed salvific work.

FORMATIVE WORKS

As noted, during this project, the author revisited the formative comic book works that the author had not revisited in at least two decades to draw memories regarding early experiences with the medium and conjure images of what it was like to be a young person of faith and engage with visual literature. In addition to this textual visitation and artifact collecting, the author has attempted to balance voice against the theoretical work of fellow scholars. This presence of other voices from a range of experiences has created a sense of literary and philosophical conversation that has been useful in this introspective journey. The author is never alone in thinking, as the primary function of communication is community.

Images of ailing, hospitalized superhero characters in *Invasion Book 3: World Without Heroes* (1988) linked with personal family illness; the direction of the Huntress to achieve justice in *Huntress* issue one (1989) coincided with a personal search for a way through trauma. At this point, only memory serves as the instrument from which the author reflects om the imaginations of youth applied to small images, and from which the author gave these images names or recognized them from popular action figure lines of the time.

All of this writing and reflecting process is textual and links with reading and writing practices, as well as practices of play, for the author. Further implications apply to the work of educators who explore the power of literacy and storytelling in their work across types of narrative and ways of composing. Further implications relate to the ways in which readers/researchers can explore their histories in literature, as texts have proven to be a traceable and locatable source of literary documentation, and have a helpful chronology in terms of their publication dates. As a reader, the author has been able to recall and point to specific examples from the publication history of comics, beginning around 1988 and stretching to present day.

Further implications point to the access to texts that occur in particular communities, as well as the lack of access in some other communities across time. In the late 1980s and through the early 1990s, comics could be found in many places, including pharmacies. In the present age, digital means can be used to access many examples. Family photographs and journaled reflections are additional artifacts of memory that can be linked to experiences, including childhood costume play, linking to the notion that to be a comics reader can involve some engagement with collecting as an avocation and enacting stories, as well. In this same way, the author asks students now to point to particular texts that they have found meaningful in literacy history activities and responses. Students often point to a few school-related texts, but they also draw upon social media, filmic, comic book, and other forms of texts. They often express surprise when this definition of text is broadened.

These documents include childhood photographs in costume, as well as some examples of childhood art. These artifacts are markers of engagement and making, as well as interesting in terms of their details that appealed to the author-as-creator. Engagement with visual literature was hardly passive, and indeed figured into many aspects of identity. It was not enough to read about characters on a page; this was a practice of becoming. These notions underpin the possibilities of comics and visual storytelling as sites for active literacy practices.

The author's continued appreciation of comics as a reader comes after a period of shame and fear of being as "less than" in terms of reading because of affinity with comics. This is a sense of readership that declined in early adulthood and which has since been reclaimed or rediscovered at the same level or almost the same level of engagement from decades prior. Much of pandemic experience has been informed and sustained by the readily available nature of digital comics, and the steady supply of titles the author continues to encounter, issuing into continued encounters with the written and visual. What Gee (2013) referred to as an identity kit, those cultural symbols and elements that are drawn together in consideration and co-construction of who people are and want to be, certainly includes these materials as part of a personal and pedagogical story in development – work which has found its outcome, at present, in the formation of a comics club and the increased centering of comics as spaces for reading and composing in the secondary North American classroom.

The linking of literacy and social practices, including faith, has been informed by a larger cultural move in Appalachia that continues to bring affiliation with religion to the forefront. the author also approaches these works as someone who has worked with adolescent readers for more than a decade and who, moreover, lived and worked in an academic community that was heavily influenced by the habituation of faith practices. It is from reflection on the power of comics to engage readers who are reluctant and who may or may not wish to engage with classic literature that a two-prong appreciation for the medium as reader and as educator has formed.

Within comics, the author sees these tensions of the canonical and complex explored, and the author also notes the potential for identity work and the consideration of tough questions when it comes to issues of faith rendered through narratives which can then lend themselves to more nuanced conversations revolving around ethics and community. A visual pedagogy has the potential to include critical awareness and dialogic community practices as readers link their engaging with both the visual and verbal, and as they take up questions of self and the world through narratives which are at once boundless in terms of what is possible on the page, and bounded by the value and direction of the human being creating the elements of the page.

These commitments lead to conversations that occur within the spaces of classrooms, but the author adds that this work is tentative, thoughtful, and always respectful and reflective.

OUTSIDER AND INSIDER

A sense of belonging combined with a sense of otherness and being othered is not without pain; often, communities are just as adept as excluding as they are including, and this final point of resonance links to inclusive teaching practices which note belonging as a primary feature of storytelling. Characters in the comics mentioned in this chapter often find themselves at odds with the wider world, either through transplantation or trauma (or both), and must make sense of the universes they inhabit. In addition to their sense-making, their work is often based on some sense of heroism and salvific function.

Perhaps this is the closest approximation to a limitations section the author might offer. Indeed, there are essential layers here to share, and it has taken the better part of a decade to examine these experiences. First is the layer of personhood, evident in the author's positionality and endemic to the authentic textual experience, which serves as a source of bias but also of insight. An emic experience with the Evangelical church and a background as a religion student serve as part of this view into self and practice, as well as the ways students continue to position themselves in terms of religious/spiritual stance. The author continues to engage with what it means to be an academic with a particular set of experiences and spiritual beliefs, which are themselves sometimes in a state of revision, as well as the ethics of faith in reading and composing. The author also contends with what it means to be a living and active member of culture.

An additional layer that occurs on the next tier of experience is that of work and life as a reader. There are certain indispensable parts in this investigation that cannot be completely unraveled because of relative perceptions in the account. These include the author encounter scripture, spiritual readings, and artifacts of popular culture in a simultaneous fashion as a person of faith, and as a student and teacher. An individual's view of these works, then, is informed by spiritual underpinnings, shaded by experiences and those experiences passed down, and always revolving around text.

Conclusion and Implications

In retrospect, the theme of hope resonates throughout many of the avenues of expression found in comics and media, and this hope is born out in an interest in social justice that the serves as one of the nexus points between work in education and in the development of faith.

This is the context of a pandemic, however strange it may be, has been fertile and necessary ground for the continued work in the classroom and in education-based research in terms of engagement with narratives of redemption and ways of understanding worlds which have found the need to be redefined in story arcs. A sense of engagement with spiritual/religious communities and comics culture as a student, teacher, and believer points to the simultaneous and changing roles of the educator, and the author has attempted to reconsider and unite many threads of identity.

The exploration of the self in relationship to text(s) is a question that continues to propel both personal and professional work, and a richer understanding of these intentional links with ways of creating and communicating might one day issue into reconsiderations of policy around the use of visual and digital media in classroom spaces en masse. It is a visual world of storytelling, and a world of sense-making in a post-pandemic time period in which illness continues to occur frequently.

What readers discover in the textual worlds presented in classrooms and located in their personal reading practices, as well as the ways that readers take up the work of communication and composing, points to the accessibility of narratives and the emerging tools of storytelling that continue to be refashioned and community-based in social media applications and in web-based, hyperlinked media. The ways that texts are centered in instruction speak to the positioning and importance that is conveyed or granted to that text. When students are drawn to a particular text and it is relegated to a secondary position through, for example, a book ban, that action has implications for the individual young reader who connects with that text.

All of this holds implications for how reading is defined by institutionally and personally, and how composing becomes a way of connecting across an accessible and often curated audience in web spaces, including building community between and among members of comics affinity groups who have found aspects of their identity reflected through the transmedial and transformational practices of taking up visual narratives.

REFERENCES

Anyon, J. (1981). Social class and school knowledge. *Curriculum Inquiry*, *11*(1), 3–42. doi:10.1080/03626784.1981.11075236

Bishop, R. S. (1990, March). Windows and mirrors: Children's books and parallel cultures. In *California State University reading conference: 14th annual conference proceedings* (pp. 3-12).

Cavalieri, J. (1989). *The Huntress*. DC Comics.

Chase, M., Son, E. H., & Steiner, S. (2014). Sequencing and graphic novels with primary-grade students. *The Reading Teacher*, *67*(6), 435–443. doi:10.1002/trtr.1242

DeHart, J. (Ed.). (2023). *The role of faith and religious diversity in educational practices*. IGI Global. doi:10.4018/978-1-6684-9184-3

DeHart, J. D. (2020). Living in a 'digital world': An ethnographic study of film and adolescent literacy education in rural secondary schools in America. *Film Education Journal*, *3*(1), 46–57. doi:10.14324/FEJ.03.1.04

Fronk, J. (2016). *Sequential religion: The history of religion in comic books & graphic novels* [Doctoral dissertation, Fashion Institute of Technology, State University of New York].

Gee, J. P. (2013). *The anti-education era: Creating smarter students through digital learning*. St. Martin's Press.

hooks, b. (1996). Teaching to transgress: Education as the practice of freedom. *Journal of Leisure Research, 28*(4), 316.

Jacobs, D. (2014). Webcomics, multimodality, and information literacy. *ImageTexT: Interdisciplinary Comics Studies, 7*(3), https://imagetextjournal.com/webcomics-multimodality-and-information-literacy

Lefèvre, P. (2009). The construction of space in comics. *A Comics Studies Reader*, 157-162.

McCreary, J. J., & Marchant, G. J. (2017). Reading and empathy. *Reading Psychology*, *38*(2), 182–202. doi:10.1080/02702711.2016.1245690

Moltmann, J. (1993). *Theology of hope: On the ground and the implications of a Christian eschatology*. Fortress Press.

Parker, K. N. (2022). *Literacy is liberation: Working toward justice through culturally relevant teaching*. ASCD.

Pawley, C. (2002). Seeking" significance": Actual readers, specific reading communities. *Book History*, *5*(1), 143–160. doi:10.1353/bh.2002.0013

Pilkey, D. (2023). *Dogman (series)*. Graphix.

Pinnegar, S., & Hamilton, M. L. (2009). *Self-study of practice as a genre of qualitative research: Theory, methodology, and practice* (Vol. 8). Springer Science & Business Media.

Polkinghorne, D. E. (1995). Narrative configuration in qualitative analysis. *International Journal of Qualitative Studies in Education : QSE, 8*(1), 5–23. doi:10.1080/0951839950080103

Street, B. (2006). Autonomous and ideological models of literacy: Approaches from New Literacy Studies. *Media Anthropology Network, 17,* 1–15.

Teampau, G. (2015). Comic books as modern mythology. *Caietele Echinox,* (28), 140–155.

Wallner, L. (2019). *Framing education: Doing comics literacy in the classroom* (Vol. 34). Linköping University Electronic Press.

Zoboi, I. (2019). *Pride: A pride & prejudice remix.* Balzer + Bray.

KEY TERMS AND DEFINITIONS

Comics: A universal term for the mingling of visual and verbal across a particular narrative form, either print or digital.

Digital Literacy: The ways in which readers navigate (and create) using technological tools. This approach includes reading, writing, and composing.

Graphic Novel: A prestige term that usually applies to a larger work in comics form, often used as a way of legitimizing the medium.

Graphica: An umbrella term that often refers to visual ways of communicating.

Transmedia: A field of examination that considers the ways in which stories are told and considered across media forms, including film, television, music, toys, and more.

Visual Literacy: A means of considering communication using pictorial form.

Web Comics: The web-based method of storytelling, drawing upon comics features for building stories.

Compilation of References

Abd Algane, M., & Jabir Othman, K. A. (2023). Utilizing artificial intelligence technologies in Saudi EFL tertiary level classrooms. *Journal of Intercultural Communication*, *23*(1), 92–99.

Afzal, A., Mouid, R., Dogar, M. M., Bhatti, M. J., & Asghar, M. (2023). Career Of Undergraduates And Status Of Education In Pakistan Under Influence Of Poverty. *Journal of Positive School Psychology*, *7*(5), 902–916.

Ahmad Tarmizi, S., Mutalib, S., Abdul Hamid, N., Abdul-Rahman, S., & Md Ab Malik, A. (2019). A Case Study on Student Attrition Prediction in Higher Education Using Data Mining Techniques. *Soft Computing in Data Science.* . http://link.springer.com/10.1007/978-981-15-0399-3_15 doi:10.1007/978-981-15-0399-3_15

Ajzen, I. (1991). The theory of planned behavior. *Organizational Behavior and Human Decision Processes*, *50*(2), 179–211. doi:10.1016/0749-5978(91)90020-T

Akçayir, M., & Akçayir, G. (2016). Üniversite Öğrencilerinin Yabancı Dil Eğitiminde Artırılmış Gerçeklik Teknolojisi Kullanımına Yönelik Görüşleri. *Erzincan Üniversitesi Eğitim Fakültesi Dergisi*, *18*(2), 1169–1186. doi:10.17556/jef.86406

Akhmedov, B., & Shuhkrat, K. (2020). Cluster methods of learning english using information technology. *Science Progress*, *1*(2), 40–43.

Akhtar, N., Kerim, B., Perwej, Y., Tiwari, A., & Praveen, S. (2021). A Comprehensive Overview of Privacy and Data Security for Cloud Storage. *International Journal of Scientific Research in Science, Engineering and Technology*, 113–152. doi:10.32628/IJSRSET21852

Aksu, H., Babun, L., Conti, M., Tolomei, G., & Uluagac, A. S. (2018, November). Advertising in the IoT Era: Vision and Challenges. *IEEE Communications Magazine*, *56*(11), 138–144. doi:10.1109/MCOM.2017.1700871

Alabbasi, D. (2018). Exploring teachers' perspectives towards using gamification techniques in online learning. *Turkish Online Journal of Educational Technology-TOJET, 17*(2), 34-45. https://eric.ed.gov/?id=EJ1176165

Alahmari, M., Jdaitawi, M. T., Rasheed, A., Abduljawad, R., Hussein, E., Alzahrani, M., & Awad, N. (2023). Trends and gaps in empirical research on gamification in science education: A systematic review of the literature. *Contemporary Educational Technology*, *15*(3), ep431. doi:10.30935/cedtech/13177

Alberth, A. (2023). How Important Is Communicating with Native English Speakers to EFL Learners' Self-Confidence in their English Language Proficiency? *Journey: Journal of English Language and Pedagogy*, *6*(2), 380–393. doi:10.33503/journey.v6i2.3169

Aldeen, Y. A. A. S., Salleh, M., & Razzaque, M. A. (2015). A survey paper on privacy issue in cloud computing. *Research Journal of Applied Sciences, Engineering and Technology*, *10*(3), 328–337. doi:10.19026/rjaset.10.2495

Al-Dosakee, K., & Ozdamli, F. (2021). Gamification in teaching and learning languages: A systematic literature review. *Revista Romaneasca Pentru Educatie Multidimensionala*, *13*(2), 559–577. doi:10.18662/rrem/13.2/436

Alfadda, H. A., & Mahdi, H. S. (2021). Measuring students' use of zoom application in language course based on the technology acceptance model (TAM). *Journal of Psycholinguistic Research*, *50*(4), 883–900. doi:10.1007/s10936-020-09752-1 PMID:33398606

Alghali, M., Najwa, H. M. A., & Roesnita, I. (2014). Challenges and benefits of implementing cloud based e-Learning in developing countries. *Proceeding of the Social Sciences Research ICSSR*, (pp. 9-10). IEEE.

Alhassan, A., Ali, N. A., & Ali, H. I. H. (2021). EFL students' challenges in English-medium business programmes: Perspectives from students and content teachers. *Cogent Education*, *8*(1), 1–15. doi:10.1080/2331186X.2021.1888671

Al-Karawi, M. (2020). English Language Learning Through Games. *Educational Challenges*, *25*(1), 9–20. doi:10.34142/2709-7986.2020.25.1.01

Almaiah, M. A., Alfaisal, R., Salloum, S. A., Hajjej, F., Thabit, S., El-Qirem, F. A., Lutfi, A., Alrawad, M., Al Mulhem, A., Alkhdour, T., Awad, A. B., & Al-Maroof, R. S. (2022). Examining the impact of artificial intelligence and social and computer anxiety in e-learning settings: Students' perceptions at the university level. *Electronics (Basel)*, *11*(22), 3662. doi:10.3390/electronics11223662

Almajalid, R. (2017). *A survey on the adoption of cloud computing in education sector*. arXiv preprint arXiv:1706.01136.

Alonso García, S., Martínez-Domingo, J. A., Berral Ortiz, B., & De la Cruz Campos, J. C. (2021). Gamificación en educación superior. Revisión de experiencias realizadas en España en los últimos años. *Hachetetepé. Revista Científica de Educación y Comunicación*, *23*(23), 1–21. doi:10.25267/Hachetetepe.2021.i23.2205

Al-Rahmi, W. M., Alias, N., Othman, M. S., Alzahrani, A. I., Alfarraj, O., Saged, A. A., & Rahman, N. S. A. (2018). Use of e-learning by university students in Malaysian higher educational institutions: A case in Universiti Teknologi Malaysia. *IEEE Access : Practical Innovations, Open Solutions*, 6, 14268–14276. doi:10.1109/ACCESS.2018.2802325

Álvarez Cadavid, G., & González Manosalva, C. (2022). Apropiación de TIC en docentes de la educación superior: Una mirada desde los contenidos digitales. *Praxis Educativa (Santa Rosa)*, 26(1), 1–25. doi:10.19137/praxiseducativa-2022-260104

Amanah, F. S., & Yunus, M. M. (2018). QR codes in ESL classroom learning. *International Journal of Innovative Research and Creative Technology*, 4(3), 74–77.

Anderson, R. W., & Lee, S. T. (2019). Technology Integration in AgileFaculty Development: A Case Study of Innovative Practices. *Journal of Educational Technology*, 42(4), 321–338.

Anuar, K., & Hajar, U. M. Z. (2024). Cloud computing scene in Malaysia. *The Malaysian Reserve*. https://themalaysianreserve.com/2023/07/27/cloud-computing-scene-in-malaysia/

Anyon, J. (1981). Social class and school knowledge. *Curriculum Inquiry*, 11(1), 3–42. doi:10.1080/03626784.1981.11075236

Aoyama, T., & Takahashi, T. (2020). International students' willingness to communicate in English as a second language: The effects of l2 self-confidence, acculturation, and motivational types. *Journal of International Students*, 10(3), 703–723. doi:10.32674/jis.v10i3.730

Araújo, I., & Carvalho, A. A. (2017). Empowering teachers to apply gamification. *2017 International Symposium on Computers in Education (SIIE)*, (pp. 1–5). IEEE. 10.1109/SIIE.2017.8259668

Araya Muñoz, I., & Majano Benavides, J. (2022). Didáctica universitaria en entornos virtuales. Experiencia en ciencias sociales. *Educare (San José)*, 26(3), 511–529. doi:10.15359/ree.26-3.28

Ares, A. M., Bernal, J., Nozal, M. J., Sánchez, F. J., & Bernal, J. (2018). Results of the use of Kahoot! gamification tool in a course of Chemistry. In *4th international conference on higher education advances (HEAD'18)* (pp. 1215-1222). Editorial Universitat Politècnica de València. 10.4995/HEAD18.2018.8179

Ariffin, N. A. N., Ramli, N., Badrul, N. M. F. H. N., Yusof, Y., & Suparlan, A. (2022). Effectiveness of gamification in teaching and learning mathematics. *Journal on Mathematics Education*, 13(1), 173–190. doi:10.22342/jme.v13i1.pp173-190

Arifin, S. R. (2018). Ethical considerations in qualitative study. *International journal of care scholars, 1*(2), 30-33.

Armstrong, J. S., & Overton, T. S. (1977). Estimating nonresponse bias in mail surveys. *JMR, Journal of Marketing Research*, 14(3), 396–402. doi:10.1177/002224377701400320

Ashtari, S., & Eydgahi, A. (2015, October). Student perceptions of cloud computing effectiveness in higher education. In *2015 IEEE 18th International Conference on Computational Science and Engineering* (pp. 184-191). IEEE. 10.1109/CSE.2015.36

Avello, M., Camacho-Miñano, M. D. M., Urquia-Grande, E., & del Campo, C. (2019). "Do You Use English in Your Daily Life?" Undergraduate Students' Perceptions of Their Extramural Use of English. *Journal of Teaching in International Business*, *30*(1), 77–94. doi:10.1080/0897593 0.2019.1627978

Avia, N. (2009). *Grade 10 Life Science Teachers' Understanding and Development of Critical Thinking Skills in Selected Schools in Namibia (MEd dissertation)*. Rhodes University.

Aydin, H. (2021). A study of cloud computing adoption in universities as a guideline to cloud migration. Sage Open, 11(3).

Aziza, P. K. (2020). The Implementation of using quick response Codes in listening comprehension for senior high school. *Retain*, *8*(1), 125–131.

Bagheri, M., & Andi, T. (2015). The relationship between medical students' attitude towards English language learning and their English language proficiency. *ICT & Innovations in Education—International Electronic Journal, 3*(1), 7-19.

Bagherzadeh, H., & Azizi, Z. (2012). Learners' Beliefs about English Language Learning: Examining the Impact of English Proficiency Level on the Motivation of Students among Non-English Major EFL Students. *Theory and Practice in Language Studies*, *2*(10), 1987–1992. doi:10.4304/tpls.2.10.2096-2102

Bakla, A. (2018). Quick response codes in foreign language instruction: Practical ideas and strategies, Inonu University. *Journal of the Faculty of Education*, *19*(3), 749–762. doi:10.17679/inuefd.475262

Balintag, C. M., & Wilang, J. D. (2020). QR codes utilization in EFL classroom: Affective language learning attributes in writing. *Script Journal: Journal of Linguistics and English Teaching*, *5*(1), 1–13. doi:10.24903/sj.v5i1.425

Balouchi, S., & Samad, A. A. (2021). No more excuses, learn English for free: Factors affecting L2 learners intention to use online technology for informal English learning. *Education and Information Technologies*, *26*(1), 1111–1132. doi:10.1007/s10639-020-10307-z

Banks, S., Hart, A., Pahl, K., & Ward, P. (2018). Co-producing research: A community development approach. In *Co-producing Research* (pp. 1–18). Policy Press.

Barrera López, E. H., & Morales Vázquez, E. (2023). Aplicación de videojuegos, en aulas virtuales ¿Es buena para aprender otro idioma? *Ciencia Latina Revista Científica Multidisciplinar*, *7*(4), 2544–2576. doi:10.37811/cl_rcm.v7i4.7072

Barron, B., & Darling-Hammond, L. (2008). Teaching for meaningful learning: A review of research on inquiry-based and cooperative learning. In *Powerful Learning: What We Know About Teaching for Understanding* (pp. 11–70). Jossey-Bass.

Begosso, L. R., & Begosso, L. C. Da Cunha, D. S., Pinto, J. V., Lemos, L., & Nunes, M. (2018). The use of gamification for teaching algorithms. In FedCSIS (Communication Papers) (pp. 225-231). doi:10.15439/2018F165

Belda Medina, J., & Calvo Ferrer, J. (2022). Preservice Teachers' Knowledge and Attitudes toward Digital-Game-Based Language Learning. *Education Sciences*, *12*(3), 1–16. doi:10.3390/educsci12030182

Bers, M., Seddighin, S., & Sullivan, A. (2013). Ready for robotics: Bringing together the T and E of STEM in early childhood teacher education. *Journal of Technology and Teacher Education*, *21*(3), 355–377.

Bhatia, M., Hooda, M., & Gupta, P. (2021). Deep Data Analytics: Future of Telehealth. In Research Anthology on Telemedicine Efficacy, Adoption, and Impact on Healthcare Delivery (pp. 274-295). IGI Global.

Bhatia, M., Choudhury, T., & Dewangan, B. K. (Eds.). (2023). *Exploring Future Opportunities of Brain-inspired Artificial Intelligence*. IGI Global. https://www.igi-global.com/book/exploring-future-opportunities-brain-inspired/305123 doi:10.4018/978-1-6684-6980-4

Bhatia, M., Manani, P., Garg, A., Bhatia, S., & Adlakha, R. (2023). Mapping Mindset about Gamification: Teaching Learning Perspective in UAE Education System and Indian Education System. *Revue d'Intelligence Artificielle*, *37*(1), 47–52. Advance online publication. doi:10.18280/ria.370107

Biedermann, S. (2015). Agile curriculum development in higher education. *Journal of Learning Design*, *8*(2), 35–44.

Bishop, R. S. (1990, March). Windows and mirrors: Children's books and parallel cultures. In *California State University reading conference: 14th annual conference proceedings* (pp. 3-12).

Bitrián, P., Buil, I., & Catalán, S. (2021). Enhancing user engagement: The role of gamification in mobile apps. *Journal of Business Research*, *132*, 170–185. doi:10.1016/j.jbusres.2021.04.028

Blumenfeld, P. C., Soloway, E., Marx, R. W., Krajcik, J. S., Guzdial, M., & Palincsar, A. (1991). Motivating project-based learning: Sustaining the doing, supporting the learning. *Educational Psychologist*, *26*(3-4), 369–398. doi:10.1080/00461520.1991.9653139

Bottino, R. (2020). Schools and the digital challenge: Evolution and perspectives. *Education and Information Technologies*, *25*(3), 2241–2259. doi:10.1007/s10639-019-10061-x

Braun, V., & Clarke, V. (2006). Using thematic analysis in psychology. *Qualitative Research in Psychology*, *3*(2), 77–101. doi:10.1191/1478088706qp063oa

Briones, D., Pallaroso, C., & Cangas, E. (2023). El impacto de los videojuegos de aventura en el aprendizaje de lenguas extranjeras y las percepciones de los alumnos. *MQRInvestigar*, *7*(2), 188–203. doi:10.56048/MQR20225.7.2.2023.188-203

British Council. (2020a). *English Language Teaching and Covid-19: A Global Snapshot of Ministries of Education Responses in the State Primary and Secondary Sector*. British Council. [Google Scholar]

British Council. (2020b). *English Language Teaching and Covid-19: A Survey of Teacher and Teacher Educator Needs During the Covid-19 Pandemic April–May 2020.* British Council. [Google Scholar]

British Council. (2020c). *English Language Teaching and Covid-19: A Global Snapshot of Ministries of Education Responses During the Period of School Reopening, in the State Primary and Secondary Sector.* British Council. [Google Scholar]

Brull, S., & Finlayson, S. (2016). Importance of gamification in increasing learning. *Journal of Continuing Education in Nursing, 47*(8), 372–375. doi:10.3928/00220124-20160715-09 PMID:27467313

Buck Institute for Education. (2021). *What is PBL?* PBL Works. https://www.pblworks.org/what-is-pbl

Bujang, S. D. A., Selamat, A., & Krejcar, O. (2021). Decision Tree (J48) Model for Student's Final Grade Prediction: A Machine Learning Approach. *IOP Conference Series. Materials Science and Engineering, 1051*(1), 012005. doi:10.1088/1757-899X/1051/1/012005

Bukralia, R., Deokar, A. V., & Sarnikar, S. (2015). *Using academic analytics to predict dropout risk in e-Learning courses.* Springer International Publishing. doi:10.1007/978-3-319-11575-7_6

Caldwell, B. (2015). *Beyond positivism.* Routledge. doi:10.4324/9780203565520

Calixto, E. (2016). In E. Calixto (Ed.), *Human Reliability Analysis. Gas and Oil Reliability Engineering* (2nd ed., pp. 471–552). doi:10.1016/B978-0-12-805427-7.00005-1

Caminero, G., Lopez-Martin, M., & Carro, B. (2019). Adversarial environment reinforcement learning algorithm for intrusion detection. *Computer Networks, 159*, 96–109. doi:10.1016/j.comnet.2019.05.013

Capraro, R. M., Capraro, M. M., & Morgan, J. (2013). *STEM Project-Based Learning: An Integrated Science, Technology, Engineering, and Mathematics (STEM) Approach.* Sense Publishers. doi:10.1007/978-94-6209-143-6

Caraballo Padilla, Y. Y. (2023). Gamificación educativa y su impacto en la enseñanza y aprendizaje del idioma inglés: Un análisis de la literatura científica. *Ciencia Latina. Revista Científica Multidisciplinar, 7*(4), 1813–1830. doi:10.37811/cl_rcm.v7i4.7011

Caravaca Llamas, C., & Sáez Olmos, J. (2021). Gamificación en la enseñanza superior: Descripción de los principales recursos para su utilización. *Edutech Review, 8*(2), 165–177. doi:10.37467/gkarevedutech.v8.3039

Cardullo, V., Wang, C. H., Burton, M., & Dong, J. (2021). K-12 teachers' remote teaching self-efficacy during the pandemic. *Journal of research in innovative teaching & learning, 14*(1), 32-45.

Casañ Pitarch, R., Girón García, C., & Holgado Sáez, C. (2022). Desarrollo de un videojuego para la enseñanza del inglés como lengua extranjera para fines específicos y el fomento de conocimientos en Educación para el Desarrollo y Ciudadanía Global en Ingeniería Industrial. *Tabanque: Revista pedagógica, 34*, 68-87. doi:10.24197/trp.1.2022.68-87

Casañ Pitarch, R. (2017). Enseñanza de lenguas extranjeras a través de videojuegos: revisión de caso experimentales y prácticos. In *Estudios de Lingüística Aplicada* (pp. 27–35). Servicio de Publicaciones de la Universidad Politécnica de Valencia.

Castells, M. (2002). *The Internet galaxy: Reflections on the Internet, business, and society*. Oxford University Press. doi:10.1093/acprof:oso/9780199255771.001.0001

Cavalieri, J. (1989). *The Huntress*. DC Comics.

Celik, B. (2023). EFL learners' perceptions on QR code enriched instruction in developing macro-skills. *International Journal of Social Sciences & Educational Studies*, *10*(3).

Cerezo Cortijo, I. (2021). La gamificación como metodología innovadora en el ámbito educativo. In *Avances y Desafíos para la Transformación Educativa* (pp. 272–280). Servicio de Publicaciones de la Universidad de Oviedo.

Chan, Y. M. (2018). Self-directed learning readiness and online video use among digital animation students [Doctoral dissertation, Multimedia University (Malaysia)].

Chango, W., Sánchez-Santillán, M., Cerezo, R., & Romero, C. (2020). Predicting Students' performance using emotion detection from face-recording video. IEDM Tech. Dig. pp. 1–3.

Chanier, T., & Lamy, M. N. (2017). Researching Technology-mediated Multimodal Interaction. The handbook of technology and second language teaching and learning, 428-443.

Chase, M., Son, E. H., & Steiner, S. (2014). Sequencing and graphic novels with primary-grade students. *The Reading Teacher*, *67*(6), 435–443. doi:10.1002/trtr.1242

Chaturvedi, I., Cambria, E., & Welsch, R. E. (2023). Teaching Simulations Supported by Artificial Intelligence in the Real World. *Education Sciences*, *13*(2), 2. Advance online publication. doi:10.3390/educsci13020187

Cheah, P. K., Diong, F. W., & Yap, Y. O. (2018). Peer Assessment in Higher Education: Using Hofstede's Cultural Dimensions to Identify Perspectives of Malaysian Chinese Students. *Pertanika Journal of Social Science & Humanities*, *26*(3).

Chee, K. M., & Tan, K. H. (2021). QR Codes as a Potential Tool in Teaching and Learning Pronunciation: A Critical Review. *Higher Education and Oriental Studies, 1*(1).

Chen, N. S., Teng, D. C. E., & Lee, C. H. (2010). Augmenting paper-based reading activities with mobile technology to enhance reading comprehension. In *2010 6th IEEE international conference on wireless, Mobile, and ubiquitous technologies in education* (pp. 201–203). IEEE. 10.1109/WMUTE.2010.39

Chen, C. H., Hung, H. T., & Yeh, H. C. (2021). Virtual reality in problem-based learning contexts: Effects on the problem-solving performance, vocabulary acquisition and motivation of English language learners. *Journal of Computer Assisted Learning*, *37*(3), 851–860. doi:10.1111/jcal.12528

Cheng, S. C., Hwang, W. Y., Wu, S. Y., Shadiev, R., & Xie, C.-H. (2010). A mobile device and online system with contextual familiarity and its effects on English learning on Campus. *Journal of Educational Technology & Society*, *13*(3), 93–109.

Chen, H. J. H., Hsu, H. L., Chen, Z. H., & Todd, A. G. (2021). Investigating the Impact of Integrating Vocabulary Exercises into an Adventure Videogame on Second Vocabulary Learning. *Journal of Educational Computing Research*, *59*(2), 318–341. doi:10.1177/0735633120963750

Chen, H. Y., Das, A., & Ivanov, D. (2019). Building resilience and managing post-disruption supply chain recovery: Lessons from the information and communication technology industry. *International Journal of Information Management*, *49*, 330–342. doi:10.1016/j.ijinfomgt.2019.06.002

Chen, H., & Davis, E. C. (2022). Fostering Collaboration and Community: A Comparative Analysis of Traditional and Agile Faculty Development Models. *Higher Education Research Quarterly*, *48*(1), 78–94.

Chen, J., Lai, P., Chan, A., Man, V., & Chan, C. H. (2022). AI-assisted enhancement of student presentation skills: Challenges and opportunities. *Sustainability (Basel)*, *15*(1), 196. doi:10.3390/su15010196

Chen, M. P., Wang, L. C., Zou, D., Lin, S. Y., Xie, H., & Tsai, C. C. (2022). Effects of captions and English proficiency on learning effectiveness, motivation and attitude in augmented-reality-enhanced theme-based contextualized EFL learning. *Computer Assisted Language Learning*, *35*(3), 381–411. doi:10.1080/09588221.2019.1704787

Chen, P., Hernández, A., & Dong, J. (2021). Impact of project-based learning on student achievement: A meta-analysis investigating moderators. *Educational Research Review*, *35*, 100367.

Chen, Y. L., & Hsu, C. C. (2020). Self-regulated mobile game-based English learning in a virtual reality environment. *Computers & Education*, *154*, 103910. doi:10.1016/j.compedu.2020.103910

Chetty, M. (2011, October). *Cause of Relapse Post Treatment for Substance Dependency Within the South African Police Services.* University of Pretoria. https://repository.up.ac.za/bitstream/handle/2263/29121/dissertation.pdf?isAllowed=y&sequence=1

Chiappe, A., Amado, N., & Leguizamón, L. (2020). Educommunication in digital environments: An interaction´s perspective inside and beyond the classroom. *Innoeduca. International Journal of Technology and Educational Innovation*, *6*(1), 34–41. doi:10.24310/innoeduca.2020.v6i1.4959

Christopoulos, A., Mystakidis, S., Pellas, N., & Laakso, M. J. (2021). ARLEAN: An augmented reality learning analytics ethical framework. *Computers*, *10*(8), 92. doi:10.3390/computers10080092

Chung, C. H., & Lin, Y. Y. (2022). Online 3D gamification for teaching a human resource development course. *Journal of Computer Assisted Learning*, *38*(3), 692–706. doi:10.1111/jcal.12641

Compilation of References

Chung, E., Subramaniam, G., & Dass, L. C. (2020). Online learning readiness among university students in Malaysia amidst COVID-19. *Asian Journal of University Education*, *16*(2), 45–58. doi:10.24191/ajue.v16i2.10294

Chu, S. K. W., Reynolds, R. B., Tavares, N. J., Notari, M., & Lee, C. W. Y. (2017). *21st century skills development through inquiry-based learning*. Springer. doi:10.1007/978-981-10-2481-8

Cocca, M., & Cocca, A. (2019). Affective Variables and Motivation as Predictors of Proficiency in English as a Foreign Language. *Journal on Efficiency and Responsibility in Education and Science*, *12*(3), 75–83. doi:10.7160/eriesj.2019.120302

Contreras, J. L. G., Torres, C. A. B., & Ojeda, Y. C. E. (2022). Using of ICT in higher education: A bibliometric analysis. *Revista Complutense de Educación*, *33*(3), 601–613. doi:10.5209/rced.73922

Correia, M., & Santos, R. (2017). *game-based learning: the use of kahoot in teacher education*. *International Symposium on Computers in Education (SIIE)*, Lisbon, Portugal. 10.1109/SIIE.2017.8259670

Cortés-Pérez, I., Zagalaz-Anula, N., López-Ruiz, M. C., Díaz-Fernández, Á., Obrero-Gaitán, E., & Osuna-Pérez, M. C. (2023). Study based on gamification of tests through *kahoot!*™ and reward game cards as an innovative tool in physiotherapy students: A preliminary study. *Health Care*, *11*(4), 578. doi:10.3390/healthcare11040578 PMID:36833112

Creswell, J. W. (2020). Educational research: Planning, conducting, and evaluating quantitative and qualitative research. Pearson Higher Ed.

Cristiano, J., Rahmani, M., Helland, K., & Puig, D. (2019). Gable–gamification for a better life. *Opportunities and challenges for European Projects, 1*, 2017-18. doi:10.5220/0008862401240132

Crompton, H. (2013). A historical overview of m-learning; Toward learner-centered education. In Z. Berge & L. Y. Muilenburg (Eds.), *Handbook of mobile learning* (pp. 3–14). Routledge.

Csiernik, R., & Birnbaum, R. (2017). *Practising social work research: Case studies for learning*. University of Toronto Press.

Dachyar, M., Zagloel, T. Y. M., & Saragih, L. R. (2019). Knowledge growth and development: Internet of things (IoT) research, 2006–2018. *Heliyon*, *5*(8), e02264. doi:10.1016/j.heliyon.2019.e02264 PMID:31517087

Damodharan, V. S. (2022). Antecedents of QR code acceptance during Covid-19: Towards sustainability. *Transnational Marketing Journal, 10*(1).

Darasawang, P., & Reinders, H. (2021). Willingness to communicate and second language proficiency: A correlational study. *Education Sciences*, *11*(9), 517. doi:10.3390/educsci11090517

Darling-Hammond, L., Flook, L., Cook-Harvey, C., Barron, B., & Osher, D. (2020, April 02). Flook, C. Cook-Harvey, B. Barron, & Osher D. (2019). Implications for educational practice of the science of Learning and development. *Applied Developmental Science*, *24*(2), 97–140. doi:10.1080/10888691.2018.1537791

Darus, P., Rasli, R. B., & Gaminan, N. Z. (2015). A review on cloud computing implementation in higher educational institutions. *International Journal of Scientific Engineering and Applied Science*, *1*(8), 459–465.

Davies, H., Hjorth, L., Andrejevic, M., Richardson, I., & DeSouza, R. (2023). QR codes during the pandemic: Seamful quotidian placemaking. *Convergence*, 13548565231160623.

Davis, F. D. (1989). Perceived usefulness, perceived ease of use and user acceptance of information technology. *Management Information Systems Quarterly*, *13*(3), 319–339. doi:10.2307/249008

Dawood, M., Tu, S., Xiao, C., Alasmary, H., Waqas, M., & Rehman, S. U. (2023). Cyberattacks and security of cloud computing: A complete guideline. *Symmetry*, *15*(11), 1981. doi:10.3390/sym15111981

De Oliveira, C. F., Sobral, S. R., Ferreira, M. J., & Moreira, F. (2021). How does learning analytics contribute to prevent students' dropout in higher education: A systematic literature review. *Big Data and Cognitive Computing*, *5*(4), 64. doi:10.3390/bdcc5040064

De Pietro, O., & Fronter, G. (2012). *Mobile tutoring for situated learning and collaborative learning in AIML application using QR-Code*. In The sixth international conference on complex, intelligent, and software systems (CISIS-2012), Palermo, Italy.

Deci, E. L., Eghrari, H., Patrick, B. C., & Leone, D. R. (1994). Facilitating internalization: The self-determination theory perspective. *Journal of Personality*, *62*(1), 119–142. doi:10.1111/j.1467-6494.1994.tb00797.x PMID:8169757

DeHart, J. (Ed.). (2023). *The role of faith and religious diversity in educational practices*. IGI Global. doi:10.4018/978-1-6684-9184-3

DeHart, J. D. (2020). Living in a 'digital world': An ethnographic study of film and adolescent literacy education in rural secondary schools in America. *Film Education Journal*, *3*(1), 46–57. doi:10.14324/FEJ.03.1.04

Dehghanzadeh, H., Fardanesh, H., Hatami, J., Talaee, E., & Noroozi, O. (2021). Using gamification to support learning English as a second language: A systematic review. *Computer Assisted Language Learning*, *34*(7), 934–957. doi:10.1080/09588221.2019.1648298

Del Padre, L., González, A., & Benítez Ayala, D. A. (2022). Uso de las TIC para el proceso enseñanza aprendizaje en la educación superior. *LATAM Revista Latinoamericana de Ciencias Sociales y Humanidades*, *3*(2), 1393–1411. doi:10.56712/latam.v3i2.191

Demkah, M., & Bhargava, D. (2019). *Gamification in education: a cognitive psychology approach to cooperative and fun learning*. Amity International Conference on Artificial Intelligence (AICAI), Dubai, United Arab Emirates. /10.1109/AICAI.2019.8701264

Dempsey, L., Gaffney, L., Bracken, S., Tully, A., Corcoran, O., McDonnell-Naughton, M., & McDonnell, D. (2022). Experiences of undergraduate nursing students who worked clinically during the COVID-19 pandemic. *Nursing Open*. Advance online publication. doi:10.1002/nop2.1289 PMID:35866179

Dhir, S., Kumar, D., & Singh, V. B. (2018). Success and Failure Factors that Impact on Project Implementation using Agile Software Development Methodology. Advances in Intelligent Systems and Computing. Springer.

Dhir, S., & Dubey, R. (2021). Identification of Barriers To The Successful Integration of ICT in Teaching and Learning. [TOJQI]. *Turkish Online Journal of Qualitative Inquiry*, *12*(5), 4428–4440.

Dhir, S., & Kumar, D. (2015, November). Agile Software Development in Defiance of Customary Software Development Process: A Valuation of Prevalence's and Challenges. *Advanced Science Letters*, *21*(11), 3554–3558. doi:10.1166/asl.2015.6590

Dhir, S., & Kumar, D. (2015, October). Factors Persuading Nuts and Bolts of Agile Estimation. *Advanced Science Letters*, *21*(10), 3118–3122. doi:10.1166/asl.2015.6534

Dima, A., Bugheanu, A. M., Boghian, R., & Madsen, D. O. (2022). Mapping Knowledge Area Analysis in E-Learning Systems Based on Cloud Computing. *Electronics (Basel)*, *12*(1), 62. doi:10.3390/electronics12010062

Dimitra, K., Kousaris, K., & Zafeiriou, C. (2023). Types of Game-Based Learning in Education: A Brief State of the Art and the Implementation in Greece. *European Educational Researcher*, *3*(2), 87–100. doi:10.31757/euer.324

Din, M. (2020). Evaluating university students' critical thinking ability as reflected in their critical reading skill: A study at bachelor level in Pakistan. *Thinking Skills and Creativity*, *35*, 100627. doi:10.1016/j.tsc.2020.100627

Djordjevic, B. (2016). Implementing agile in higher education administration. Agile processes in software *Engineering and extreme programming*, 283-296.

Donoso Cedeño, M. M., Echeverría Zurita, L. O., Moreira Pérez, R. W., & Ponce Anchundia, L. S. (2023). Innovación en la enseñanza del inglés en la educación superior: Desafíos, oportunidades y buenas prácticas. *Revista Científica Arbitrada Multidisciplinaria PENTACIENCIAS*, *5*(7), 165–174. doi:10.59169/pentaciencias.v5i7.924

Dörnyei, Z., & Chan, L. (2013). Motivation and vision: An analysis of future L2 self images, sensory styles, and imagery capacity across two target languages. *Language Learning*, *63*(3), 437–462. doi:10.1111/lang.12005

Doyle, L., Brady, A. M., & Byrne, G. (2009). An overview of mixed methods research. *Journal of Research in Nursing*, *14*(2), 175–185. doi:10.1177/1744987108093962

Drachsler, H., & Greller, W. (2012). *The pulse of learning analytics: Understandings and expectations from the stakeholders. Proceedings of the 2nd International Conference on Learning Analytics and Knowledge*, Vancouver, British Columbia, Canada. 10.1145/2330601.2330634

Dusek, G., Yurova, Y., & Ruppel, C. P. (2015). Using social media and targeted snowball sampling to survey a hard-to-reach population: A case study. *International Journal of Doctoral Studies*, *10*, 279. doi:10.28945/2296

Dwivedi, D. N., & Anand, A. (2021). The Text Mining of Public Policy Documents in Response to COVID-19: A Comparison of the United Arab Emirates and the Kingdom of Saudi Arabia. *Public Governance / Zarządzanie Publiczne, 55*(1), 8-22. doi:10.15678/ZP.2021.55.1.02

Dwivedi, D. N., Mahanty, G., & Pathak, Y. K. (2023). AI Applications for Financial Risk Management. In M. Irfan, M. Elmogy, M. Shabri Abd. Majid, & S. El-Sappagh (Eds.), The Impact of AI Innovation on Financial Sectors in the Era of Industry 5.0 (pp. 17-31). IGI Global. doi:10.4018/979-8-3693-0082-4.ch002

Dwivedi, D. N., Mahanty, G., & Vemareddy, A. (2023). Sentiment Analysis and Topic Modeling for Identifying Key Public Concerns of Water Quality/Issues. In: Harun, S., Othman, I.K., Jamal, M.H. (eds) *Proceedings of the 5th International Conference on Water Resources (ICWR) – Volume 1. Lecture Notes in Civil Engineering.* Springer, Singapore. 10.1007/978-981-19-5947-9_28

Dwivedi, D. N., Pandey, A. K., & Dwivedi, A. D. (2023). Examining the emotional tone in politically polarized Speeches in India: An In-Depth analysis of two contrasting perspectives. *South India Journal Of Social Sciences, 21*(2), 125-136. https://journal.sijss.com/index.php/home/article/view/65

Dwivedi, D. N., & Anand, A. (2022). A Comparative Study of Key Themes of Scientific Research Post COVID-19 in the United Arab Emirates and WHO Using Text Mining Approach. In S. Tiwari, M. C. Trivedi, M. L. Kolhe, K. Mishra, & B. K. Singh (Eds.), *Advances in Data and Information Sciences. Lecture Notes in Networks and Systems* (Vol. 318). Springer. doi:10.1007/978-981-16-5689-7_30

Dwivedi, D. N., Mahanty, G., & Vemareddy, A. (2022). How Responsible Is AI?: Identification of Key Public Concerns Using Sentiment Analysis and Topic Modeling. [IJIRR]. *International Journal of Information Retrieval Research, 12*(1), 1–14. doi:10.4018/IJIRR.298646

Dwivedi, D. N., & Pathak, S. (2022). Sentiment Analysis for COVID Vaccinations Using Twitter: Text Clustering of Positive and Negative Sentiments. In S. A. Hassan, A. W. Mohamed, & K. A. Alnowibet (Eds.), *Decision Sciences for COVID-19. International Series in Operations Research & Management Science* (Vol. 320). Springer. doi:10.1007/978-3-030-87019-5_12

Dwivedi, D. N., Wójcik, K., & Vemareddyb, A. (2022). Identification of Key Concerns and Sentiments Towards Data Quality and Data Strategy Challenges Using Sentiment Analysis and Topic Modeling. In K. Jajuga, G. Dehnel, & M. Walesiak (Eds.), *Modern Classification and Data Analysis. SKAD 2021. Studies in Classification, Data Analysis, and Knowledge Organization.* Springer. doi:10.1007/978-3-031-10190-8_2

Dwivedi, D., & Vemareddy, A. (2023). Sentiment Analytics for Crypto Pre and Post Covid: Topic Modeling. In A. R. Molla, G. Sharma, P. Kumar, & S. Rawat (Eds.), Lecture Notes in Computer Science: Vol. 13776. *Distributed Computing and Intelligent Technology. ICDCIT 2023.* Springer. doi:10.1007/978-3-031-24848-1_21

Eastin, M. S., Cicchirillo, V., & Mabry, A. (2015). Extending the digital divide conversation: Examining the knowledge gap through media expectancies. *Journal of Broadcasting & Electronic Media*, *59*(3), 416–437. doi:10.1080/08838151.2015.1054994

Ebadi, S., & Amini, A. (2022). Examining the roles of social presence and human-likeness on Iranian EFL learners' motivation using artificial intelligence technology: A case of CSIEC chatbot. *Interactive Learning Environments*, ●●●, 1–19. doi:10.1080/10494820.2022.2096638

Edelson, D. C., Gordon, D. N., & Pea, R. D. (1999). Addressing the challenges of inquiry-based learning through technology and curriculum design. *Journal of the Learning Sciences*, *8*(3-4), 391–450. doi:10.1080/10508406.1999.9672075

Evans, C., O'Connor, C., Graves, T., Kemp, F., Kennedy, A., Allen, P., Bonnar, G., Reza, A., & Aya, U. (2020). Teaching Under Lockdown: The Experiences of London English Teachers. [Google Scholar]. *Changing English*, *27*(3), 244–254. doi:10.1080/1358684X.2020.1779030

Farley, A., Yang, H. H., Min, L., & Ma, S. (2020). Comparison of Chinese and Western English language proficiency measures in transnational business degrees. *Language, Culture and Curriculum*, *33*(3), 319–334. doi:10.1080/07908318.2019.1630423

Farsawang, P., & Songkram, N. (2023). Fostering technology integration and adaptability in higher education: Insights from the COVID-19 pandemic. *Contemporary Educational Technology*, *15*(4), ep456. doi:10.30935/cedtech/13513

Felicia, A., Wong, W. K., Loh, W. N., & Juwono, F. H. (2021). Increasing Role of IoT in Education Sector: A Review of Internet of Educational Things (IoEdT). *International Conference on Green Energy, Computing and Sustainable Technology (GECOST)*. (pp. 1-6). IEEE. 10.1109/GECOST52368.2021.9538781

Flores-Aguilar, G., Prat-Grau, M., Fernández-Gavira, J., & Muñoz-Llerena, A. (2023). I learned more because I became more involved": Teacher's and students' voice on gamification in physical education teacher education. *International Journal of Environmental Research and Public Health*, *20*(4), 3038. doi:10.3390/ijerph20043038 PMID:36833730

Flores, E. G. R., Mena, J., Montoya, M. S. R., & Velarde, R. R. (2020). The use of gamification in xMOOCs about energy: Effects and predictive models for participants' learning. *Australasian Journal of Educational Technology*, *36*(2), 43–59. doi:10.14742/ajet.4818

Fogg, B. J. (2019). Fogg behavior model. *Behavior Design*. https://behaviordesign.stanford.edu/resources/fogg-behavior-model

Fronk, J. (2016). *Sequential religion: The history of religion in comic books & graphic novels* [Doctoral dissertation, Fashion Institute of Technology, State University of New York].

Frustaci, M., Pace, P., Aloi, G., & Fortino, G. (2017). Evaluating critical security issues of the IoT World: Present and future challenges. *IEEE Internet of Things Journal*, *5*(4), 2483–2495. doi:10.1109/JIOT.2017.2767291

Galloway, N., & Ruegg, R. (2020). The provision of student support on English Medium Instruction programmes in Japan and China. *Journal of English for Academic Purposes, 45*, 100846. doi:10.1016/j.jeap.2020.100846

Gapazo, J. P., Talan, M. G., Ganotice, F., & Chua, C. L. (2021). The genius hour program in enhancing critical thinking, self-directed learning and academic performance. *Journal of Ethnic and Cultural Studies, 8*(1), 220–236.

Garay, J., & Ávila, C. (2021). Videojuegos y su influencia en el rendimiento académico. *Episteme Koinonía, 4*(8), 1–10. doi:10.35381/e.k.v4i8.1343

García Intriago, S. S., & Rodríguez Zambrano, A. D. (2022). *Revisión de estudios sobre el uso de la gamificación en educación especial*. Mawil Publicaciones Impresas y Digitales.

García, C., Martín Peña, M. L., & Díaz Garrido, E. (2019). Gamificar una asignatura sin tecnología avanzada. *Working Papers on Operations Management, 10*(2), 20-35. doi:10.4995/wpom.v10i2.12662

Gardner, R. C. (2010). *Motivation and second language acquisition: The socio-educational model* (Vol. 10). Peter Lang.

Garzón, J., & Acevedo, J. (2019). Meta-analysis of the impact of augmented reality on students' learning gains. *Educational Research Review, 27*, 244–260. doi:10.1016/j.edurev.2019.04.001

Gdowska, K., Gaweł, B., Dziabenko, O., & Blazhko, O. (2018). Gamification in teaching humanities – „GameHub" project. *Zeszyty Naukowe Wydziału Elektrotechniki i Automatyki Politechniki Gdańskiej, 58*, 27–32. 19.04-20.04.2018

Gee, J. P. (2013). *The anti-education era: Creating smarter students through digital learning*. St. Martin's Press.

George Reyes, C. E. (2020). Uso de las TIC en la Educación Superior: Incorporación en el modelo educativo de la Universidad Autónoma del Estado de Hidalgo. *Debates en Evaluación y Currículum, 5*, 1–13.

George Reyes, C. E. (2021). Incorporación de las TIC en la educación. Recomendaciones de organismos de cooperación internacional 1972-2018. *Revista Caribeña de Investigación Educativa, 5*(1), 101–115. doi:10.32541/recie.2021.v5i1.pp101-115

Getie, A. S. (2020). Factors affecting the attitudes of students towards learning English as a foreign language. *Cogent Education, 7*(1), 1738184. doi:10.1080/2331186X.2020.1738184

Ghanea, M., Pisheh, H. R. Z., & Ghanea, M. H. (2011). The relationship between learners-motivation (integrative and instrumental) and English proficiency among Iranian EFL learners. *International Journal of Educational and Pedagogical Sciences, 5*(11), 1368–1374.

Ghasemi, A. A., Ahmadian, M., Yazdani, H., & Amerian, M. (2020). Towards a model of intercultural communicative competence in Iranian EFL context: Testing the role of international posture, ideal L2 self, L2 self-confidence, and metacognitive strategies. *Journal of Intercultural Communication Research*, *49*(1), 41–60. doi:10.1080/17475759.2019.1705877

Ghazy, A., Wajdi, M., Sada, C., & Ikhsanudin, I. (2021). The use of game-based learning in English class. *Journal of Applied Studies in Language*, *5*(1), 67–78. doi:10.31940/jasl.v5i1.2400

Ginaya, G., Rejeki, I. N. M., & Astuti, N. N. S. (2018). The effects of blended learning to students' speaking ability: A study of utilizing technology to strengthen the conventional instruction. *International journal of linguistics, literature and culture*, *4*(3), 1-14.

Gligori N., Uzelac A. & Krco. S. (2023). *Smart Classroom: Real-Time Feedback on Lecture Quality.*

Gligoric, N., Uzelac, A., Krco, S., Kovacevic, I., & Nikodijevic, A. (2018). System for recognizing lecture quality based on analysis of physical parameters. Vol 35. Issue 3. June 2018.

Gómez García, L., & Urraco Solanilla, M. (2022). Relación entre los videojuegos y las aplicaciones y la adquisición de vocabulario en inglés como lengua extranjera. *Revista Iberoamericana de Tecnología en Educación y Educación en Tecnología*, *31*(31), 60–68. doi:10.24215/18509959.31.e6

Gómez-Carrasco, C. J., Monteagudo-Fernández, J., Moreno-Vera, J. R., & Sainz-Gómez, M. (2020). Evaluation of a gamification and flipped-classroom program used in teacher training: Perception of learning and outcome. *PLoS One*, *15*(7), e0236083. doi:10.1371/journal.pone.0236083 PMID:32673373

González Pérez, A., & Álvarez Serrano, A. (2022). Aprendizaje basado en juegos para aprender una segunda lengua en educación superior. *International Journal of Technology and Educational Innovation*, *8*(2), 114–128. doi:10.24310/innoeduca.2022.v8i2.13858

Goosen, L. (2015). Educational Technologies for Growing Innovative e-Schools in the 21st Century: A Community Engagement Project. In D. Nwaozuzu, & S. Mnisi (Ed.), *Proceedings of the South Africa International Conference on Educational Technologies* (pp. 49 - 61). Pretoria: African Academic Research Forum.

Goosen, L., & Van Heerden, D. (2013). Project-Based Assessment Influencing Pass Rates of an ICT Module at an ODL Institution. In E. Ivala (Ed.), *Proceedings of the 8th International Conference on e-Learning*. 1, pp. 157-164. Cape Town: Academic Conferences and Publishing.

Goosen, L. (2018a). Trans-Disciplinary Approaches to Action Research for e-Schools, Community Engagement, and ICT4D. In T. A. Mapotse (Ed.), *Cross-Disciplinary Approaches to Action Research and Action Learning* (pp. 97–110). IGI Global. doi:10.4018/978-1-5225-2642-1.ch006

Goosen, L. (2018b). Ethical Information and Communication Technologies for Development Solutions: Research Integrity for Massive Open Online Courses. In C. Sibinga (Ed.), *Ensuring Research Integrity and the Ethical Management of Data* (pp. 155–173). IGI Global. doi:10.4018/978-1-5225-2730-5.ch009

Goosen, L. (2022). Augmented/Virtual Reality Technologies and Assistive/Humanoid Robots: Students With Autism Spectrum Disorders. In S. Dhamdhere & F. Andres (Eds.), *Assistive Technologies for Differently Abled Students* (pp. 239–267). IGI Global. doi:10.4018/978-1-7998-4736-6.ch012

Goosen, L., & Naidoo, L. (2014). Computer Lecturers Using Their Institutional LMS for ICT Education in the Cyber World. In C. Burger, & K. Naudé (Ed.), *Proceedings of the 43rd Conference of the Southern African Computer Lecturers' Association (SACLA)* (pp. 99-108). Port Elizabeth: Nelson Mandela Metropolitan University.

Gressick, J., & Langston, J. B. (2017). The gilded classroom: Using gamification to engage and motivate undergraduates. *The Journal of Scholarship of Teaching and Learning*, *17*(3), 109–123. doi:10.14434/v17i3.22119

Griol, D., & Molina, J. M. (2016). From VoiceXML to multimodal mobile Apps: Development of practical conversational interfaces. *Advances in Distributed Computing and Artificial Intelligence Journal*, *3*(5), 43–53. doi:10.14201/ADCAIJ2016534353

Group, D. L. R. (2021). *Creating Environments Conducive to Project-Based Learning.* DLR Group. https://www.dlrgroup.com/insights/creating-environments-conducive-project-based-learning/

Gupta, A. et al., 2021. Understanding Consumer Product Sentiments through Supervised Models on Cloud: Pre and Post COVID. *Webology,* *18*(1), pp.406–415. . doi:10.14704/WEB/V18I1/WEB18097

Gupta, A., Dwivedi, D. N., & Shah, J. (2023). Applying Artificial Intelligence on Investigation. In: Artificial Intelligence Applications in Banking and Financial Services. Future of Business and Finance. Springer, Singapore. doi:10.1007/978-981-99-2571-1_9

Gupta, A., Dwivedi, D. N., & Shah, J. (2023). Applying Machine Learning for Effective Customer Risk Assessment. In: Artificial Intelligence Applications in Banking and Financial Services. Future of Business and Finance. Springer, Singapore. doi:10.1007/978-981-99-2571-1_6

Gupta, A., Dwivedi, D. N., & Shah, J. (2023). Artificial Intelligence-Driven Effective Financial Transaction Monitoring. In: Artificial Intelligence Applications in Banking and Financial Services. Future of Business and Finance. Springer, Singapore. doi:10.1007/978-981-99-2571-1_7

Gupta, A., Dwivedi, D. N., & Shah, J. (2023). Data Organization for an FCC Unit. In: Artificial Intelligence Applications in Banking and Financial Services. Future of Business and Finance. Springer, Singapore. doi:10.1007/978-981-99-2571-1_4

Gupta, A., Dwivedi, D. N., & Shah, J. (2023). Ethical Challenges for AI-Based Applications. In: Artificial Intelligence Applications in Banking and Financial Services. Future of Business and Finance. Springer, Singapore. doi:10.1007/978-981-99-2571-1_10

Gupta, A., Dwivedi, D. N., & Shah, J. (2023). Financial Crimes Management and Control in Financial Institutions. In: Artificial Intelligence Applications in Banking and Financial Services. Future of Business and Finance. Springer, Singapore. doi:10.1007/978-981-99-2571-1_2

Gupta, A., Dwivedi, D. N., & Shah, J. (2023). Machine Learning-Driven Alert Optimization. In: Artificial Intelligence Applications in Banking and Financial Services. Future of Business and Finance. Springer, Singapore. doi:10.1007/978-981-99-2571-1_8

Gupta, A., Dwivedi, D. N., & Shah, J. (2023). Overview of Money Laundering. In: Artificial Intelligence Applications in Banking and Financial Services. Future of Business and Finance. Springer, Singapore. doi:10.1007/978-981-99-2571-1_1

Gupta, A., Dwivedi, D. N., & Shah, J. (2023). Overview of Technology Solutions. In: Artificial Intelligence Applications in Banking and Financial Services. Future of Business and Finance. Springer, Singapore. doi:10.1007/978-981-99-2571-1_3

Gupta, A., Dwivedi, D. N., & Shah, J. (2023). Planning for AI in Financial Crimes. In: Artificial Intelligence Applications in Banking and Financial Services. Future of Business and Finance. Springer, Singapore. doi:10.1007/978-981-99-2571-1_5

Gupta, A., Dwivedi, D. N., & Shah, J. (2023). Setting up a Best-In-Class AI-Driven Financial Crime Control Unit (FCCU). In: Artificial Intelligence Applications in Banking and Financial Services. Future of Business and Finance. Springer, Singapore. doi:10.1007/978-981-99-2571-1_11

Gupta, A., & Gupta, N. (2022). *Research methodology*. SBPD Publications.

Habib, M. N., Jamal, W., Khalil, U., & Khan, Z. (2021). Transforming universities in interactive digital platform: Case of city university of science and information technology. *Education and Information Technologies*, *26*(1), 517–541. doi:10.1007/s10639-020-10237-w PMID:32837236

Halliday, M. A. K. (1985). *Spoken and written language*. Deakin University Press.

Hamed, P. K., & Preece, A. S. (2020). Google Cloud Platform Adoption for Teaching in HEIs: A Qualitative Approach. *OAlib*, *7*(11), 1–23. doi:10.4236/oalib.1106819

Han, D. (2021). An Analysis of Korean EFL Learners' Experience on English Classes Using AI Chatbot. *Robotics & AI Ethics*, *6*(3), 1–9. doi:10.22471/ai.2021.6.3.01

Handayani, P. W., Raharjo, S. R., & Putra, P. H. (2021). Active Student Learning through Gamification in a Learning Management System. *Electronic Journal of e-Learning*, *19*(6), 601–613. doi:10.34190/ejel.19.6.2089

Han, S. Y., Capraro, R., & Capraro, M. M. (2014). How science, technology, engineering, and mathematics project based learning affects high-need students in the US. *Learning and Individual Differences*, *36*, 8–15.

Han, S., Capraro, R., & Capraro, M. M. (2015). How science, technology, engineering, and mathematics (STEM) project-based learning (PBL) affects high, middle, and low achievers differently: The impact of student factors on achievement. *International Journal of Science and Mathematics Education*, *13*(5), 1089–1113. doi:10.1007/s10763-014-9526-0

Harada, V. H., Kirio, C., & Yamamoto, S. (2015). Project-based learning: Rigor and relevance in high schools. *Library Media Connection*, *33*(6), 14–16.

Harfoushi, O. (2017). Influence of Cloud Based Mobile Learning Applications on User Experiences: A Review Study in the Context of Jordan. *International Journal of Interactive Mobile Technologies, 11*(4), 202. doi:10.3991/ijim.v11i4.6938

Hart, C. (2018). Doing a literature review: Releasing the research imagination. *Sage (Atlanta, Ga.)*.

Hellas, A., Ihantola, P., Petersen, A., Ajanovski, V., Gutica, M., Hynninen, T., Knutas, A., Leinonen, J., Messom, C., & Liao, S. Predicting academic performance: a systematic literature review. *Proceedings Companion of the 23rd Annual ACM Conference on Innovation and Technology in Computer Science Education*. (175-199). ACM. 10.1145/3293881.3295783

Henriksen, D. (2017). Creating STEAM with Design Thinking: Beyond STEM and Arts Integration. Steam4U. *STEAM Education Monograph Series, 1*(1), 1–11.

Henry, P. G. (2022). *The Experiences of Educators in Low-Income New York City Middle Schools Navigating Classroom Instruction and Decisions for Homeless Students: A Phenomenological Study* [PhD thesis, Liberty University].

Hill, R. P., & Langan, R. (Eds.). (2014). *Handbook of research on marketing and corporate social responsibility*. Edward Elgar Publishing. doi:10.4337/9781783476091

Hlaing, H. K. T., Phyu, S. P., & Yi, M. T. S. (2018). Thida. Effective Classroom Management Information System to Improve Teaching and Learning Approach. *International Journal of Advanced Research in Computer Science and Software Engineering, 8*(8).

hooks, b. (1996). Teaching to transgress: Education as the practice of freedom. *Journal of Leisure Research, 28*(4), 316.

Hsu, T. C. (2017). Learning English with augmented reality: Do learning styles matter? *Computers & Education, 106*, 137–149. doi:10.1016/j.compedu.2016.12.007

Huang, F., Teo, T., & Zhou, M. (2020). Chinese students' intentions to use the Internet-based technology for learning. *Educational Technology Research and Development, 68*(1), 575–591. doi:10.1007/s11423-019-09695-y

Huang, W., Hew, K. F., & Fryer, L. K. (2022). Chatbots for language learning—Are they really useful? A systematic review of chatbot-supported language learning. *Journal of Computer Assisted Learning, 38*(1), 237–257. doi:10.1111/jcal.12610

Hung, W., Jonassen, D. H., & Liu, R. (2008). Problem-based learning. Handbook of research on educational communications and technology, 485-506.

Hursen, C., & Bas, C. (2019). Use of gamification applications in science education. *International Journal of Emerging Technologies in Learning, 14*(1), 4. doi:10.3991/ijet.v14i01.8894

Hussein, L. A., & Hilmi, M. F. (2020). Cloud computing-based e-learning in Malaysian universities. *International Journal of Emerging Technologies in Learning (Online), 15*(8), 4. doi:10.3991/ijet.v15i08.11798

Hwang, G. J., Wu, C. H., Tseng, J. C. R., & Huang, I. (2011). Development of a ubiquitous learning platform based on a real-time help-seeking mechanism. *British Journal of Educational Technology*, *42*(6), 992–1002. doi:10.1111/j.1467-8535.2010.01123.x

IBM. (2024). *What are Iaas, Paas and Saas?* IBM Newsroom. https://www.ibm.com/topics/iaas-paas-saas

Ibrahim, H., Liu, F., Asim, R., Battu, B., Benabderrahmane, S., Alhafni, B., Adnan, W., Alhanai, T., AlShebli, B., Baghdadi, R., Bélanger, J. J., Beretta, E., Celik, K., Chaqfeh, M., Daqaq, M. F., Bernoussi, Z. E., Fougnie, D., Garcia de Soto, B., Gandolfi, A., & Zaki, Y. (2023). Perception, performance, and detectability of conversational artificial intelligence across 32 university courses. *Scientific Reports*, *13*(1), 12187. doi:10.1038/s41598-023-38964-3 PMID:37620342

Infante Plaza, A. A. (2023). La gamificación como una herramienta necesaria en el aprendizaje de los estudiantes. *Espíritu Emprendedor TES*, *7*(4), 74–91. doi:10.33970/eetes.v7.n4.2023.360

Isa, W. W. M., Suhaimi, A. I. H., Noordin, N., Harun, A. F., Ismail, J., & Teh, R. A. (2019). Factors influencing cloud computing adoption in higher education institution. *Indonesian Journal of Electrical Engineering and Computer Science*, *17*(1), 412–419.

Ishak, S. A., Hasran, U. A., & Din, R. (2023). Ishak,Hasran UA, Din R. Media Education through Digital Games: A Review on Design and Factors Influencing Learning Performance. *Education Sciences*, *13*(2), 102. doi:10.3390/educsci13020102

J. C. Lester, E. Y. Ha, S. Y. Lee, B. W. Mott, J. P. Rowe & J. L. Sabourin (2017). Serious games get smart: Intelligent game-Based learning environments. *AI Mag., 34*(4).

Jaafar, J. A., Latiff, A. R. A., Daud, Z. M., & Osman, M. N. H. (2023). Does revenue diversification strategy affect the financial sustainability of Malaysian Public Universities? A panel data analysis. *Higher Education Policy*, *36*(1), 116–143. doi:10.1057/s41307-021-00247-9

Jackson, L. R., & Patel, A. M. (2023). Personalized Learning in Faculty Development: A Framework for Tailoring Professional Growth Opportunities. *Journal of Faculty Development*, *40*(2), 167–183.

Jacobs, D. (2014). Webcomics, multimodality, and information literacy. *ImageTexT: Interdisciplinary Comics Studies, 7*(3), https://imagetextjournal.com/webcomics-multimodality-and-information-literacy

Jalbani, A. N., Ahmad, A., & Maitlo, S. K. (2023). A Comparative Study to Evaluate ESL Learners' Proficiency and Attitudes towards English Language. *Global Language Review*, *VIII*(II), 446–455. doi:10.31703/glr.2023(VIII-II).36

Jayabalan, J., Dorasamy, M., & Raman, M. (2021). Reshaping higher educational institutions through frugal open innovation. *Journal of Open Innovation*, *7*(2), 145. doi:10.3390/joitmc7020145

Jewitt, C. (2009). *The Routledge Handbook of Multimodal Analysis*. Routledge.

Jia, C., Hew, K., Bai, S., & Huang, W. (2021). Adaptation of a conventional flipped course to an online flipped format during the Covid-19 pandemic: Student learning performance and engagement. *Journal of Research on Technology in Education.* . https://www.tandfonline.com/doi/full/10.1080/15391523.2020.1847220 doi:10.1080/15391523.2020.1847220

Jiang, L., Zhang, L. J., & May, S. (2019). Implementing English-medium instruction (EMI) in China: Teachers' practices and perceptions, and students' learning motivation and needs. *International Journal of Bilingual Education and Bilingualism, 22*(2), 107–119. doi:10.1080/13670050.2016.1231166

Jobin, A., Ienca, M., & Vayena, E. (2019). The global landscape of AI ethics guidelines. *Nature Machine Intelligence, 1*(9), 389–399. https://www.nature.com/articles/s42256-019-0088-2. doi:10.1038/s42256-019-0088-2

Johnson, E., Larner, A., Merritt, D., Vitanova, G., & Sousa, S. (2020). Assessing the impact of game modalities in second language acquisition. *Journal of Universal Computer Science, 26*(8), 880–903. doi:10.3897/jucs.2020.048

Johnson, M. B., & Brown, L. K. (2021). A Comprehensive Review of Agile Training Programs in Academic Settings. *Educational Leadership Review, 18*(3), 56–72.

Jung, H. J. (2015). Fostering an English teaching environment: Factors influencing English as a foreign language teachers' adoption of mobile learning. *Informatics in Education-An International Journal, 14*(2), 219–241. doi:10.15388/infedu.2015.13

Kabilan, M. K., Annamalai, N., & Chuah, K. M. (2023). Practices, purposes and challenges in integrating gamification using technology: A mixed-methods study on university academics. *Education and Information Technologies, 28*(11), 14249–14281. doi:10.1007/s10639-023-11723-7 PMID:37361777

Kallio, H., Pietilä, A. M., Johnson, M., & Kangasniemi, M. (2016). Systematic methodological review: Developing a framework for a qualitative semi-structured interview guide. *Journal of Advanced Nursing, 72*(12), 2954–2965. doi:10.1111/jan.13031 PMID:27221824

Kamal, H., Dhir, S., Hasteer, N., & Soni, K. M. (2023). *Analysis of Barriers to ICT4D Interventions in Higher Education through Interpretive Structural Modeling.* 2022 4th International Conference on Advances in Computing, Communication Control and Networking (ICAC3N), Greater Noida, India. 10.1109/ICAC3N56670.2022.10074596

Kamran, R., Farid, M., Naveed, A., Tufail, S., Shafique, A., Mushtaq, S., & Khan, J. S. (2023). MEDICAL EDUCATION: Future Health Professionals Readiness and Awareness Towards Interprofessional Education in a Health Care Institution of Lahore. [JIIMC]. *Journal of Islamic International Medical College, 18*(1), 56–62.

Kang, H. (2022). Effects of Artificial Intelligence (AI) and native speaker interlocutors on ESL learners' speaking ability and affective aspects. *Multimedia-Assisted Language Learning, 25*(2), 9–43.

Kang, K., & Wang, S. (2018). Analyze and predict student dropout from online programs. In *Proceedings of the 2nd International Conference on Compute and Data Analysis* (pp. 6-12). ACM. 10.1145/3193077.3193090

Kapoor, M. C. (2016). Types of studies and research design. *Indian Journal of Anaesthesia*, *60*(9), 626–630. doi:10.4103/0019-5049.190616 PMID:27729687

Karataş, İ., & Simsek, N. (2021). Adaptive learning systems: Surveying the landscape from general to discipline-specific systems. *Computers and Education: Artificial Intelligence*, *2*, 100014.

Kassab, M., DeFranco, J., & Laplante, P. (2020). A systematic literature Review on Internet of things in education: Benefits and challenges. *Journal of Computer Assisted Learning*, *36*(2), 115–127. doi:10.1111/jcal.12383

Kassab, M., DeFranco, J., & Voas, J. (2018, September/October). Smarter Education. *IT Professional*, *20*(5), 20–24. doi:10.1109/MITP.2018.053891333

Kassim, A. F. (2020). *Educators' views on the effectiveness of alternatives to corporal punishment to maintain discipline: a case of four high schools in the OR Tambo District* [MEd dissertation, University of Fort Hare. http://vital.seals.ac.za:8080/vital/access/services/Download/vital:39060/SOURCE1

Kaur, A., Bhatia, M., & Stea, G. (2022). A survey of smart classroom literature. *Education Sciences*, *12*(2), 86. doi:10.3390/educsci12020086

Kaur, P., Stoltzfus, J., & Yellapu, V. (2018). Descriptive statistics. *International Journal of Academic Medicine*, *4*(1), 60. doi:10.4103/IJAM.IJAM_7_18

Kaya, O. S., & Ercag, E. (2023). The impact of applying challenge-based gamification program on students' learning outcomes: Academic achievement, motivation and flow. *Education and Information Technologies*, *28*(8), 1–26. doi:10.1007/s10639-023-11585-z PMID:36691635

Khan, M. K., Sheraz, K., Sultan, U., & Mushtaq, A. (2022). Investigating the Impact of Technology Involvement in Education from Student's Perspective: Technology Impact Analysis on Students in Academia. *Proceedings of the Pakistan Academy of Sciences: A. Physical and Computational Sciences, 59*. 10.53560/PPASA(59-3)788

Khan, S. H., Li, P., Chughtai, M. S., Mushtaq, M. T., & Zeng, X. (2023). The role of knowledge sharing and creative self-efficacy on the self-leadership and innovative work behavior relationship. *Journal of Innovation & Knowledge*, *8*(4), 100441. doi:10.1016/j.jik.2023.100441

Khasawneh, M. A. S., & Jadallah Abed Khasawneh, Y. (2023). The potentials of artificial intelligence in stimulating motivation and improving performance of undergraduates in foreign languages. *Journal of Namibian Studies: History Politics Culture*, *34*, 7059–7077.

Khoo, E., & Kang, S. (2022). Proactive learner empowerment: Towards a transformative academic integrity approach for English language learners. *International Journal for Educational Integrity*, *18*(1), 1–24. doi:10.1007/s40979-022-00111-2

Kim, S., Yoo, E., & Kim, S. (2023). *A Study on the Prediction of University Dropout Using Machine Learning.* arXiv preprint arXiv:2310.10987. DOI:/arXiv.2310.10987 doi:10.48550

Kim, J. Y., Shim, J. P., & Ahn, K. M. (2011). Social networking service: Motivation, pleasure, and behavioral intention to use. *Journal of Computer Information Systems*, *51*(4), 92.

Kim, J., & Castelli, D. (2021). Effects of Gamification on Behavioral Change in Education: A Meta-Analysis. *International Journal of Environmental Research and Public Health*, *18*(7), 1–14. doi:10.3390/ijerph18073550 PMID:33805530

Kim, T. Y., & Kim, Y. (2021). Structural relationship between L2 learning motivation and resilience and their impact on motivated behavior and L2 proficiency. *Journal of Psycholinguistic Research*, *50*(2), 417–436. doi:10.1007/s10936-020-09721-8 PMID:32691245

Kress, G. (2000a). Design and transformation: New theories of meaning. In B. Cope & M. Kalantzis (Eds.), *Multiliteracies: Literacy learning and the design of social futures* (pp. 153–161). Routledge.

Kress, G. (2000b). Multimodality. In B. Cope & M. Kalantzis (Eds.), *Multiliteracies: Literacy learning and the design of social futures* (pp. 182–202). Routledge.

Kress, G. (2010). *Multimodality: A social semiotic approach to contemporary communication.* Routledge.

Kress, G. R., & van Leeuwen, T. (2001). *Multimodal Discourse: the modes and media of contemporary communication.* Edward Arnold.

Kress, G., Jewitt, C., Bourne, J., Franks, A., Hardcastle, J., Jones, K., & Reid, E. (2005). *English in Urban Classrooms: A Multimodal Perspective on Teaching and Learning.* Routledge.

Kress, G., Jewitt, C., Ogborn, J., & Tsatsarelis, C. (2001). *Multimodal teaching and learning.* Continuum Press.

Kristiani, T., & Usodo, B. (2022). Exploration of the use of quizizz gamification application: Teacher perspective. *International Journal of Elementary Education*, *6*(2). doi:10.23887/ijee.v6i2.43481

Kruger, W. M. (2020). *Placement factors contributing to the well-being of social work interns in a government setting.* North-West University.

Kukulska-Hulme, A., Lee, H., & Norris, L. (2017). Mobile learning revolution: Implications for language pedagogy. In The handbook of technology and second language teaching and learning, 217-233.

Kumar, J. A., Bervell, B., & Osman, S. (2020). Google classroom: Insights from Malaysian higher education students' and instructors' experiences. *Education and Information Technologies*, *25*(5), 4175–4195. doi:10.1007/s10639-020-10163-x

Kumatongo, B., & Muzata, K. K. (2021). Research paradigms and designs with their application in education. *Journal of Lexicography and Terminology*, *5*(1), 16–32.

Kurelovic, E. K., Rako, S., & Tomljanovic, J. (2013). Cloud Computing in Education and Student's Needs. *Proceedings of 36th Internation Convention on Information and Communication Technology*, Opatija, Croatia.

Kuru Gönen, S. İ., & Zeybek, G. (2022a). Using QR code enhanced authentic texts in EFL extensive reading: A qualitative study on student perceptions. *Education and Information Technologies*, *27*(2), 2039–2057. doi:10.1007/s10639-021-10695-w

Kuru Gönen, S. İ., & Zeybek, G. (2022b). Training on multimodal mobile-assisted language learning: A suggested model for pre-service EFL teachers. *Computer Assisted Language Learning*, 1–22. doi:10.1080/09588221.2022.2157016

Kusuma, G. P., Wigati, E. K., Utomo, Y., & Suryapranata, L. K. P. (2018). Analysis of gamification models in education using MDA framework. *Procedia Computer Science*, *135*, 385–392. doi:10.1016/j.procs.2018.08.187

Lagus, J., Longi, K., Klami, A., & Hellas, A. (2018). Transfer-learning methods In programming course outcome prediction. *ACM Trans. Comput. Educ.*, *18*(4), 1–18. doi:10.1145/3152714

Lainjo, B. (2023). Predictive Analytics in Higher Education for Student Retention and Success. *IACSIT International Journal of Engineering and Technology*, *3*(1). doi:10.47747/ijets.v3i1.866

Lam, L., Lau, N. S., & Ngan, L. C. (2013). An investigation of the factors influencing student learning motivation with the facilitation of cloud computing in higher education context of Hong Kong. *Hybrid learning: Theory, application and practice, 12*, 13.

Lamb, M., & Arisandy, F. E. (2020). The impact of online use of English on motivation to learn. *Computer Assisted Language Learning*, *33*(1-2), 85–108. doi:10.1080/09588221.2018.1545670

Lampropoulos, G., Keramopoulos, E., Diamantaras, K., & Evangelidis, G. (2022). Augmented Reality and Gamification in Education: A Systematic Literature Review of Research, Applications, and Empirical Studies. *Applied Sciences (Basel, Switzerland)*, *12*(13), 6809. doi:10.3390/app12136809

Langshaw, S. J. (2017). *Relationship between the self-efficacy and self-directed learning of adults in undergraduate programs* [Doctoral dissertation, Capella University].

Larmer, J., & Mergendoller, J. R. (2010). Seven essentials for project-based learning. *Educational Leadership*, *68*(1), 34–37.

Law, C., & So, S. (2010). QR codes in education. *Journal of Educational Technology Development and Exchange*, *3*(1), 85–100. doi:10.18785/jetde.0301.07

Law, K. M., Geng, S., & Li, T. (2019). Student enrollment, motivation and learning performance in a blended learning environment: The mediating effects of social, teaching, and cognitive presence. *Computers & Education*, *136*, 1–12. doi:10.1016/j.compedu.2019.02.021

Lee, D. K., In, J., & Lee, S. (2015). Standard deviation and standard error of the mean. *Korean Journal of Anesthesiology*, *68*(3), 220–223. doi:10.4097/kjae.2015.68.3.220 PMID:26045923

Lee, H., & Hwang, Y. (2022). Technology-enhanced education through VR-making and metaverse-linking to foster teacher readiness and sustainable learning. *Sustainability (Basel)*, *14*(8), 4786. doi:10.3390/su14084786

Lefèvre, P. (2009). The construction of space in comics. *A Comics Studies Reader*, 157-162.

Le, N., & Dinh, H. (2020). Augmented reality: A brief introduction, its potentials, and implications in language education. In J. Perren, K. Kelch, J. Byun, S. Cervantes, & S. Safavi (Eds.), *Applications of CALL theory in ESL and EFL environments* (pp. 291–352). IGI Global.

Lester, J. C., Ha, E. Y., Lee, S. Y., Mott, B. W., Rowe, J. P., & Sabourin, J. L. (2017). Serious games get smart: Intelligent game-Based learning environments. *AI Magazine*, *34*(4), 31–45. doi:10.1609/aimag.v34i4.2488

Libbrecht, P., & Goosen, L. (2015). Using ICTs to Facilitate Multilingual Mathematics Teaching and Learning. In R. Barwell, P. Clarkson, A. Halai, M. Kazima, J. Moschkovich, N. Planas, & M. Villavicencio Ubillús (Eds.), *Mathematics Education and Language Diversity* (pp. 217–235). Springer. doi:10.1007/978-3-319-14511-2_12

Lin, H. C. K., Chao, C. J., & Huang, T. C. (2015). From a perspective on foreign language learning anxiety to develop an affective tutoring system. *Educational Technology Research and Development*, *63*(5), 727–747. doi:10.1007/s11423-015-9385-6

Liu, T. Y., Tan, T. H., & Chu, Y. L. (2008). QR code and augmented reality-supported mobile English learning system. In Workshop of mobile multmedia processing (pp. 37–52). Heidelberg.

Liu, C., Hou, J., Tu, Y. F., Wang, Y., & Hwang, G. J. (2023). Incorporating a reflective thinking promoting mechanism into artificial intelligence-supported English writing environments. *Interactive Learning Environments*, *31*(9), 5614–5632. doi:10.1080/10494820.2021.2012812

Liu, H., Zhang, X., & Fang, F. (2023). Young English learners' attitudes towards China English: Unpacking their identity construction with implications for secondary level language education in China. *Asia Pacific Journal of Education*, *43*(1), 283–298. doi:10.1080/02188791.2021.1908228

Liu, I. F. (2020). The impact of extrinsic motivation, intrinsic motivation, and social self-efficacy on English competition participation intentions of pre-college learners: Differences between high school and vocational students in Taiwan. *Learning and Motivation*, *72*, 101675. doi:10.1016/j.lmot.2020.101675

Liu, X., Zhu, Y., You, H., & Hong, J. C. (2023). The relationships among metacognitive strategies, acculturation, learning attitude, perceived value, and continuance intention to use YouTube to learn English. *Computer Assisted Language Learning*, 1–21. doi:10.1080/09588221.2023.2297037

Li, Z., Lou, X., Chen, M., Li, S., Lv, C., Song, S., & Li, L. (2023). Students' online learning adaptability and their continuous usage intention across different disciplines. *Humanities & Social Sciences Communications*, *10*(1), 1–10. doi:10.1057/s41599-023-02376-5

López Carrillo, D., Calonge García, A., Rodríguez Laguna, T., Ros Magán, G., & Lebrón Moreno, J. A. (2019). Using gamification in a teaching innovation project at the university of alcalá: A new approach to experimental science practices. *Electronic Journal of e-Learning*, *17*(2), 93–106. doi:10.34190/JEL.17.2.03

López Espinosa, J. R., González Bello, E. O. (2021). Educación superior, innovación y docencia: alcances y limitaciones de la virtualidad como estrategia institucional. *Revista Iberoamericana para la investigación y el desarrollo educativo, 12*(23), 1-34. doi:10.23913/ride.v12i23.1051

Lourens, A., & Bleazard, D. (2016). Applying predictive analytics in identifying students at risk: A case study. *South African Journal of Higher Education*, *30*(2), 129–142. doi:10.20853/30-2-583

Lovato, C., & Junior, O. S. (2011). Motivation in Second Language Acquisition-Gardners Socio-Educational Model. In *9th Symposium on Graduate Education. Piracicaba, Br.* IEEE.

Mabogo, R. (2021). *Evaluation of the impacts of clay brick production on water quality and socio-economic issues in Dididi Village, Limpopo Province, South Africa* [MSc dissertation, University of South Africa].

MacIntyre, P. D., Gregersen, T., & Mercer, S. (2020). 'Language Teachers' Coping Strategies During the Covid-19 Conversion to Online Teaching: Correlations with Stress, Wellbeing and Negative Emotions.' [Google Scholar]. *System*, *94*, 1–13. doi:10.1016/j.system.2020.102352

Madhavi, E., Sivapurapu, L., Koppula, V., Rani, P. E., & Sreehari, V. (2023). Developing Learners' English-Speaking Skills using ICT and AI Tools. *Journal of Advanced Research in Applied Sciences and Engineering Technology*, *32*(2), 142–153. doi:10.37934/araset.32.2.142153

Maftuna, A. (2020). Self-confidence in oral performance. *Бюллетень науки и практики, 6*(4), 444-452.

Magal-Royo, T., Giménez-López, J. L., Pairy, B., García-Laborda, J., & Gonzalez-del Rio, J. (2011). Multimodal application for foreign language teaching. In *Interactive Collaborative Learning (ICL), 2011 14th International Conference on* (pp. 145-148). IEEE. 10.1109/ICL.2011.6059564

Mahlangu, B. G., & Goosen, L. (2023). The Impact of a Lack of Information and Communication Technologies at Rural Schools: Digitalization in a Changing Education Environment. In A. Arinushkina, A. Morozov, & I. Robert (Eds.), *Contemporary Challenges in Education: Digitalization, Methodology, and Management* (pp. 254–275). IGI Global. doi:10.4018/979-8-3693-1826-3.ch019

Majid, U. (2018). Research fundamentals: Study design, population, and sample size. *Undergraduate research in natural and clinical science and technology journal, 2*, 1-7.

Malhotra, N. K., Nunan, D., & Birks, D. F. (2017). *Marketing research: An applied approach*. Pearson.

Malik, A. R., Pratiwi, Y., Andajani, K., Numertayasa, I. W., Suharti, S., Darwis, A., & Marzuki. (2023). Exploring Artificial Intelligence in Academic Essay: Higher Education Student's Perspective. *International Journal of Educational Research Open*, *5*, 100296. doi:10.1016/j.ijedro.2023.100296

Mampage, A., Karunasekera, S., & Buyya, R. (2022). A holistic view on resource management in serverless computing environments: Taxonomy and future directions. *ACM Computing Surveys*, *54*(11s), 1–36. doi:10.1145/3510412

Manegre, M., & Gutiérrez-Colón, M. (2023). Foreign language learning through collaborative writing in knowledge building forums. *Interactive Learning Environments*, *31*(3), 1364–1376. doi:10.1080/10494820.2020.1836499

Mangla, A. S., Bhatia, M., Bhatia, S., & Kumar, P. (2022). Current State of Engineering Education in India: Student Teacher Scenario in Online Mode. Rising Threats in Expert Applications and Solutions. *Lecture Notes in Networks and Systems*, *434*, 465–476. doi:10.1007/978-981-19-1122-4_49

Mangla, A. S., Bhatia, M., Bhatia, S., & Kumar, P. (2022). *Current State of Engineering Education in India: Student Teacher Scenario in Online Mode. Rising Threats in Expert Applications and Solutions: Proceedings of FICR-TEAS*. Springer Nature. https://link.springer.com/chapter/10.1007/978-981-19-1122-4_49

Marinensi, G., Di Lallo, M., & Botte, B. (2023). Gamification as a strategy to increase student engagement in Higher Education: exploring teachers' perspective. In S. Capogna, G. Makrides, & V. Stylianakis (Eds.), *The European Higher Education Area facing the Digital Challenge*.

Martinez, S. L., & Stager, G. (2013). *Invent to learn: Making, tinkering, and engineering in the classroom*. Constructing Modern Knowledge Press.

Martín-Sómer, M., Moreira, J., Cintia Casado. (2021). *Use of kahoot! to keep students' motivation during online classes in the lockdown period caused by covid 19, education for chemical engineers*. IEEE. doi:10.1016/j.ece.2021.05.005

Martí-Parreño, J., Seguí-Mas, D., & Seguí-Mas, E. (2016). Teachers' attitude towards and actual use of gamification. *Procedia: Social and Behavioral Sciences*, *228*, 682–688. doi:10.1016/j.sbspro.2016.07.104

Mary, A. C., & Rose, P. J. (2020). The impact of graduate student's perceptions towards the usage of cloud computing in higher education sectors. *Univ. J. Educ. Res*, *8*(11), 5463–5478. doi:10.13189/ujer.2020.081150

Masadeh, T. S. (2022). Teaching English as a Foreign language and the Use of Educational Games. *Asian Journal of Education and Social Studies*, *30*(3), 26–34. https://doi.org/. doi:10.9734/ajess/2022/v30i330721

Mathevula, M. D., & Uwizeyimana, D. E. (2014). The challenges facing the integration of ICT in teaching and learning activities in South African rural secondary schools. *Mediterranean Journal of Social Sciences*, *5*(20), 1087–1097. doi:10.5901/mjss.2014.v5n20p1087

McCabe, M., & Tedesco, S. (2012). Using QR codes and mobile devices to foster a learning environment for mathematics education. *International Journal of Technology Inclusive and Inclusive Education*, *1*(6), 37–43. doi:10.20533/ijtie.2047.0533.2012.0006

McCreary, J. J., & Marchant, G. J. (2017). Reading and empathy. *Reading Psychology*, *38*(2), 182–202. doi:10.1080/02702711.2016.1245690

McGuire, P., & Kenney, J. (2015). The Collaborative Project-Based Model: Supporting technology integration in K-12 with Professional Learning Communities. *Technology and Teacher Education Conference 2015*. Research Gate.

Md. Khambari, M. N. (2019). Instilling innovativeness, building character, and enforcing camaraderie through interest-driven challenge-based learning approach. *Research and Practice in Technology Enhanced Learning*, *14*(1), 19. doi:10.1186/s41039-019-0115-2

Melvina, M., & Julia, J. (2021). Learner Autonomy and English Proficiency of Indonesian Undergraduate Students. *Cypriot Journal of Educational Sciences*, *16*(2), 803–818. doi:10.18844/cjes.v16i2.5677

Mentz, E., & Goosen, L. (2007). Are groups working in the Information Technology class? *South African Journal of Education*, *27*(2), 329–343.

Mesbahi, M. R., Rahmani, A. M., & Hosseinzadeh, M. (2018). Reliability and high availability in cloud computing environments: A reference roadmap. *Human-centric Computing and Information Sciences*, *8*(1), 1–31. doi:10.1186/s13673-018-0143-8

Milutinović, M., Labus, A., Stojiljković, V., Bogdanović, Z., & Despotović-Zrakić, M. (2015). Designing a mobile language learning system based on lightweight learning objects. *Multimedia Tools and Applications*, *74*(3), 903–935. doi:10.1007/s11042-013-1704-5

Mircea, M., & Andreescu, A. I. (2011). Using cloud computing in higher education: A strategy to improve agility in the current financial crisis. *Communications of the IBIMA*, 1–15. doi:10.5171/2011.875547

Mir, M., Hussain, M., & Jariko, M. (2023). Contexts and Faculty Belief Matters: Problems in Pedagogical Shifts among Faculty Members of Business Schools: A Study on Pakistan Higher Education Institutions (HEIs), Karachi Sindh, Pakistan. *KASBIT Business Journal*, *16*(2), 19–40.

Mitchell, Á., & Cunningham, L. (2014, October). Impact of cloud computing in Ireland's institutes of higher education. In *eChallenges e-2014 Conference Proceedings* (pp. 1-11). IEEE.

Mohamad Noor, M. B., & Hassan, W. H. (2019). Current research on Internet of Things (IoT) security: A survey. *Computer Networks*, *148*, 283–294. doi:10.1016/j.comnet.2018.11.025

Mohamad, S. N. M., Sazali, N. S. S., & Salleh, M. A. M. (2018). Gamification approach in education to increase learning engagement. *International Journal of Humanities. Arts and Social Sciences*, *4*(1), 22–32. doi:10.20469/ijhss.4.10003-1

Mohd Nordin, A. R., Mohd Fadzil, A. K., Syarilla Iryani, A. S., Syadiah Nor, W. S., & Jazurainifariza, J. (2017). The *Direction of Cloud Computing for Malaysian Education Sector in 21th Century.*

MOHE. (2019). Higher Education Statistics 2019. Ministry of Higher education, Putrajaya.

Molina García, P. F., Molina García, A. R., & Gentry Jones, J. (2021). La gamificación como estrategia didáctica para el aprendizaje del idioma inglés. *Dominio de las Ciencias*, *7*(1), 722–730. doi:10.23857/dc.v7i1.1672

Moltmann, J. (1993). *Theology of hope: On the ground and the implications of a Christian eschatology.* Fortress Press.

Montiel-Ruiz, F. J., & Solano-Fernández, I. M. (2023). Social networks and gamification in physical education: A case study. *Contemporary Educational Technology*, *15*(1), ep401. doi:10.30935/cedtech/12660

Moon, M.-H., & Kim, G. (2023). Predicting University Dropout Rates Using Machine Learning Algorithms. *Journal of Economics and Finance Education*, *32*(2), 57–68. doi:10.46967/jefe.2023.32.2.57

Moreira Santos, M.G. & Cedeño Zambrano, E.G. (2023). El uso de las tecnologías de la información y comunicación (TIC) como estrategia en la enseñanza y aprendizaje en la educación superior. *RECIAMUC, 7*(2), 101-109. https://doi.org/.(2).abril.2023.101-109 doi:10.26820/reciamuc/7

Moseikina, M., Toktamysov, S., & Danshina, S. (2022). Modern technologies and gamification in historical education. *Simulation & Gaming*, *53*(2), 135–156. doi:10.1177/10468781221075965

Mujahidah, N., & Yusdiana, Y. (2023). Application of Albert Bandura's Social-Cognitive Theories in Teaching and Learning. *Edukasi Islami: Jurnal Pendidikan Islam, 12*(02).

Muñoz, J. L. R., Ojeda, F. M., Jurado, D. L. A., Peña, P. F. P., Carranza, C. P. M., Berríos, H. Q., & Vasquez-Pauca, M. J. (2022). Systematic review of adaptive learning technology for learning in higher education. *Eurasian Journal of Educational Research*, *98*(98), 221–233.

Mushtaq, M. S., Mushtaq, M. Y., & Iqbal, M. W. (2020). Use of authentic learning tools in delivery of scientific education. [IJCSIS]. *International Journal of Computer Science and Information Security*, *18*(11), 1–8.

MushtaqM. T. (2021). The Impact of Emotions on Consumer Behaviour in Post Covid Environment: A Neuromarketing Perspective. *Conference contribution.* Cardiff Metropolitan University. doi:10.25401/cardiffmet.14614266.v1

Nadolny, L. (2017). Interactive print: The design of cognitive tasks in blended augmented reality and print documents. *British Journal of Educational Technology*, *48*(3), 814–823. doi:10.1111/bjet.12462

Nakashololo, T. M. (2021). *A decision support framework for selecting big data analytics tools in an organisation*. Cape Peninsula University of Technology.

Nasri, N. M., & Mydin, F. (2017). Universiti students' view of self-directed learning in an online learning context. *Advances in Social Sciences Research Journal*, *4*(24).

Navarro, J. L., & Tudge, J. R. (2023). Technologizing Bronfenbrenner: Neo-ecological theory. *Current Psychology (New Brunswick, N.J.)*, *42*(22), 19338–19354. doi:10.1007/s12144-022-02738-3 PMID:35095241

Neumann, H., Padden, N., & McDonough, K. (2019). Beyond English language proficiency scores: Understanding the academic performance of international undergraduate students during the first year of study. *Higher Education Research & Development*, *38*(2), 324–338. doi:10.1080/07294360.2018.1522621

Ngugi, J. K., & Goosen, L. (2021). Innovation, Entrepreneurship, and Sustainability for ICT Students Towards the Post-COVID-19 Era. In L. C. Carvalho, L. Reis, & C. Silveira (Eds.), *Handbook of Research on Entrepreneurship, Innovation, Sustainability, and ICTs in the Post-COVID-19 Era* (pp. 110–131). IGI Global. doi:10.4018/978-1-7998-6776-0.ch006

Nguyen, T. N. Q., & Vo, N. T. T. (2021). The need of applying English learning apps to help Van Lang University students improve their spoken English performance. *AsiaCALL Online Journal*, *12*(2), 72–86.

Ni, A., & Cheung, A. (2023). Understanding secondary students' continuance intention to adopt AI-powered intelligent tutoring system for English learning. *Education and Information Technologies*, *28*(3), 3191–3216. doi:10.1007/s10639-022-11305-z PMID:36119127

Niemiec, C. P., Ryan, R. M., & Deci, E. L. (2010). Self-determination theory and the relation of autonomy to self-regulatory processes and personality development. Handbook of personality and self-regulation, 169-191.

Nieto-Escamez, F. A., & Roldán-Tapia, M. D. (2021). Gamification as online teaching strategy during COVID-19: A mini-review. *Frontiers in Psychology*, *12*, 648552. doi:10.3389/fpsyg.2021.648552 PMID:34093334

Nikolaidis, P., Ismail, M., Shuib, L., Khan, S., & Dhiman, G. (2022). *Predicting Student Attrition in Higher Education through the Determinants of Learning Progress: A Structural Equation Modelling Approach. Sustainability*. MDPI. . https://www.mdpi.com/2071-1050/14/20/13584 doi:10.3390/su142013584

Nižetić, S., Šolić, P., López-de-Ipiña González-de-Artaza, D., & Patrono, L. (2020). Internet of Things (IoT): Opportunities, issues and Challenges towards a smart and sustainable future. *Journal of Cleaner Production*, *274*, 122877. doi:10.1016/j.jclepro.2020.122877 PMID:32834567

Nousiainen, T., Kangas, M., Rikala, J., & Vesisenaho, M. (2018). Teacher competencies in game-based pedagogy. *Teaching and Teacher Education*, *74*, 85–97. doi:10.1016/j.tate.2018.04.012

Noviana, N., & Oktaviani, L. (2022). The correlation between college student personality types and English proficiency ability at Universitas Teknokrat Indonesia. *Journal of English Language Teaching and Learning*, *3*(1), 54–60. doi:10.33365/jeltl.v3i1.1709

Nurmalitasari, A. & Mohd Noor, M. (2023). The Predictive Learning Analytics for Student Dropout Using Data Mining Technique: A Systematic Literature Review. *Advances in Technology Transfer Through IoT and IT Solutions*. Springer. doi:10.1007/978-3-031-25178-8_2

Nurmalitasari, L. Z. & Mohd Noor, M. (2021). Reduction of Data Dimensions in The PLA Process. *2021 15th International Conference on Ubiquitous Information Management and Communication (IMCOM)*. (1-8). IEEE. https://ieeexplore.ieee.org/document/9377391/ doi:10.1109/IMCOM51814.2021.9377391

Obeidat, M. M., & Alomari, M. D. (2020). The Effect of Inductive and Deductive Teaching on EFL Undergraduates' Achievement in Grammar at the Hashemite University in Jordan. *International Journal of Higher Education*, *9*(2), 280–288. doi:10.5430/ijhe.v9n2p280

Ogbonna, E., & Harris, L. C. (2000). Leadership style, organizational culture and performance: Empirical evidence from UK companies. international Journal of human resource management, 11(4), 766-788.

Oliveira, W., Hamari, J., Shi, L., Toda, A. M., Rodrigues, L., Palomino, P. T., & Isotani, S. (2022). Tailored gamification in education: A literature review and future agenda. *Education and Information Technologies*, *28*(1), 373–406. doi:10.1007/s10639-022-11122-4

Oqaidi, K., Aouhassi, S., & Mansouri, K. (2022). A Comparison between Using Fuzzy Cognitive Mapping and Machine Learning to Predict Students' Performance in Higher Education. *2022 IEEE 3rd International Conference on Electronics, Control, Optimization and Computer Science (ICECOCS)*. IEEE. doi:10.1109/ICECOCS55148.2022.9983470. https://ieeexplore.ieee.org/document/9983470/ doi:10.1109/ICECOCS55148.2022.9983470

Ortega, F., & Vásquez, C. (2021). Análisis del impacto de la enseñanza basada en juegos en el compromiso de los estudiantes en la clase de inglés. *Ingenio Libre*, *9*(19), 66–88.

Ortiz-Rojas, M., Chiluiza, K., & Valcke, M. (2019). Gamification through leaderboards: An empirical study in engineering education. *Computer Applications in Engineering Education*, *27*(4), 777–788. doi:10.1002/cae.12116

Osipovskaya, E., & Miakotnikova, S. (2020). Using gamification in teaching public relations students. Auer, M., Tsiatsos, T. (eds) the challenges of the digital t ransformation in education. icl 2018. Advances in Intelligent Systems and Computing, (vol 916). Springer, Cham. doi:10.1007/978-3-030-11932-4_64

Oyewo, S. A., & Goosen, L. (2024). Relationships Between Teachers' Technological Competency Levels and Self-Regulated Learning Behavior: Investigating Blended Learning Environments. In R. Pandey, N. Srivastava, & P. Chatterjee (Eds.), *Architecture and Technological Advancements of Education 4.0* (pp. 1–24). IGI Global. doi:10.4018/978-1-6684-9285-7.ch001

Ozdemir, E., & Papi, M. (2022). Mindsets as sources of L2 speaking anxiety and self-confidence: The case of international teaching assistants in the US. *Innovation in Language Learning and Teaching*, *16*(3), 234–248. doi:10.1080/17501229.2021.1907750

Özdener, N. (2018). Gamification for enhancing Web 2.0 based educational activities: The case of pre-service grade school teachers using educational Wiki pages. *Telematics and Informatics*, *35*(3), 564–578. doi:10.1016/j.tele.2017.04.003

Öztürk, M., & Çakıroğlu, Ü. (2021). Flipped learning design in EFL classrooms: Implementing self-regulated learning strategies to develop language skills. *Smart Learning Environments*, *8*(1), 2. doi:10.1186/s40561-021-00146-x

Padilla Escobedo, J. C., & Ayala Jiménez, G. G. (2021). Competencias digitales en profesores de educación superior de Iberoamérica: una revisión sistemática. *Revista Iberoamericana para la investigación y el desarrollo educativo, 12*(23), 1-19. doi:10.23913/ride.v12i23.1096

Pardo Cueva, M., Chamba Rueda, L. M., Higuerey Gómez, Á., & Jaramillo Campoverde, B. G. (2021). Las TIC y rendimiento académico en la educación superior: Una relación potenciada por el uso del Padlet. *Revista Ibérica de Sistemas e Tecnologias de Informação*, *28*, 934–944.

Parker, K. N. (2022). *Literacy is liberation: Working toward justice through culturally relevant teaching*. ASCD.

Parra González, M. E., Segura Robles, A., Vázquez Cano, E., & López Meneses, E. (2020). Gamificación para fomentar la activación del alumnado en su aprendizaje. *Revista Linguagem e Tecnologia*, *13*(3), 278–293. doi:10.35699/1983-3652.2020.25846

Párraga Solórzano, R.J., Vargas Serrano, J.V., Solórzano Alcivar, E.A. & Gómez Rivas, I.B. (2022). Recursos didácticos digitales en la enseñanza del idioma inglés. *Universidad, Ciencia y Tecnología, 26*(116), 84-92). doi:10.47460/uct.v26i116.647

Patwa, N., Seetharaman, A., Sreekumar, K., & Phani, S. (2018). Learning Analytics: Enhancing the quality of higher education. *Res. J. Econ.*, *2*(2), 13–29.

Pawley, C. (2002). Seeking" significance": Actual readers, specific reading communities. *Book History*, *5*(1), 143–160. doi:10.1353/bh.2002.0013

Pedaste, M., Mäeots, M., Siiman, L. A., de Jong, T., van Riesen, S. A., Kamp, E. T., Manoli, C. C., Zacharia, Z. C., & Tsourlidaki, E. (2015). Phases of inquiry-based learning: Definitions and the inquiry cycle. *Educational Research Review*, *14*, 47–61. doi:10.1016/j.edurev.2015.02.003

Pektaş, M., & Kepceoğlu, İ. (2019). What do prospective teachers think about educational gamification? *Science education international, 30*(1). doi:10.33828/sei.v30.i1.8

Peng, A., & Patterson, M. M. (2022). Relations among cultural identity, motivation for language learning, and perceived English language proficiency for international students in the United States. *Language, Culture and Curriculum*, *35*(1), 67–82. doi:10.1080/07908318.2021.1938106

Perez, B., Castellanos, C., & Correal, D. (2018, May). Applying data mining techniques to predict student dropout: a case study. In *2018 IEEE 1st colombian conference on applications in computational intelligence (colcaci)* (pp. 1-6). IEEE. 10.1109/ColCACI.2018.8484847

Pérez, E., & Gertrudis, F. (2021). Ventajas de la gamificación en el ámbito de la educación formal en España. Una revisión bibliográfica en el periodo de 2015-2020. *Contextos Educativos. Review of Education*, *28*(28), 203–227. doi:10.18172/con.4741

Perwitasari, I. D., & Hendrawan, J. (2023). Design of a library book lending information system using qr code technology. *Prosiding Universitas Dharmawangsa*, *3*(1), 577–584.

Petrovych, O., Zavalniuk, I., Bohatko, V., Poliarush, N., & Petrovych, S. (2023). Motivational readiness of future teachers-philologists to use the gamification with elements of augmented reality in education. *International Journal of Emerging Technologies in Learning*, *18*(3), 4–21. doi:10.3991/ijet.v18i03.36017

Pholotho, T., & Mtsweni, J. (2016, May). Barriers to electronic access and delivery of educational information in resource constrained public schools: A case of Greater Tubatse Municipality. *IST-Africa Week Conference Proceedings* (pp. 1-9). IEEE.

Pholotho, T. J. (2017). *Toward a Broadband Services Delivery Model over Wireless Technologies to Resource-Constrained Public High Schools in South Africa (MTech)*. University of South Africa.

Pilkey, D. (2023). *Dogman (series)*. Graphix.

Pinnegar, S., & Hamilton, M. L. (2009). *Self-study of practice as a genre of qualitative research: Theory, methodology, and practice* (Vol. 8). Springer Science & Business Media.

Polas, M. R. H., & Raju, V. (2021). Technology and entrepreneurial marketing decisions during COVID-19. *Global Journal of Flexible Systems Managment*, *22*(2), 95–112. doi:10.1007/s40171-021-00262-0

Polit, D. F., & Beck, C. T. (2020). Trustworthiness and rigor in qualitative research. In *Nursing research: generating and assessing evidence for nursing practice* (pp. 567–584). Lippincott Williams & Wilkins.

Polkinghorne, D. E. (1995). Narrative configuration in qualitative analysis. *International Journal of Qualitative Studies in Education : QSE*, *8*(1), 5–23. doi:10.1080/0951839950080103

Poveda Pineda, D. F., & Cifuentes Medina, J. E. (2020). Incorporación de las tecnologías de información y comunicación (TIC) durante el proceso de aprendizaje en la educación superior. *Formación Universitaria*, *13*(6), 95–104. doi:10.4067/S0718-50062020000600095

Prasanth, A., & Alqahtani, H. (2023). Predictive Models for Early Dropout Indicators in University Settings Using Machine Learning Techniques. In *2023 IEEE International Conference on Emerging Technologies and Applications in Sensors (ICETAS)*. IEEE. DOI:10.1109/ICETAS59148.2023.10346531

Prince, M. J., & Felder, R. M. (2006). Inductive teaching and learning methods: Definitions, comparisons, and research bases. *Journal of Engineering Education*, *95*(2), 123–138. doi:10.1002/j.2168-9830.2006.tb00884.x

Putz, L. M., Hofbauer, F., & Treiblmaier, H. (2020). Can gamification help to improve education? Findings from a longitudinal study. *Computers in Human Behavior*, *110*, 106392. doi:10.1016/j.chb.2020.106392

Qasem, Y. A., Abdullah, R., Jusoh, Y. Y., Atan, R., & Asadi, S. (2019). Cloud computing adoption in higher education institutions: A systematic review. *IEEE Access : Practical Innovations, Open Solutions*, *7*, 63722–63744. doi:10.1109/ACCESS.2019.2916234

Qasem, Y. A., Abdullah, R., Yaha, Y., & Atana, R. (2020). Continuance use of cloud computing in higher education institutions: A conceptual model. *Applied Sciences (Basel, Switzerland)*, *10*(19), 6628. doi:10.3390/app10196628

Qiao, S., Yeung, S., Zainuddin, Z., Ng, D. T. K., & Chu, S. K. W. (2023). Examining the effects of mixed and non-digital gamification on students' learning performance, cognitive engagement and course satisfaction. *British Journal of Educational Technology*, *54*(1), 394–413. doi:10.1111/bjet.13249

Quast, K. (2020). Gamification, foreign language teaching and teacher education. *Revista Brasileira de Lingüística Aplicada*, *20*, 787–820. doi:10.1590/1984-6398202016398

Qureshi, M. I., Khan, N., Raza, H., Imran, A., & Ismail, F. (2021). *Digital technologies in education 4.0. Does it enhance the effectiveness of learning?*

Rafiee, M., & Abbasian-Naghneh, S. (2021). E-learning: Development of a model to assess the acceptance and readiness of technology among language learners. *Computer Assisted Language Learning*, *34*(5-6), 730–750. doi:10.1080/09588221.2019.1640255

Rajesh, M. (2017). A systematic review of cloud security challenges in higher education. *The Online Journal of Distance Education and e-Learning : TOJDEL*, *5*(1).

Ramírez-Donoso, L., Pérez-Sanagustín, M., Neyem, A., Alario-Hoyos, C., Hilliger, I., & Rojos, F. (2023). Fostering the use of online learning resources: Results of using a mobile collaboration tool based on gamification in a blended course. *Interactive Learning Environments*, *31*(3), 1564–1578. doi:10.1080/10494820.2020.1855202

Rangongo, M. F. (2021). *Work-life conflict experiences and cultural expectations of women managers in the public sector of Limpopo Province.* University of Limpopo. http://ulspace.ul.ac.za/bitstream/handle/10386/3623/rangongo_mf_2021.pdf?isAllowed=y&sequence=1

Rasool, G., & Winke, P. (2019). Undergraduate students' motivation to learn and attitudes towards English in multilingual Pakistan: A look at shifts in English as a world language. *System*, *82*, 50–62. doi:10.1016/j.system.2019.02.015

Reyes, E., Gálvez, J. C., & Enfedaque, A. (2021). Learning course: Application of gamification in teaching construction and building materials subjects. *Education Sciences*, *11*(6), 287. doi:10.3390/educsci11060287

Riasati, M. J. (2018). Willingness to speak English among foreign language learners: A causal model. *Cogent Education*, *5*(1), 1455332. doi:10.1080/2331186X.2018.1455332

Rikala, J., & Kankaanranta, M. (2012). The use of quick response codes in the classroom. In M. Specht, M. Sharples, & J. Multisilta (Eds.), *Proceedings of the 11th Conference on Mobile and Contextual Learning* (pp. 148–155)., Retrieved from https://ceur-ws.org/Vol-955/papers/paper_40.pdf

Robinson, J. (2010). *Triandis' theory of interpersonal behaviour in understanding software piracy behaviour in the South African context* [Doctoral dissertation, University of the Witwatersrand].

Roca Castro, Y. D., & Véliz Robles, F. M. (2022). Innovación en la Enseñanza del Idioma Inglés a Nivel de Educación Superior en Postpandemia. *Domino de las Ciencias*, *8*(2), 361–377. doi:10.23857/dc.v8i2.2759

Rodríguez Cajamarca, L. P., García Herrera, D. G., Guevara Vizcaíno, C. F., & Erazo Álvarez, J. C. (2020). Alianza entre aprendizaje y juego: Gamificación como estrategia metodológica que motiva el aprendizaje del Inglés. *Revista Arbitrada Interdisciplinaria KOINONIA*, *5*(1), 370–391. doi:10.35381/r.k.v5i1.788

Rosa, E. M., & Tudge, J. (2013). Urie Bronfenbrenner's theory of human development: Its evolution from ecology to bioecology. *Journal of Family Theory & Review*, *5*(4), 243–258. doi:10.1111/jftr.12022

Rose, H., Curle, S., Aizawa, I., & Thompson, G. (2020). What drives success in English medium taught courses? The interplay between language proficiency, academic skills, and motivation. *Studies in Higher Education*, *45*(11), 2149–2161. doi:10.1080/03075079.2019.1590690

Rosmayanti, V., Ramli, R., & Rafiqa, R. (2023). Building beginners' self-confidence in speaking at private high school in Makassar. *EduLite: Journal of English Education. Literature and Culture*, *8*(1), 192–208.

Rumjaun, A., & Narod, F. (2020). Social Learning Theory—Albert Bandura. *Science education in theory and practice: An introductory guide to learning theory*, 85-99.

Rupashi, B., Saru, D., Nitasha, H., & Soni, K. M. (2023). [IJIET.]. *Analysis of Barriers in Conduct of Lab Based Courses in Remote Teaching Learning Paradigm.*, *13*(3), 475–481.

Ryan, R. M., & Deci, E. L. (2017). Self-determination theory: Basic psychological needs in motivation. Development, and Wellness. Guilford Press, 10(978.14625), 28806.

Ryan, R. M., & Deci, E. L. (2000). Self-Determination Theory and the Facilitation of Intrinsic Motivation, Social Development, and Well-Being. *The American Psychologist*, *55*(1), 68–78. doi:10.1037/0003-066X.55.1.68 PMID:11392867

Ryan, R. M., & Deci, E. L. (2022). Self-determination theory. In *Encyclopedia of quality of life and well-being research* (pp. 1–7). Springer International Publishing. doi:10.1007/978-3-319-69909-7_2630-2

Safdar, S., Ren, M., Chudhery, M. A. Z., Huo, J., Rehman, H. U., & Rafique, R. (2022). Using cloud-based virtual learning environments to mitigate increasing disparity in urban-rural academic competence. *Technological Forecasting and Social Change, 176,* 121468. doi:10.1016/j.techfore.2021.121468

Sagita, I. K. (2021). Applying Conversation Method and Self-Confidence and Its Effect to Learning Achievement. *Journal Corner of Education, Linguistics, and Literature, 1*(2), 122–131. doi:10.54012/jcell.v1i2.11

Sailer, M., & Homner, L. (2020). The gamification of learning: A meta-analysis. *Educational Psychology Review, 32*(1), 77–112. doi:10.1007/s10648-019-09498-w

SAIS. (2022). *Our Commitment to Innovation.* SAIS. https://sais-singapore.sg/innovative-learning

Sajinčič, N., Sandak, A., & Istenič, A. (2022). Pre-service and in-service teachers' views on gamification. *International Journal of Emerging Technologies in Learning (IJET), 17*(3). doi:10.3991/ijet.v17i03.26761

Salado, L., Amavisca, S., Richart, R., & Rodríguez, R. (2019). Alfabetización digital de estudiantes universitarios en las modalidades presencial y virtual. *Revista Electrónica de Investigación e Innovación Educativa, 5*(1), 30–47. doi:10.6018/red.444751

Saleem, A. N., Noori, N. M., & Ozdamli, F. (2022). Gamification applications in e-learning: A literature review. *Tech Know Learn, 27*(1), 139–159. doi:10.1007/s10758-020-09487-x

Sánchez-Mena, A., & Martí-Parreño, J. (2017). Drivers and barriers to adopting gamification: Teachers' perspectives. *Electronic Journal of e-Learning, 15*(5), 434–443. https://eric.ed.gov/?id=EJ1157970

Santos González, D. C. (2023). La gamificación en el aprendizaje de segundas lenguas extranjeras: FLE y su aprendizaje en la enseñanza pública de España. *Revista Educación. Investigación. Innovación y Transferencia, 1*(1), 68–91. doi:10.26754/ojs_reiit/eiit.202318813

Santos-Villalba, M. J., Olivencia, J. J. L., Navas-Parejo, M. R., & Benítez-Márquez, M. D. (2020). Higher education students' assessments towards gamification and sustainability: A case study. *Sustainability (Basel), 12*(20), 1–20. doi:10.3390/su12208513

Sardegna, V. G., Lee, J., & Kusey, C. (2018). Self-efficacy, attitudes, and choice of strategies for English pronunciation learning. *Language Learning, 68*(1), 83–114. doi:10.1111/lang.12263

Sari, F. M., & Wahyudin, A. Y. (2019). Undergraduate Students' Perceptions Toward Blended Learning through Instagram in English for Business Class. *International Journal of Language Education, 3*(1), 64–73. doi:10.26858/ijole.v1i1.7064

Sarstedt, M., & Mooi, E. (2014). A concise guide to market research. The Process. *Data, 12.*

Sato, R. (2023). Examining fluctuations in the WTC of Japanese EFL speakers: Language proficiency, affective and conditional factors. *Language Teaching Research*, 27(4), 974–994. doi:10.1177/1362168820977825

Saunders, M. (2014). *Research Methods for Business Students* (6th ed.).

Savery, J. R. (2015). Overview of problem-based learning: Definitions and distinctions. Essential readings in problem-based learning: Exploring and extending the legacy of Howard S. *Barrows*, 9, 5–15.

Scheerder, A., van Deursen, A., & van Dijk, J. (2017). Determinants of Internet skills, uses and outcomes: A systematic review of the second-and third-level digital divide. *Telematics and Informatics*, 34(8), 1607–1624. doi:10.1016/j.tele.2017.07.007

Schnitzler, K., Holzberger, D., & Seidel, T. (2020). All better than being disengaged: Student engagement patterns and their relations to academic self-concept and achievement. *European Journal of Psychology of Education*. doi:10.1007/s10212-020-00500-6

Sedgwick, P. (2014). Cross Sectional Studies: Advantages and Disadvantages. *BMJ (Clinical Research Ed.)*, (348), 1–2.

Seidel, E., & Kutieleh, S. (2017). Using predictive analytics to target and improve first year student attrition. *Australian Journal of Education*, 61(2), 200–218. doi:10.1177/0004944117712310

Sellke, T., Bayarri, M. J., & Berger, J. O. (2001). Calibration of ρ values for testing precise null hypotheses. *The American Statistician*, 55(1), 62–71. doi:10.1198/000313001300339950

Semartiana, N., Putri, A., & Rosmansyah, Y. (2022). A systematic literature review of gamification for children: game elements, purposes, and technologies. In *International Conference on Information Science and Technology Innovation (ICoSTEC)* (Vol. 1, No. 1, pp. 72-76). IEEE. 10.35842/icostec.v1i1.12

Septiani, E., Petrus, I., & Mirizon, S. (2021). The Correlations Among Teachers' Competences, Students' Learning Motivation, and Students' English Proficiency. *Eralingua: Jurnal Pendidikan Bahasa Asing Dan Sastra*, 5(1), 143. doi:10.26858/eralingua.v5i1.14316

Sepulveda-Escobar, P., & Morrison, A. (2020). Online Teaching Placement During the COVID-19 Pandemic in Chile: Challenges and Opportunities. [Google Scholar]. *European Journal of Teacher Education*, 43(4), 587–607. doi:10.1080/02619768.2020.1820981

Shafie, H., Majid, F. A., & Ismail, I. S. (2019). Technological pedagogical content knowledge (TPACK) in teaching 21st century skills in the 21st century classroom. *Asian Journal of University Education*, 15(3), 24–33. doi:10.24191/ajue.v15i3.7818

Shafiq, D. A., Marjani, M., Habeeb, R. A. A., & Asirvatham, D. (2022). Predictive Analytics in Education: A Machine Learning Approach. In *2022 3rd International Multidisciplinary Conference on Computer and Energy Science (SpliTech)* (pp. 1-6). IEEE. [DOI:10.1109/MACS56771.2022

Shahzad, A., Golamdin, A. G., & Ismail, N. A. (2016). Opportunity and challenges using the cloud computing in the case of Malaysian higher education institutions. [IJMSIT]. *The International Journal of Management Science and Information Technology*, (20), 1–18.

Shahzad, A., Hassan, R., Aremu, A. Y., Hussain, A., & Lodhi, R. N. (2021). Effects of COVID-19 in E-learning on higher education institution students: The group comparison between male and female. *Quality & Quantity*, *55*(3), 805–826. doi:10.1007/s11135-020-01028-z PMID:32836471

Shakeabubakor, A. A., Sundararajan, E., & Hamdan, A. R. (2015). Cloud computing services and applications to improve productivity of university researchers. *International Journal of Information and Electronics Engineering*, *5*(2), 153. doi:10.7763/IJIEE.2015.V5.521

Shang, C., Moss, A. C., & Chen, A. (2023). The expectancy-value theory: A meta-analysis of its application in physical education. *Journal of Sport and Health Science*, *12*(1), 52–64. doi:10.1016/j.jshs.2022.01.003 PMID:35051641

Sharma, P., & Dhir, S. (2016). Functional & Non-Functional Requirement Elicitation and Risk Assessment for Agile Processes. *International Journal of Control Theory and Applications*, *9*(18), 9005–9010.

Shih, Y. C., & Reynolds, B. L. (2018). The effects of integrating goal setting and reading strategy instruction on English reading proficiency and learning motivation: A quasi-experimental study. *Applied Linguistics Review*, *9*(1), 35–62. doi:10.1515/applirev-2016-1022

Showkat, N., & Parveen, H. (2017). Non-Probability and Probability Sampling. *Media & Communication Studies*.

Shuqfa, Z., & Harous, S. (2019). *Data Mining Techniques Used in Predicting Student Retention in Higher Education: A Survey 2019 International Conference on Electrical and Computing Technologies and Applications (ICECTA)*. IEEE. https://ieeexplore.ieee.org/document/8959789/ doi:10.1109/ICECTA48151.2019.8959789

Siani, A., & Harris, J. (2023). Self-Confidence and STEM Career Propensity: Lessons from an All-Girls Secondary School. *Open Education Studies*, *5*(1), 20220180. doi:10.1515/edu-2022-0180

Siemon, D., & Eckardt, L. (2017). Gamification of teaching in higher education. In S. Stieglitz, C. Lattemann, S. Robra-Bissantz, R. Zarnekow, & T. Brockmann (Eds.), *Gamification. Progress in IS*. Springer. doi:10.1007/978-3-319-45557-0_11

Silalahi, M. (2019). Improving students' interest in learning English by using games. *International Journal of Theory and Application in Elementary and Secondary School Education*, *1*(1), 50–56. doi:10.31098/ijtaese.v1i1.24

Singapore Ministry of Education. (2018). *Reimagining Learning and Teaching for the 21st Century*. MoE. https://www.moe.gov.sg/news/speeches/teaching21–reimagining-learning-and-teaching-for-the-21st-century

Skinner, B. F. (1971). Operant conditioning. *The encyclopedia of education, 7*, 29-33.

Smith, J. A. (2020). Agile Faculty Development: Enhancing Teaching and Learning in Higher Education. *The Journal of Higher Education, 35*(2), 123–140.

Solís Castillo, J. C., & Marquina Lujan, R. J. (2022). Gamificación como alternativa metodológica en la educación superior. *Revista ConCiencia EPG, 7*(1), 66–83. doi:10.32654/CONCIENCIAEPG.7-1.5

Soni, V. D. (2019). Security issues in using iot enabled devices and their Impact. *Int. Eng. J. Res. Dev., 4*(2), 7.

Srivani, V., Hariharasudan, A., Nawaz, N., & Ratajczak, S. (2022). Impact of Education 4.0 among engineering students for learning English language. *PLoS One, 17*(2), e0261717. doi:10.1371/journal.pone.0261717 PMID:35108282

Srivastava, P., Dhir, S., Hasteer, N., & Soni, K. M. (2023). *Examining Parameters that Influence the Choice of Learners in Selecting Massive Open Online Courses.* 2023 2nd Edition of IEEE Delhi Section Flagship Conference (DELCON). Rajpura. India. 10.1109/DELCON57910.2023.10127325

Stott, A., & Neustaedter, C. (2013). Analysis of gamification in education. *Surrey, BC, Canada, 8*(1), 36. http://clab.iat.sfu.ca/pubs/Stott-Gamification.pdf

Street, B. (2006). Autonomous and ideological models of literacy: Approaches from New Literacy Studies. *Media Anthropology Network, 17*, 1–15.

Studer, P., & Konstantinidou, L. (2015). Language attitudes and language proficiency of undergraduate students in English-medium instruction. *Revue Tranel (Travaux neuchâtelois de linguistique)*, 215-231.

Sultan, N. (2010). Cloud computing for education: A new dawn? *International Journal of Information Management, 30*(2), 109–116. doi:10.1016/j.ijinfomgt.2009.09.004

Sun, L., Asmawi, A., Dong, H., & Zhang, X. (2023). Empowering Chinese undergraduates' business english writing: Unveiling the efficacy of DingTalk-Aided Problem-based language learning during Covid-19 period. *Education and Information Technologies*, 1–33.

Sun, Y., & Gao, F. (2020). An investigation of the influence of intrinsic motivation on students' intention to use mobile devices in language learning. *Educational Technology Research and Development, 68*(3), 1181–1198. doi:10.1007/s11423-019-09733-9

Su, Y. C. (2021). College Students' Oral Communication Strategy Use, Self-perceived English Proficiency and Confidence, and Communication Anxiety in Taiwan's EFL Learning. *Educational Studies (Ames), 57*(6), 650–669. doi:10.1080/00131946.2021.1919677

Svihla, V., & Reeve, R. (2016). Facilitating problem framing in project-based learning. *The Interdisciplinary Journal of Problem-Based Learning, 10*(2). doi:10.7771/1541-5015.1603

Taherdoost, H. (2016). *Validity and reliability of the research instrument; how to test the validation of a questionnaire/survey in a research. How to test the validation of a questionnaire/survey in a research (August 10, 2016).Tchifilionova* (Vol. 2011). Security and Privacy Implications of Cloud Computing-Lost in the Cloud.

Tanoli, M. A., Khan, M. I., & Majoka, M. I. (2021). English as Medium of Instruction at Primary Level: Problems Faced by Teachers and Students. *Sir Syed Journal of Education & Social Research*, *4*(2), 167–174.

Tate, E. (2018). *AR/VR forecast to reach 90 million users by 2020*. EdTechnology. https://edtechnology.co.uk/categories/research

Tawafak, R. M., Al-Obaydi, L. H., Klimova, B., & Pikhart, M. (2023). Technology integration of using digital gameplay for enhancing EFL college students' behavior intention. *Contemporary Educational Technology*, *15*(4), ep452. doi:10.30935/cedtech/13454

Teampau, G. (2015). Comic books as modern mythology. *Caietele Echinox*, (28), 140–155.

Tehseen, S., Ramayah, T., & Sajilan, S. (2017). Testing and controlling for common method variance: A review of available methods. *Journal of management sciences, 4*(2), 142-168.

Thornton, P., & Houser, C. (2002). M-learning: Learning in transit. In P. Lewis (Ed.), *The changing face of CALL: A Japanese perspective* (pp. 229–243). Swets & Zeitlinger.

Toda, A. M., Klock, A. C. T., Oliveira, W., Palomino, P. T., Rodrigues, L., Shi, L., Bittencourt, I., Gasparini, I., Isotani, S., & Cristea, A. I. (2019). Analysing gamification elements in educational environments using an existing gamification taxonomy. *Smart Learn. Environ.*, *6*(1), 16. doi:10.1186/s40561-019-0106-1

Topçiu, M., & Myftiu, J. (2015). Vygotsky theory on social interaction and its influence on the development of pre-school children. *European Journal of Social Science Education and Research*, *2*(3), 172–179. doi:10.26417/ejser.v4i1.p172-179

Tridinanti, G. (2018). The correlation between speaking anxiety, self-confidence, and speaking achievement of Undergraduate EFL students of private university in Palembang. *International Journal of Education and Literacy Studies*, *6*(4), 35–39. doi:10.7575/aiac.ijels.v.6n.4p.35

Tudge, J. R., Merçon-Vargas, E. A., Liang, Y., & Payir, A. (2022). The importance of Urie Bronfenbrenner's bioecological theory for early childhood education. In *Theories of early childhood education* (pp. 50–61). Routledge. doi:10.4324/9781003288077-5

Usman, M., Ahmad, M., & Ali, M. (2020). Inclusive Education of Children with Special Needs: Practices, Opportunities and Barriers. *Pakistan Journal of Education*, *37*(1), 75–94.

Uunona, G. N., & Goosen, L. (2023). Leveraging Ethical Standards in Artificial Intelligence Technologies: A Guideline for Responsible Teaching and Learning Applications. In M. Garcia, M. Lopez Cabrera, & R. de Almeida (Eds.), *Handbook of Research on Instructional Technologies in Health Education and Allied Disciplines* (pp. 310–330). IGI Global. doi:10.4018/978-1-6684-7164-7.ch014

Van Heerden, D., & Goosen, L. (2012). Using Vodcasts to Teach Programming in an ODL Environment. *Progressio*, *34*(3), 144–160.

van Leeuwen, T. (2005). *Introducing Social Semiotics*. Routlegde.

Vélez-Agosto, N. M., Soto-Crespo, J. G., Vizcarrondo-Oppenheimer, M., Vega-Molina, S., & García Coll, C. (2017). Bronfenbrenner's bioecological theory revision: Moving culture from the macro into the micro. *Perspectives on Psychological Science*, *12*(5), 900–910. doi:10.1177/1745691617704397 PMID:28972838

Vélez, K. G. C., Cedeño, M. A. P., & Ponce, G. V. B. (2020). Enseñanza de inglés como lengua extranjera (EFL) en el desarrollo de la destreza speaking a través de clases virtuales en la educación superior. *Revista Cognosis*, *5*, 167–178. doi:10.33936/cognosis.v5i0.2785

Venegas Álvarez, G. S., & Proaño Rodríguez, C. E. (2021). Las TIC y la formación del docente de educación superior. *Dominio de las Ciencias*, *7*(1), 575–592. doi:10.23857/dc.v7i1.1662

Vicente, L. C. (2020). Elena de la G., Teresa O., M Julia F. & Luis O.-B. *IEEE Transactions on Learning Technologies*, *13*(4), 704–717.

Vigil, K. M. (2017). *Quick response (QR) codes for audio support in foreign language learning.* [Doctoral dissertation, Boston University].

Wallner, L. (2019). *Framing education: Doing comics literacy in the classroom* (Vol. 34). Linköping University Electronic Press.

Waluyo, B., & Rofiah, N. L. (2021). Developing Students' English Oral Presentation Skills: Do Self-Confidence, Teacher Feedback, and English Proficiency Matter? *Mextesol Journal*, *45*(3), n3.

Wang, C., Ahmad, S. F., Ayassrah, A. Y. B. A., Awwad, E. M., Irshad, M., Ali, Y. A., & Han, H. (2023). An empirical evaluation of technology acceptance model for Artificial Intelligence in E-commerce. *Heliyon*, *9*(8), e18349. doi:10.1016/j.heliyon.2023.e18349 PMID:37520947

Wang, N., Chen, J., Tai, M., & Zhang, J. (2021). Blended learning for Chinese university EFL learners: Learning environment and learner perceptions. *Computer Assisted Language Learning*, *34*(3), 297–323. doi:10.1080/09588221.2019.1607881

Wang, Q., & Xue, M. (2022). The implications of expectancy-value theory of motivation in language education. *Frontiers in Psychology*, *13*, 992372. doi:10.3389/fpsyg.2022.992372 PMID:36425822

Wang, Y. H. (2023). Can gamification assist learning? A study to design and explore the uses of educational music games for adults and young learners. *Journal of Educational Computing Research*, *60*(8), 2015–2035. doi:10.1177/07356331221098148

Woiceshyn, J., & Daellenbach, U. (2018). Evaluating inductive vs deductive research in management studies: Implications for authors, editors, and reviewers. Qualitative research in organizations and management: An International Journal, 13(2), 183-195.

Wong, L.-H., & Looi, C.-J. (2010). Vocabulary learning by mobile-assisted content creation and social meaning-making: Two case studies. *Journal of Computer Assisted Learning*, *26*(5), 421–433. doi:10.1111/j.1365-2729.2010.00357.x

Wu, M. L., Zhou, Y., & Li, L. (2023). The effects of a gamified online course on pre-service teachers' confidence, intention, and motivation in integrating technology into teaching. *Education and Information Technologies*, *28*(10), 12903–12918. doi:10.1007/s10639-023-11727-3 PMID:37361757

Wurdinger, S., & Qureshi, M. (2015). Enhancing College Students' Life Skills through Project Based Learning. *Innovative Higher Education*, *40*(3), 279–286. doi:10.1007/s10755-014-9314-3

Wut, T. M., Xu, J., Lee, S. W., & Lee, D. (2022). University student readiness and its effect on intention to participate in the flipped classroom setting of hybrid learning. *Education Sciences*, *12*(7), 442. doi:10.3390/educsci12070442

Xia, Q., Chiu, T. K., Chai, C. S., & Xie, K. (2023). The mediating effects of needs satisfaction on the relationships between prior knowledge and self-regulated learning through artificial intelligence chatbot. *British Journal of Educational Technology*, *54*(4), 967–986. doi:10.1111/bjet.13305

Xi, N., & Hamari, J. (2019). Does gamification satisfy needs? A study on the relationship between gamification features and intrinsic need satisfaction. *International Journal of Information Management*, *46*, 210–221. doi:10.1016/j.ijinfomgt.2018.12.002

Xu, Z., Banerjee, M., Ramirez, G., Zhu, G., & Wijekumar, K. (2019). The effectiveness of educational technology applications on adult English language learners' writing quality: A meta-analysis. *Computer Assisted Language Learning*, *32*(1-2), 132–162. doi:10.1080/09588 221.2018.1501069

Yadav, D., Bansal, A., Bhatia, M., Hooda, M., & Morato, J. (Eds.). (2021). *Diagnostic applications of health intelligence and surveillance systems*. IGI Global. doi:10.4018/978-1-7998-6527-8

Yang, S., & Pu, R. (2022). The effects of contextual factors, self-efficacy and motivation on learners' adaptability to blended learning in college english: A structural equation modeling approach. *Frontiers in Psychology*, *13*, 847342. doi:10.3389/fpsyg.2022.847342 PMID:35465522

Yau, H. K., Cheng, A. L. F., & Ho, W. M. (2015). Identify the Motivational Factors to Affect the Higher Education Students to Learn Using Technology. *Turkish Online Journal of Educational Technology-TOJET*, *14*(2), 89–100.

Yelland, N. J. (2018). A pedagogy of multiliteracies: Young children and multimodal learning with tablets. *British Journal of Educational Technology*, *49*(5), 847–858. doi:10.1111/bjet.12635

Yildirim, I. (2017). The effects of gamification-based teaching practices on student achievement and students' attitudes toward lessons. *The Internet and Higher Education*, *33*, 86–92. doi:10.1016/j. iheduc.2017.02.002

Yildiz, İ., Topçu, E., & Kaymakci, S. (2021). The effect of gamification on motivation in the education of pre-service social studies teachers. *Thinking Skills and Creativity*, *42*, 100907. doi:10.1016/j.tsc.2021.100907

Yunus, M., Lau, E. Y. Y., Khair, A. H. M., & Yusof, N. M. (2020). Acquisition of vocabulary in primary schools via GoPic with QR code. *International Journal of English Language and Literature Studies*, *9*(3), 121–131. doi:10.18488/journal.23.2020.93.121.131

Yu, Z., Xu, W., & Sukjairungwattana, P. (2023). Motivation, learning strategies, and outcomes in mobile English language learning. *The Asia-Pacific Education Researcher*, *32*(4), 545–560. doi:10.1007/s40299-022-00675-0

Zainuddin, Z., Chu, S. K. W., Shujahat, M., & Perera, C. J. (2020). The impact of gamification on learning and instruction: A systematic review of empirical evidence. *Educational Research Review*, *30*, 100326. doi:10.1016/j.edurev.2020.100326

Zeybek, G. (2020). Multimodal mobile-assisted language learning classroom applications: A study in pre-service teacher education. [Doctoral Dissertation, Anadolu University, Eskişehir].

Zhai, C., & Wibowo, S. (2023). A systematic review on artificial intelligence dialogue systems for enhancing English as foreign language students' interactional competence in the university. *Computers and Education: Artificial Intelligence*, *100134*, 100134. doi:10.1016/j.caeai.2023.100134

Zhang, H., Dai, Y., & Wang, Y. (2020). Motivation and second foreign language proficiency: The mediating role of foreign language enjoyment. *Sustainability (Basel)*, *12*(4), 1302. doi:10.3390/su12041302

Zhang, Y. (2023). Teaching Strategies of College English Listening based on Affective Filter Hypothesis. *The Educational Review, USA, 7*(1), 26–30. doi:10.26855/er.2023.01.007

Zhang, Y., Yang, M., Zheng, D., Lang, P., Wu, A., & Chen, C. (2018). Efficient and secure big data storage system with leakage resilience in cloud computing. *Soft Computing*, *22*(23), 7763–7772. doi:10.1007/s00500-018-3435-z

Zhan, Z., He, L., Tong, Y., Liang, X., Guo, S., & Lan, X. (2022). The effectiveness of gamification programming education: Evidence from a meta-analysis. *Computers and Education: Artificial Intelligence*, *3*(1), 1–11. doi:10.1016/j.caeai.2022.100096

Zhao, Y., & Lai, C. (2023). Technology and second language learning: Promises and problems. In *Technology-mediated learning environments for young English learners* (pp. 167–206). Routledge. doi:10.4324/9781003418009-8

Zhou, S., & Thompson, G. (2023). Exploring role of English proficiency, self-efficacy, and motivation in listening for learners transitioning to an English-medium transnational university in China. *System*, *113*, 102998. doi:10.1016/j.system.2023.102998

Compilation of References

Zhu, Y., Zhang, J. H., Au, W., & Yates, G. (2020). University students' online learning attitudes and continuous intention to undertake online courses: A self-regulated learning perspective. *Educational Technology Research and Development*, *68*(3), 1485–1519. doi:10.1007/s11423-020-09753-w

Zoboi, I. (2019). *Pride: A pride & prejudice remix*. Balzer + Bray.

Zou, B., Liviero, S., Hao, M., & Wei, C. (2020). Artificial intelligence technology for EAP speaking skills: Student perceptions of opportunities and challenges. *Technology and the psychology of second language learners and users*, 433-463. doi:10.1007/978-3-030-34212-8_17

Zourmpakis, A. I., Kalogiannakis, M., & Papadakis, S. (2023). Adaptive gamification in science education: An analysis of the impact of implementation and adapted game elements on students' motivation. *Computers*, *12*(7), 143. doi:10.3390/computers12070143

Zourmpakis, A. I., Papadakis, S., & Kalogiannakis, M. (2022). Education of preschool and elementary teachers on the use of adaptive gamification in science education. *International Journal of Technology Enhanced Learning*, *14*(1), 1–16. doi:10.1504/IJTEL.2022.120556

Zulfikar, T., Dahliana, S., & Sari, R. A. (2019). An Exploration of English Students' Attitude towards English Learning. *English Language Teaching Educational Journal*, *2*(1), 1–12. doi:10.12928/eltej.v2i1.947

Zvitambo, K. (2021, April). *Dissertation Writing: A Student Guide*. ISPPME. https://isppme.com/wp-content/uploads/2021/04/Reseaarch-Project-Guidelines.docx

About the Contributors

Muhammad Mushtaq is an experienced Senior Lecturer with a demonstrated history of working in the Higher Education Industry. Skilled in Marketing Management, Data Analytics, SEO, Social Media Marketing, AI, Marketing Automation and Technology Adoption, Content Marketing, Performance Marketing, Psychology, Market Research, Consumer Behaviour, Neuromarketing, and Statistical Analysis. Strong education professional with a Doctorate of Philosophy (PhD) in Marketing from Swansea University.

***

Amir Rizaan Rahiman (A. R. Rahiman) currently works as the Senior Lecturer and Lead Coordinator for Student Mobility at the Faculty of Computer Science and Information Technology, UPM, Malaysia. His expertise lies in Mathematical Computational, Real-Time Systems, Mobile Computing Applications, and Distributed Computing. With extensive teaching and research experience, he has been selected as a guest lecturer at several overseas universities.

Amir Aatieff currently working in the Department of Computer Science at the Kulliyyah of Information and Communications Technology, International Islamic University Malaysia, holds a Ph.D. from Loughborough University, UK, specializing in AI, particularly in Multi-Agent Systems. His expertise covers areas such as Coalition Formation, Heuristic Methods, Automation for Digital Content Management, Industrial Automation, Medical Information Systems, ICT for Sustainable Development, and Mobile/IoT Integration. With a diverse skill set, Dr. Amir Aatieff brings valuable insights to both theoretical and applied aspects of AI and technology.

Ishani Basak born on 14 th of November,1992 completed her schooling from Gokhale Memorial Girls High School and St. John Diocesan Girls HS school. She completed her graduation and masters in English from University of Calcutta. She also completed her B.Ed and M.Ed from WBUTTEPA.She had a teaching experience of 2 years in the school of Kolkata along with ESL training. She cracked UGC Net for assistant professor on 2022 and currently pursuing PHD in Education from Christ University Bengaluru. Her area of interest is educational technology and psychological problems suffered by children in their adolescence. ORCID Link

Jason D. DeHart is a passionate educator and has served as a middle grades teacher for eight years. He also served as an assistant professor of reading education at Appalachian State University from 2019-2022, and has taught reading education courses at The University of Tennessee, Knoxville and Lee University in Cleveland, Tennessee. DeHart's research interests include multimodal literacy, including film and graphic novels, and literacy instruction with adolescents. His work has recently appeared in SIGNAL Journal, English Journal, and The Social Studies.

Dwijendra Nath Dwivedi is a professional with 20+ years of subject matter expertise creating right value propositions for analytics and AI. He currently heads the EMEA+AP AI and IoT team at SAS, a worldwide frontrunner in AI technology. He is a post-Graduate in Economics from Indira Gandhi Institute of Development and Research and is PHD from crackow university of economics Poland. He has presented his research in more than 20 international conference and published several Scopus indexed paper on AI adoption in many areas. As an author he has contributed to more than 8 books and has more than 25 publications in high impact journals. He conducts AI Value seminars and workshops for the executive audience and for power users.

Isabel María Garcia Conesa has a degree in English Studies from the University of Alicante and a PhD from the National University of Distance Education (UNED). She is currently working as a full time lecturer at the Centro Universitario de la Defensa in San Javier (Spain). She has been awarded a scholarship by the Franklin Institute (University of Alcala de Henares, Spain) and the Radcliffe Institute for Advanced Study (Harvard University, USA), where she conducted a pre-doctoral research stay in the year 2012. Among her main lines of research, we can highlight the role of different women in literature and culture of the United States in contrast to Francophone writers with publication in Spanish journals like Revista Estudios Humanísticos (University of León), Tonos Digital (University of Murcia), Dossiers Feministes (University Jaime I), Prisma Social, Raudem (University of Almeria), Camino Real (University of Alcala de Henres), or Nomadas (University Complutense of Madrid). She also focuses on the study of the history of the teaching of English and gender studies with publications in journals such as Revista Feminismo (University of Alicante) or even Quaderns Digitals.

Leila Goosen is a full professor in the Department of Science and Technology Education of the University of South Africa. Prof. Goosen was an Associate Professor in the School of Computing, and the module leader and head designer of the fully online signature module for the College for Science, Engineering and Technology, rolled out to over 92,000 registered students since the first semester of 2013. She also supervises ten Masters and Doctoral students, and has successfully completed supervision of 43 students at postgraduate level. Previously, she was a Deputy Director at the South African national Department of Education. In this capacity, she was required to develop ICT strategies for implementation. She also promoted, coordinated, managed, monitored and evaluated ICT policies and strategies, and drove the research agenda in this area. Before that, she had been a lecturer of Information Technology (IT) in the Department for Science, Mathematics and Technology Education in the Faculty of Education of the University of Pretoria. Her research interests have included cooperative work in IT, effective teaching and learning of programming and teacher professional development.

Abdurrahman Jalil is currently working as a senior lecturer in the School of Information Science, College of Computing, Informatics, and Mathematics at Universiti Teknologi MARA. His expertise lies in Mobile Application, Software Engineering, Web Development, and Information Science. With several years of experience in the industry and over ten years of experience in academic institutions, he brings a wealth of practical and academic knowledge to his role.

Suresh Karayil has been in English Language Teaching since 1998. Has experience of teaching at Secondary, Higher Secondary and Tertiary levels. Holds a Masters in English Language and Literature from Acharya Nagarjuna University, Guntur, Andhra Pradesh State, India. Obtained a Post Graduate Diploma in Teaching English from Central Institue of English and Foreign Languages, Hyderabad, Telangana State, India, (Currently EFLU, Hyderabad). As part of the research for the Doctoral Thesis, conducted a parametric study to ascertain that News Paper Content can be embedded into the English Language Classroom of Engineering Programs to achieve quick and effective vocabulary learning. Currently working on analyzing the practicality of incorporating Narrow Reading Activity into the curriculum of Engineering Programs in the states of Andhra Pradesh and Telangana, India.

Raenu Kolandaisamy, currently working at the Institute of Computer Science and Innovation, UCSI University as a Director, he holds a Ph.D. from the University Malay (UM), Malaysia, specializing in computer sciences, particularly in security. His expertise covers areas such as cybersecurity, Networking, IoT, blockchain and Mobile/IoT integration. With a diverse skill set, Dr. Raenu brings valuable insights into both theoretical and applied aspects of security and technology.

Maran Marimuthu, an Associate Professor at Universiti Teknologi PETRONAS, holds a Ph.D. in Finance from Universiti Malaya. Specializing in capital structure, he teaches courses in Financial Management and Corporate Finance. With a proven track record, Dr. Maran has supervised 3 master's and 6 Ph.D. students, aiming for 4 more Ph.D. completions in 2023. He has an impressive publication record of over 150 articles, co-authored books on Finance, and serves as a Trainer and Consultant in the Oil and Gas industry, including Petonas, focusing on socio-economic and cost analysis.

Sebastian Mathai is the Associate Professor in the Department of International Studies, Political Science and History at CHRIST University.

Prakasha G. S. is an Assistant Professor at School of Education, Christ University, Bangalore, India. He has 20 years of teaching and research experience in Education. His areas of interest lie in quantitative research methodology, Teaching-learning, Assessment and Evaluation, Educational Technology, Teacher education, and Higher education. He has published in peer-reviewed journals indexed in reputed databases. He has presented papers in national and international conferences. He is involved in research activities, which have national and international emphasis.

Sanskriti Rawat (9 December 1996) is a research scholar at the School of Education, Christ University, Central Campus, Bangalore, India. Her areas of interest in research include educational psychology, educational technology, teacher education, and English language teaching and learning.

Glaret Shirley Sinnappan currently holds the position of Assistant Professor at Tunku Abdul Rahman University of Management and Technology. With a Ph.D. from the University of Malaya (UM), Malaysia, she possesses extensive expertise in Information Systems, Instruction Technology, Artificial Intelligence (AI), Data Mining, and Machine Learning. Dr. Glaret's diverse skill set equips her to offer valuable insights into both theoretical and applied aspects of Information Technology.

Gülin Zeybek is a doctor in ELT (Anadolu University) and is currently working in School of Foreign Languages at Isparta University of Applied Sciences. She earned her BA degree in English Language Teaching at Boğaziçi University and holds two MA degrees in both areas of Foreign Language Education and Educational Technologies. Her research interests center on pre-service teacher education, Multimodal Mobile Assisted Language Learning, and various technology integrations such as Augmented Reality and Artificial Intelligence into foreign language teaching. She has worked as a foreign language teacher trainer for over 10 years. She has published various research papers nationally and internationally.

Index

Recommended Reference Books

IGI Global's reference books are available in three unique pricing formats:
Print Only, E-Book Only, or Print + E-Book.

Order direct through IGI Global's Online Bookstore at **www.igi-global.com** or through your preferred provider.

Premier Reference Source

Online Distance Learning Course Design and Multimedia in E-Learning

ISBN: 9781799897064
EISBN: 9781799897088
© 2022; 302 pp.
List Price: US$ 215

Premier Reference Source

Global and Transformative Approaches Toward Linguistic Diversity

ISBN: 9781799889854
EISBN: 9781799889878
© 2022; 383 pp.
List Price: US$ 215

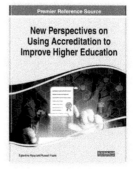

Premier Reference Source

New Perspectives on Using Accreditation to Improve Higher Education

ISBN: 9781668451953
EISBN: 9781668451960
© 2022; 300 pp.
List Price: US$ 215

Premier Reference Source

Impact of School Shootings on Classroom Culture, Curriculum, and Learning

ISBN: 9781799852001
EISBN: 9781799852018
© 2022; 355 pp.
List Price: US$ 215

Premier Reference Source

Modern Reading Practices and Collaboration Between Schools, Family, and Community

ISBN: 9781799897507
EISBN: 9781799897521
© 2022; 304 pp.
List Price: US$ 215

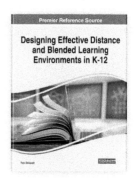

Premier Reference Source

Designing Effective Distance and Blended Learning Environments in K-12

ISBN: 9781799868293
EISBN: 9781799868316
© 2022; 389 pp.
List Price: US$ 215

Do you want to stay current on the latest research trends, product announcements, news, and special offers?
Join IGI Global's mailing list to receive customized recommendations, exclusive discounts, and more.
Sign up at: **www.igi-global.com/newsletters.**

Publisher of Timely, Peer-Reviewed Inclusive Research Since 1988

IGI Global
PUBLISHER of TIMELY KNOWLEDGE

www.igi-global.com   ✉ Sign up at www.igi-global.com/newsletters   f facebook.com/igiglobal   t twitter.com/igiglobal

Ensure Quality Research is Introduced to the Academic Community

Become an Reviewer for IGI Global Authored Book Projects

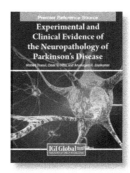

The overall success of an authored book project is dependent on quality and timely manuscript evaluations.

Applications and Inquiries may be sent to:
development@igi-global.com

Applicants must have a doctorate (or equivalent degree) as well as publishing, research, and reviewing experience. Authored Book Evaluators are appointed for one-year terms and are expected to complete at least three evaluations per term. Upon successful completion of this term, evaluators can be considered for an additional term.

If you have a colleague that may be interested in this opportunity, we encourage you to share this information with them.

Submit an Open Access Book Proposal

Have Your Work Fully & Freely Available Worldwide After Publication

Seeking the Following Book Classification Types:
Authored & Edited Monographs • Casebooks • Encyclopedias • Handbooks of Research

Gold, Platinum, & Retrospective OA Opportunities to Choose From

Easily Track Your Work in Our Advanced Manuscript Submission System With **Rapid Turnaround Times**

Double-Blind Peer Review by Notable Editorial Boards (*Committee on Publication Ethics* (COPE) Certified

Publications Adhere to All **Current OA Mandates & Compliances**

Affordable APCs *(Often 50% Lower Than the Industry Average)* Including Robust Editorial Service Provisions

Direct Connections with **Prominent Research Funders** & OA Regulatory Groups

Institution Level OA Agreements Available (Recommend or Contact Your Librarian for Details)

Join a **Diverse Community of 150,000+ Researchers Worldwide** Publishing With IGI Global

Content Spread Widely to Leading Repositories (AGOSR, ResearchGate, CORE, & More)

 Retrospective Open Access Publishing

You Can Unlock Your Recently Published Work, Including Full Book & Individual Chapter Content to Enjoy All the Benefits of Open Access Publishing

Learn More

Publishing Tomorrow's Research Today
IGI Global
e-Book Collection

Including Essential Reference Books Within Three Fundamental Academic Areas

Business & Management
Scientific, Technical, & Medical (STM)
Education

- Acquisition options include Perpetual, Subscription, and Read & Publish
- No Additional Charge for Multi-User Licensing
- No Maintenance, Hosting, or Archiving Fees
- Continually Enhanced Accessibility Compliance Features (WCAG)

| Over **150,000+** Chapters | Contributions From **200,000+** Scholars Worldwide | More Than **1,000,000+** Citations | Majority of e-Books Indexed in Web of Science & Scopus | Consists of Tomorrow's Research Available Today! |

Recommended Titles from our e-Book Collection

Innovation Capabilities and Entrepreneurial Opportunities of Smart Working
ISBN: 9781799887973

Advanced Applications of Generative AI and Natural Language Processing Models
ISBN: 9798369305027

Using Influencer Marketing as a Digital Business Strategy
ISBN: 9798369305515

Human-Centered Approaches in Industry 5.0
ISBN: 9798369326473

Modeling and Monitoring Extreme Hydrometeorological Events
ISBN: 9781668487716

Data-Driven Intelligent Business Sustainability
ISBN: 9798369300497

Information Logistics for Organizational Empowerment and Effective Supply Chain Management
ISBN: 9798369301593

Data Envelopment Analysis (DEA) Methods for Maximizing Efficiency
ISBN: 9798369302552

Request More Information, or Recommend the IGI Global e-Book Collection to Your Institution's Librarian

For More Information or to Request a Free Trial, Contact IGI Global's e-Collections Team: eresources@igi-global.com | 1-866-342-6657 ext. 100 | 717-533-8845 ext. 100

Are You Ready to
Publish Your Research ?

IGI Global
PUBLISHER of TIMELY KNOWLEDGE

IGI Global offers book authorship and editorship opportunities across 11 subject areas, including business, computer science, education, science and engineering, social sciences, and more!

Benefits of Publishing with IGI Global:

- Free one-on-one editorial and promotional support.

- Expedited publishing timelines that can take your book from start to finish in less than one (1) year.

- Choose from a variety of formats, including Edited and Authored References, Handbooks of Research, Encyclopedias, and Research Insights.

- Utilize IGI Global's eEditorial Discovery® submission system in support of conducting the submission and double-blind peer review process.

- IGI Global maintains a strict adherence to ethical practices due in part to our full membership with the Committee on Publication Ethics (COPE).

- Indexing potential in prestigious indices such as Scopus®, Web of Science™, PsycINFO®, and ERIC – Education Resources Information Center.

- Ability to connect your ORCID iD to your IGI Global publications.

- Earn honorariums and royalties on your full book publications as well as complimentary content and exclusive discounts.

Join Your Colleagues from Prestigious Institutions, Including:

Australian National University

Massachusetts Institute of Technology

JOHNS HOPKINS UNIVERSITY

HARVARD UNIVERSITY

COLUMBIA UNIVERSITY IN THE CITY OF NEW YORK

Learn More at: www.igi-global.com/publish

or by Contacting the Acquisitions Department at: acquisition@igi-global.com

Individual Article & Chapter Downloads

US$ 37.50/each

Easily Identify, Acquire, and Utilize Published Peer-Reviewed Findings in Support of Your Current Research

- Browse Over *170,000+ Articles & Chapters*

- *Accurate & Advanced* Search

- Affordably Acquire *International Research*

- *Instantly Access* Your Content

- Benefit from the *InfoSci® Platform Features*

THE UNIVERSITY
of NORTH CAROLINA
at CHAPEL HILL

It really provides an excellent entry into the research literature of the field. It presents a manageable number of highly relevant sources on topics of interest to a wide range of researchers. The sources are scholarly, but also accessible to 'practitioners'.

- Ms. Lisa Stimatz, MLS, University of North Carolina at Chapel Hill, USA

Milton Keynes UK
Ingram Content Group UK Ltd.
UKHW021429160324
439418UK00007B/89